THE
BABY AND TODDLER
HEALTH GUIDE

Denise
Cullen.

THE BABY AND TODDLER HEALTH GUIDE

AN ENCYCLOPEDIA OF ILLNESSES, CAUSES, SYMPTOMS AND TREATMENTS

PROFESSOR PETER ABRAHAMS

amber
BOOKS

First published in 2006 by
Amber Books Ltd
Bradley's Close
74–77 White Lion Street
London N1 9PF
United Kingdom
www.amberbooks.co.uk

ISBN-13: 978-1-904687-65-8
ISBN-10: 1-904687-65-2

Distributed in the UK by
Bookmart Ltd
Blaby Road
Wigston
Leicester LE18 4SE

Design: Hawes Design
General Editor: Jane de Burgh
Project Editor: Michael Spilling

Printed in the Czech Republic

Contents

Introduction   8

Caring For Your Baby   10

Checking a Newborn Baby   12

Jaundice in Newborns   14

Care in Infancy   16

Lung Problems in Newborn Babies   18

Checking a Baby at Six Weeks   20

Breast Milk and the Newborn   22

Sleep Patterns in Babies   24

Newborn Baby Reflexes   26

Baby Immune Systems   28

Baby's Skull   30

Immunizing Infants   32

Developmental Delay   34

Learning to Eat   36

Feeding and Weaning Problems   38

Failure to Thrive   40

Infant Skin Problems   42

Nappy Rash   44

Minor Abnormalities in Newborns   46

Caring for Premature Babies   48

Problems Associated with Prematurity   50

Eight Month Baby Check   52

Teething   54

Hearing Problems in Infants   56

Developing Walking Skills   58

Your Growing Child   60

Growth in the First 18 Months   62

Developmental Progress to 18 Months   64

Learning to Talk   66

Developing Language Skills   68

Developmental Progress from 18 to 36 Months   70

Potty Training   72

Bed-wetting   74

Entering Childhood   76

Development of Vision   78

Stimulation and Play   80

Temperament and Personality   82

Temper Tantrums   84

Good Eating Habits   86

Pre-school Children   88

Developmental Progress up to Five Years   90

Starting School   92

Losing the First Set of Teeth   94

Growth Rates in Childhood   96

Inherited Characteristics   98

Common Problems With Children	100
Sticky Eyes in Children	102
Squints in Children	104
Upper Airway Problems	106
Tonsillitis	108
Croup	110
Asthma in Children	112
Treating Childhood Asthma	114
Glue Ear and Grommets	116
Dental Problems in Children	118
Tongue Tie	120
Constipation in Children	122
Urinary Tract Infections in Children	124
Treating Eczema	126
Measles	128
Mumps	130
Rubella	132
Chickenpox	134
Hand, Foot and Mouth Disease	136
Head Lice	138
Dyspraxia	140
Dyslexia	142
Diagnosing Dyslexia	144

Diseases, Conditions and their Treatment	146
Gastro-Intestinal System	
Gastroenteritis	148
Appendicitis	150
Intussusception	152
Hirschsprung's Disease	154
Inguinoscrotal Disorders	156
Bones, Muscles and Joints	
Congenital Dislocation of the Hip	158
Talipes	160
Juvenile Idiopathic Arthritis	162
Rickets	164
Osteogenesis Imperfecta	166
Muscular Dystrophy	168
Rheumatic Fever	170
Blood and Immune System	
Anaemia in Childhood	172
Thalassaemia	174
Treating Thalassaemia	176
Children with HIV	178
Caring for Children with HIV	180
Diagnosing Acute Leukaemia	182
Treating Acute Leukaemia	184

Heart and Lungs

Heart Murmurs   186

Newborn Heart Disease   188

Treating Congenital Heart Disease   190

Chronic Chest Problems   192

Acute Viral Bronchiolitis   194

Pneumonia in Childhood   196

Pertussis   198

Tuberculosis in Children   200

Inheriting Cystic Fibrosis   202

Managing Cystic Fibrosis   204

Nervous System

Viral Encephalitis   206

Epilepsy in Childhood   208

Hydrocephalus   210

Meningitis   212

Causes of Meningitis   214

Meningococcal Septicaemia   216

Poliomyelitis   218

Reye's Syndrome   220

Spina Bifida   222

Autism   224

Attention Deficit Hyperactivity   226
Disorder

Cerebral Palsy   228

Difficulties Associated   230
with Cerebral Palsy

Down's Syndrome   232

Miscellaneous

Accidental Poisoning   234

Alcohol and Drug Poisoning   236

Head Injuries   238

Types of Head Injury   240

Sudden Infant Death Syndrome   242

Childhood Cancers   244

Paediatric Intensive Care   246

Index   248

Introduction

One of life's great challenges is starting a family, and pregnancy and birth are only the beginning of a long and fascinating process. Ask any prospective parents about their main concerns during a pregnancy and they will almost certainly express the·desire to have a healthy baby, who will develop normally and lead a happy life.

For most parents these basic desires are met; a healthy child is born and immediately begins the process of adaptation to a constantly changing environment. Regular checks on physical, mental and social development are routinely carried out during early childhood and serve to reassure parents that all is going well. Physical checks begin just

after birth, when the baby is given its first medical examination. At six weeks and eight months, further developmental checks are carried out to assess hearing, vision and growth – most babies triple in weight and grow in length by 30cm (12in) in the first year! These checks also ascertain whether the baby is learning new skills, such as how to coordinate

Learning to walk is one of the great milestones in a child's life, and usually occurs between the ages of 9 and 16 months.

movement and respond to stimuli.

During the first 18 months of life, important milestones are reached; first crawling and then walking and talking. From the age of two onwards, when children begin to grasp the concepts of language and communication, they start to establish their individuality by forming opinions, making decisions and establishing lasting relationships outside the family unit.

Independence increases as a child learns to feed him or herself and use the potty rather than wear nappies. Sometimes, a child will not do as well as expected; he or she may have feeding or weaning problems, or may fail to grow or develop as quickly as other children. However, each child is an individual, and not achieving the 'norm' is not necessarily a problem. With help and support, minor setbacks can be effectively resolved at an early stage.

COMMON CHILDHOOD ILLNESS

Over the years, children experience the many common illnesses and conditions that are part of growing up. Coughs, colds, sore throats and minor infections are passed around playgroups and schools like sweets and although the course of these illnesses is unpleasant, they are not harmful in the long term.

In fact, minor illnesses help to strengthen the immune system and create life-long resistance to many of the hundreds of viruses and bacteria that we are exposed to in our daily lives. Some illnesses, such as diphtheria and whooping cough, can be prevented altogether through immunization. Babies are vaccinated against these and other diseases when they are only 2 months old and immunizations continue throughout childhood. Efficient national and international vaccination programmes have resulted in the virtual eradication of potentially fatal conditions such as smallpox and poliomyelitis in developed countries (although other parts of

Although the causes are little understood, colic, involving uncontrollable crying in the evenings, is a common ailment among babies.

the world are not so fortunate). In the last 20 years, immunisation against potentially serious illnesses such as measles and rubella has led to a huge decrease in their incidence, and mortality, although recent adverse publicity about the MMR vaccine resulted in a wave of new cases after many parents failed to get their children immunized.

COPING WITH MORE SERIOUS CONDITIONS

Whilst all families experience the inevitable minor illnesses in their children, some parents are faced with more serious challenges. Rare developmental problems such as autism and attention deficit disorder, although not life-threatening, can be difficult to cope with, both

for the children themselves and for their families. Physical or developmental disabilities like cerebral palsy or Down syndrome inevitably involve significant adjustments to day-to-day life that affect all members of the family, although many children with disabilities lead full and active lives and often live independently when they become adults. Rarely, children are born with a congenital heart or lung disease, or they develop a life-threatening illness such as cancer.

Infectious diseases can also prove more serious than the coughs and colds routinely experienced in childhood. For example, meningitis is a much-feared illness that can have devastating consequences if not diagnosed and treated

promptly. A serious illness in a child is an intensely emotional experience for parents, who inevitably feel responsible for their child's distress.

There is, however, always a wealth of support available. Highly specialised services exist for children, and health professionals trained in paediatric care are sensitive to the needs of the whole family during an undoubtedly stressful time. The good news is that nowadays many childhood conditions can be cured, or unpleasant symptoms alleviated, with modern medical and surgical treatments, and international research into even more effective therapies is ongoing.

Jane de Burgh
Medical Editor

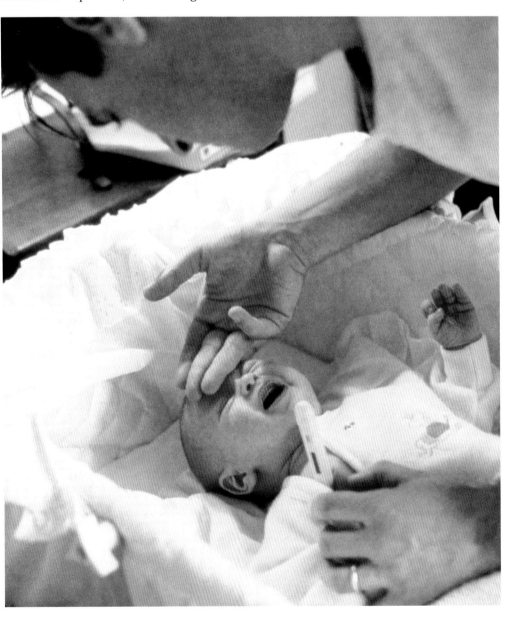

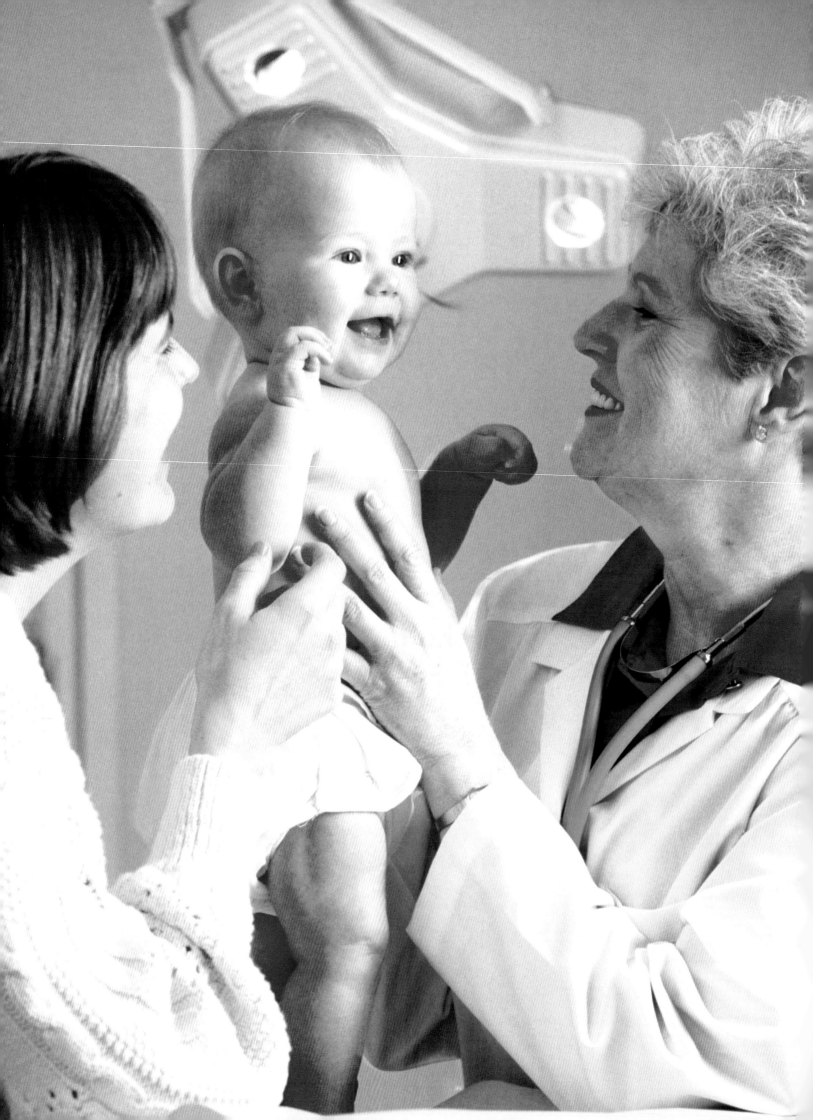

Chapter One

Caring for Your Baby

Watching your baby grow and develop is a time of both excitement and anxiety. The regular physical, mental and developmental checks that he or she will undergo in the first 8 months of life are described in this section. You can read about the minor setbacks that may occur during this time – jaundice, nappy rash, and feeding and teething problems, for example, are all common and easily resolved. The pages dealing with immunisation will help you to understand this important process in protecting your baby from potentially serious illnesses. Premature babies may have different problems, but expert care and modern technology usually guarantee a healthy recovery.

Checking a newborn baby

Every baby has routine checks within minutes of birth to identify any life-threatening problem, to establish that the baby is healthy and to reassure the parents. Up to four sets of checks are carried out in the first week of life.

The first checks on a newborn are carried out by the midwife or doctor at delivery. Breathing must be properly established, and this and other functions are assessed in a standard way. Babies are given an Apgar score at one minute and then five minutes after birth.

APGAR CHECKS

The five elements checked are breathing, heart rate, colour, muscle tone and reflexes. Each is given a score of 0, 1 or 2. The maximum Apgar score is 10 and seven or more is quite normal. Babies scoring five or less need to be given oxygen to help them establish their breathing.

When the baby is short of oxygen, breathing is irregular or absent, heart rate is below 100 and the skin is blue or pale.

MEASUREMENTS

Shortly after birth, all babies are weighed, the circumference of the head is recorded, the baby's length is measured, and the midwife does a quick check for any obvious congenital abnormalities.

The Apgar score

The Apgar score was devised by an American paediatrician, Dr Virginia Apgar, to provide a standard way of monitoring a baby's condition.

Breathing	Regular, crying	2
	Slow, irregular	1
	Absent	0
Heart rate	Over 100	2
	Slow, below 100	1
	Absent	0
Colour	Pink	2
	Body pink, extremities blue	1
	Blue, pale	0
Muscle tone	Moving actively	2
	Moving extremities only	1
	Limp	0
Reflexes	Cough or sneeze	2
(often to a catheter	Grimace	1
in the nostril)	None	0

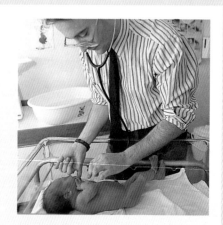

Placing his little finger in a baby's mouth, a doctor checks the baby's muscle tone.

The baby's weight can indicate potential health problems. Any weight between 2,500 grams and 4,500 grams (5½-10 lbs) is normal. Low birthweight babies may need extra care. A very large baby may indicate that the mother has diabetes.

Measuring the circumference of a baby's head. Head size depends on a baby's size but an average for a 7½ lb baby would be about 35 cm (14 in). An abnormally small or large head may indicate brain problems.

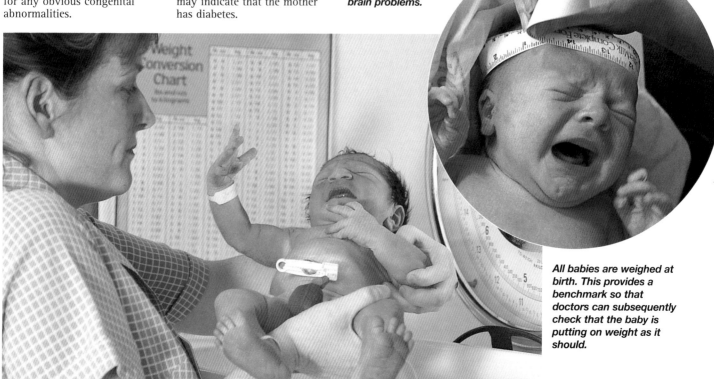

All babies are weighed at birth. This provides a benchmark so that doctors can subsequently check that the baby is putting on weight as it should.

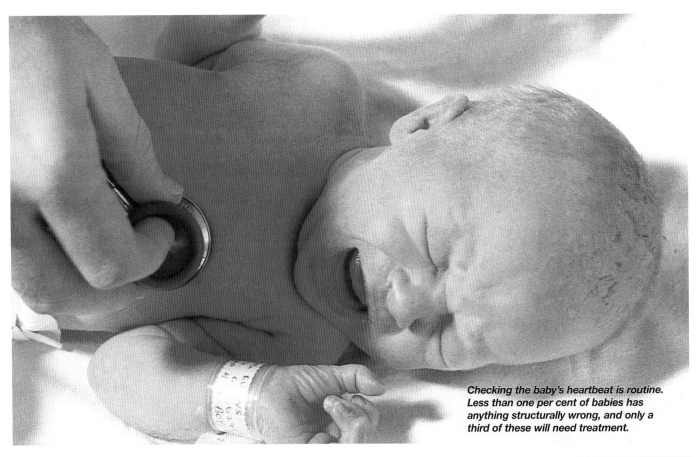

Checking the baby's heartbeat is routine. Less than one per cent of babies has anything structurally wrong, and only a third of these will need treatment.

First medical checks

A careful examination is made of every baby in the first 24 hours. Usually this is done by a member of the paediatric team, but it may be carried out by a midwife, particularly if the mother is to be discharged within six hours.

MEDICAL HISTORY
The mother's medical notes are checked for any abnormalities discovered during pregnancy, and the mother is asked about any illnesses in the family. The baby is undressed and observed carefully from top to toe.

HEART
Using a stethoscope, the heart is checked first, before the baby gets upset and starts crying – reactions that alter heart rate.

BLOOD FLOW
The pulses in the groin are felt to make certain there is no blockage in the aorta, the main artery of the body – a condition that is known as coarctation of the aorta.

JAUNDICE
Jaundice – now increasingly common – can damage the brain, so a check is made of the whites of the baby's eyes.

ABNORMALITIES
Some congenital abnormalities – such as missing fingers – are obvious but some of the more dangerous problems are not. Cleft palate is often associated with a cleft lip, but it is easy to miss a cleft at the back of the palate. To have a thorough look, the doctor will carefully depress the baby's tongue with a wooden spatula.

BLOCKAGES
Any blockage in the digestive tract is a problem. Atresia of the bowel (blockage of the bowel) needs urgent surgery. Atresia of the oesophagus (blockage of the gullet) causes regurgitation of saliva. If the baby is showing this symptom, a tube is passed into the stomach to check that there is no block. Atresia further down the gut, such as duodenal atresia (just below the stomach), makes the baby vomit green bile. A blockage even further down the gut leads to a distension of the abdomen. The anus is inspected to make sure that it is present and open.

HIPS
The hip is a ball-and-socket joint, and may be dislocated. It is relatively easy to treat early in life and is more common in girls, those with a family history of such things, and after breech delivery. All babies have a gentle examination to see if either of the hips can be dislocated. There are now ways of assessing the hip by ultrasound if there is thought to be any problem.

GENITALS
The genitalia are carefully examined to make sure that the vagina is present in a girl and that the penis is normal and the testes have descended in a boy. Any abnormality may require surgery to correct it.

Discharge examination

The baby is given a discharge examination before leaving hospital, but it may be done at home by the family practitioner. This checks that nothing has been missed and that no illness has developed.

Jaundice, for instance, caused by excess bilirubin (a bile pigment) in the blood, is extremely common in breast-fed or premature babies. A blood test may be needed to check the bilirubin level.

UMBILICAL CORD
The umbilical cord separates from the baby at any time from three days to two weeks after birth. If the belly button (the umbilicus) becomes infected it will be very red and swollen with a discharge.

FEEDING
It is important for the baby's growth that breast-feeding is properly established, and this is also assessed during the check.

Guthrie test

All babies have a blood test after they are six days old. It is called the Guthrie test. The baby's heel is pricked and drops of blood are put on a special card. The test is to look for two treatable causes of mental handicap. An absent thyroid causes a high level of thyroid-stimulating hormone (TSH) in the blood. The other condition is phenylketonuria, where there is a block in the chemistry of phenylalanine, one of the amino acids in the body. Brain damage can be avoided by putting the baby on a special diet.

Jaundice in newborns

A yellow discoloration of the skin (jaundice) often occurs in healthy newborn babies and it soon disappears. However, GPs examine jaundiced babies regularly to rule out any serious problems.

Jaundice is caused by an increase in blood levels of bilirubin, which is a waste product made when haemoglobin in red blood cells is broken down. Newborn babies have immature liver enzymes and are unable to chemically transform (metabolize) this bilirubin effectively for later excretion. Babies who are born underweight and those born to diabetic mothers are particularly likely to become jaundiced.

After a difficult delivery, babies sometimes develop a bruise-like haemorrhage under the scalp (cephalhaematoma), and may become jaundiced when the extra blood is re-absorbed. If the umbilical cord is not clamped early enough, too many red blood cells may pass to the baby (polycythaemia), and this can also lead to jaundice.

PHYSIOLOGICAL JAUNDICE

A natural build up of unmetabolized bilirubin is termed physiological jaundice. It results from a natural decline in the number of red blood cells over the first few days of life and because a baby's liver enzymes are, initially, not fully unaccustomed to dealing with the broken down products.

Normal physiological jaundice always develops after the first 24 hours of life. Now that mothers and babies are discharged early

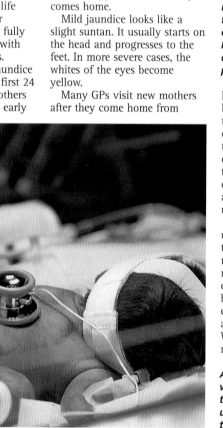

from hospital, most cases of jaundice appear after the baby comes home.

Mild jaundice looks like a slight suntan. It usually starts on the head and progresses to the feet. In more severe cases, the whites of the eyes become yellow.

Many GPs visit new mothers after they come home from

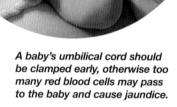

Many newborns develop jaundice – it affects more than half of all full-term babies and over 80 per cent of babies that are delivered prematurely.

hospital. If the baby is jaundiced, the GP may examine the baby to look for anaemia or an enlarged liver. If the baby's urine is dark or the faeces pale, blood and urine tests are needed urgently.

Physiological jaundice usually disappears by the time the baby is two weeks old. The most important treatment is to make sure the baby is getting enough milk. If the mother is breast-feeding, she should be encouraged to continue or seek advice if there are difficulties. Weighing the baby regularly reveals whether there is an

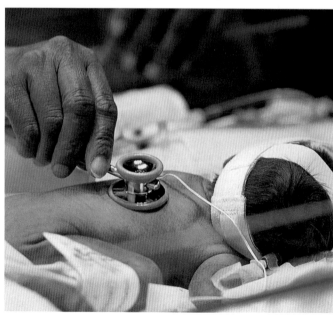

A small percentage of newborns with jaundice may need treatment in an intensive care unit – ultraviolet light is one of the treatments available.

A baby's umbilical cord should be clamped early, otherwise too many red blood cells may pass to the baby and cause jaundice.

adequate fluid and calorie intake.

If the jaundice is severe, or the baby seems drowsy or has difficulty feeding, the midwife will take blood to measure the bilirubin level. Charts help the doctor decide whether phototherapy (light treatment) is needed to help break the bilirubin down.

Causes of jaundice

Occasionally, prolonged jaundice in newborns can be caused by a serious illness, so further tests to establish the exact cause may be have to be carried out.

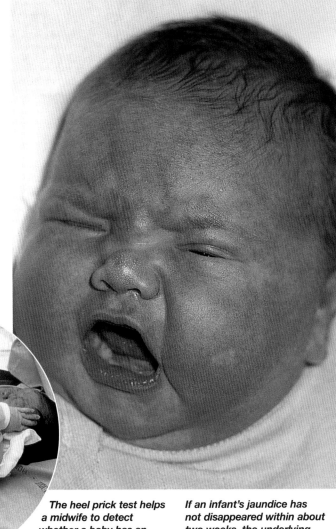

Jaundice occurring on the first day of life is always abnormal. It is usually due to breakdown of the baby's red blood cells by haemolysis. This can be confirmed by a blood test known as a Coombs' test.

Haemolytic disease of the newborn may occur if the mother has a different blood group to the baby and produces antibodies which cross the placenta (ABO or rhesus incompatibility). This is now rare because rhesus-negative mothers are given anti-D injections after childbirth to prevent them making these antibodies.

RELATED FACTORS
Sometimes there will be a family history of jaundice. Most cases of prolonged jaundice occur in breast-fed babies, although the cause is still unknown. Breast milk jaundice affects 5 per cent of breast-fed babies and is not harmful, so mothers should continue breast-feeding. However, prolonged jaundice may be caused by serious illness, and investigations are needed.

INVESTIGATIONS AND CAUSES
First, blood tests are done to determine whether the bilirubin is conjugated (with linked-up molecules) or unconjugated, and urine is tested. If the bilirubin is

conjugated, further tests are needed. These may include an ultrasound scan of the liver or a liver biopsy.

Serious causes include liver disease and biliary atresia (blocked bile ducts). The latter must be diagnosed early because surgery may be life-saving if done within the first six weeks. Occasionally these babies need a liver transplant.

Chronic congenital infections such as cytomegalovirus and toxoplasmosis may cause prolonged jaundice. Jaundice may also be caused by hereditary metabolic diseases such as cystic fibrosis and galactosaemia.

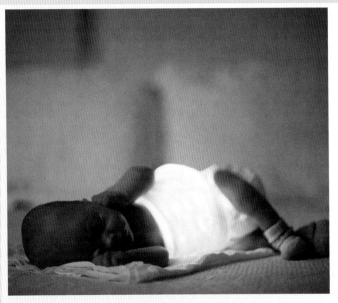

The heel prick test helps a midwife to detect whether a baby has an underactive thyroid gland (hypothyroidism).

If an infant's jaundice has not disappeared within about two weeks, the underlying cause will need further investigation.

Treating jaundice in babies

Phototherapy lamps work on the principle that yellow bilirubin absorbs light of blue wavelengths, which changes it into non-toxic by-products. Phototherapy involves separating the baby from the mother and sometimes has side effects including dehydration and loose faeces, so extra fluids are needed.

A newer device is a body suit emitting blue light – this is worn under a baby's clothes and avoids separation problems.

Conjugated bilirubin that has been metabolized by the liver is

Phototherapy means that a baby has to be separated from the mother during treatment, so this should only be used in more serious cases.

no longer harmful. However, if the level of unconjugated bilirubin becomes very high, a small amount may cross into the brain, where it is toxic (kernicterus). Kernicterus may cause deafness and/or cerebral palsy, but this can be prevented by prompt exchange transfusions of blood.

An exchange transfusion is a practical procedure used as a last resort to prevent kernicterus. Warmed rhesus-negative blood from a donor which has been cross-matched against the mother's blood and baby's blood is transfused into the baby's umbilical vein at the same rate that the baby's own blood is removed. This removes toxic unconjugated bilirubin and any antibodies present, and corrects any anaemia.

Care in infancy

Care in infancy is the medical care given to a baby prior to its first birthday. This involves regular health checks, screening for various conditions and treatment of any specific medical problems that arise.

Care in infancy involves looking after the child in the most vulnerable part of its life, the first year, when it is wholly dependent on surrounding adults for everything: food, warmth, care and protection.

INFANT CARE PROFESSIONALS

GPs and health visitors are the source of most medical advice in the community. In addition, families may also use the receptionist or practice nurse in some instances as sources of general childcare information.

Most child surveillance is the responsibility of GPs, rather than clinic-based medical officers. The GPs role is to assess the seriousness of a child's condition and to decide whether the child requires referral to a hospital unit. The majority of conditions do not require hospitalization, and are managed solely by the primary healthcare team.

PROVISION OF PRIMARY HEALTHCARE

Parents are naturally anxious about the health of their infant, and may well seek the help of their family doctor. Childhood problems constitute a major part of any GP's workload. Some infants require only a single visit, whereas others may need regular check-ups. Some parents will take their child to the surgery because they think it is unwell, in addition to regular developmental check-ups.

The GP will look for signs of serious ill-health, such as dehydration and infection (especially ear and chest infections). If the GP is carrying out a normal surveillance of the

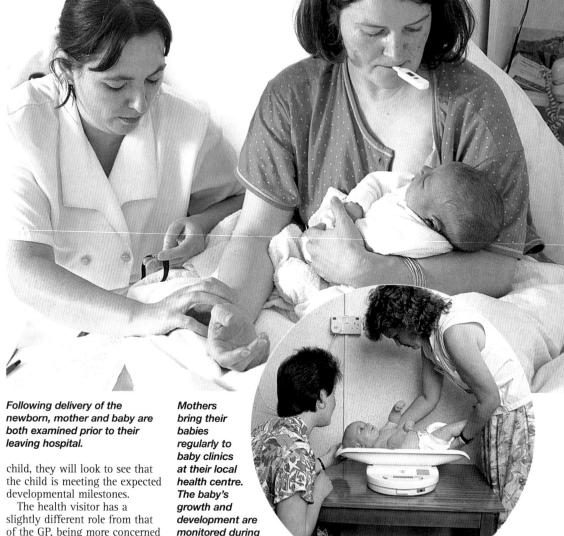

Following delivery of the newborn, mother and baby are both examined prior to their leaving hospital.

Mothers bring their babies regularly to baby clinics at their local health centre. The baby's growth and development are monitored during the first few months of life, and any problems are referred to the GP.

child, they will look to see that the child is meeting the expected developmental milestones.

The health visitor has a slightly different role from that of the GP, being more concerned with promoting general health within the family. As well as examining the physical health of the child, the health visitor is interested in the child's general well-being and that of the family, particularly the mother.

The health visitor may be especially helpful to first-time mothers, providing them with information on how to access the available community services. Initially, the new mother will be supported by the midwife for the first ten days, then the health visitor will become involved after this time. There are a number of ways in

which health services are delivered across the UK, but there is usually one initial home visit by the health visitor. After that, many families contact health visitors if they want further home visits. In addition to this, families are encouraged to attend a baby clinic.

At about eight months of age, all babies receive a comprehensive screening check by the health visitor. If a significant problem is found at any stage during the first year, the child will be referred for secondary medical care under a paediatrician in a hospital.

One of the health visitor's tasks is to call at the home of newborn babies. As well as checking that the infant is developing normally, they give support and information to the mother.

Health screening

Immediately after birth, the infant receives a neonatal check, which involves monitoring its heartbeat and making sure there is no hip dislocation. The newborn is given another examination within 24 hours, and receives another check at six weeks of age.

After eight months, the parents receive a visit from their health visitor, and raise any concerns they have about their baby's health. If the infant is progressing healthily, there are no further examinations in its first year of life. But if, for example, the infant is not putting on enough weight, further visits to the primary healthcare team will be necessary. Between eight and nine months old, all children will have their hearing tested.

PROBLEM AREAS
■ **Feeding** problems include difficulties in weaning (changing from a liquid to a solid diet), babies not putting on weight, or not taking enough milk.

The infant may suffer from constipation, vomiting or burping. Parents often worry that the child is vomiting, but in fact often the baby is just posseting (regurgitating a small amount of digested food).
■ **Sleeping** problems include infant colic. A common condition, it gives the baby severe abdominal pain, and often prevents the child from sleeping. Colic is caused by wind in the intestine, and results in the baby crying a lot. This can be very distressing for the parents, since there is nothing they can do to alleviate their child's discomfort.

Another sleeping problem is that some babies reverse their sleeping clock, waking and sleeping at an opposing time to their parents.

They are wakeful at night and families end up exhausted as a result.
■ **Colds** that develop in babies can be a worrying time for parents. Babies tend to stop feeding when their nose is blocked because ingesting food prevents them from breathing. Parents may conclude that the cold is something more serious, and often pay a visit to their baby clinic for reassurance.
■ **Skin rashes** may be due to a primary skin disorder, such as eczema, or secondary to other illnesses, such as viral infection.

When handling a newborn, the midwife wears overalls and a surgical mask to prevent infection. The infant's umbilical cord has been clamped with a clip about 2.5 cm from its abdomen. The stump falls off within a couple of weeks to leave a scar, which is called the navel or umbilicus.

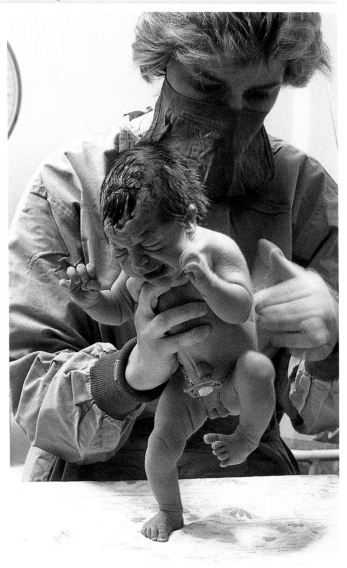

Colic in newborn babies

Crying is the natural way that a newborn baby communicates discomfort and parents usually become adept at knowing instinctively what is needed. For a baby who has colic, however, there are times when nothing seems to help, and this places huge strain on already overtired parents.

Colic is a griping discomfort in the abdomen that causes a baby to draw up his or her legs towards the abdomen and cry inconsolably. One of the main features of colic is that it has a regular pattern; the episodes occur regularly and last for several hours, often during the evenings. The good news is that the problem usually disappears once the baby is three months or more old.

What can be done?
To date there is no firm evidence as to what exactly causes colic. Despite this, there are several tactics you can use to alleviate your baby's distress.

■ Sucking can prove immense relief and a baby may settle if you let him or her suck your little finger or a sterilized dummy. Certainly, it will keep your baby quiet until he or she falls asleep.
■ A dark, quiet environment and gentle rocking motions may help to avoid over-stimulation and encourage sleep, although the parent will need to be persistent. Gentle tummy massage can be beneficial in some babies.

■ Gripe remedies are generally discouraged by medical experts as they are not thought to be of use.
■ Support is essential during difficult periods. Stressed parents can benefit from occasionally asking friends and family to help, allowing brief periods of respite.
■ A breast-feeding mother may want to check her own diet for foods that may be upsetting the baby. A bottle fed baby could benefit from switching to an alternative brand. It may help to consult a health visitor about adapting feeds.
■ Finally, if you are concerned that there may be a more serious problem, it is important to seek help from your family doctor.

Lung problems in newborn babies

Birth involves the progression from fetal life to an independent external existence. The baby's lungs must begin to fill with air to sustain life for the first time, and this can sometimes be a difficult physiological transition.

At the moment of birth, a baby is removed from the stable environment of the womb, where oxygenation and waste removal are provided by the placenta. From here, the baby enters a situation in which the lungs inflate with air, blood exchanges gases with the air in the lungs, and blood delivers oxygen to the tissues and carries away waste carbon dioxide.

In this distressing process, the lungs undergo the great transition from being fluid-filled to inflating with air. The heart also changes in order to accommodate the huge increase in blood flowing to the lungs. As the first breath is taken, oxygen levels in the blood increase, and changes are set in motion that will eventually establish the adult circulation.

LEARNING TO BREATHE

It is now known that babies 'practise' breathing movements in the uterus in preparation for external life. It is the stress of labour, however, that primes the newborn for breathing. One of the main stimuli that causes the infant to breathe after birth is cold air coming in contact with the skin, and most babies will take a breath within a few seconds of delivery.

In premature babies, respiratory drive may be poor, especially following Caesarean section when the mother (and therefore the baby) have had a general anaesthetic. Simple measures – such as blowing oxygen on the face – are often sufficient to establish respiration, but further support by face-mask ventilation or even endotracheal intubation may be required.

Although respiratory problems are common in the newborn, doctors always have to bear in mind that the same symptoms can be due to cardiac disease.

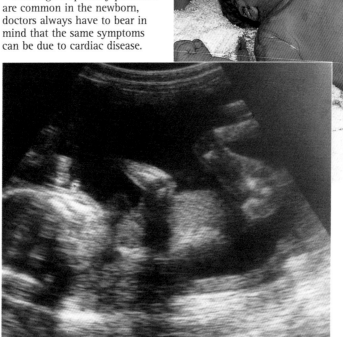

It is very common for babies to be born with amniotic fluid in their lungs. A doctor will use a endotracheal tube, inserted into the lungs via the mouth, to drain the fluid.

In the womb, the unborn baby obtains all its oxygen requirements from the mother via the placenta. The lungs are not used for breathing till birth.

Symptoms of lung problems in the first few hours

Following birth, many physiological complications with the lungs can be expected. These include:
■ Raised respiratory rate
■ Grunting – the emission of a short noise on expiration; it is an attempt by the baby to prevent collapse of the lungs in expiration
■ Cyanosis – a blue colour of the skin and mucosa due to inadequate oxygen supply in the blood. After birth, cyanosis of the extremities is common and of no real significance; however, central (torso) cyanosis requires urgent action.

All babies with signs of respiratory distress other than a very mild and transient tachypnoea (increased breathing rate) must be admitted to a neonatal unit for investigation. This will involve:
■ A detailed history of the latter stages of pregnancy and delivery
■ Close observation to assess the severity of the signs
■ Blood gas analysis, an investigation to assess the baby's oxygen saturation and carbon dioxide levels
■ Chest X-rays to show evidence of meconium aspiration, infection, surfactant deficiency,

pneumothorax or a congenital lung defect
■ Other vital measurements, such as blood sugar levels, temperature and blood pressure
■ An echocardiogram (ultrasound image of the heart) in cases of suspected cardiac problems.

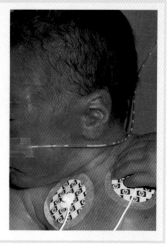

Cyanosis is caused by an inadequate supply of oxygen in the blood, resulting in a blue discoloration of the skin. This is because blood low in oxygen is a dark red-blue, unlike fully oxygenated blood, which is bright red.

Causes of neonate lung problems

The cardiorespiratory system may be very weak at birth, and there are numerous problems that can cause long-term damage and even death if not identified and treated immediately.

Meconium aspiration

Meconium is a tarry, dark green material, composed of cellular debris. It is the unborn baby's first faeces, and it is found in the intestines – its passage into the amniotic fluid is a sign of fetal distress.

The presence of meconium in amniotic fluid will alert obstetricians to speed up delivery. This is because there is a danger that meconium-stained liquid will be aspirated into the lung as the baby takes its first breath after birth. Suction must therefore be applied to the baby's nose and mouth as soon as the head is visible to minimize the risk of aspiration.

If the fluid in the lungs is heavily meconium-stained, and regular respiration has

not been established, the trachea must be directly suctioned using an endotracheal tube and an aspirator (suction device).

Meconium in the lower airways and alveoli of the lungs causes a severe chemical pneumonitis, and respiratory failure can develop. The inflammation causes air to become trapped in the lungs, with a risk of pneumothorax and a rise in pulmonary artery pressure causing a reversion to the fetal circulation.

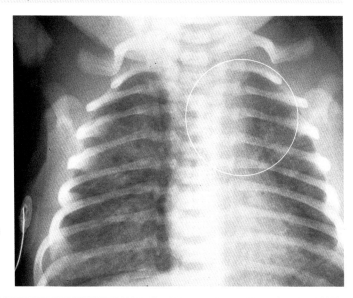

Amniotic fluid and meconium (circled) can be seen in the lungs of this newborn. It represents a serious threat to health as respiratory failure can develop, which can be fatal.

Rapid breathing in newborn babies

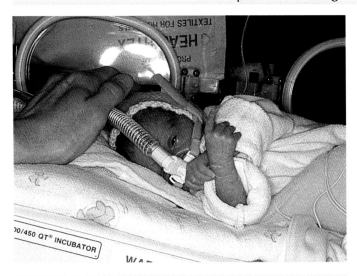

Transient tachypnoea (rapid breathing) is probably the most common cause of respiratory distress in neonates. It is caused by retained fetal lung fluid. The production of lung fluid in the fetus *in utero* is usually 'switched off' by steroid hormones and catecholamines (physiological substances, such as dopamine and adrenaline, which mainly act as neurotransmitters).

These chemicals usually come into effect during labour, and

A face mask is used to administer oxygen to a baby diagnosed with transient tachypnoea. This condition is common after Caesarean births.

this also causes absorption of the fluid across the alveoli. Retention of this fluid within the lungs at the time when they should fill with air causes respiratory distress.

Classically, this complication occurs after Caesarean section, which deprives the fetus of the process of labour and the stimuli that triggers the release of hormones and catecholamines. It is also more common with the use of certain drugs at the end of pregnancy. A maximum of a 40 per cent concentration of oxygen, administered via a face mask as soon as possible after diagnosis, is necessary to treat transient tachypnoea.

Infections

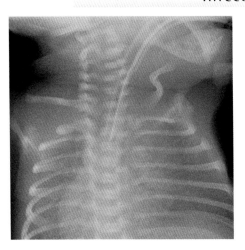

There are several infections from the maternal genital tract that can be acquired during birth – such as Gram-negative organisms or the group B Streptococci. An infection may cause a severe pneumonia, septicaemia or meningitis.

All infants with respiratory distress must be treated for infection until it is excluded by investigations, as any delay in treatment can be fatal.

Streptococcus can cause severe problems, such as pneumonia. This is identified as generalized shadowing on an X-ray.

Rarer respiratory problems

There are a number of rare but serious respiratory conditions that can also affect newborn babies. These include:
■ Surfactant deficiency. Rare in full-term babies but does occur after Caesarean section and in infants of diabetic mothers
■ Primary pulmonary hypertension. Hypoxia resulting from the failure of the circulation to change from the fetal pattern
■ Upper airway obstruction, such as choanal atresia
■ Pneumothorax. The collection of air between the chest wall and the lung, causing partial or total

collapse of the lung. Very rarely requires treatment
■ Congenital diaphragmatic hernia. Herniation of abdominal contents through a congenital defect in the diaphragm. If this occurs early in gestation, the underlying lung does not develop (pulmonary hypoplasia). This is a rare abnormality affecting about 1 in 3,000 births. Severity of symptoms depends on how well the underlying lung is developed
■ Other congenital anomalies, such as cystic adenomatoid malformation of the lung, are rare but can also occur.

Checking a baby at six weeks

Six weeks after birth, all babies undergo a full physical and developmental assessment. The aim is to identify any abnormalities that might not have been apparent at the birth examination.

As part of the Child Health Promotion programme, all babies have a full physical and developmental examination at around six to eight weeks of age. This check-up is usually done by a GP with a special interest in child health, and is sometimes combined with the mother's postnatal examination or the baby's first immunizations.

The aim of the six-week examination is to identify any abnormalities that may not have been found at the birth assessment, and to identify any potential developmental problems or disability as early as possible. The examination is usually recorded in the baby's child health record book.

CHECK-UP

The doctor will already have details about any problems during the delivery or during pregnancy or any family history of handicap. The check-up includes an assessment of vision, hearing and feeding. It also includes an examination for cardiac murmurs, hip instability and undescended testicles.

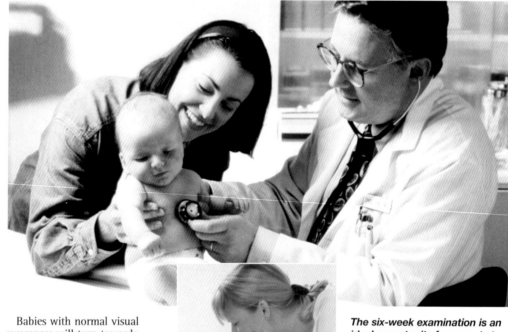

Babies with normal visual awareness will turn towards light or follow the mother's gaze. They will also startle to any sudden loud noise if they have normal hearing. During the visit, the doctor will observe the baby's alertness and watch it interacting with its mother.

The six-week examination is an ideal opportunity for parents to discuss any minor worries they may have with the GP.

Most six-week-old babies have begun to smile at their parents. They will be able to look into the mother's eyes.

Feeding

Before the examination, the baby will be weighed. The doctor will plot the baby's weight on the growth chart in the child health record book. He or she will also inquire whether the baby is breast-fed, bottle-fed, or both.

If there are any problems with weight gain, the doctor will discuss feeding in more detail. This will include the amount of milk taken by the baby, the number and frequency of feeds and any resulting vomiting.

The average weight of a baby doubles by the age of five months, and will have trebled by the end of the first year.

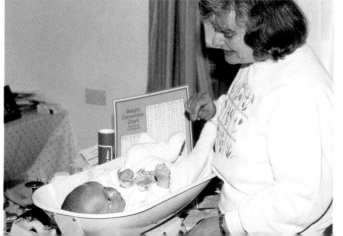

Sleeping patterns

The baby's feeding and sleeping patterns will also influence the amount of sleep that the parents are getting, and this may influence the extent to which the mother is coping in general. The doctor may ask questions designed to identify mothers who may be at risk of post-natal depression so that support and treatment can be offered early.

AVOIDING RISKS

The doctor will also check that the baby is being put down to sleep on his or her back or side, because sleeping prone (on the tummy) is known to significantly increase the risk of cot death (also known as sudden infant death syndrome). Other factors that may be discussed are ways to avoid overheating the baby and parental smoking.

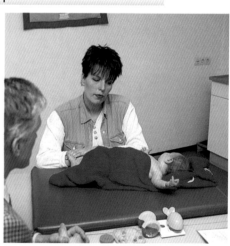

Doctors recommend that a baby should be put to sleep on its back. This is to avoid any possible impairment of breathing if the baby is on its stomach.

Physical examination

The doctor will methodically examine the baby's hands to check the number of digits and the creases in the palm. Babies usually (but not always) have two horizontal palmar creases; Down's syndrome babies may have only one crease and a shortened thumb.

The doctor will also check the fontanelle (soft spots) on the baby's skull, and measure the head circumference to exclude the possibility of hydrocephalus (water on the brain).

CHECKING FOR DEFECTS
The doctor will carefully examine the baby's eyes for any abnormalities of the iris or congenital cataracts. He or she will also examine the inside of the baby's mouth for any small defects in the palate and will check the ears for any minor deformities.

The doctor measures the baby's head circumference. This helps assess growth and is also a check for hydrocephalus.

The baby's eyesight will be tested to check that he or she has normal visual awareness and can track movement.

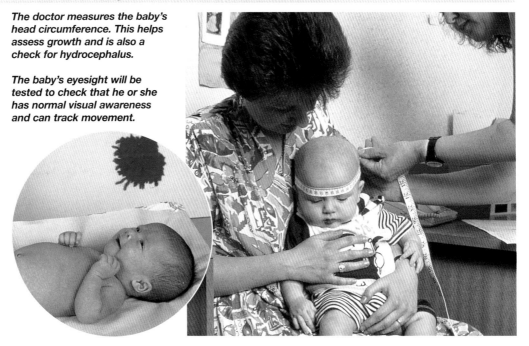

Checking the heart

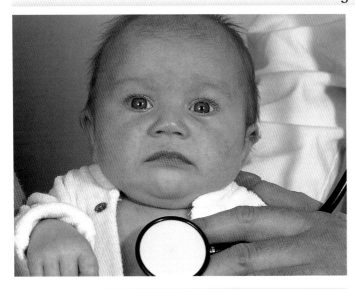

The cardiac examination is vital at the six-week check to detect any heart murmurs that may not have been audible at the new birth examination.

HEART MURMURS
Circulatory changes at birth may mask a small hole between the cardiac chambers, which may go unnoticed for several weeks. Although mild heart murmurs are entirely innocent in otherwise healthy babies, all babies with a murmur will be referred to a paediatrician for

A cardiac examination is vital at six weeks. This is because the circulatory system undergoes major changes at birth.

investigations. These may include a chest X-ray and ECG and, if necessary, an echocardiogram and an ultrasound scan, which clearly shows the anatomy of the heart.

Babies with serious cardiac problems are likely to show symptoms such as breathlessness, difficulty in feeding or central cyanosis, which causes blue discoloration of the lips and tongue.

CHECKING PULSES
After listening to the heart, the doctor will feel the femoral pulses in the baby's groin. Any asymmetry may be a sign of a narrowing of the aorta (the body's largest artery).

Abdominal examination

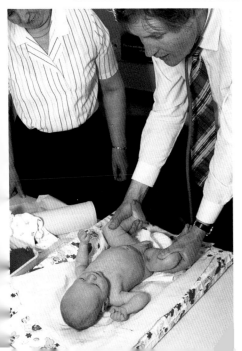

The doctor checks the abdomen for any bladder distension, the hips for dislocation and the genitals for any deformity. If in doubt, the GP will arrange for further referrals.

UNDESCENDED TESTICLES
At birth, around two per cent of full-term male infants have undescended testicles which will come down on their own in the first year. If the testicles do not descend, the baby will be referred to a surgeon for the condition to be corrected.

The doctor will examine the baby's hips for dislocation. A dislocated hip will produce a 'clunk'-like sound when going back into its socket.

Further checks

The doctor handles the baby and looks for any hint of floppiness or stiffness, which can be a sign of neurological problems. The normal mobility and symmetry of all the limbs is checked.

The GP will discuss all the findings with the parents and fill in the child health record. If there are any problems, a referral may be organized.

Parents can ask about the immunization programme as well. If there are no problems, then the next routine examination is a health visitor review at eight months of age.

The feet will be checked for any possible malformations. Most deformities can be surgically corrected, if detected early on.

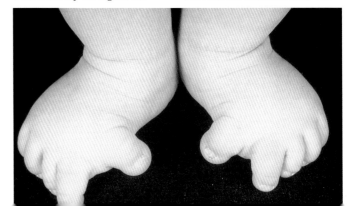

Breast milk and the newborn

Humans, like all mammals, are designed to be fed on their mother's breast milk when first born. Breast milk is tailor-made for growing babies, and this natural option provides newborns with ideal nourishment.

Breast-feeding is generally recognized as the method of first choice for feeding a newborn baby. However, it is not an automatic choice, and many babies grow into healthy adults having never been breast-fed. Cultural values and social factors play a role in determining whether a woman decides to breast-feed and how long she does so.

RICH DIET
The benefits of breast-feeding lie largely in the constituents of the milk. Low in sodium and phosphates, breast milk contains large amounts of carbohydrates. It is less likely than bottled milk to induce allergic reactions, and contains an iron-binding protein that inhibits the growth of *E. coli*, a bacterium that can cause gastro-intestinal infection.

There are also emotional and physical advantages in breast-feeding, as it nurtures the bond between mother and baby. It can also confer physical benefits on the mother as well as the child. Studies show lower incidences of breast cancer in women who breast-feed, and there is evidence of lower incidences of inflammatory bowel disease and diabetes mellitus in adults who were breast-fed as babies.

Packed with vitamins and minerals, and armed with bacteria-busting antibodies, breast milk helps a newborn baby develop immunity and fight infection, especially in its respiratory tract and gut.

Breast-feeding is a demand-led process: when a child is hungry, it demands to be fed, no matter where the mother is at the time. In some countries, breast-feeding in public is frowned upon; in others, it is acceptable and it is common to see a mother breast-feeding her child publicly.

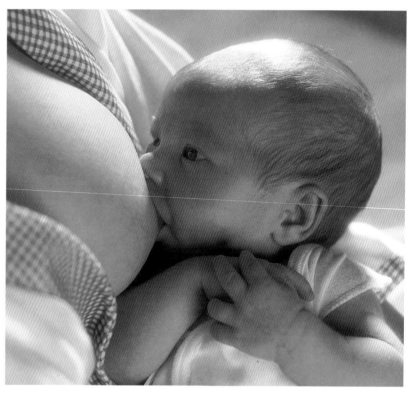

MILK PRODUCTION
The amount of milk produced varies depending on the baby's demands. Each feed has a watery, thirst-quenching 'foremilk', followed by a fat-rich, filling 'hindmilk'.

It is very difficult to overfeed a breast-fed baby, whereas it is common to see babies on 'formula' who are overfed. Unless the mother is having problems producing adequate amounts of milk, feeding on demand allows the baby to satisfy its nutritional requirements when needed.

The 'normal' range of feeding habits is wide. Babies feed for various lengths of time and do not take the same volume of milk from one feed to the next. The length of time between feeds varies, and, provided that the baby is fed on demand, there are no fixed rules regarding how often the baby should be fed.

Contrary to popular belief, women with breasts of all shapes and sizes can breast-feed. Women with small breasts are usually pleasantly surprised that they can adequately feed their babies, while those with the largest breasts may often experience difficulties.

Health implications of being breast-fed

Breast milk is sterile and contains antibodies that can boost immunity. Bottles used for feeding infants must be carefully sterilized to prevent infection.

Breast milk is naturally sterile, which means that there is a much lower incidence of gastro-enteritis (inflammation of the stomach) in breast-fed babies. There is also no need to sterilize and prepare bottles – a blessing in the middle of the night.

Breast-feeding is recommended in developing countries because of the risks associated with poor hygiene. The World Health Organization rates breast-feeding as one of the most important strategies for reducing infant mortality. In

these countries, bottle-fed babies are three times as likely to die from gut or respiratory infections as breast-fed babies.

Breast-feeding may also improve the neurological development of pre-term infants, and evidence suggests that the health of an adult is related to their nutritional intake as a baby. Claims have been made that breast-feeding reduces the incidences of sudden infant death syndrome, but this has yet to be substantiated through independent testing.

EARLY DIFFICULTIES

Starting breast-feeding is not always easy. In the first three days, the breasts produce colostrum, which is thick and bright yellow in colour compared with the more dilute, white milk produced from day four. Colostrum is very high in fat and protein, and is full of enzymes and antibodies. A little of it goes a long way, and the baby feeds on each breast for a very short time to begin with.

This is the first hurdle that many new mothers fall at. Concerned that their child cannot possibly be getting enough sustenance from such tiny amounts, they add a bottle of formula to make sure the baby is full.

Breast-feeding is a demand-led process, so the less the baby feeds from the breast, the less milk the breasts produce. Thus, with the addition of a bottle, the breasts start to reduce the amount they produce. If the baby gets frustrated at the small amount they are now getting, the mother may be convinced that she is unable to breast-feed, and change wholly to formula.

The more abundant, whiter milk appears around day three. Some mothers' breasts engorge at this stage, and, as milk accumulates, the breast becomes tender. When the mother eventually manages to get her desperate infant 'fixed' to her nipple, this can cause her great discomfort.

SUCCESSFUL FEEDING

The mother's mental and physical state also affects the success of breast-feeding. If the mother is very anxious, even with the baby latched to her breast, she may not 'let down' the milk because of her nervousness. Hot flannels, gentle massage or immersing the breasts in warm water may help to 'let down' the milk.

The early stages of breast-feeding can be difficult and require good support and a strongly motivated mother. The ability to breast-feed is learned, not inherited, so it is important that the mother is given encouragement and information on the correct techniques.

Successful lactation is helped by encouraging the mother to feed the baby as soon after birth as possible. Frequent suckling also prompts the release of prolactin from the pituitary gland, which stimulates milk production. The mother should empty the breast during a feed to encourage further production.

SOCIAL ISSUES

In the UK, breast-feeding is most common among women who have a strong support network – including the midwife, health visitor and community nurse – and are well-informed about the

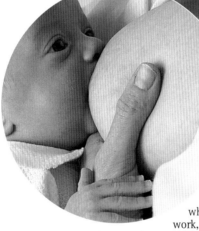

In order to feed, a baby must be 'fixed' properly to its mother's breast. The baby must take in its mouth the entire nipple and the areola – the brownish or pink ring surrounding the nipple.

most successful techniques. Some mothers are unable to devote the time it takes to breast-feed because of domestic or work commitments. And for those mothers who have to go back to work, few companies offer crèche facilities.

The duration of breast-feeding is largely determined by the mother's culture. In some African countries, five years is perfectly normal, while in the

The breast pump is designed to provide the mother with a hygienic and convenient means of expressing milk. If the mother's breasts become too sore to breast-feed, she can express milk for bottle-feeding.

UK many children are breast-fed for two years. The baby itself may dictate when breast-feeding ends. After a baby has started on solids, which usually begins from 16 weeks, it is perfectly normal for it to reduce feeding from its mother's breasts.

Breast milk for bottle-feeding

Bottle-feeding with expressed milk presents an ideal opportunity for a father to bond with his child, as well as giving the mother a rest if her nipples are cracked and sore.

There are some situations in which breast-feeding is impossible, at least in the early stages. Premature babies often cannot breast-feed, but the mother may express her milk for feeding via a nasogastric tube or by bottle until they are able to suckle properly.

Women who experience cracked nipples or breast engorgement may find the baby's sucking painful. To relieve the pain, the mother may express milk for bottle-feeding or use a breast shield, which is a rubber cap with a teat in the middle. If the mother continues breast-feeding with severely cracked nipples, the baby may ingest her blood. This can result in haematemesis (blood in the vomit) and melaena (black, tarry faeces), which can cause parents great concern. These problems are easily avoided by the mother bottle-feeding with milk that she has expressed until she can recommence breast-feeding.

There are several methods of expressing breast milk. It can be done manually by massaging the breast, or mechanically using a breast pump.

The breast pump is placed firmly over the nipple and the plunger retracted to create a vacuum which draws the milk into a container. There are several variations on this device, including an electrically operated pump that allows the mother to alter the pressure and length of suction on the nipple.

Sleep patterns in babies

Babies require far more sleep than older children and adults.
What seem to be chaotic sleep patterns in babies are in fact vital for
the ongoing process of growth, development and maturation.

Newborn babies sleep for approximately 16 hours in every 24, but some need more than this and others need less. Premature babies usually sleep for more than 16 hours a day, but within a year their sleep requirement will match that of full-term babies. In the womb, some paediatricians believe that the unborn baby is asleep virtually all of the time with a very short time actually spent awake.

The length of time spent asleep at night depends on a child's age and personality, and on any rests during the daytime. At three months of age, most babies have three or four sleep periods; at one year old, two or three periods; by the age of three, many babies will not want an afternoon sleep. More placid babies will sleep more than this, and continue with an afternoon rest for a year or two longer. More active children sleep less and may not want an afternoon nap by the age of two.

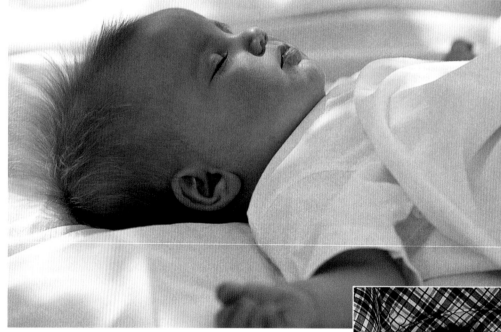

Young babies sleep for much of the day in the first few months of life. As they grow older, the total time spent asleep reduces.

WHAT IS SLEEP?
Sleep is different from a loss of consciousness. When we are unconscious, our brains barely respond to any outside stimulation, such as light, temperature or noise. During sleep, however, our brains are still active, aware of the passage of time and able to respond to physical states, such as hunger, cold or anxiety, as well as to certain sounds.

EARLY SLEEP PATTERNS
Some people believe that newborn babies are either asleep or feeding. However, a newborn is awake for six to eight hours out of every 24, often for an hour or so at a time. Some babies are more wakeful than others. The development of a baby's sleeping and waking cycle, and the maturation of the different sleep states, are closely linked to the integrity of the developing central nervous system.

The length of time that a baby spends asleep depends on the maturity of the brain as much as the baby's need for food. At first, babies rarely sleep for longer than three to five hours, but by the age of four months, most will sleep for between six to ten hours and can also stay awake for several hours.

The big problem for many parents, although not for the child, is that their baby's sleep patterns very often do not coincide with the normal adult sleep pattern. Whereas adults like to sleep for perhaps seven to nine hours each night without interruption, a baby may wake

Newborns need up to 16 hours of sleep a day. A tired baby will be able to sleep even when it is on the move, such as in a pram.

at 1 am and not sleep for several hours or until the early hours of the morning. There is nothing abnormal in this sleep pattern.

Babies cannot fall asleep on demand just because someone else expects it. Adults, however, after several weeks or even months of interrupted sleep, will start to show the normal signs of sleep deprivation, including

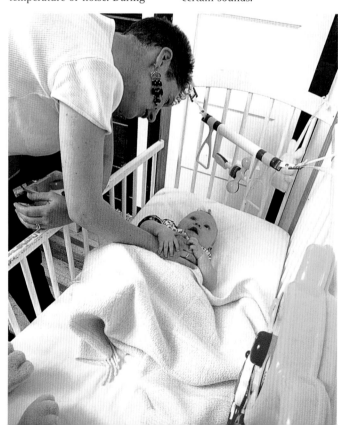

Babies often sleep a great deal during the day. This can mean that they are awake for long periods at night.

irritability and forgetfulness. Unfortunately, a baby has no concept of an adult's timetable and their need to sleep and go to work.

A baby will sleep when it wants to for as long as it wants to. If it has not had enough sleep, it will fall asleep while being fed, while travelling in a car or being pushed in a buggy. It will even fall asleep in a sling on the mother's back while she continues to work. It is thought that the baby feels secure and is reassured by the physical contact and warmth of its mother.

Some babies cry on waking, while others do not. Babies may cry on waking for a variety of reasons: because they are bored, hungry, too hot or cold, uncomfortable, need changing, are suffering with colic, are still tired or because they want physical contact with a parent.

Other babies wake quite contented and just look around and gurgle to themselves until a parent comes in to feed them.

Older babies require less sleep, and daytime naps may interfere with sleep at night. However, overtiredness can cause young children to become distressed.

WHY IS SLEEP NECESSARY?

Sleep is vital for survival. Small animals die after a few days without sleep. A baby needs to sleep in order to grow, develop and mature. However, it is only the brain that needs the sleep state. All the other organs of the body can cope with rest and food alone. But the brain requires sleep in order to function properly.

After decades of research into sleep and the mystery of why the brain needs it, the question remains unresolved – except for the common sense answer of rest. Even in sleep, however, the brain remains active at some low level.

DO BABIES DREAM?

Newborns show the same external signs of dreaming as do older children and adults. In adults, the outward sign of a dreaming state is movement of the eyeballs under the closed lids. This is known as rapid eye movement (REM) sleep.

Newborns also show REMs during active sleep. Even premature babies as young as 32 weeks of gestational age (that is, eight weeks premature) show REM sleep. Curiously, newborns spend about half of their sleep time in REM sleep, while in young adults only about 20 per cent of the time spent asleep is REM sleep.

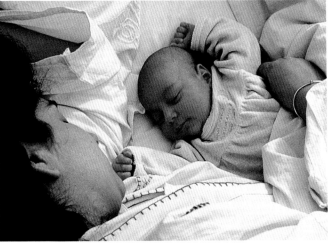

Newborn babies spend about 50 per cent of sleep time in REM sleep. This drops to about 30 per cent by the time the child is 18 months to two years old.

A baby will be comforted by the warmth and physical contact of lying with a parent. This can be a good strategy for encouraging a restless baby to fall asleep.

Bedtime difficulties

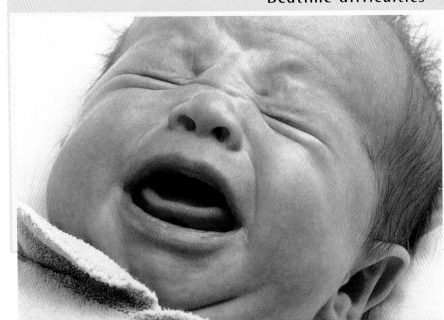

Some babies are very reluctant to be put to bed for the night. When left to cry in bed, around 10 per cent of babies become acutely agitated and as a result are less able to sleep than before. Some babies even vomit as a result, which can cause further concern for the parents.

In older children (usually between two and four), night terrors can occur. These are distinct from nightmares, and the child appears to wake in a state of absolute fear, occasionally screaming, and with its eyes wide open. However, the episode ceases as soon as full wakefulness is reached, and the child has no recollection of it the following morning.

Some babies find it difficult to get to sleep without the presence of a parent. A regular bedtime routine often resolves the problem.

Newborn baby reflexes

A newborn exhibits many reflex actions that disappear as the baby matures. Some reflexes are vital to the baby's survival, such as the instinctive ability to find the breast and suckle, but others have no apparent use.

The large and well-developed human cerebral cortex is the part of the brain that distinguishes us from other animals. Reflex actions, however, do not involve the cortex. They are involuntary, and occur in response to a stimulus, such as touch or pain, whether we want them to or not.

PRIMITIVE RESPONSES

The primitive reflexes are a group of automatic nervous responses seen mainly in newborns and the elderly. They stem from the primitive parts of the brain – the mid-brain and the medulla – which lie beneath the cerebral cortex. In babies, the cortex is underdeveloped, and so the automatic responses are much more apparent.

The absence of primitive reflexes in newborns may be an indication of spinal cord or muscle disease. However, the continued presence of any or some of the primitive reflexes after six months may indicate a neurological problem, such as cerebral palsy. These will not be isolated signs, and the baby will have other problems, too.

A baby will grasp a finger placed in its palm, and release it if the back of its hand is stroked. This is an involuntary reaction to a touch stimulus.

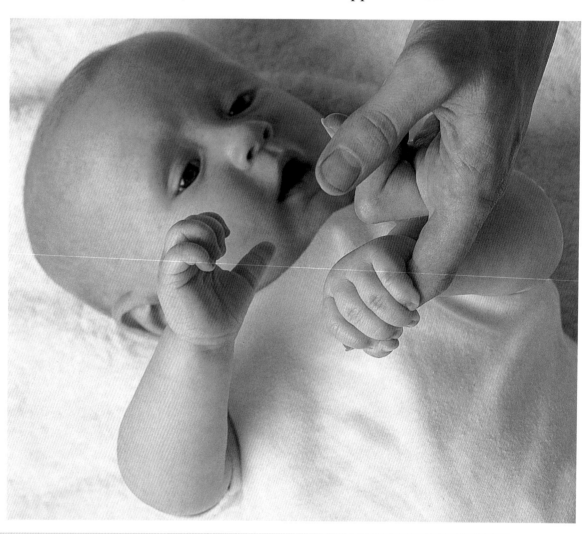

Reflexes vital for survival

Some primitive reflexes are vital for the baby's survival, and are termed 'adaptive'. For example, a newborn will automatically turn its head and open its mouth if a finger is pressed on the cheek near the mouth. This is the 'rooting reflex' that enables the baby to latch onto the mother's nipple when it touches its cheek.

The baby will also suck furiously if a finger or dummy is placed in its mouth. It is also able to swallow at the same time as sucking. These skills are essential

A baby sucking its thumb demonstrates the suck and swallow reflex. This primitive reflex making feeding possible is essential for survival.

for the baby to survive.

At approximately six months, the developing cortex of the brain starts to exert an inhibitory activity over the primitive reflexes, allowing more elaborate forms of intentional activity. This causes the primitive reflexes to recede.

It seems that many of the primitive reflexes do not have any obvious or useful function. It may well be that they hark back to a much earlier stage of human development, and reflect evolutionary changes over time.

Premature babies born before 32 weeks do not have easily identifiable primitive reflexes, but as the baby develops, the reflexes become stronger and more consistent.

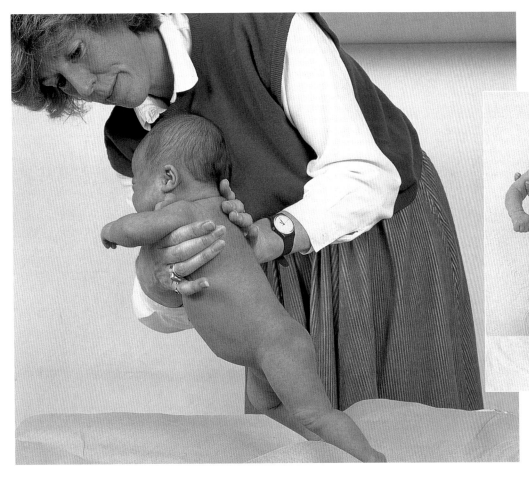

The walking reflex is prompted by placing the legs on a table and leaning the baby forwards by 10–20 degrees. This reaction is lost as the baby achieves voluntary control.

Pressure on the sole of the feet produces instinctive extension of the baby's leg. This is easily demonstrated in a baby under six months.

TESTING FOR REFLEXES

The grasp, or cling, reflex can be induced by drawing a finger across a baby's palm. This action causes it to clench the finger so tightly that it can be pulled up from a lying position. Although this is of no practical use to modern humans, it was perhaps useful to our ancestors millions of years ago. A strong, instinctive grip is certainly useful to a baby monkey clinging to its mother's back.

The 'asymmetric tonic neck reflex' involves lying the baby on its back; when the baby's head is turned 90 degrees to the right or left, the arm and leg on the same side stretch out (extend) while the arms and legs on the opposite side bend (flex).

The 'Moro reflex' is probably the best-known test. The baby is laid down on the forearm and hand of the examiner and the head is held in the other hand. When the baby's head is 'dropped' a few centimetres, its arms flail out and then flex again. The absence of a Moro reflex usually points to a serious problem with the baby's neurological development.

Another reflex is the 'extensor thrust, placing and walking reflex.' This is useful for checking that the baby's legs are functioning correctly. The baby is held in both hands and lowered towards a solid surface. Pressure on the soles of its feet should cause the lower limbs to suddenly extend and push out. If the legs are held against the edge of a table, the baby will bend its leg to place the foot. Leaning the baby forwards at an angle of 10–20 degrees will induce a 'walking' movement.

OTHER SIGNS

The 'glabellar tap' reflex is elicited by repeatedly tapping the forehead above the bridge of the nose. This makes the baby blink with each tap, and it does not cease to blink (habituate), as an adult would.

Another sign is the 'snout reflex', whereby tapping the lips causes the baby to make a pout with its mouth, ready for feeding.

REFLEXES IN THE ELDERLY

As babies grow and develop, the primitive reflexes disappear. As we age, however, they may start to re-emerge. The cerebral cortex deteriorates over time and loses its inhibitory control over the reflexes. This is seen in people with certain forms of dementia, such as Alzheimer's disease.

The reflexes are most obvious in the final stages, but they are not specific enough to be used as a diagnostic test for disease. They may simply be a sign of an ageing brain.

The grasp reflex is seen in infants of up to four months. This surprisingly strong reflex indicates that the nervous system is operating correctly.

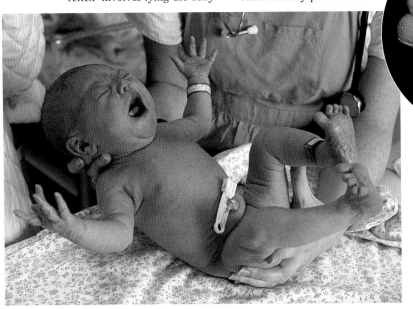

During a routine check-up, all the baby's reflexes will be examined. The Moro reflex occurs when the baby's head is suddenly dropped a few centimetres. The arms and legs will flail out and flex.

Baby immune systems

In the womb, the foetus is initially protected from disease by its mother's immune system. During the weeks before birth, the mother's antibodies are transferred to the baby, protecting it for the first months of life.

The foetus is protected by its mother's immune system in the womb, and is not directly exposed to most pathogens, the micro-organisms that cause disease. However, some infections acquired by the mother, such as rubella (German measles), can have devastating consequences on the developing foetus.

BEFORE BIRTH

The cells of a foetus' immune system are detectable within six weeks of gestation but they are 'naive' (without experience) and do not mature until exposed to foreign proteins and organisms.

Antibodies – the components of the immune system which trigger responses against infection – are transferred from the mother to the foetus from mid-pregnancy onwards, and are detectable in the newborn until about nine months of age. If the mother is immune to certain infections, such as chickenpox or measles, the baby will be protected for its first few months.

ABSENCE OF ANTIBODIES

Severe infections can occur in a newborn if maternal antibodies fail to protect the foetus from, for example, group B streptococcus bacteria, which are carried on the skin and in the birth canal.

Some women do not produce the protective antibodies which, when transferred to their foetus, would protect the newborn child.

Streptococci can cause life-

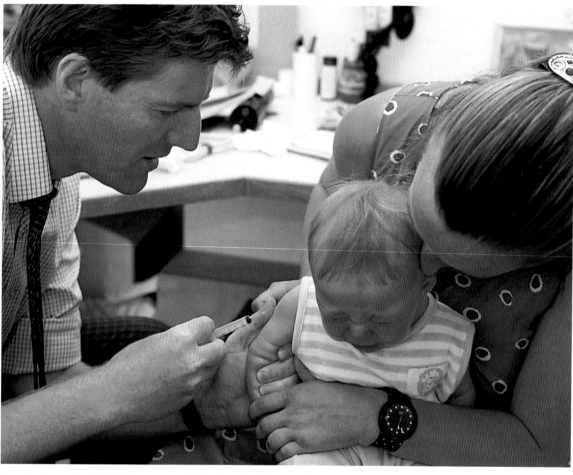

threatening neonatal infection leading to meningitis, severe pneumonia or septicaemia.

DURING INFANCY

During the first year of life, the levels of maternally-transferred antibody that the baby was born with fall. However, mothers who breast-feed continue to pass on antibodies in their milk.

The baby's own antibody production rises sharply. Production of immunoglobulin,

Children dislike injections, but the programme of immunization against potentially lethal diseases is an important way of boosting their defences against illness in the years before they develop full immunity.

a blood protein antibody, begins. There are several types of immunoglobulin and these include IgM (the first line of antibody defence) and IgA (the antibody that protects body surfaces).

It takes many years for adult levels of antibody protection to build up. Therefore, infants have low levels of defence against many antigens, substances regarded by the body as foreign or potentially dangerous.

INFECTIONS AND DEFENCES

The child–adult antibody difference means that a young child is susceptible to infection with certain micro-organisms,

Danger of infection in premature babies

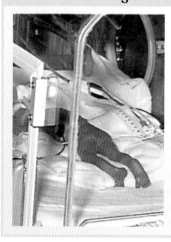

Premature babies are nurtured in an incubator. This gives the baby a controlled environment, protecting it against infections which would otherwise endanger its survival.

Premature babies may have specific difficulties in coping with infection:

■ Their very thin skin is not covered in the thickened protective keratin layer until up to 14 days after birth.
■ The baby may undergo many invasive procedures, including

drips and blood tests, that further disrupt the skin, giving micro-organisms the opportunity to invade.
■ The baby is handled by many hospital staff (unlike a baby at home with parents only). This highlights the importance of good hygiene practice.
■ They may lack the protective maternal antibodies normally transferred late in pregnancy; if delivery is early, the baby will not have received them.
■ Bone marrow production of immune cells is overwhelmed if an infection takes hold.

such as *Haemophilus influenzae* type B (Hib). This is a genus of bacteria frequently found in the respiratory tract. IgG type 2 immunoglobulin (relatively deficient in infants) is the predominant antibody that deals with such infections.

Haemophilus influenzae type B causes serious infections such as epiglottitis, periorbital cellulitis and meningitis, and until recently killed up to 80 children a year in the UK. Since 1992, the Hib vaccination programme has almost eliminated this infection.

Ongoing exposure to foreign organisms and proteins allows the development of immune memory cells in the child.

Two types of lymphocytes – white blood cells that fight infection – are rapidly produced: B-cells, which produce circulating antibodies, and T-cells, the immune response directed against infected body cells.

An increased susceptibility to infections such as *Candida albicans* (thrush) and *Mycobacterium tuberculosis* (TB) persists for much of childhood.

PATTERNS OF INFECTION

Parents often worry about their baby's health, fearing that cold-like symptoms signal a deeper problem. In fact, frequent colds are common in normal children, especially those who mix with many other children or who have siblings.

Further investigation might be warranted, however, in the following situations:
■ Frequent infections, leading to a failure to thrive.
■ An unusually severe case of a common infection, such as severe candida or chickenpox.
■ Infection with an unusual organism, or one that does not normally infect an immune-competent host, such as *Pneumocystis carinii*. This is a pneumonia-causing micro-organism associated with AIDS and other defects of cellular immunity.

In such instances, the doctor will examine the child to check how well its immune defences are working.

IMMUNE DEFICIENCY SYNDROMES

There are a number of immune deficiency syndromes, including:
■ Low antibody levels, diminishing the ability to mount sufficient antibody protection.
■ Severe combined immune

deficiency (SCID) – a rare disorder due to insufficient white blood cells for fighting infection; it requires a bone-marrow transplant.
■ White cell abnormality, resulting in a failure to destroy pathogens.
■ Specific complement deficiency – inhibits the action of a defensive substance in the blood (the complement).

The genetic basis of many of these conditions is now well established. In fact, antenatal diagnosis may even be possible.

Immune deficiency may also be due to infection of the baby during or shortly after

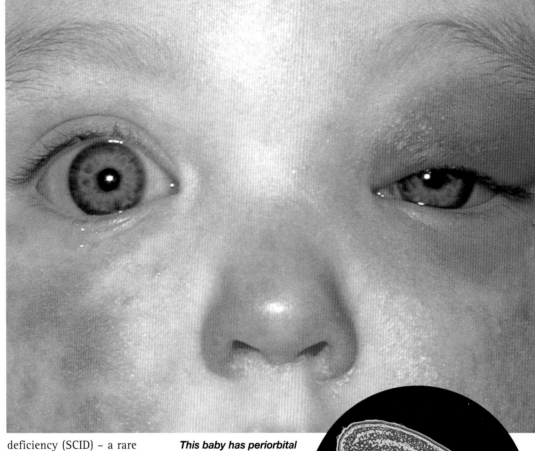

This baby has periorbital cellulitis, an eye condition brought on by the bacterium Haemophilus influenzae *type B. Cellulitis is an infection of the deep dermis of the skin. In this case, the area affected is around the eye socket. Treatment usually involves penicillin.*

pregnancy with HIV. This virus attacks the helper T-cells, which are mainly responsible for cell-mediated immunity. Thus the baby is left vulnerable to the many infections with which it is bound to come into contact.

A single Haemophilus influenzae *type B bacterium can colonize a child's upper respiratory tract in the first few months of life.*

Child immunity – the doctor's key tasks

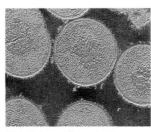

This false-colour electron micrograph shows the bacteria Streptococcus pneumoniae. *It can cause pneumonia or meningitis in newborn babies with too few antibodies.*

Doctors must ascertain the extent to which an infant is protected against illness. They will check the following:
Examinations
■ Growth parameters, such as measuring the length, head circumference and weight of the child
■ Any signs of chronic infection, especially of the mouth, skin, ears and chest
Investigations
■ White cell count
■ Immunoglobulin levels
■ Specific antibodies against vaccinated antigens

■ The number and function of infection-fighting lymphocyte T-cells and B-cells
Key questions for the doctor to ask:
1 Was the child normal at birth?
2 Has the child thrived in infancy?
3 Did the umbilical cord fall off as normal?
(Failure of the umbilical cord to separate can be a sign of defective functioning of the white blood cells that ingest invading micro-organisms.)
4 What infections has the child had so far?

Baby's skull

The newborn's skull has the same bones as an adult's skull, although it is much smaller. There are, however, significant differences in the proportions of the skull, the size and shape of the bones, and how they are joined.

If all the bones of the child's skull were to grow equally until reaching their adult size, then we would end up looking very different. What actually happens is that there is a marked change in the proportions of the skull, with the bones growing at different rates. The face in particular changes radically.

PROPORTIONS

In the newborn skull, the neurocranium (that houses and protects the brain) is about eight times as large as the viscerocranium, or face (which includes the jaws), whereas, in the adult it is only three times as large. This is because the brain develops rapidly and reaches adult proportions early in life, while the jaws, teeth and associated musculature develop over a longer period of time.

At birth, the circumference of the skull is, on average, about 33 cm and the capacity of the brain case is 400 ml. By two years of age, the circumference is about 47 cm and the brain capacity already nearly 1,000 ml, compared with the adult skull circumference of about 55 cm and a capacity of about 1,400 ml.

The orbit (eye socket) in the newborn is comparatively large and its floor is almost level with that of the nasal cavity.

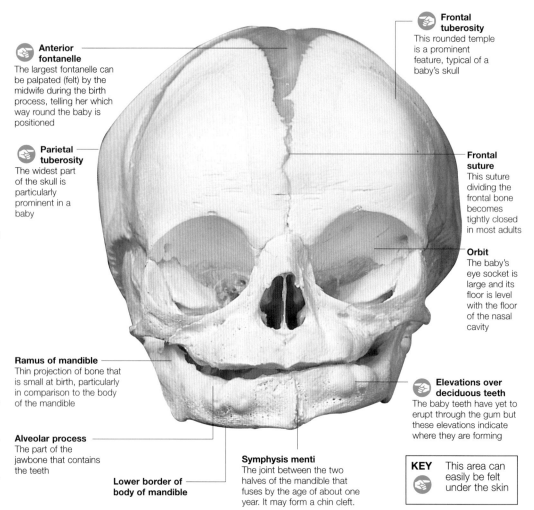

Frontal tuberosity
This rounded temple is a prominent feature, typical of a baby's skull

Anterior fontanelle
The largest fontanelle can be palpated (felt) by the midwife during the birth process, telling her which way round the baby is positioned

Parietal tuberosity
The widest part of the skull is particularly prominent in a baby

Frontal suture
This suture dividing the frontal bone becomes tightly closed in most adults

Orbit
The baby's eye socket is large and its floor is level with the floor of the nasal cavity

Ramus of mandible
Thin projection of bone that is small at birth, particularly in comparison to the body of the mandible

Elevations over deciduous teeth
The baby teeth have yet to erupt through the gum but these elevations indicate where they are forming

Alveolar process
The part of the jawbone that contains the teeth

Symphysis menti
The joint between the two halves of the mandible that fuses by the age of about one year. It may form a chin cleft.

Lower border of body of mandible

KEY This area can easily be felt under the skin

Development of the fetal skull

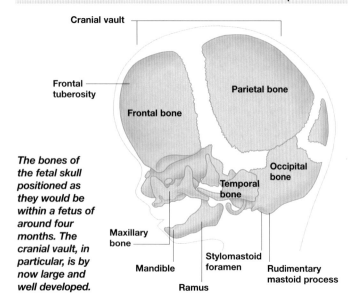

Cranial vault

Frontal tuberosity

Frontal bone

Parietal bone

Occipital bone

Temporal bone

Maxillary bone

Mandible

Stylomastoid foramen

Rudimentary mastoid process

Ramus

The bones of the fetal skull positioned as they would be within a fetus of around four months. The cranial vault, in particular, is by now large and well developed.

The bones of the skull of the newborn are smaller than their adult counterparts, the exceptions being the ossicles of the middle ear (malleus, incus and stapes), which are adult size at birth. Many of the bones are slightly different shapes from those in the adult due to their relative proportions.

In the baby, the bones of the cranial vault are more curved and the frontal and parietal tuberosities (at the temple, and above and behind the ear) are especially prominent.

The mandibular fossa, a depression in the temporal bone where the lower jaw hinges (temporomandibular joint), is flat. The mastoid process behind the ear canal is poorly developed. Consequently, the stylomastoid foramen of the temporal bone, is superficial. One of the nerves that supplies the facial muscles passes through this foramen. An occasional problem is a forceps delivery in which the baby's head is held behind the ears. This may compress the nerve and result in temporary facial paralysis.

The newborn's mandible has no defined chin, but is composed mostly of the alveolar process containing the developing teeth. Each maxillary (upper jaw) bone also consists mainly of its alveolar process.

The first teeth (deciduous) do not begin to erupt until about six months after birth. These teeth have all erupted by three years. The second (permanent) set may not be complete until the age of 20.

Joints of the baby's skull

Fontanelles are a prominent feature of the skull of the newborn.

Fontanelles are the fibrous membranes that fill in the gaps between the growing bones of the vault of the skull. These, and the wide sutures, permit sliding and overriding of the bones of the cranium during the passage of the head through the narrow birth canal. This often leads to temporary distortion of the skull at birth.

There are six fontanelles, each one located at the corners of the parietal bones.

FONTANELLE POSITIONS

Along the midline at the top of the cranium are the anterior and posterior fontanelles. The anterior is the largest of all the fontanelles and is diamond-shaped. It lies between the frontal bone and the parietal bones. At the back of the head is the small, triangular posterior fontanelle.

On each side of the skull are the paired sphenoidal (anterolateral) and mastoid (posterolateral) fontanelles. Both are small and irregular in shape. The posterior and sphenoidal fontanelles close up within three months of birth, the mastoid fontanelle closes at about one year, and the anterior fontanelle at about one-and-a-half years.

PALPATING FONTANELLES

During labour, when the head is engaged in the birth canal, the anterior and posterior fontanelles can be palpated (felt) and identified by the doctor or midwife. In the ideal labour position, the anterior fontanelle should be in front, and a reversal of this position indicates rotation of the baby within the uterus. This may result in a difficult labour.

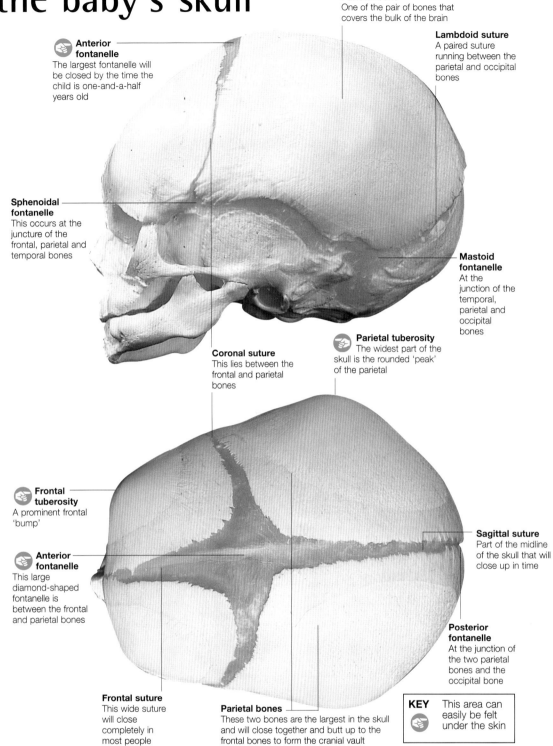

Parietal bone
One of the pair of bones that covers the bulk of the brain

Lambdoid suture
A paired suture running between the parietal and occipital bones

Anterior fontanelle
The largest fontanelle will be closed by the time the child is one-and-a-half years old

Sphenoidal fontanelle
This occurs at the juncture of the frontal, parietal and temporal bones

Mastoid fontanelle
At the junction of the temporal, parietal and occipital bones

Coronal suture
This lies between the frontal and parietal bones

Parietal tuberosity
The widest part of the skull is the rounded 'peak' of the parietal

Frontal tuberosity
A prominent frontal 'bump'

Anterior fontanelle
This large diamond-shaped fontanelle is between the frontal and parietal bones

Sagittal suture
Part of the midline of the skull that will close up in time

Posterior fontanelle
At the junction of the two parietal bones and the occipital bone

Frontal suture
This wide suture will close completely in most people

Parietal bones
These two bones are the largest in the skull and will close together and butt up to the frontal bones to form the cranial vault

KEY This area can easily be felt under the skin

The ways in which a child's skull grows

The bones of the growing skull develop in one of two ways. Some bones, such as those of the vault of the skull and face, may develop directly from a soft connective tissue membrane by the process of intramembranous ossification. Other bones, such as those found in the midline of the base of the skull (the ethmoid and parts of the sphenoid and occipital bones) are derived from pre-existing cartilage, and this is known as endochondral ossification.

The bones of the skull are joined by fibrous joints called sutures that allow for growth. The enlarging brain and eyeballs both generate a force sufficient to separate the bones at their sutures. Bone is then deposited at the edges of the sutures, stabilizing the skull at its new size.

When the brain stops its main phase of growth after about seven years, sutural growth also slows down and the skull enlarges at a slower rate by bone remodelling. Bone is deposited on the outer surface of the skull and reabsorbed on the inner surface. This gradually changes the shape of bones during continued growth.

In the child's skull, certain bones take some years to fuse and form a single bone, because the ossification occurs at more than one site.

For example, the frontal bone is initially separated into two by a midline suture which disappears at about the age of four. The mandible is also in two halves, separated by a midline mandibular symphysis, which fuses between the ages of one and two. At birth, the occipital bone is divided into four parts, and complete fusion does not occur until around six years.

Immunizing infants

Modified bacteria or viruses are used in the form of vaccines
to stimulate the body into producing specific antibodies. Immunity is
sustained by an ongoing programme of vaccination.

Routine immunization of infants has virtually eradicated several serious infectious diseases in the UK. New babies are protected from these diseases in the first few months of life by antibodies that cross the placenta from the mother. This immunity is boosted by breastfeeding, but wears off once the child is weaned.

VACCINES

Vaccines are manufactured using a tiny amount of bacteria or virus that has been modified so that it stimulates antibody production but does not cause the actual illness. If the child is ever exposed to the disease in the future, his or her body will rapidly produce protective antibodies to provide immunity.

For some vaccines, this immunity gradually wanes, and further doses are required to provide longstanding immunity. This includes the diphtheria, tetanus, and polio vaccines, which are first given to babies and then again to pre-school children.

Diphtheria, tetanus and polio are administered a further time at the age of 15 years.

PRIMARY PROGRAMME

The current primary programme of immunization consists of three sets of vaccinations starting at two months of age and repeated at monthly intervals. This consists of a combined vaccine (DTP-Hib) against diphtheria, whooping cough (pertussis), tetanus and Hib (*Haemophilus influenzae* type b); a separate vaccine against meningitis C; and three drops of polio vaccine given orally.

Although these illnesses are now rare in the UK, high uptake of vaccination is essential to prevent new outbreaks. Travel may also present a risk to those who are not immunized.

It is important not to delay in vaccinating premature babies, as they have an immature immune system and are especially vulnerable to infection. Vaccines are extremely effective at producing antibodies, even in newborns.

The UK's primary vaccination programme begins when babies are two months old. Widespread immunization has led to near-eradication of certain diseases.

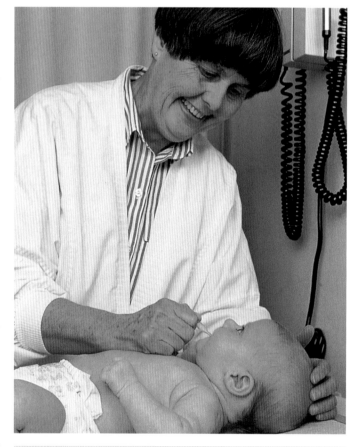

Immunization schedule

From birth (if at risk only)	BCG (TB)	One injection
At 2, 3 and 4 months	Diphtheria Tetanus Whooping cough Hib (DTP-Hib) Meningitis C	Two injections
At 2, 3 and 4 months	Polio	Orally
12–15 months	Measles Mumps Rubella	One injection

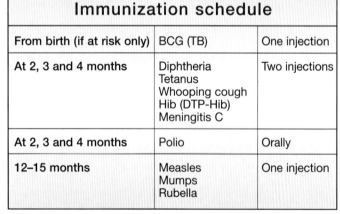

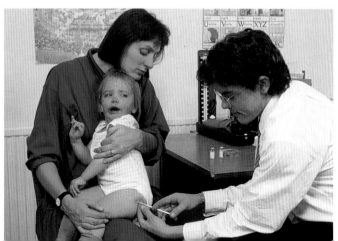

Other vaccines

Certain injections are given to children at a later date or when they are considered to be at risk.

BCG VACCINE

With the re-emergence of tuberculosis (TB) in certain inner city areas, BCG injection is offered to newborns who are considered to be at risk. This includes children travelling to and from countries where TB remains common.

BCG is administered by injecting the vaccine just under the skin in the left upper arm. It is normal for a small swelling to develop, which may discharge pus. This is not a sign of infection and no treatment is required other than keeping the area clean and dry.

A skin prick test is usually

The MMR injection is given to children at 12–15 months and repeated before the child starts school. Short-term side effects are generally mild.

taken before administering BCG, to test for previous exposure to TB. This is not necessary in children under 12 weeks of age. After a BCG injection it is important not to give further injections into the same arm for three months, but the timing of other vaccines is not relevant.

MMR VACCINE

The measles, mumps and rubella (MMR) vaccine is a live attenuated (weakened) vaccine given at 12–15 months of age. One week after vaccination, babies sometimes develop a mild measles-like illness consisting of a temperature and a rash that lasts around 48 hours. This is not infectious and the child should be treated for mild fever with infant paracetamol.

Occasionally, swelling occurs in the cheeks or under the jaw after around three weeks. This is a reaction to the mumps component of the vaccine and will settle without treatment.

Side effects of vaccines

Babies often cry or are irritable and develop a mild fever after their primary injections. In these cases, there are several measures a parent can take:
■ Administer infant paracetamol in a dose of 60 mg (2.5 ml) to reduce temperature and relieve any discomfort. The dose can be repeated after four hours
■ Remove the baby's clothes and sponge the skin with tepid water to reduce fever
■ Give extra fluids.
It is appropriate to ring for medical advice if the symptoms do not settle.

LOCAL REACTION

It is common to develop local redness or a swelling at the site of the DTP-Hib injection that may persist for a few weeks. The GP should be informed if this reaction exceeds 8 cm in diameter, although a reaction is only considered to be severe if it extends the entire circumference of the arm. In this case, specialist advice should be sought before further immunization.

POLIO VACCINE

Polio drops have a bitter taste and babies sometimes posset or vomit the dose. If this occurs within an hour of taking the vaccine and there is some doubt over absorption, the dose may need to be repeated.

Polio vaccine is excreted in the faeces for up to six weeks and there have been very rare cases of unimmunized adults contracting polio through changing nappies. This should only, therefore, be done by fully immunized carers. Likewise, if there is a family member who has an immune deficiency, the infant should have a special non-live polio injection.

CONTRAINDICATIONS

There are few true contra-indications to vaccination unless the baby is acutely unwell. The doctor should be told if the child has any allergies, an immune deficiency, or is taking any medication such as long-term oral steroid treatment. In these situations vaccinations may be deferred.

Infant paracetamol can be given to reduce fever. A pharmacist can supply an oral syringe to measure the dose accurately and to administer the medicine.

Risks of vaccines

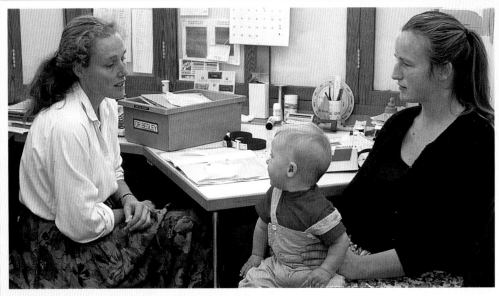

From time to time there are well-publicized scares about the safety of vaccines. However, there is very good research evidence that the risk of the illnesses themselves vastly outweighs any theoretical risk.

After a scare linking whooping cough vaccine to rare cases of brain damage in the 1970s, there was a drastic drop in vaccine uptake. Consequently, a serious whooping cough epidemic developed, which caused a number of unnecessary deaths and cases of brain damage. Subsequent research proved the safety of the whooping cough vaccine currently in use, but the immunization programme took several years to recover.

MMR controversy

The current controversy over the MMR vaccine risks similar consequences. One researcher

The publication of research questioning the safety of the MMR vaccine has led to some parents refusing to vaccinate their children.

hypothesized a link between the MMR vaccine, childhood autism and Crohn's disease. This finding has not been duplicated by other large, good quality studies, and experts at the Medical Research Council and the CSM (Committee on Safety of Medicines) have concluded that the evidence does not support a link.

Autism

Autism is a developmental disorder that usually becomes apparent in the second year of life, when children begin to communicate and interact with other people. It is thought to have a largely genetic component.

As MMR is given shortly before the age that autism usually becomes obvious, the link is believed by most immunization experts to be coincidental rather than causative. There is no evidence that splitting the vaccine into individual components is safe practice and this is discouraged by national policy, because it leaves children vulnerable to life-threatening diseases for longer.

Herd immunity

Withholding immunizations is a serious decision that leaves children at risk of infection and reduces 'herd' immunity of the population.

Any parental concerns should be discussed with the health visitor or GP, who can refer them to the local immunization specialist if necessary.

Developmental delay

In their first year, babies undergo assessment to ensure that they are progressing normally. If certain 'milestones' are not achieved, a team of health professionals will investigate the reasons for this delay.

Every baby develops at their own pace. There is no absolute age at which a baby should reach a developmental milestone, such as being able to sit or crawl, but rather a normal age range. A baby who seems slow in one aspect of development, such as walking, may turn out to start talking early, for example.

The term 'developmental delay' is used for children who are not progressing within expected limits. If there are problems it is important to detect them early so that any special needs can be met. For this reason, there is a well-established child health promotion programme for children up to five years old.

Premature babies are not expected to reach milestones at their actual age. Instead, a corrected age is calculated from their expected date of delivery.

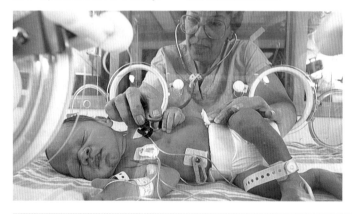

Checking an infant's length, weight and head circumference gives an indication of how well it is growing in the first year.

EXAMINATION

Soon after a birth, the paediatrician will examine the baby thoroughly, and will check the infant twice in the first year to monitor its ongoing development.

Any baby who had a difficult birth or required special care in the neonatal period will be monitored particularly closely. The 6–8 weeks check is usually done by a GP, and the eighth-month developmental review is usually performed by a health visitor.

In most areas of the UK, these examinations are recorded in a personal child health record book, which the parent retains and which acts as a permanent record of a child's development and immunizations.

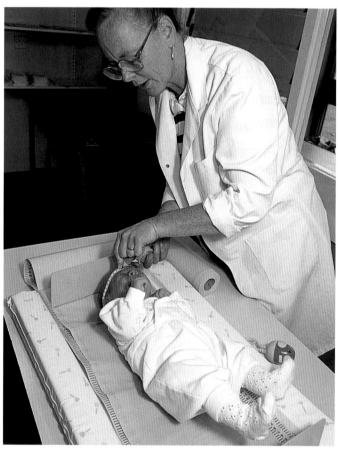

AREAS OF DEVELOPMENT

In the first year of life, babies rapidly learn motor skills and start to develop speech and language and early social skills. Motor development can be divided into gross motor skills, such as crawling, and fine motor skills, such as picking up small objects, which also requires good vision. To learn speech, a baby copies sounds and therefore must be able to hear normally.

Although children develop at different rates, they follow the same sequence, such as first learning to roll, then sit, before crawling and then walking.

Causes of developmental delay

About three per cent of children are considered to have developmental delay. This may affect all areas of development, or it can be specific to a single area. Sometimes no cause can be found and the child outgrows the problem, but it should not be assumed that this will happen.

There are numerous medical causes for developmental delay, including genetic diseases, cerebral palsy and autism, together with social causes, such as lack of stimulation. Most children who have a serious mental handicap will be diagnosed in the first year of life, but occasionally this may only become clear at a much later stage, such as when there are speech problems. Autism is an abnormality of social behaviour, which usually appears in the second year of life in children who previously seem to be developing normally.

Babies are tested for hypotonia – lack of muscle tone – by observing how the infant wriggles and flexes. Hypotonia indicates a number of conditions, including Down's syndrome.

Developmental checks

The two most important medical examinations for a baby after the neonatal period are the six- to eight-week check and the eight-month check. By a range of simple tests, a doctor can monitor an infant's general health.

At the six–eight week check, the doctor will ask the parents questions to ascertain each area of development. At this age, most babies will look at their parents' faces and follow their gaze around the room. If a baby does not seem visually aware at this age, it will be referred to an ophthalmologist for an eye examination. By six weeks, babies will start to make loud noises, and many babies will be starting to make cooing sounds. If parents are concerned about their child's hearing, or there is a family history of hearing problems, the hearing can be tested from birth by an audiologist measuring electrical emissions from the cochlea in the inner ear. Early diagnosis of hearing problems is crucial, so that speech development can be optimized if there is a problem by using hearing aids and speech therapy.

The six–week check will also include evaluating head control and muscle tone, which can be used to detect a physical problem.

EIGHT–MONTH CHECK

By the time of the eight-month check, it is usually much clearer if a baby is developing normally. Most babies will be rolling and sitting and a few will be starting to crawl. It is now possible to assess early fine motor grasp, with some babies using their whole hand to pick up small objects and some starting to use a pencil grip with two fingers.

Most babies will be babbling and some will be saying 'mama' and 'dada'. Babies whose hearing was not tested in the neonatal period will have a distraction hearing test at around this age.

If a baby seems slow to develop in any area, at either the six–eight week or the eight month examination, there is no immediate cause for concern. In

By the age of eight months, most babies will be able to sit upright unsupported. Failure to do so could be indicative of a musculoskeletal disorder.

most cases, the parents will simply be asked by the doctor or health visitor to bring the baby for a further check-up in a few weeks. However, if there are still concerns at this stage, the baby is likely to be referred to a specialist for a second opinion.

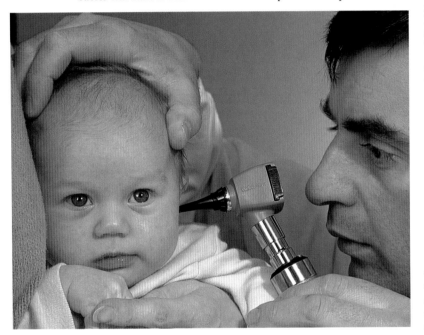

Checking the health of a baby's ears is very important. Any problem with hearing could interfere with the normal process of learning to speak.

Specialist referral

If a baby seems completely physically normal, it will usually be referred to a community paediatrician for a more detailed developmental assessment. This will involve scoring systems, such as the Griffiths Mental Development Scales, which are suitable for children from birth to eight years.

The test assesses the child in five areas: locomotor, personal-social, hearing and language, eye and hand, and performance. Various toy tests, tasks and pictures are used, depending on the child's age.

SPECIAL NEEDS

A child development centre has access to a multidisciplinary team, including a speech therapist, physiotherapist, occupational therapist and social worker, depending on the specific problem areas. The aim is to identify any special needs, so that the child can make the best of its ability, and to provide emotional and practical support for the family to help them come to terms with difficulties.

If there are concerns about the ability of the child to integrate into a mainstream school, the local education authority will be informed so that a full assessment and a statement of educational needs can be made.

Part of the assessment of a baby's physical and mental development at the six–eight week test stage involves dangling an object over the baby's head. This tests the baby's sight and their ability to track movement.

Problems with a child's development may be noticed at home while a parent plays with the child. These may include hand-eye co-ordination, such as playing with a musical toy.

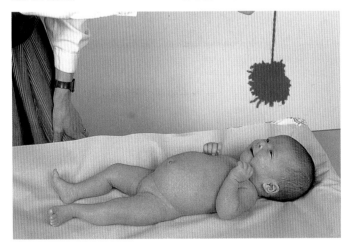

Learning to eat

After only 10 days, a newborn baby will have drunk its own body weight in milk. But babies soon require over 100 Calories per day for every kilogram they weigh, and to maintain this, they need to start eating solid foods.

For the first 16 weeks of life, babies are dependent on milk for all their nutritional requirements. Their reflexes are geared to help them find the nipple, and suck and swallow at the same time. Hunger drives them to cry when another feed is required, and milk produces instant hunger gratification.

As the baby develops and grows, its hunger becomes more difficult to satisfy with milk alone. The baby also begins to notice when other members of the household are eating, and may even try to grab a mug or spoon if held on a parent's lap at meal times. This signifies that the baby will soon be ready to try new tastes.

TELL-TALE SIGNS
Usually, a baby will be ready for solid food at around four to six months of age. It may show dissatisfaction after a bottle-feed, and take every opportunity to put things into its mouth to fully investigate them. This is a major step in the baby's development, as it signifies the beginning of its relative independence from its parents. However, this is a slow process, as the baby will only eat when it feels like it.

Even if the baby is keen to start on solid foods, there are risks to starting too early. For example, the high concentration of salt and other minerals in the food may damage a baby's kidneys. Also, allergies such as eczema are more common in babies started on solids before three months old – as are

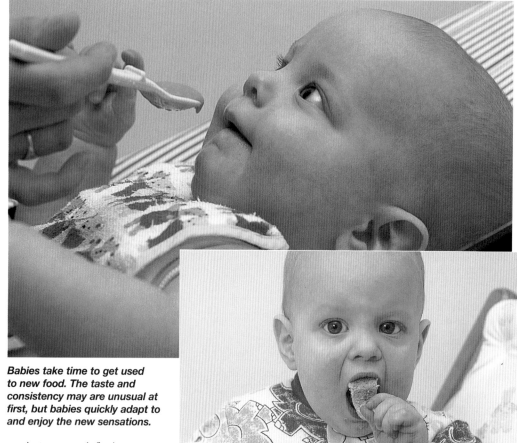

Babies take time to get used to new food. The taste and consistency may are unusual at first, but babies quickly adapt to and enjoy the new sensations.

respiratory tract infections.

There are also several complex activities involved in eating, such as chewing, swallowing and movements of the tongue and jaw. These actions require a certain degree of development of the jaw and facial muscles, and take a few months to learn. Therefore, babies of less than three months are simply not physiologically ready for solids.

FOODS TO AVOID
In developed countries, babies usually start weaning on a gluten-free cereal, such as baby rice. Gluten is a mixture of proteins found in wheat, and it is an important part of the baking process. Babies under six months may be sensitive to gluten, and must avoid food containing wheat or rye. If infants have trouble digesting these foods, they may suffer full-blown coeliac disease (an intestinal malabsorption disease due to permanent gluten intolerance) in later life.

In the early stages of eating solids, the baby will usually feed

Effective finger feeding is an important part of a baby's development. It involves hand-eye co-ordination, manual dexterity and a degree of independence from parents.

once a day on one teaspoon of baby rice mixed in with its normal milk. This is a very smooth mixture which does not need chewing. A number of parents choose to introduce these first meals at breakfast, when the baby is alert and ready for new ideas, rather than just before bedtime when it may be tired and less willing to tolerate anything unusual.

A baby will adapt to solid foods more easily if it feeds an hour or two after a bottle- or breast-feed. This ensures that it is not too hungry and therefore unwilling to do anything but drink milk.

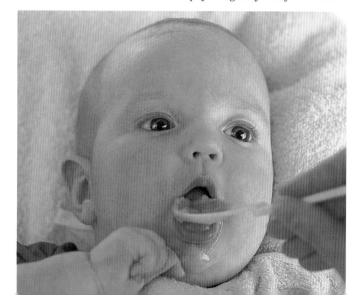

A baby may be frustrated by spoon feeding at first as it has to wait for each spoonful to be put into their mouth. However, it soon adapts to this new feeding pattern.

CHANGING FROM FLUIDS TO SOLIDS

Even when solid food has been introduced into the diet, the urge to suckle continues and a baby will often put a finger, thumb or several fingers in its mouth with every mouthful of food. The baby needs time to adjust to this method of feeding.

At first, it may find eating solids a frustrating experience: it has been used to a continuous flow of nourishment from the breast or bottle, and now the flow of feeding is interrupted by waiting for each spoonful. However, it will gradually become used to the experience and begin to anticipate food with the action of being placed in a chair with a bib and the noises of food preparation.

ENERGY REQUIREMENTS

Compared with an adult, a newborn will require about double the Calorie intake per kilogram of bodyweight. This equates to about 100 Calories per kilogram per day. Parents may be tempted to load as many Calories as possible into the baby, but it will still rely heavily on milk intake for most of its Calories. Once the baby is taking a few spoonfuls of solids once per day, the number of meals per day can be increased.

After six months, the baby will be able to handle lumpier foods, and may want a drink other than milk when it is eating. Soft drinks should be avoided, as the sweet juices rot young teeth, especially when given in a bottle, and provide very little sustainable energy.

Around this time, the baby will start trying to feed itself, and this is the time to wrap the kitchen in washable plastic and be prepared to find food in every one of the baby's orifices as well as, hopefully, in its mouth. Not letting a baby have a spoon will ultimately lead to frustration and loss of temper, and possibly a refusal to eat.

EXPLORING NEW FOODS

A baby has surprisingly hard gums, and after six to seven months, teeth may also start to show. When this happens, a baby will be able to start eating finger foods such as banana or bread sticks. It will, however, need constant supervision in case it chokes.

There is potential for problems centred around a toddler's eating habits, but the way that the first year is handled strongly influences the future eating habits of the child. Patience spent at this time goes a long way later in childhood.

Babies have limited manual dexterity and co-ordination, and cannot easily manipulate tools like spoons or forks. As they grow older, they develop the skills needed to feed themselves.

When feeding from the breast, the baby's natural response is to place the tongue out and under the nipple to draw in fluid. When the diet includes solids, this response pushes food out of the mouth.

Chronology of food tolerance

Babies benefit from handling their food, as this helps develop their motor skills. It also prepares them for using tools, and teaches them to feed themselves.

4–6 months: After a few days of small amounts of baby rice, a baby will be ready for new textures and flavours in its diet. The best foods are mashed vegetables or fruit. Babies may be particularly partial to carrot, apple or potato. These should be carefully peeled, steamed or boiled and then puréed, and allowed to cool.

6–7 months: Some foods are better left until the baby is over six months old, as they are more likely to sensitize the baby and cause allergies. Therefore, foods containing gluten (such as pasta or bread), dairy products and strong tasting foods can be introduced gradually at this age.

7–9 months: Older babies are able to tolerate and enjoy slightly coarser food, such as minced or mashed chicken, fish or lamb. Finger foods, such as rice crackers or cheese, will develop manual feeding skills and encourage the baby to feed itself. This can be an engrossing and enjoyable experience for the baby; it is also an important stage of development as it involves a degree of independence from the parents' involvement in feeding.

Food such as pasta, which contains gluten, should be avoided until the baby is over six months. If the baby is younger than this, it might be sensitive to gluten.

Feeding and weaning problems

Babies may develop feeding difficulties either in the first few weeks of life or when they start to take solid foods. Most problems respond well to medical advice and are short-lived.

For many new parents, feeding a new baby may be problematic in the early days. As infancy progresses, difficulties with weaning and with establishing a healthy balanced diet often arise. Fortunately, most problems can be resolved with advice and support from the midwife, health visitor and doctor.

BREAST-FEEDING PROBLEMS

Breast-feeding should be encouraged because it confers immunity on the baby and reduces the risk of allergies. However, although two thirds of women begin by breast-feeding, only 50 per cent are still doing so by the time the infant is two weeks of age. This is due to a number of problems that may occur, which include:

■ Sore and cracked nipples – many mothers are unprepared for the initial discomfort caused by prolonged sucking. The correct technique is important as the baby must 'latch on' correctly, with the neck slightly extended and most of the areola (dark area of tissue surrounding the nipple), as well as the nipple, in the mouth

■ Mastitis – mastitis is an infection of the breast, which may follow a cracked nipple. It causes pain and redness in the breast and is often associated with a fever. Treatment is with appropriate antibiotics, and breast-feeding can continue unless it is too uncomfortable

■ Misinterpreting need – breast-feeding on demand is usually recommended. However, babies suck for comfort as well as for food; crying may therefore be misinterpreted as hunger, when it is actually due to discomfort from too much milk or simply a desire for contact with their mother

■ Failure to thrive – some mothers worry that their baby is not obtaining enough milk, so they give the baby extra nourishment in the form of formula milk. This is not generally advisable, as the baby's sucking action stimulates milk production and the less the baby tries to feed, the more scarce the

milk supply becomes. If a breast-fed baby is not gaining weight normally, the usual advice is to encourage the baby to suck more frequently in the first instance, before resorting to supplementary feeds.

Regular weighing at the local child health clinic is helpful to monitor weight gain and to

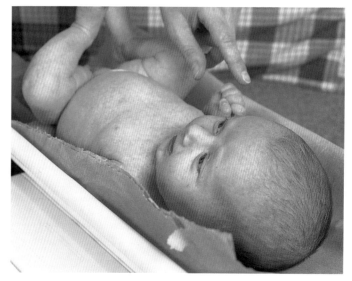

Babies are weighed regularly to check that they are progressing normally. A baby should gain about 200 g (6 oz) per week after the first two weeks of life.

identify any babies who are failing to thrive. Mothers must take care to eat healthily and not diet excessively.

Bottle-feeding problems

Babies are often fed using a bottle, either through choice or because of difficulty with breast feeding. However, formula feed itself can cause problems.

Many women opt for bottle-feeding, either as a first choice, or because of difficulties in breast-feeding. Infant formula milk is produced by modifying cows' milk to make it similar (in terms of fat and protein content) to breast milk.

FORMULA STRENGTH

Parents often think that changing the formula can help to solve feeding difficulties, but this is more likely to cause further problems. Formula milk should always be made up to the recommended strength, as adding additional powder can put a strain on the kidneys, and excessively diluting the formula

provides inadequate calories.

As a rough guide, a baby's weight gain is around 200 g (6 oz) per week, although this may fluctuate. If a baby is failing to gain weight well, the milk intake should be recorded and monitored over several weeks.

COWS' MILK ALLERGY

True cows' milk allergy in infants is rare and may present as a rash around the mouth or diarrhoea. If a baby has a cows' milk allergy, milk should not be re-introduced until after the child is one year of age; medical supervision is then necessary in case of an allergic reaction.

Babies sometimes develop transient lactose intolerance after an episode of gastroenteritis, and are unable to drink cows' milk for a period of time. Soya formula milks can be helpful in such situations.

Digestive problems

Most digestive problems are minor, such as constipation or a slight regurgitation
of milk following a feed. Occasionally, more serious difficulties may occur, such as
pyloric stenosis or hernias, which can be treated effectively by surgery.

Most babies sometimes regurgitate (posset) a little milk after feeds, whether they are breast- or bottle-fed. Posseting may be caused by overfeeding or inadequate winding of the baby. It is a nuisance, but is generally normal as long as the baby is gaining weight well.

REFLUX

Oesophageal reflux is a more dramatic regurgitation. It is caused by underactivity of the sphincter between the oesophagus and the stomach, which normally acts as a one-way valve. Affected babies regurgitate after every feed and must be propped up for at least

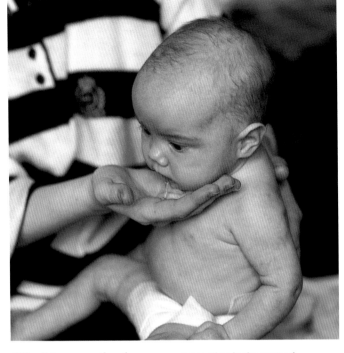

twenty minutes after a feed. Elevating the head of the mattress (by placing a thin pillow underneath) is helpful. Reflux may be helped by adding a prescribed thickening agent to the feed; most babies grow out of the condition by about six months of age.

These conditions must be distinguished from projectile vomiting. This can be a symptom of pyloric stenosis, in which the muscle at the outlet of the stomach becomes thickened. Pyloric stenosis presents at around four weeks of age and is associated with poor weight gain. The condition is diagnosed by ultrasound scan and is easily treated surgically by dividing the affected muscle.

Vomit that is blood- or bile-stained should always be reported, as it may be a sign of obstruction of the bowel, caused by a hernia, for example.

CONSTIPATION

Constipation refers to a hard stool that is

Heavily diluted juice can be given to babies who are suffering from constipation. Infants should be at least one month of age.

difficult to pass, rather than infrequent bowel motions; it is normal in breast-fed babies for several days to elapse between bowel motions.

A baby with constipation may be helped by additional fluids in the form of boiled, cooled water. Pure fruit juice, diluted to a ratio of at least 1: 6, may be given after four weeks of age. For

Posseting is the normal regurgitation of small amounts of milk. It differs from persistent vomiting, which may be a sign of a more serious condition.

babies who have already been weaned, fruit purées may help relieve constipation. Sugar water is an old-fashioned remedy, and should not be given.

Weaning problems

Weaning from milk to solid food should begin gradually from around four months of age. Babies have immature digestive systems and problems may arise if weaning is started before three

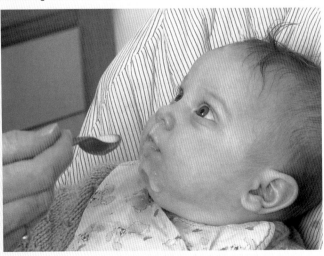

months of age. For hungry babies, it is better to increase the amount of milk given than to wean them too early. Late weaning beyond six months is associated with iron deficiency

anaemia, particularly for breast-fed babies, as breast milk has a low iron content.

First foods

First foods, such as baby rice, should be introduced by spoon in small quantities after the milk feed. At this age, the main nutrition is from milk, and solids are a supplement rather than a substitute.

From around seven months of age, lumpier foods and finger foods can be carefully introduced. Babies can begin to eat puréed, home-made foods as long as there is no salt added. It is important to introduce a variety of foods of different flavours, to

Babies should be introduced to solid food from about four months of age. Gluten or egg products are not recommended before six months of age.

prevent babies from becoming 'faddy'. At this age, it is helpful to leave plenty of time for meals and to try to avoid showing frustration.

From about nine months of age, a baby's milk intake should drop to around one pint (20 floz/568 ml) a day. Excessive milk consumption is often a reason for poor eating at this age and it may be helpful to leave milk drinks until after a meal and to discourage feeding from bottles during the night.

Coeliac disease

Coeliac disease causes an intolerance to gluten in the diet, leading to malabsorption and fatty, offensive-smelling stools. Affected babies are well until gluten products are introduced into the diet, at which stage they show poor weight gain and develop vitamin deficiency.

Failure to thrive

Failure to thrive describes the situation when a baby does not grow or gain weight as normal. This is often due to insufficient amounts of food, but it may indicate an underlying disease.

The first two years of life are a time of rapid growth and development. Most babies double their birth weight by around four months, and treble it by the end of the first year. Failure to thrive is the medical term used for those children who are not growing and gaining weight adequately. A baby who is underweight will be weighed several times over a period of weeks by the health visitor to monitor weight gain and try and identify any difficulties with feeding.

CENTILE CHARTS

All new parents are given a child record book. This book contains growth charts for weight, height and head circumference. These growth charts show centile lines representing the range of normal weight gain for healthy infants at different ages. The middle line, or 50th centile, represents the average weight; other lines indicate the expected weights of most babies. At the extremes of these ranges are bands representing the weight of the heaviest two per cent (98th centile) and lightest two per cent (second centile).

One measurement on its own is not adequate, and several weights are needed before a

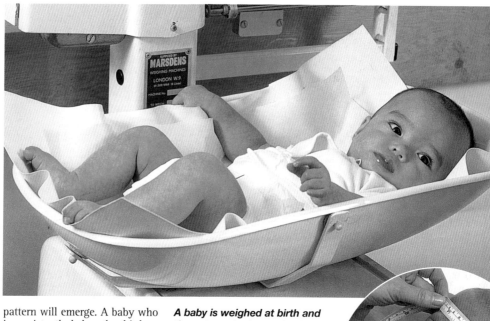

pattern will emerge. A baby who is persistently below the third centile may just be small or may be failing to thrive.

COMMON CAUSES

In most cases, failure to thrive is due to either the baby not taking enough milk or not being offered enough, either through inexperience or neglect. In a small percentage of cases, it may be a sign of chronic disease such as malabsorption, heart disease or kidney problems.

A baby is weighed at birth and then at regular intervals; these measurements are compared to a growth chart. Failure of a child to grow and gain weight may indicate an underlying disease.

Head circumference is regularly measured. Babies whose weight is on a much lower centile than their head circumference should be monitored, although this is often simply a family trait.

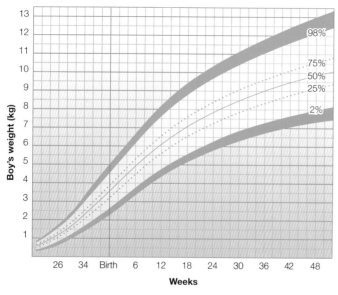

This simplified centile chart shows how the weight of a baby boy is expected to increase in a predictable way. If a previously healthy baby suddenly deviates from its centile, failure to thrive is a possible cause.

Breast-feeding problems

A common feeding problem is simply poor breast-feeding technique. Breast-feeding can be painful, and many women get sore nipples and a few suffer from mastitis (inflammation, usually caused by bacterial infection). Most difficulties settle rapidly with perseverance and advice from health visitors or breast-feeding counsellors.

If a baby is not gaining weight, the health professional may want to watch the mother feeding her baby to see if it is latching on to the breast properly.

If poor weight gain persists over a period of several weeks and there are concerns about the baby's health, the health professional may occasionally recommend supplementing feeding with formula milk. This should not be perceived in any way as a failure on the part of the mother.

Breast-feeding is a co-operative act between mother and child, both of whom may experience problems at first. This may result in an insufficient supply of milk.

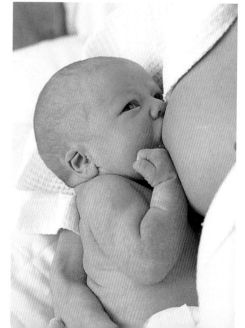

Bottle-feeding problems

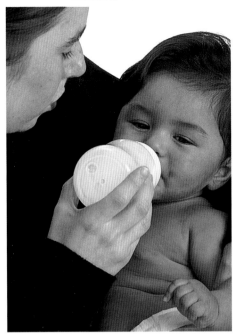

In bottle-fed babies, it is obviously much easier to measure the amount of milk taken at a feed. An average baby requires 150 ml/kg per day (around 2.5 oz per lb), and the average weekly weight gain is around 200 g. It is normal for weight gain to vary slightly each week and to appear to increase in steps. Simple problems can sometimes be identified, such as the hole in the teat being too small or feeds being made up incorrectly.

Poor hygiene in the preparation of bottle feeds is an important and potentially serious cause of poor nutrition due to recurrent bouts of gastro-enteritis.

The amount of milk consumed by a bottle-fed infant is easy to gauge. It is, however, vital that formula milk is made up properly to provide adequate calories.

Toddler feeding problems

Once solids are introduced, problems with food refusal become an important cause of failure to thrive. It is quite easy for poor eating patterns to become fixed, and many toddlers develop food fads.

Toddlers do not have the same nutritional requirements as adults. Many well-intentioned parents feed their small children with 'healthy' high-fibre low-fat foods, which fill the child up without providing sufficient calories or protein for growth. Children under two years should have an energy-rich diet which includes whole milk, full-fat cheese, eggs and red meat.

Once a child is eating solids, it may develop poor eating habits and refuse the meals provided. It is important that the food a child eats is energy- and protein-rich.

Medical problems

Failure to thrive should not be put down to a feeding problem if the baby seems unwell in any way. Babies who are not gaining weight and are vomiting regularly, or who have abnormal stools or seem breathless, should be seen by their GP.

Medical conditions that can cause failure to thrive include:

■ Excessive vomiting
Healthy babies who are gaining weight normally vomit small amounts of milk after feeding; this is known as posseting. In a

condition called oesophageal reflux this problem is exaggerated and treatment may be required, such as thickening feeds with an infant antacid preparation.

Projectile vomiting is associated with pyloric stenosis; a thickening of the muscular opening of the stomach, which can be corrected by a simple surgical procedure.

■ Diarrhoea
Diarrhoea in an underweight child may suggest a malabsorption, such as coeliac disease. This is a sensitivity to gluten, a wheat

protein. This usually occurs after around six months, as this is the age when it is recommended that gluten-containing solids are introduced.

It is important to remember that breast-fed babies usually have mustard-coloured, loose faeces until they start to eat solid food. Similarly, many healthy young children have undigested food in their faeces (for example, peas and sweetcorn), so-called toddler diarrhoea, caused by food passing rapidly through the intestinal tract.

■ Congenital heart disease
Breathlessness when feeding and cyanosis – a blue discoloration of the skin and mucous membranes – are both serious signs which can be associated with congenital heart disease. If there is any suspicion of this, it should be reported to a doctor as soon as possible.

■ Cystic fibrosis
Cystic fibrosis is another condition which may be a cause of failure to thrive. It is usually associated in infancy with recurrent chest infections and diarrhoea.

There are numerous other possible causes of failure to thrive, including neurological diseases and genetic and metabolic conditions, but these are very unlikely in a baby who otherwise seems healthy and is developing normally.

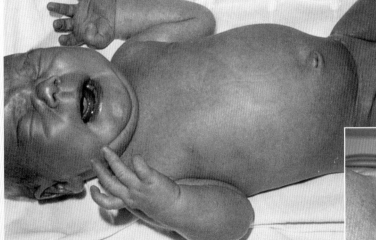

Cyanosis, a blue tinge to the skin, is caused by insufficient oxygenation of the tissues. It may be due to a congenital heart condition, which can result in a failure to thrive.

If failure to thrive is a result of inadequate nutrition, prompt treatment will prevent long-term developmental problems. The first six months of life is the time of maximum brain growth.

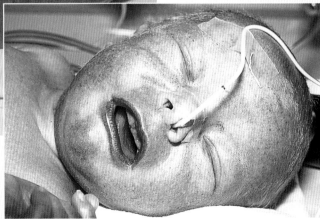

Infant skin problems

Babies are prone to a number of skin disorders in the first year of life. Although few of these are serious, the cause needs to be determined, and medical treatment may be necessary in some cases.

Many healthy babies develop unsightly rashes on their face or body in the first few months of life. Most rashes disappear without any treatment, but it is important to differentiate those that are self-rectifying from those that need treatment with prescription-only creams.

Babies have very sensitive skin and may react to the mildest of fragrances. It is also helpful to avoid biological washing powders, which contain enzymes that can irritate babies' skin and fabric softeners which are fragranced.

DRY SKIN

Soap can strip the natural oils from a baby's skin and cause dryness. This is also the case with many baby bath products, which often contain detergents. It is usually quite sufficient to bathe a baby in water alone, but if the baby is suffering from dry skin, a pharmacist or health visitor may recommend a bath emollient and a simple, cheap, unscented moisturizer such as an aqueous (water-based) cream.

SWEAT RASH

A sweat rash (miliaria) is very common in newborn babies. Babies have underdeveloped sweat glands and can overheat easily. Small raised spots may develop over the face and trunk, but these usually settle spontaneously.

It is essential not to overdress small babies, as overheating is also thought to be a risk factor for cot death.

It is important to avoid bathing with soap if a baby has dry skin. A pharmacist may suggest a mild bath emollient as an alternative.

Infections

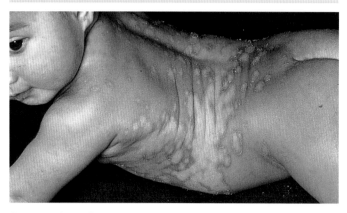

Common skin infections include:
■ Impetigo neonatorum. This is a rare, highly infectious skin infection of young babies. It is easily recognized because of the typical small, pus-filled blisters.
■ Thrush (candidiasis). This can occur as a secondary infection to nappy rash, sometimes with white patches in the baby's mouth. This rash is different from an ammoniacal nappy rash because it affects the skin

Impetigo can be serious in newborn babies. Prompt medical advice is needed if a baby develops pus-filled spots.

creases and there may be spots spreading away from the immediate bottom area.
■ Scabies. This is a mite infestation that causes an extremely itchy rash, usually on the palms or soles in infants. It is transmitted by close contact, so usually affects more than one family member.

Candidiasis, often known as thrush, is a fungal infection. It is common in the nappy area, and sometimes the mouth is affected.

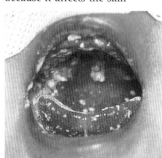

Neonatal problems

Skin problems associated with newborns include:
■ **Urticaria** – this is a fluctuating blotchy rash that is sometimes seen in the first few days of life. It occurs mainly on the trunk and usually disappears spontaneously.
■ **Milia** – these are raised white spots, 1–2 mm in diameter, which appear on the noses of newborn babies. They are caused by immature sebaceous glands and disappear within a few weeks.
■ **Strawberry naevi** – these are raised red patches that are rarely present at birth but usually appear in the first few weeks of life. They may occur on the body, neck or face. Although they tend to develop in the first year, they outgrow their blood supply and usually disappear before school age. Laser treatment may be needed if a naevus occurs around the eyes.
■ **'Stork patches'** – these are reddish birthmarks that are often present from birth at the nape of the neck. They invariably fade with time and are not a long-term cosmetic problem.
■ **Mongolian blue spots** – these are bluish patches commonly found in babies with dark skin. They usually occur around the base of the spine and buttocks and tend to fade with time.

Mongolian blue spots are common in newborn babies with darker skin. They usually fade as a baby gets older.

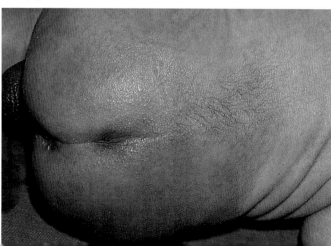

Inflammatory conditions

Eczema and dermatitis are common in infants and may be alarming in appearance.
Successful treatments are available for both conditions, and many cases improve or
even resolve completely as the child grows older

Eczema is an extremely common rash in small children, but fortunately most children grow out of the problem. It is often found in families who are atopic, that is, having a history of asthma, hay fever or eczema.

INFANT ECZEMA
Infants with eczema have very dry skin and develop itchy red patches on their body or face. In older children, the rash often affects the creases of the elbows and those behind the knees.

The mainstay of treatment is to use regular emollients and soap substitutes. If this is not sufficient, a GP may prescribe a short course of 1.0 per cent hydrocortisone cream, which is a very mild steroid, to reduce the inflammation on the body. For the face, a weaker strength (0.05 per cent) of hydrocortisone is usually recommended.

SPECIALIST TREATMENT
Occasionally, in more severe cases, the rash may become extensive and require stronger therapy. A GP may refer the child to a paediatrician or dermatologist for specialist treatment, such as occlusive bandaging.

In eczema, much of the damage is done by scratching, and so scratch mittens are useful for babies. Breast-feeding is thought to provide some protection against developing eczema. Elimination diets, however, are rarely helpful in children and there is a danger of nutritional deficiencies.

CRADLE CAP
Cradle cap, or infantile seborrhoeic dermatitis, commonly affects the scalp, but may also affect the face, chest and skin creases of the arms and legs. It may cause thick yellow scales on the scalp, and a red scaly rash on the body. In most cases, it settles by around three months of age. Mild cases respond to olive oil or arachis oil massaged into the scalp and rinsed with baby shampoo.

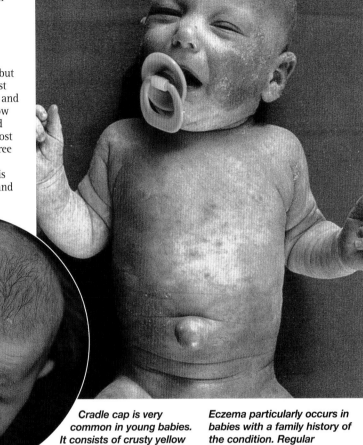

Cradle cap is very common in young babies. It consists of crusty yellow scales over the scalp, and sometimes a rash on the body.

Eczema particularly occurs in babies with a family history of the condition. Regular application of emollient creams is the most important treatment.

Transient rashes

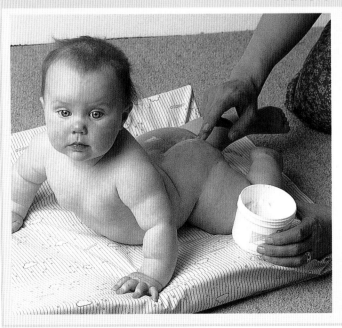

Common causes of transient rashes and skin problems include:

■ **Nappy rash**
Most nappy rashes are a reaction to ammonia in urine. This type of dermatitis is less common nowadays because of the use of absorbent disposable nappies.

Typically, the skin crease areas of the baby's bottom are not affected, which gives a clue to the diagnosis. Nappy rash usually settles down if the nappy is changed more frequently and, if possible, left off completely for short periods.

It is important to avoid

Simple barrier creams are helpful for most babies with a nappy. Frequent nappy changes and leaving the nappy off for as long as possible will also help.

fragranced baby wipes and revert to thorough washing with cotton wool and water if the baby has a sore bottom. Using a simple nappy rash cream, such as zinc and castor oil, also acts as a barrier to protect the baby.

■ **Viral rashes**
Many viruses that cause a temperature in children will also cause a rash. Often, the GP will be unable to identify the specific virus, but the vast majority of rashes will settle down without treatment.

Most viral rashes will fade if pressed firmly with the bottom of a glass tumbler, with the exception of chickenpox and meningial rashes. If any rash fails this tumbler test in an unwell child, it is essential to seek immediate medical attention to make sure that it is not a case of meningitis.

Nappy rash

A baby's skin is very sensitive and the nappy area is particularly susceptible to irritation. Most babies, at some stage, will experience nappy rash, which may be due to infection or allergies.

Nearly all babies get nappy rash or a sore bottom at some time. The nappy area appears red and inflamed and the skin may be either dry or moist. Some babies with sensitive skin are affected more frequently and need special attention.

Nappy rash is most commonly caused by irritation or chafing of the skin by a wet or dirty nappy. Other causes of nappy rash are yeast infections, diarrhoea, allergy and skin conditions such as seborrhoeic dermatitis and eczema.

AMMONIA DERMATITIS

If a baby's wet nappy is left on too long, bacteria can break down chemicals in the urine and generate ammonia, which burns the skin. The nappy area develops a flat, red rash and the skin may become broken. This sort of nappy rash does not affect the skin creases of the thighs and buttocks, because the urine does not touch these areas.

PRACTICAL MEASURES

Ammonia nappy rash seems less common nowadays, because disposable nappies keep the skin relatively dry for longer periods than traditional towelling nappies. However, the baby is less likely to cry when it is wet, and therefore the nappy may be left on too long.

These rashes usually improve with regular use of a layer of a simple barrier cream such as zinc and castor oil or one of the many similar products available,

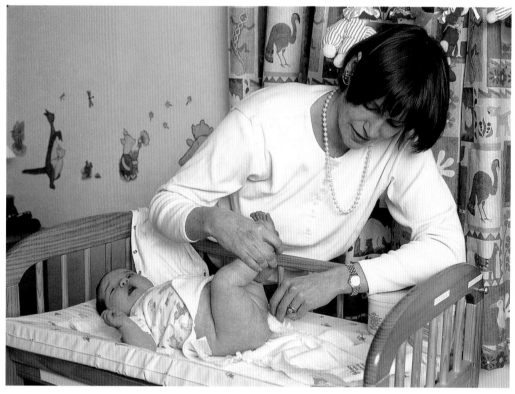

some of which contain an antiseptic. To treat ammonia nappy rash, the nappy should be changed much more frequently, at least every two to three hours.

HEALING SORE AREAS

Leaving the nappy off and letting the baby play on a plastic changing mat or crawl around on an easily cleaned floor allows the air to get to the sore area and aids healing.

If the baby has a nappy rash

it is important to clean his bottom with cotton wool and warm water only.

WHAT TO AVOID

Although modern baby wipes are convenient, they can sting sore skin and can worsen nappy rash. If it is essential to use baby wipes when travelling, non-fragranced hypoallergenic wipes cause fewer problems.

If a baby has diarrhoea, this may cause marked irritation due

Most nappy rashes are caused by prolonged contact with a soiled or wet nappy. Regular changing, and the use of barrier creams can help to avoid rashes.

to the acid in the faeces, even if the nappies are changed frequently.

If the nappy rash does not improve within a few days it is important to ask the health visitor or GP if there are signs of secondary infection.

Yeast infection

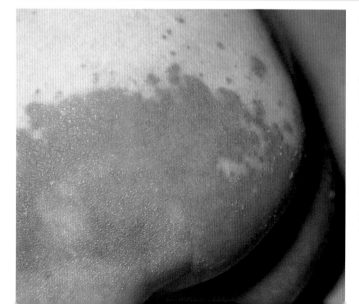

A nappy rash that fails to settle may be infected with candida (thrush). This tends to be an angrier red rash and there may be distinct separate spots called satellite lesions. The spots combine, forming a raised rash with a clear border.

A clue to diagnosis is that thrush also affects the skin creases, which are spared in ammonia dermatitis.

A common cause of nappy rash is the yeast infection known as candida, or thrush. This results in a raised red rash which can also affect the skin creases.

TREATING INFECTION

Thrush infection is very common and is not a sign of bad hygiene. Candida is a yeast that is normally found in the bowel, but may overgrow and cause infection. Babies who are taking antibiotics are more likely to develop thrush.

It is important to check the baby's mouth for signs of thrush and the mother's nipples if she is breast-feeding. Candidal nappy rash responds well to antifungal creams such as clotrimazole. Sometimes hydrocortisone is added if the rash is particularly inflamed.

Less common types of nappy rash

Nappy rash can be caused by factors other than the skin coming into
contact with urine or faeces. A baby may also develop a rash due to specific
skin complaints, allergies to cleaning products or bacterial infections.

There are several less common
types of nappy rash which may
affect babies' skin. Once
diagnosed, these conditions are
easily treated and the symptoms
alleviated.

SEBORRHOEIC DERMATITIS
Babies who are prone to cradle
cap (a scaly rash on the scalp),
may get a similar rash on the
face and sometimes in the nappy
area; this is caused by overactive
sebaceous glands.

Characteristically there is
redness, greasiness and scaling,
but the rash is not usually itchy
or sore. The rash is raised and
may extend across the groin and
lower abdomen and can look
very severe. If it becomes more
inflamed then there is usually
secondary infection.

Seborrhoeic dermatitis
invariably starts in the first 12
weeks and disappears by the end
of the first year. The treatment is
usually hydrocortisone cream.

ECZEMA
Babies with infantile eczema
may develop dry, red patches in
the nappy area. Indeed this may
be the first sign of eczema in an
infant. The mainstay of
treatment is the regular use of
emollients and mild
hydrocortisone cream if needed.

Using medicated eczema bath
oils is also helpful, but soaps
should be avoided.

CONTACT DERMATITIS
Babies with sensitive skin or
mild eczema may react to baby
wipes, detergents and fragranced
products. Even if nappies are
changed diligently, the baby
may develop an irritant rash.

When towelling nappies are
used, babies may develop an
allergy to the washing powder.
Biological washing powders are
often the culprit, or fragranced
fabric softeners. It is important
to make sure that the nappies
are rinsed thoroughly and it may
help to change to disposable
nappies. Alternatively, if
disposable nappies are already
being used, it may help to try a
different brand in case they are
irritating the skin, or change to
towelling nappies.

Soaps and bubble baths dry
the skin and should be avoided
if the baby has eczema or if the
skin is irritated. Warm water is
adequate for cleansing. Baby
wipes contain chemicals that
can actually cause nappy rash if
the baby has sensitive skin and
should be avoided.

BACTERIAL INFECTION
Rarely, if the skin in the bottom
area becomes broken or
scratched, bacteria can penetrate
the surface. In this situation the
skin becomes red and swollen
and the baby may be irritable or
develop a fever. If there are
yellow pustules in the nappy

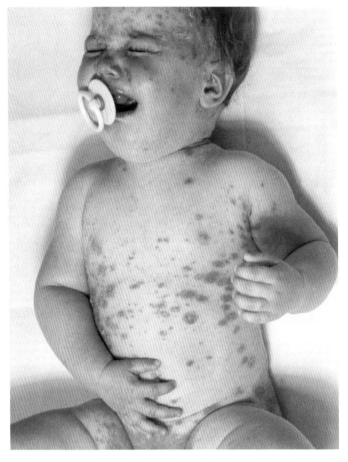

area, this is highly suggestive
of bacterial infection. It is
important to seek medical
advice, because the baby is
likely to need antibiotics.

*Seborrhoeic dermatitis is a skin
condition that affects some
babies in the first 12 weeks of
life. This particular rash can
spread up the abdomen.*

Preventing nappy rash

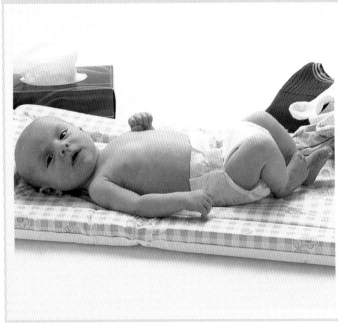

For all types of nappy rash, the
basic principle is to keep the
nappy area dry.

It is essential to change the
nappy frequently. Some babies
seem happy to sit in a soiled
nappy without crying, so parents
will often need to check by smell.

Thorough washing of the
nappy area after a soiled nappy is
removed is important, as is
thorough drying. The use of
talcum powder is not

*Some babies may not cry when
their nappy is wet. Parents
should change nappies
regularly to avoid nappy rash.*

*Barrier cream should be
applied as soon as the first
signs of nappy rash occur. The
cream helps to protect the
affected area of skin.*

recommended because of the
small risk of inhalation.

Fastening the nappy too tightly
or wearing tight waterproof
plastic pants will prevent air
circulating freely and thus
increase the risk of a rash. At the
first sign of problems it is
important to increase the use of a
barrier cream to protect the skin.

Minor abnormalities in newborns

There are numerous minor abnormalities that may be noticed by the parents, midwife or the doctor at the birth examination. However, these are very rarely serious and most resolve within a short time.

During the first few days of life, parents may become worried about unexpected small problems with their new baby. Most of these problems are self-limiting, but some babies may need monitoring to see if further action is needed.

BLOODSHOT EYES

Newborn babies sometimes have slightly bloodshot eyes, known as subconjunctival haemorrhages. These are caused by the pressure on the baby's face in the birth canal during delivery. They are no cause for concern and usually settle down within the first week or so.

RED STAINING IN THE NAPPY

Although alarming, a red discoloration in the nappy of a newborn baby is normally harmless. It is usually caused by innocent substances in the urine called urates. Another

cause may be slight bleeding from the umbilical cord when it is separating.

VAGINAL BLEEDING AND DISCHARGE

Harmless vaginal bleeding can occur in girls at around four days old. This is an oestrogen withdrawal bleed; it is caused by the baby no longer being exposed to the oestrogen present in the mother's blood. Vaginal discharge is also common in the early days of life.

If there is any unexpected bleeding, it is essential to check that the baby has had adequate vitamin K supplements to prevent the rare but serious complications of haemorrhagic disease of the newborn.

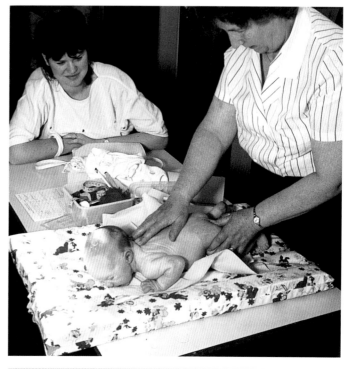

A midwife will thoroughly check a newborn baby for evidence of congenital abnormalities. The majority of these will be harmless and transitory.

Breast enlargement

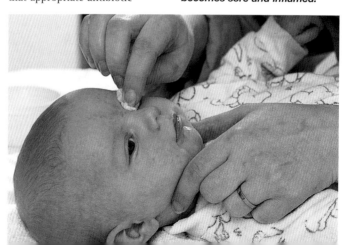

Swollen breasts can occur in both male and female infants, and occasionally a discharge known as 'witch's milk' is seen. This is due to circulating maternal hormones and may last several weeks, but settles as long as it is left alone.

It is important not to try to squeeze the milk out, because this may cause infection.

Breast enlargement in newborns is due to a reaction to the mother's oestrogen during gestation. The swelling subsides soon after birth.

Antibiotics are needed if there is redness around the nipple that is beginning to spread. Rarely, an abscess may form in the breast, requiring surgical drainage.

Eye problems

Sticky eyes are extremely common in young babies because the tear ducts are not yet completely open. This problem usually responds to bathing with cotton wool and boiled, cooled water.

Occasionally, a discharging eye in the first week of life can be a sign of a serious eye infection, such as chlamydia, transmitted from the mother during delivery. To be on the safe side, the midwife may take a swab from the baby's eye, so that appropriate antibiotic

treatment can be given.

Sometimes blocked tear ducts can result in conjunctivitis, the eye becoming red and the discharge more mucky. If this secondary infection occurs, antibiotic drops are needed. To prevent infection, parents can be taught to massage the tear duct gently before cleaning the eye.

Neonatal conjunctivitis is very common. The conjunctiva – which lines the front of the eye and the inside of the eyelid – becomes sore and inflamed.

Umbilical problems

UMBILICAL HERNIA
An umbilical hernia occurs if there is a small weakness in the abdominal wall that causes the navel (umbilicus) to protrude outwards. It is most noticeable when the baby cries or strains, but is not painful and very rarely causes any problems. Umbilical hernias virtually always close without surgery by the age of five years.

UMBILICAL GRANULOMA
The umbilical cord separates and drops off at around the end of the first week of life. Occasionally this area can become sticky, which may be a sign of an infection. Swabs can determine if antibiotic treatment is needed. Keeping the area clean and dry is the main treatment unless the baby becomes unwell.

An umbilical granuloma is a small, red piece of scar tissue that is sometimes seen after the umbilical cord separates. If it persists it is easily treated by cauterization with a silver nitrate stick. This is a painless procedure because the granuloma tissue does not contain nerve fibres and the doctor will protect the surrounding skin with lubricating jelly.

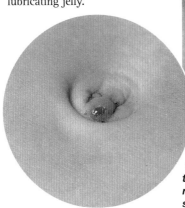

An umbilical granuloma is caused by the severance of the umbilical cord. Occasionally this scar tissue can persist, requiring cauterization with silver nitrate.

In an infant with congenital umbilical hernia, part of the gut protrudes through the umbilicus (navel), causing it to bulge. Such hernias are more common in Afro-Caribbean babies.

Tongue-tie

In tongue-tie, the frenulum (circled) is shorter than usual and extends towards the front of the tongue. Treatment includes operating to divide the frenulum.

The lingual frenulum is the small cord that joins the base of the tongue to the floor of the mouth. In some babies this is shorter than usual, which can restrict the movements of the tongue, hence the name tongue-tie. This tends to run in families and one of the parents may have had a tongue-tie that was cut during childhood. However, surgery in infancy has largely gone out of fashion, apart from its use in feeding difficulties.

In most cases, tongue-tie will gradually improve over the first year of life without treatment. The child will be watched until it begins speaking to see if there are any problems with articulating certain sounds. A speech therapy assessment may be helpful to see if speech is merely immature or whether there is a structural problem that needs a simple surgical release.

Positional talipes

Some babies are born with a foot pointing downwards and the heel facing inward, because of the way the baby was lying in the uterus. If this is easily correctable by massaging the foot then it is known as positional talipes.

TREATMENT
The treatment is to stretch the foot at every nappy change, whereupon the problem should resolve in a few weeks. It may be helpful to consult a paediatric physiotherapist for further advice.

If the foot cannot be straightened then there may be a structural problem such as club-foot (talipes equinovarus) and the baby will be referred to an orthopaedic surgeon for diagnosis and treatment.

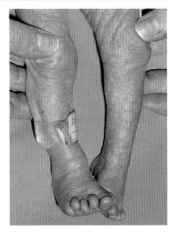

Positional talipes is caused by the unborn baby's position in the uterus. This type of talipes is easily corrected by gentle massage of the foot and leg.

Testicular hydrocele

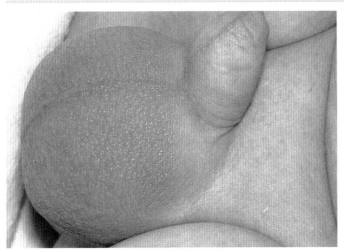

A testicular hydrocele is a collection of fluid around the testicle, sometimes found in newborn boys. During fetal life, the testicles are surrounded by a fluid-filled sac and descend into the scrotum at around the eighth month of gestation. In most cases, the sac closes and the fluid is reabsorbed, but occasionally the fluid persists and is known as a hydrocele.

Hydroceles are painless and

This infant is suffering from bilateral hydrocele; both testes are surrounded by accumulated fluid. The condition usually resolves without complications.

most will disappear on their own within a year. If the hydrocele is still present after this time, surgery will be considered.

Sometimes the neck of the sac remains open and the hydrocele varies in size, becoming smaller in the morning and larger as the day goes on. This is referred to as a communicating hydrocele, and it is still connected to the abdomen.

If there is a hydrocele present the doctor will examine the baby carefully to distinguish this from an inguinal (groin) hernia. This type of hernia is usually an intermittent lump that appears when the baby cries or strains.

Caring for premature babies

Infants born after less than 37 weeks' gestation are considered to be premature, or 'pre-term'. Fortunately, advances in obstetrics mean that the chances of survival are higher than ever before.

The normal gestation period for the human fetus is 37–42 weeks. However, approximately 10 per cent of all pregnancies end before 37 weeks.

The causes of premature or pre-term delivery include complications that would necessitate early delivery for the mother's health (particularly pre-eclampsia, abnormally high blood pressure in pregnancy) and early rupture of the membranes, which can be due to infection. Twins and multiple pregnancies result in a much higher incidence of early delivery. However, in many cases, the exact cause of early onset of labour remains obscure.

CHANCES OF SURVIVAL

If a premature delivery is expected, particularly at the extreme end of the current survival limits (23–26 weeks), clear communication between labour ward staff and the neonatal unit is essential. The situation is highly stressful for parents, and one of the most important functions of the neonatologist (a specialist in newborn babies) is to inform them of the likely sequence of

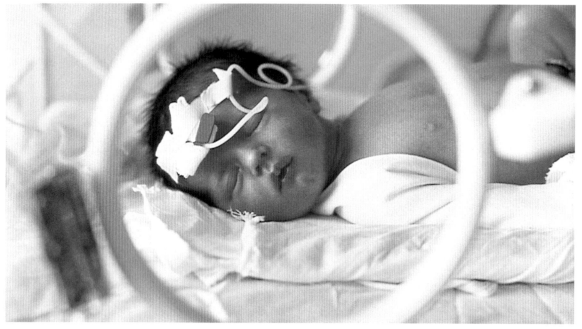

events following the birth.

The family will most likely wish to discuss the survival prospects for the baby. Survival becomes possible from 23 weeks, and its chance increases progressively up to 30 weeks.

It must be made clear that the degree of severity of an individual baby's condition is very hard to predict, but the population figures (see below) can be very helpful. A baby at any gestation can be sick, but significant problems are to be anticipated in those of less than 30 weeks (corresponding to birth weight of 1.2–1.5 kg).

Premature babies are placed in incubators to increase their chances of survival. Within this hygienic, closed environment, the temperature, oxygen and humidity levels are carefully controlled, and the child can still be accessed through port-holes.

Preparing for delivery

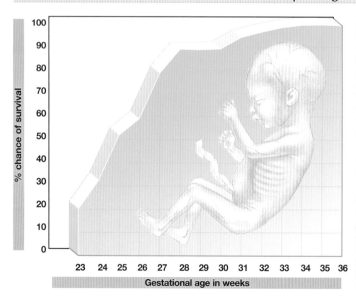

Gestational age in weeks

If problems with the pregnancy have been foreseen, and the early delivery is elective, the neonatal unit intensive care staff can prepare in advance. If the hospital has no such facility, the mother should be transferred to an appropriate hospital if possible. To delay the birth, drugs can be administered.

Once the baby is born, the neonatal team will be ready to receive it from the obstetrician

A baby's chance of survival depends on its degree of prematurity. It is thought that 23 weeks in utero is the minimum gestation period for a baby, but only 20 per cent of babies born at this stage will survive.

or midwife. Their immediate task is to resuscitate and stabilize its condition.

Oxygenation of the blood, glucose level, fluid balance and temperature control are the key functions to optimize. From the moment of delivery, the baby (who may weigh as little as 500 g/1lb) is separated from the warm, stable environment of the uterus and deprived of the oxygen and glucose supply that the placenta provides. The premature infant's ability to maintain stable physiological systems is extremely limited.

Once the baby's vital signs are satisfactory, the baby is transferred to the neonatal unit in a portable incubator with a ventilator.

Open platforms and incubators

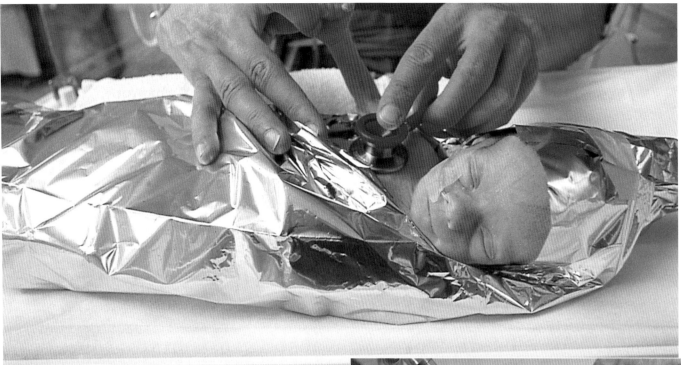

It is essential to maintain the premature baby's body temperature. The warm and humidified atmosphere of the incubator may be sufficient, but sometimes an aluminium thermal blanket is also needed.

Before 30 weeks, a baby's skin is extremely thin, has a transparent quality and is almost fully permeable to water. Steps must therefore be taken to reduce evaporation from the infant's skin, which would cause dehydration and hypothermia. The baby can be nursed on a heated open platform or in an incubator. Many units nurse babies on open platforms only until they are stable, and then transfer them to an incubator.

Open platform advantages
■ Easy to observe the infant
■ Good access for medical procedures, such as drips and blood tests

Disadvantages
■ More difficult to control temperature and humidity
■ Staff may over-handle baby
■ Baby exposed to noise and light 24 hours a day

CARE OF THE FAMILY
When a baby is born before 30 weeks' gestation, a long period of hospitalization is anticipated in a unit which may be far from the family home. Great demands are placed on the parents, especially if the baby suffers any problems, and facilities are provided to maximize their ability to visit. Siblings are welcomed in the neonatal unit to see their tiny sister or brother, and visiting by other relatives, particularly grandparents, is encouraged.

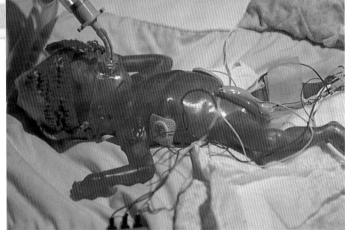

The 'open platform' allows easy access for the monitoring leads, drip tubes and the respirator equipment that is used in the first critical hours following delivery. After this time, the baby may be moved to an incubator.

'Kangaroo care'

Pre-term infants are likely to be separated from their mothers in order to receive the appropriate medical care. It is recognized that the distress of this enforced separation of mother and baby can be reduced by skin to skin handling, whereby the baby is nursed for long periods against the mother's skin. This mode of

It is important for mothers and babies not to be separated while the child is in a special care unit. Parents must be allowed to talk to and touch their child, allowing important bonds to form.

care – often termed 'kangaroo care', analogous to the kangaroo keeping her young in her pouch – can be instituted once the medical team are happy that the infant is sufficiently stable. It gives the mother a better opportunity to bond with her baby.

A further benefit of this mode of care is that it can enhance the mother's production of breast milk. If the baby cannot suckle, the milk can still be 'expressed' and stored until the baby is well enough to be fed via the gastro-intestinal tract, rather than intravenously.

Problems associated with prematurity

Premature babies are extremely vulnerable to heart, lung and digestive system failure. Infection, slow growth and developmental delays are additional problems. They are also more likely to remain underweight and small in size.

We all breathe without conscious effort in a rhythmic fashion due to impulses from a specialized area in the brain stem. This control mechanism is unreliable in premature infants, particularly during acute illness. A significant problem of prematurity is apnoea, when the baby temporarily stops breathing. Respiratory stimulants can be used until this problem becomes resolved.

RETINOPATHY

Retinopathy is partly due to high levels of oxygen in the blood, induced by artificial ventilation, and involves the growth of new blood vessels in the developing retina. The retina can even detach, causing blindness. Although all babies require adequate oxygen, too much is harmful.

LOW BLOOD PRESSURE

Many premature babies have low blood pressure due to a lack of circulating blood volume and poor cardiac contraction. Blood pressure monitoring enables appropriate amounts of blood to be transfused; drugs can also be administered to raise vascular tone and cardiac performance.

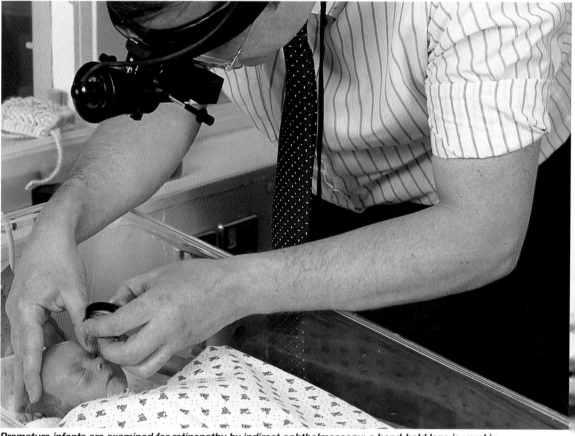

Premature infants are examined for retinopathy by indirect ophthalmoscopy: a hand-held lens is used in conjunction with an ophthalmoscope mounted in a headset worn by the doctor.

Respiratory distress syndrome (RDS)

RDS manifests as poor oxygenation with signs of increased or increasing respiratory effort, caused by a lack of surfactant in the lungs. The incidence declines with increasing maturity and is more frequent with Caesarean births and in infants of diabetic mothers.

Surfactant is a fatty substance (phosopholipid) produced by the cells lining the alveoli (air sacs of the lungs) from 26 weeks in the uterus. It lines the air sacs and prevents their collapse in expiration. This is the same effect that detergent has in producing perfect spherical bubbles.

Production of surfactant may be enhanced by giving cortico-steroids to the mother when premature delivery is anticipated: its production and release are enhanced by the stress response of the baby to labour.

If the infant has a borderline sufficiency of surfactant and struggles with breathing, the supply is rapidly destroyed and progressive ventilatory failure will develop. However, surfactant is now available commercially and can be directly introduced into the airway.

The treatment of RDS involves good general neonatal care to prevent hypothermia, acidosis, hypoglycaemia and hypoxia; this will reduce the incidence and severity of RDS. If other functions are well maintained, surfactant production will match demand.

Respiratory support may include the administration of an air/oxygen blend under pressure through small cannulae in the nostrils. This prevents collapse of the airways and alveoli during expiration. Artificial ventilation, via an endo-tracheal tube through the nose or mouth, allows the lungs to be inflated under careful control.

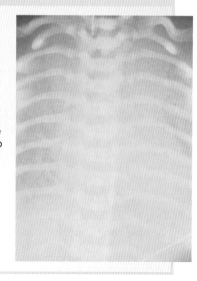

Lungs of a patient with RDS often have a cloudy appearance on X-ray. The heart outline cannot easily be distinguished from the lung because the lung is poorly aerated and relatively solid.

NECROTIZING ENTEROCOLITIS

This is an inflammatory disease of the intestinal tract which can lead to distention and perforation of the bowel. The exact cause is obscure, but poor blood supply to the intestines antenatally, and cardiovascular instability post-natally are factors. Babies who survive require long term intravenous nutrition before the gut recovers.

ANAEMIA

The production of red blood cells (in bone marrow) is suppressed in premature infants, and great demands are placed on the baby's blood production to replace the volume taken in the frequent samples for testing.

The total blood volume of a premature baby is only 50–80 millilitres per kilo. Therefore a baby with a birth weight of 750 grams has only about 40 ml of blood. Frequent transfusions are required in such infants, and iron and folic acid supplements are given to aid the production of red cells.

INTRAVENTRICULAR HAEMORRHAGE

A combination of cardiovascular instability and slow or faulty blood-clotting can lead to intracranial haemorrhage (bleeding in the brain). This may occur in the most unstable babies, and it can be detected using cranial ultrasound scanning. Severe haemorrhage can lead to loss of brain tissue, with formation of cysts and hydrocephalus (excess fluid around the brain).

BRADYCARDIAS

Brief falls in heart rate may be seen, and are associated with periods of apnoea. This can be a sign of infection or worsening lung disease, but unless the falls in heart rate are severe and prolonged they are rarely life-threatening.

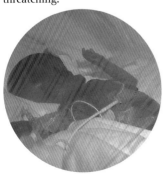

An incubator provides a premature baby with the necessary conditions for survival. Air purity is controlled and the baby's vital signs are monitored.

Fetal circulation

Fetal heart

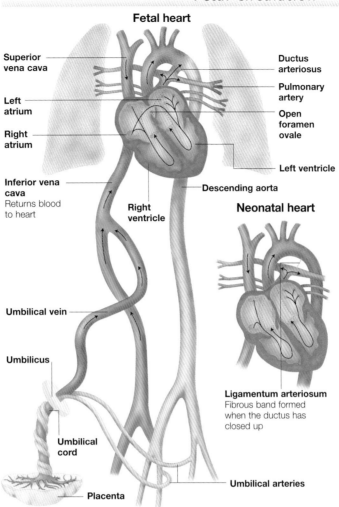

Superior vena cava

Ductus arteriosus

Pulmonary artery

Open foramen ovale

Left atrium

Right atrium

Left ventricle

Inferior vena cava
Returns blood to heart

Descending aorta

Right ventricle

Neonatal heart

Umbilical vein

Umbilicus

Ligamentum arteriosum
Fibrous band formed when the ductus has closed up

Umbilical cord

Umbilical arteries

Placenta

The patent (open) ductus arteriosus is a blood vessel that connects the aorta and the pulmonary artery, and acts to allow blood to bypass the lungs in the fetus. It should normally close shortly after birth, but this may not happen in a premature infant, especially when they have been very sick.

If the duct remains patent, the baby's heart will have to work harder to fulfil the demands of this extra channel. Clinically, what occurs is a very fast heart rate and 'bounding' pulse. A patent duct will delay weaning off ventilatory support. The administration of medication, such as Indomethacin (a non-steroidal anti-inflammatory drug), can assist closure, but in some cases surgery is required.

In the fetus, blood is oxygenated via the placenta rather than in the lungs. Two adaptations of the fetal circulation allow blood to bypass the lungs until they are filled with air at birth. Some blood passes directly between the right atrium and the left atrium through a hole in the heart wall (foramen ovale). Other blood pumped by the right ventricle to the pulmonary artery is diverted by the ductus arteriosus to the aorta.

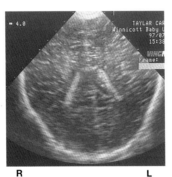

R   L

◀ *Cranial ultrasound scanning is used to check for suspected brain damage, which will not show up on an X-ray. This scan reveals a healthy brain.*

▶ *In contrast, this ultrasound scan shows intracranial haemorrhage as the white areas on the right half of the infant's brain. This can lead to loss of brain tissue, cyst formation and excess fluid around the brain.*

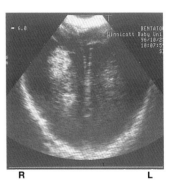

R   L

Chronic lung disease

There are many factors that contribute to the damage to baby's lungs. This is very common in those born at less than 30 weeks. Principal among these are:

- Pressure and stretch forces applied to the airways by a ventilator
- High concentrations of inspired oxygen
- Inflammation caused by infections

The recovery from chronic lung disease may be a slow process and can involve a long period when the baby requires supplementary oxygen. This can be provided at home if an oxygen concentrator is fitted.

The greatest health risk to premature babies with lung damage is intercurrent viral infections, particularly with respiratory syncitial virus, which causes bronchiolitis and carries a high mortality during winter.

Chronic lung disease can develop in babies who require prolonged artificial ventilation. This X-ray shows distended lungs, scarred lung tissue and cyst development.

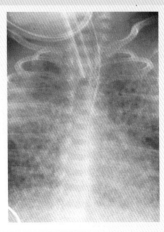

Eight-month baby check

By the age of eight months, it is usual for babies to see a health visitor for a general health examination. The aim of the visit is to identify any health or development problems infants may have.

To monitor their growth and development, all babies must undergo an eight-month review by their health visitor. This is an opportunity for parents to discuss problems with their infant's feeding or sleeping and to voice any concerns about the baby's progress. The health visitor asks questions regarding the baby's development. As this is not a regular check-up by a doctor, there is less emphasis on the physical aspects of the examination.

PACE OF DEVELOPMENT

Parents are often concerned when their baby is slower to sit, crawl or talk than other babies of the same age. However, it is important to remember that all infants develop at their own pace. It is normal for babies to achieve certain developmental milestones within a range of several months. If a baby was premature, this is taken into account when considering its developmental progress.

The aim of the eight-month review is to identify babies who are failing to meet the normal expectations for the age range, so that any remediable causes can be found and any potential learning difficulties recognized.

SITTING UP

The health visitor will ask to see a demonstration of the baby rolling over and sitting unsupported. Babies will support their own weight if pulled into the standing position, and some babies have begun to crawl by this age.

If a normal baby cannot sit up by itself by the age of nine months, this is considered to be a sign of developmental delay, and a more detailed assessment by a paediatrician is needed.

At the eight-month visit, the health visitor will check the baby for its alertness. She will also watch how the baby responds to playing with test objects.

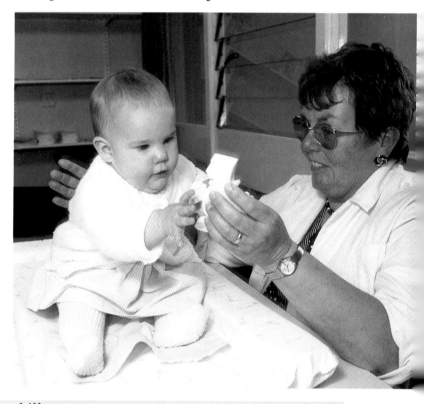

Motor skills

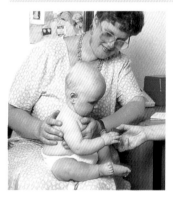

Eight-month-old babies' hands are checked for normal functioning. In particular, their ability to grasp is noted.

Most eight-month-old babies behave quite similarly if offered a 2.5 cm block to play with. They reach out and take it, pass it from hand to hand and then put it in their mouth. The health visitor will repeat this exercise to ensure that the baby uses both hands equally, as babies should not favour one hand at this early age. The health visitor will ask whether the baby is beginning to pick up small

By the time a baby reaches eight months, its motor skills are quite well developed. Objects can be grasped and put in the mouth.

objects and may test this by using a raisin, for example.

Initially, infants use an immature palmar grip, whereby they pick up objects using their whole hand. By eight months, some babies have started to use a more delicate pincer grip using just the thumb and forefinger.

FOLLOW-UP

Sometimes, babies do not co-operate with these tests because of illness. In these circumstances the health visitor will rely on the history that the parent gives, but if in doubt, may ask the parent to bring the baby again in a few weeks for a follow-up check.

Vision

For the baby to develop fine motor skills, it is important that it should have normal vision. At this age, a baby will look around and show interest in very tiny objects, such as small cake decorations. The health visitor will enquire whether the baby's eyes always move together, and will also ask about any family history of squint. If a squint is

not diagnosed, then one eye may become lazy. Thus, it is important to pick this up early on and refer for specialist advice from an orthoptist.

The health visitor will check the baby's eyes for squint. The reflection of light from the baby's eyes is examined using a torch or an ophthalmoscope.

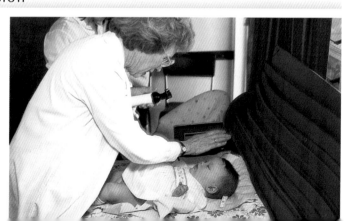

Assessing the baby

The health visitor will check the baby's overall well-being; this will include assessing vision, hearing and general feeding and sleeping habits. The health visitor will chart the baby's growth patterns in a personalized health record book.

At around eight months of age most babies start to make two-syllable babbling noises such as 'dada' and 'gaga'. Traditionally, the review included a distraction hearing test that uses this principle, but this is being gradually phased out in favour of a neonatal oto-acoustic emission hearing test.

DEFECTIVE HEARING
Babies may develop catarrh in the middle ear (glue ear) following a cold, which may affect their hearing. If in doubt, a distraction test can be performed and/or a referral to the local audiologist can be made. Babies with a family history of deafness must be observed carefully.

Babies respond to sound by turning their head to look for the source. Here, a health visitor is checking an older baby's hearing by a distraction test.

Sleeping

It can be very difficult for a mother to cope with continued lack of sleep or a baby's excessive crying. This is a risk factor for post-natal depression.

Although many babies sleep through the night by eight months of age, a number of them still wake up several times and may still have night feeds. The resulting tiredness for the mother can lead to the development of post-natal depression.

SLEEP PATTERNS
The health visitor can offer advice on how to respond to a baby's frequent episodes of waking, which can further help to promote a better sleep pattern. In some areas, there are sleep and behaviour support groups that can be very helpful.

Feeding

Most mothers will have had the baby weighed and have discussed its feeding habits at the local health visitor clinic. By nine months, the baby's milk intake has decreased to about 600 ml a day, and it should begin eating three meals daily.

Breast-fed babies will require an alternative source of iron by this stage, either in formula milk or in a mixed supplemented weaning diet containing vegetables and meat.

By the age of eight months, babies will have been eating solid food for some time. A mixed diet helps avoid food fads.

Physical examination

Part of the eight-month review is to check whether the baby's hip muscles are tight, which may be a sign of congenital dislocation (developmental dysplasia of the hip – DDH).

It is also important to check that a boy's testicles are definitely present in the scrotum and refer on to the GP if in doubt. In many cases the

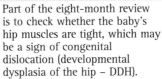

As part of the eight-month examination, babies undergo a general physical check-up. Their hips especially are checked for possible dislocation.

testicles descend spontaneously by one year of age, but if this does not occur, a surgical referral is needed to consider surgical correction.

GROWTH CHARTED
The health visitor will also plot the baby's weight, height and head circumference on the growth charts in the child health record book. Since a single weight measurement may not be representative, if there are concerns that the baby may be failing to thrive, weight gain will be monitored over several weeks.

Health record

At the end of the eight-month examination, the health visitor will complete the review section of the child health record. The booklet contains a section recording all the baby's immunizations, so that the health visitor can check whether they have been completed on time.

General health promotion topics to be discussed may also include accident prevention, skin and dental care, and advice about the risks of parental smoking.

Teething

In common with most other mammals, humans develop two sets of teeth during their lifetime. The first set – the milk teeth – appear in babies between seven months and two years of age.

The development and appearance of teeth in babies is so variable that teething is not regarded as a developmental milestone.

On average, the first tooth appears in the seventh month, but some babies still have no teeth by 12 months of age. One in every 2,000 children is born with one or more teeth already in place. In most children, however, the teeth appear sporadically.

Children have 20 primary or deciduous teeth, commonly known as milk teeth, and nearly all of them will have erupted by the time the child is two years old. Milk teeth tend to be smaller and generally whiter than adult teeth.

WHEN TEETHING BEGINS

The onset of teething is frequently associated with irritability in the child. The pain of teething may be referred (toothache is often felt in the ear) and the child may fiddle with or pull its ears for this reason. Salivation increases during teething and, as a result, fluid is lost; this, along with dribbling, makes babies thirsty. Acidity in the mouth also increases and this can cause a rash around the mouth.

Although teething may be uncomfortable, it does not produce illness, and fevers are often wrongly attributed to it.

The 20 milk teeth comprise eight incisors, four canines and eight molars. They typically appear in this order:
- Lower central incisors at 6–8 months
- Upper central incisors at 7–9 months
- Lateral incisors at 9–13 months
- First molars at 12–15 months
- Canines at 16–18 months
- Second molars at 20–30 months.

When a breast-feeding baby has teeth, they do not usually hurt the mother: the baby's tongue protrudes and is placed under the nipple, protecting it from the lower teeth.

Babies' teeth begin to develop very early, at around the sixth week of gestation. The baby is

The two lower incisors are usually the first to erupt. A teething ring can divert a baby from chewing toys and fingers, and ease the pain of teething.

Generally, girls acquire their first teeth earlier than boys. The lower teeth usually appear before their upper equivalents. The pain of erupting teeth may be a cause of some distress.

How teeth develop

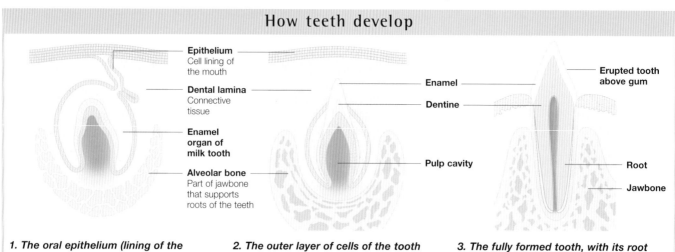

Epithelium
Cell lining of the mouth

Dental lamina
Connective tissue

Enamel organ of milk tooth

Alveolar bone
Part of jawbone that supports roots of the teeth

Enamel

Dentine

Pulp cavity

Erupted tooth above gum

Root

Jawbone

1. The oral epithelium (lining of the mouth) folds into the dental lamina (connective tissue of the jaw), forming a tooth-producing organ.

2. The outer layer of cells of the tooth organ produce enamel. The layer of cells underneath secretes dentine and rises upwards, producing the pulp cavity.

3. The fully formed tooth, with its root embedded in the jawbone, begins to protrude from the gum into the mouth. This process is known as eruption.

Growth of primary teeth

By the time a baby is seven months old, it is able to chew effectively using its hard gums. It will also be making use of any teeth that have erupted.

born with the beginnings of the permanent teeth already in place beneath the gums, below the buds of the milk teeth. The adult teeth form very slowly and, when they are fully formed, they push up through the gums, displacing the first set of teeth.

IMPORTANCE OF BABY TEETH

As the baby grows older, the primary teeth guide the growth of the jawbones and the second permanent set of teeth. If the primary teeth are lost prematurely, the jaw may not develop correctly and the new teeth may consequently emerge either crooked or crowded together.

If a baby chips a tooth, a dentist should be able to smooth down the rough surface to prevent any irritation to the mouth and gums.

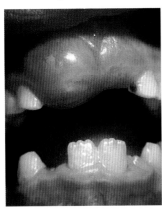

The site of an emerging incisor can be seen at the front of the upper jaw. An eruption cyst has formed around the new tooth.

6–8 months:
The first teeth to erupt are the lower central incisors.

7–9 months:
The upper central incisors start to emerge.

9–13 months:
The lateral incisors erupt, the lower ones before the upper.

12–15 months:
The first milk molar teeth erupt; the child now has 12 teeth.

16–18 months:
The canine teeth (again, lower followed by upper) erupt.

20–30 months:
The second molars appear, completing the set of milk teeth.

CARING FOR BABY TEETH

More teeth are lost through gum disorders than from tooth decay and accidents, and plaque (bacterial layer on the teeth) is usually the cause of this. Tooth enamel is hard and glossy and plaque is easily removed. However, plaque can collect around the margin of the gum, inflame it and eventually loosen the connection between gum and tooth until a pocket forms and the tooth works loose.

Regular and careful tooth-brushing, every day in the morning and at bedtime, helps to keep the plaque down: this should be done from the very first appearance of the teeth and regular dental check-ups are important. Children need supervision while brushing their teeth until they are about eight years old. The brushing action and assistance is more important than the specific type or brand of toothpaste used.

It is important that babies are not given bottles containing sugary drink, as this bathes the teeth in sugar solution for long periods of time. Unsweetened fruit juices should be given in a cup instead, once the baby is old enough to drink from one.

Teething problems

Teething is often a difficult time for babies because of the discomfort of the teeth emerging through the gums. Problems include:
- Increased saliva and dribbling – this will make the child thirsty
- Poor sleep: the child often wakes in the night because it is thirsty
- Urge to bite on any hard object, including adult's fingers
- Irritability
- Swollen red area where the tooth is coming through
- Area of gum that may feel hard to the touch.

Teething remedies
- Anaesthetic gels
- Soothing the pain by rubbing the sore gums
- Chews and ovenbaked biscuit sticks
- Paracetamol syrup.

Gently rubbing anaesthetic gel over the affected gum may soothe the discomfort and distress of teething.

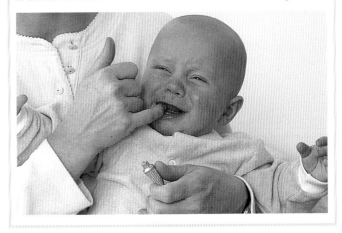

Hearing problems in infants

Each year a small number of babies are born with a permanent hearing problem. Good hearing is essential for language development, so it is vital that hearing loss is identified as soon as possible.

Hearing problems are usually diagnosed during a routine hearing screening test at eight months. Until this time, some parents are not aware that their baby is hearing-impaired because the baby responds to visual stimuli, such as their faces, rather than their voices.

TESTING BABIES' HEARING

Until recently, it was not possible to test a baby's hearing until after six months of age. Furthermore, the average age for fitting hearing aids was 18 months. In fact, many children were not diagnosed until they were over two years old.

Recent technological advances have made it possible to test the hearing of newborns, giving an opportunity, if necessary, to fit a hearing aid before the age of six months. This neonatal screening test is gradually being introduced in the UK and should have a major impact on early speech development.

HEARING DEVELOPMENT

By the six-week developmental assessment, babies with normal hearing will respond to sudden loud noises by blinking or widening their eyes. The doctor will ask the parents about this 'startle reflex' at the check-up, and query whether there are any hearing problems in the family.

RESPONDING TO SOUNDS

Babies turn in the direction of loud sounds from about three months. By six months, they respond to quieter sounds, and it is this response that forms the basis of the eight-month hearing test. At nine months, babies start to make babbling sounds. Older toddlers should respond to simple, quiet instructions without any visual clues.

Hearing is essential for speech development in babies. Thus, any hearing problem should be diagnosed quickly and a suitable hearing aid fitted.

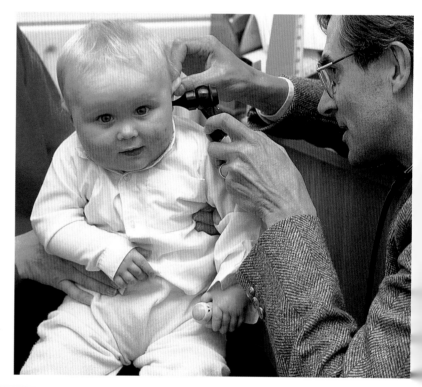

Causes of hearing impairment

Wax in the ear canal
A common cause of deafness; it is easily remedied

Nerve damage
The nerves supplying the inner ear can be damaged, for example, by a viral infection during pregnancy

Glue ear
Infection in the middle ear causes a build-up of secretions that blocks sound waves

Damaged cochlea
The cochlea is vital for detecting sound. Damage may be congenital or it can result from meningitis

Babies may be born with a congenital hearing problem or they may develop hearing impairment as they get older. Hearing problems can arise from the inner, middle or outer ear.

SENSORINEURAL DEAFNESS
Sensorineural deafness develops when there is damage to the cochlea in the inner ear, the nerves that supply the inner ear or the part of the brain involved with hearing. There are several causes for this type of deafness:
■ Congenital hearing loss – this may be genetic
■ Infections caught during pregnancy such as rubella, cytomegalovirus and toxoplasmosis
■ A difficult delivery that causes

Sounds are transmitted from outside the ear to the cochlea, where they are detected. Any problems with the transmission of sound waves can result in hearing loss.

severe birth asphyxia (suffocation) – this can also damage hearing
■ Neonatal jaundice – if the levels of the yellow pigment bilirubin in the blood become very high, there is a risk of deafness
■ Complication of bacterial meningitis infection.

CONDUCTIVE DEAFNESS
Conductive deafness occurs when sounds cannot be transmitted to the cochlea because of a problem in the outer or middle ear, such as:
■ Wax in the outer ear canal – this is an easily remediable cause of earache and deafness. Wax is usually discharged naturally from the ear
■ Glue ear – older infants and toddlers sometimes develop fluid in their middle ear after a cold
■ Perforated eardrum – infection in the ear or trauma can lead to a tear in the membrane between the middle and outer ear.

Hearing tests

All babies undergo a hearing screening test in the first year of life. Traditionally the infant distraction hearing test has been carried out between seven and nine months of age by health visitors, often in conjunction with the eight-month developmental assessment.

INFANT DISTRACTION TEST

For this test, the baby sits on its mother's lap while one health visitor sits in front of the baby and distracts him/her with a toy. The toy is then removed and the second health visitor makes a noise with a rattle, chime or voice from one side behind the baby's head, out of its field of vision. The baby should turn to look in the direction of the sound. The test is repeated in both ears with sounds of different intensity.

At eight months, babies may have a routine infant distraction hearing test. The test checks whether the baby turns to respond to a noise behind him.

A newborn's hearing can be tested sleeping. A probe sends signals that bounce off the cochlea and return as echoes; these can later be analysed.

If the baby has a cold or is uncooperative and does not respond as expected, the test is usually repeated in a few weeks.

AUDIOLOGY ASSESSMENT

At this stage, if in doubt the baby will be referred to an audiologist for a specialist assessment. Fluid can be seen in the ear with an auriscope, and middle ear problems can be distinguished from nerve deafness with a simple device called an impedance audiometer.

NEONATAL TEST

The infant distraction hearing test is currently being superseded in some areas by the neonatal screening test that can assess the function of the inner ear. This is a painless test which only takes a couple of minutes, and can be done on newborn babies before they leave hospital or in the first three months of life.

To do the test, a probe that emits clicking sounds is placed in the ear of a sleeping baby. In a normally functioning ear, the cochlea generates an echo that can be detected and recorded. This neonatal hearing test is

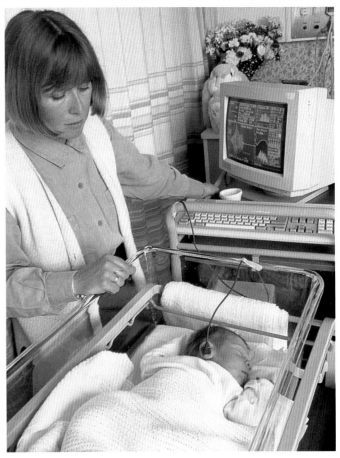

very accurate in predicting normal hearing. However, new babies sometimes fail the test because of debris left in the ear after delivery, which can block the echo. If this happens the test is repeated a few weeks later.

If there are still concerns about the baby's hearing, more sophisticated tests are available which can measure the degree of hearing loss.

LATER TESTS

Babies who have passed the neonatal screening test do not usually need to have the eight-month infant distraction test. However, hearing problems can develop later on. So, if there are any parental concerns or if there are risk factors such as a family history of hearing loss or of meningitis, the eight-month test will still be recommended.

Severe hearing impairment

As soon as a severe hearing impairment is diagnosed in a baby, hearing aids, which act as amplifiers, will be fitted. Young babies can tolerate hearing aids very well, but toddlers often go through a negative phase when they refuse to wear their aid, so patience and perseverance are needed.

■ Speech therapy

Children with hearing difficulties are offered speech and language therapy as part of a multidisciplinary programme.

In some children with profound

A baby with a severe hearing impairment can be fitted with a hearing aid. The earlier a hearing aid is fitted the easier it will be for the baby to learn to speak.

bilateral hearing loss, hearing aids do not improve hearing enough to enable speech development. It is essential that these children and their families learn to communicate through sign language as soon as possible.

■ Cochlear implants

Some children in this category may be suitable for cochlear implant surgery, which is only performed in a few specialist hospitals. This technique involves implanting an electrode, which bypasses the non-functioning parts of the inner ear.

Although cochlear implants do not restore normal hearing, the recipient can be trained to interpret the sounds so that communication can be improved considerably.

Developing walking skills

The achievement of a normal gait (manner of walking) is a vital part of a child's development. It signals a degree of independence from parents and allows the child to explore its immediate surroundings.

Humans have evolved over millions of years from a four-legged to a two-legged animal. Our bipedal gait, the way in which we walk on two legs, is a peculiarly human characteristic.

Unlike quadrupeds, we have only two points of contact with the ground and so are inherently unstable. We remain upright and balanced only due to constant activity in the muscles of the legs and back.

HOW WE WALK

Normal gait involves a smooth, stable, energy-efficient action avoiding large displacements of the centre of gravity of the body (which lies just in front of the base of the spine in adults, but is higher in children). As we move forward we lift one foot, so losing a contact point, and the body leans and begins to fall forward.

The lifted foot is placed on the ground, heel and then toes, a step in front of the moving body, thus supporting it as it continues its forward motion. The trailing foot can now be lifted and placed ahead of the first foot in time to act as support for the still moving body. In this way the body is prevented from falling, the

movement instead being continuous forward motion.

In addition to the movement in the legs, there is rotation and tilting of the pelvis, rotation of

the upper body and, to a greater or lesser extent, swinging of the arms. All these movements combine to form the familiar, normal gait.

A child's first steps are a major developmental milestone. Praise from a parent will encourage a child to 'practise' walking, helping to build strength.

Control of gait

The smooth, co-ordinated body movements that enable us to walk is achieved in older children and adults without conscious effort. The brain receives information from sensory nerves in the muscles, joints and vestibular (balance) centres to tell it what is happening at each given moment. Visual input warns of changes in terrain or obstacles ahead so that the gait can adapt accordingly. All this information is sent to the cerebellum, a primitive

part of the brain concerned with the control and co-ordination of automatic actions, and this sends out signals to the muscles to ensure that they act smoothly together to give fluid movements.

The cerebrum makes the initial decision to start or stop walking, and it can also override the cerebellum when necessary. In this way, we can take control over the process of walking if a more deliberate action is required, such as in walking on an icy surface.

A baby's gait is usually clumsy and faltering. The arms are held out for balance, and each step is slow and deliberate as walking is not yet automatic.

As a child develops, it becomes stronger and more confident in its walking abilities. Motion is fluid and unconscious, but falls still happen.

For patterns of movement to become automatic, as walking must be, it is first necessary that a child learns and practises voluntary, deliberate movements requiring conscious effort. With repetition, a child's cerebellum becomes 'programmed' so that it can continue the actions initiated by the cerebrum without further conscious effort, thus freeing the higher brain to concentrate on other things.

From birth to about the age of seven, when normal gait is almost fully developed, a child's body and brain undergo an intensive practical training in order to achieve effortless locomotion. During this period, babies and children will gradually develop a normal gait as their muscles grow and develop, as their brain matures and as they become increasingly aware of their environment.

NATURAL INSTINCTS

Newborn babies have a set of primitive reflexes which include some that appear to mimic the action of standing and walking. If a baby is held upright so that its feet just touch the floor, it will start moving its legs as if stepping, even though it cannot yet balance or support its own weight. Although this reflex will disappear by the age of four months, this stage is believed to be important preparation for the later development of walking.

By five months, a baby will be able to bounce up and down on its parent's lap while its weight is supported. Over the next few months it learns to roll, crawl and sit up. As it spends more time sitting, and thus supporting

As skills improve, a child is able to process visual information about the environment – such as a change in terrain – and change its gait accordingly.

An early stage of learning to walk is 'cruising'. A baby is able to stand but cannot yet walk with confidence – it moves around by steadying itself against items of furniture.

the vertical spine for the first time, its back will develop the normal backward thoracic (upper back) curvature.

By about eight months, a baby may well try to pull itself up to a standing position or, if propped up against a support, it will maintain that position. As it starts to stand unaided and thus bear its own weight, the normal forward curvature of the lumbar (lower back) spine develops.

Around the time of the first birthday, a baby will take its first unaided steps and the characteristic gait of the new walker is seen. Movements are jerky, the arms are bent and used for balance, the body sways from side to side and the baby's feet are placed widely apart and turned out to give a wider base.

REFINING BASIC SKILLS

During the second year, a baby begins to master the action of walking and the gait becomes more confident. Balance improves and it develops the ability to walk backwards, as well as up and down stairs with support. Its arms are now by its side but do not yet move in a co-ordinated way with the rest of the body. The feet are placed down on the ground flat, rather than heel and toe, and they often still turn out slightly. Intoeing, the turning in of the feet, may also be seen, but this usually disappears within the next year.

By the age of three, the basic walking movements have been repeated often enough so that they no longer require deliberate thought. The arms swing in opposing directions and the feet are placed on the ground in the heel-and-toe action of the adult gait. As the hip muscles strengthen, the child is able to support its weight on one foot for longer, which allows for increased stride length. There is also much better control over the speed of walking.

Over the next few years, the child becomes increasingly confident and able to control its body. Walking is simple, and it can now run, jump, climb, hop and learn to negotiate obstacles with ease. With each repetition of these actions, they become easier and more automatic until children of six or seven have almost completely attained the normal adult gait.

Physical activity is vital for growing children. Learning to walk is one of the first steps in developing a sense of independence from parents.

Some children lack confidence with walking to begin with, even though they may be physically capable. As with most areas of development, a child will progress at its own speed.

Chapter Two

Your Growing Child

As your baby grows and moves into the next stage of childhood, he or she will start to learn new skills, such as walking and running, talking and using the potty. Your child will become a social being, interacting with others and forming friendships with other children. Sometimes, establishing independence and understanding the curious ways of others can be frustrating for children, and temper tantrums are common. However, this is a rewarding time for parents who can take an active role in their child's social education. This chapter of the book describes these learning processes and also the physical development that a child undergoes in the early years.

Growth in the first 18 months

Between birth and adulthood, a baby's head doubles in size, its arms quadruple in size, its trunk triples in length, and its legs grow to five times their birth length.

At 20 weeks' gestation, the unborn baby grows at about 10 cm per month. After birth, however, the baby grows 20 cm a year, and this rate steadily decreases until late adolescence, whereupon it ceases.

Babies are assessed for growth in terms of their height (or length), weight and head circumference. They do not grow at the same rate, any more than they are born the same weight. In general, a baby's height reflects that of its parents.

Babies' growth rates are normally steady (see graph) when viewed from the overall perspective of a year, but in terms of weeks, growth tends to stop and start, leading to what is known as growth spurts. Fluctuations in babies' growth rates are common. In some weeks, a baby may gain as much as 225 g; in other weeks there may be no gain at all.

MEASURING GROWTH

Babies cannot be measured for height until they can stand (normally between 13 and 18 months), so they are usually weighed and measured for length. A measuring mat is used in most baby clinics. The baby's head is placed against a vertical plate attached to the mat and the knees are temporarily held down to gauge the position of the heels.

Most healthy full-term baby boys weigh between 2.7 kg and 4.3 kg. Girls generally weigh between 2.6 kg and 4.1 kg. Low birth weight is defined as less than 2.5 kg. An average head circumference for a baby weighing 3.3 kg is 35 cm. The head circumference is measured just above the temples.

GENETIC FACTORS

The size that a baby will eventually grow to is determined by the genetic characteristics of both parents. However, the weight at birth is determined more by the mother's size and weight than the father's. During gestation, the father's genetic contribution is suppressed and the baby grows to fit its mother's shape. After delivery, the baby grows rapidly to accommodate the genes inherited from the father and, by the time the child is two years old, it will start to show the contribution from both parents. By age five, a child's head is 80 per cent of the predicted adult head size. Therefore, the heads of newborns and toddlers are disproportionately large compared to

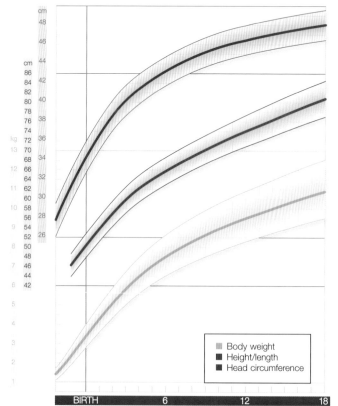

Growth chart for girls

The chart above shows typical growth patterns and normal variations for girls to 18 months old. The horizontal axis gives the age in months. The shaded area to the left of 'Birth' represents the last two months of the prenatal period.

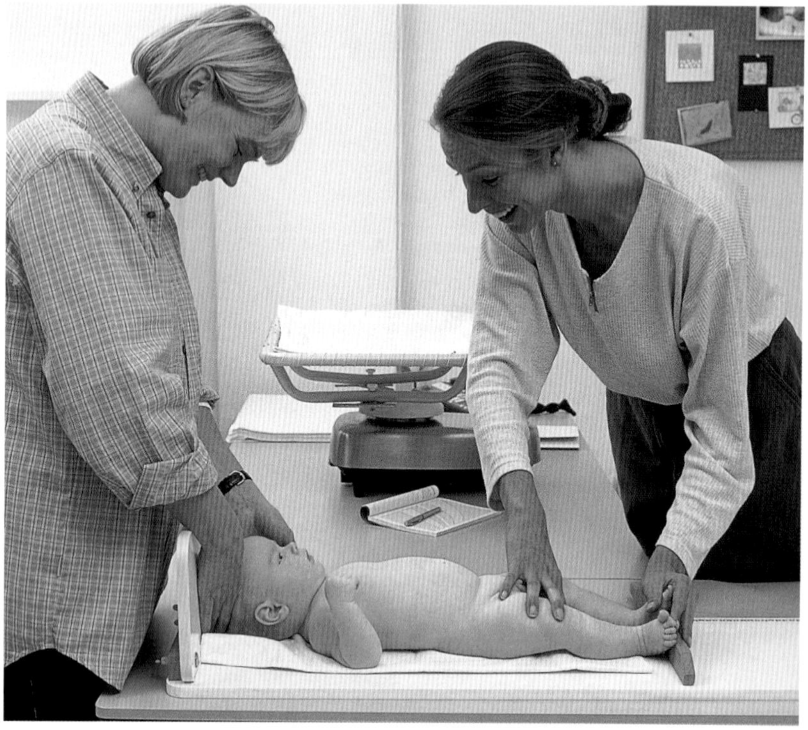

Legend:
- Body weight
- Height/length
- Head circumference

BIRTH   6   12   18

Baby clinics regularly monitor growth. Height and weight measurements are recorded and compared to published charts.

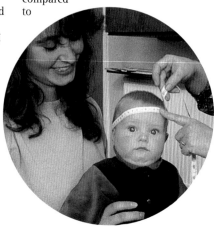

A standard reference is the head circumference. It is measured above the temples and over the occiput, the protrusion at the back of the skull.

Changing proportions

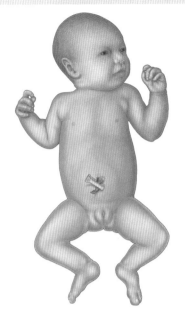

Newborn: The newborn's head is a quarter of its overall body length, and a third of its total weight.

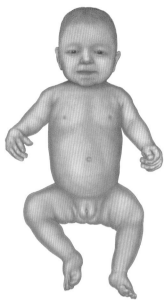

Nine months: The baby has almost tripled in weight since birth, and the relative size of the head and body decrease.

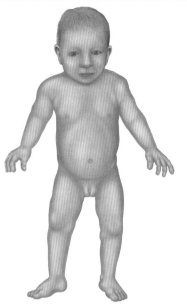

18 months: The torso and limbs have grown rapidly, so that the head appears smaller in comparison to the body.

COMMON PATTERNS OF GROWTH

Babies gain both weight and height very rapidly in the first two years. The usual rule of thumb is that an infant will double its birth weight by the age of five months, and triple its weight in the first year.

Babies usually increase in length by 25–30 cm within the first year. This rapid growth continues until babies are about two years old. It then levels off to a steady pace until the onset of adolescence, when there is a marked growth spurt. The same pattern can be seen in the development of the bones, both in the increasing number and in their hardness.

The growth of the head is made possible by open growth plates between the skull bones. Two soft areas – the fontanelles – are the areas of greatest potential growth. Initially, the baby's head represents about one-third of the entire weight and one-quarter of its body length. In adults, the head represents about one-eighth to one-tenth of the total height.

DETERMINING HEIGHT

There is virtually no difference in height between girl and boy toddlers, but by the end of adolescence boys and girls differ by an average of 12.5 cm. It has long been held that a child will have reached half its adult height by the age of two: this is true in the majority of cases, but it is not always the case.

To determine a baby's eventual adult height, a general rule of thumb is to combine the height of the parents, divide the total by two, and add 10 cm for boys and subtract 10 cm for girls for the final figure.

When assessing a child whose measurements are unusual, birth weight and the build of the parents are the principal non-disease factors to be considered.

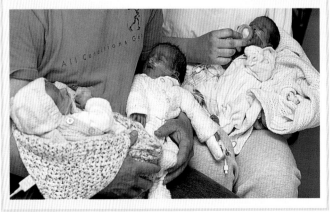

Babies are weighed at regular intervals to check whether they are gaining sufficient weight. Growth patterns may vary over weeks.

HEIGHT AND WEIGHT

A number of factors can affect how a child grows, including:
■ In-built genetic and hormonal programming, including size of both parents
■ The pituitary gland (secretes growth hormone and activating hormones that influence the rate of growth) and the thyroid gland (thyroxin, produced by the thyroid gland) are involved in physical growth
■ Twins and multiple births
■ Nutrition, before and after birth
■ Harmonious environment, allowing baby to thrive
■ Maternal age and number of previous deliveries.

Growth problems

The following factors can cause problems with growth:
■ Severe malnutrition: due, for example, to poverty, child abuse, food fads or excessive vomiting
■ Kwashiorkor: malnutrition due to a lack of protein and energy-rich foods (rare in this country)
■ Obesity
■ Turner's syndrome
■ Thyroid disorders: the thyroid gland secretes thyroxin, which influences overall growth rate
■ The baby is born preterm, or prematurely

■ Excessive alcohol consumption or smoking by the mother during pregnancy
■ Growth hormone deficiency and other disorders of the pituitary gland
■ Placental insufficiency
■ Pre-eclampsia: raised blood pressure during pregnancy.

Twins and triplets are born premature and underweight, because the mother's placenta can only provide sufficient nourishment for a limited time.

Developmental progress to 18 months

By 18 months of age, children are mobile, communicative, socially aware and inquisitive. They are able to feed themselves, understand instructions and are starting to be aware of bodily functions.

The milestones of childhood development are traditionally classified as follows: handling skills, general understanding, speech, bladder and bowel control, feelings and needs. Toddlers reach a point in time when development has equipped them with a number of skills which together create the picture of a typical 18-month-old.

The major milestones acquired in the first 18 months include:
■ The first smile
■ Recognition of individuals and other evidence of memory
■ Ability to sleep through the night
■ Ability to handle a cup
■ Independent movement – although not necessarily walking
■ Speech or speech-like communication
■ Awareness of bladder and bowel movements – although usually without total control
■ Signs of an independent will.

SMILING AND RECOGNITION

Babies will smile for the first time between the age of five and six weeks, usually at their mother. By 12 weeks a baby will smile when spoken to, and by 16 weeks it will laugh aloud. By 20 weeks babies smile at their own

Some, but not all, babies will be able to identify simple pictures in a book by 18 months. They may also know as many as 50 single words by this age.

By 18 months, most babies are insatiably curious about their environment. However, they have no concept of risk or danger, and need supervision to avoid accidents.

image in the mirror. From five to six months onwards, a baby knows how to express recognition and pleasure through smiling.

A baby first recognizes their principal carer, usually the mother. They are said to be able to do this by sound of voice and by smell from the earliest hours after birth, and by sight within the first few weeks of life. As children develop, the number of individuals they are able to recognize by sight increases. This ability to demonstrate visual recognition is linked to the development of memory.

EVIDENCE OF MEMORY

Memory starts to function in the newborn to a limited extent, and it is only from about 16 weeks of age that general comprehension and memory become more evident.

Newborn babies register a great deal of information, but what impairs their memory is their inability to retain information. Being able to remember something efficiently depends on coding (or tagging), and to achieve this, information is structured within a context, in compartments. It is not possible for babies and young children to

Painting is a complex but rewarding activity for young children. It demonstrates fine motor skills, concentration and developing cognitive abilities.

remember an enormous number of unrelated pieces of information. It is only as a child starts to integrate their picture of the world, using all of the five senses, into a coherent entity, that memory begins to function fully.

Many babies are shy or possessive; some may be very distressed when briefly separated from their parents.

INDEPENDENT MOBILITY

Of the many milestones acquired, it is the level of communication skills and independent mobility that probably distinguish an 18-month-old child from a younger baby. By 12 months, babies can walk sideways while holding on to furniture for support and can walk when both hands are held. By 18 months, a toddler can propel itself forwards at speed on its bottom and may even be running and walking.

Independent mobility opens a world of discovery to the inquisitive child. This brings with it some hazards. With new-found mobility, a toddler can often expose itself to dangers, such as kitchen knives and cleaning fluids. As co-ordination

develops, a toddler may also try to climb out of its cot, risking a fall. At this age, it is not capable of suppressing its impulse to touch and explore and parents will probably try to rearrange the child's environment to make it safer.

COMMUNICATION

The utterance of the first recognizable word is a momentous occasion in a baby's development. This may come at about 11 months. By 12 months, babies may be able to say two or three words with meaning.

Babies are able to understand much more than they can speak as development of language precedes the ability to speak. At 32 weeks, for example, babies will understand the word 'no'. At nine months, they may respond to questions such as 'Where is Daddy?' by pointing, and by 12 months they can understand perhaps a dozen words.

Eighteen-month-old children can climb stairs while holding a rail, run, seat themselves in a chair (often by the process of climbing up, standing, turning round and sitting down), throw a ball without falling over, build a tower of three cubes, manage a spoon, scribble, take off gloves and socks and unzip a fastener.

They will also understand sufficiently to point to a picture of a car or a dog in a book. Using picture cards, they will point correctly to one when asked 'Where is the dog?', and can

name simple objects. They can respond to orders, although they may have reached a point where they start to test a parent's authority and ignore the word 'no'.

At 18 months, a baby can make it quite clear that it is a small human being with a clearly defined temperament, personality and a free will.

Curiosity can lead toddlers into dangerous situations. Restrictions to the child's freedom can be frustrating to their growing sense of independence.

Signs of an independent will

The signs of independent will start to emerge within the first few months of birth and are clearly evident within the first six months of life. By this age, the baby can express eagerness and anger, pleasure and rage.

By 12 months, a baby's growing independence leads to displays of rage when thwarted. By the age of 15 months, it is clearly impatient when confronted with inhibition of any kind. The toddler's mood alternates quickly from being dependent on adults to independent action and a rejection of an adult's overtures.

Babies expect their desires to be satisfied instantly, even if the time or place makes this impossible. If their demands are not met, tantrums will inevitably ensue.

Babies can become jealous when a parent is distracted. They will often compete for attention when they see their parents engaged in other activities.

Learning to talk

Mastering speech is a long process, but a baby will master the foundations of language in the first 18 months of life. The unintelligible cooing and babbling noises that a baby makes is the beginning of this learning process.

The development of language is a gradual process, and involves learning both to understand and to express ideas using speech. A baby usually starts to say the first few meaningful words by the age of 10 months, but it will have been learning the basics of language since birth.

RECOGNIZING SOUND

Babies of as young as one month can discriminate between different two-syllable sounds, such as 'la-da' and 'la-ga'. Before six months, babies can also differentiate sound patterns not found in their native language. After this age, the ability is lost and they focus solely on the sounds of their 'mother tongue'.

Babies' ability to make noises, rather than to discriminate between different noises, begins later, as understanding is always ahead of expression. However, even from the age of two months, they start to laugh and make cooing noises – mainly vowel sounds, such as 'uuuuuuuu'.

REVEALING EMOTION

At a few weeks of age, babies begin to 'coo', often responding to a parent's smile; this is an exchange of emotions rather than language. Between three and six months of age, they turn purposefully towards sounds and voices, appearing to enjoy some sounds more than others.

The earliest indication that a baby can hear is when it stops all activity on hearing sudden or loud noises, often appearing startled. Hearing is an important factor in speech development, and if the baby has hearing problems, speech development may be delayed.

Babies of this age also makes different noises themselves, ranging from cries of annoyance to squeals of delight. Many babies make tuneful sing-song noises, 'talking' to objects and amusing themselves. They also chuckle and laugh, and this variation in noises indicates a developing selectivity in emotional response.

EXPLORING SOUND

After seven months babies begin to 'babble', repeating the same sound strung together over and over – for example, 'babababa'. Babbling is an important preparation for speech as it seems that babies learn the 'tune' before the language. They imitate the tone of the conversations around them, finishing a babbling sentence on a rising tone, as if asking a question.

At seven months, babies 'babble' sounds, even those that are not part of their language. However, they soon concentrate on the language sounds that they hear around them.

Learning by copying

Babies will often touch their parent's mouth while they are talking. They focus intently on lip movements, watching how the mouth forms sounds.

Mimicry is an important part of learning speech. A toy telephone allows the baby to practise communication by copying the behaviour of adults.

Babies are instinctively able to focus on faces as part of their social development. Many seem to enjoy the wide range of noises that a parent can make.

From nine months onwards, babies attend to everyday noises with interest, and they are able to recognize individuals by voice. They deliberately use vocalization in an attempt to communicate desires and frustrations and to attract attention.

Babies focus intently on adult faces, and may mimic mouth movements and sounds. At about one year of age, the babble develops a conversational rhythm and babies try to imitate situations where they have observed adult speech, babbling into a toy telephone, for example, then passing it to a parent for a response.

EXPRESSING IDEAS

Babies are able, through their behaviour, to indicate that they understand the context and meaning of a variety of words and instructions, such as 'drink', 'cat' and 'give to daddy'. Between 9 and 12 months, babies will also start to display recognition of objects by using them appropriately, such as drinking from a toy cup or brushing their hair with a brush.

They will start to use gestures and sounds together from around 9–10 months old. Thus, babies who want to be picked up

A child pointing at an object will often be frustrated by not being able to express its demands clearly. This is an incentive to expand its vocabulary.

Picture books allow children to learn how words and objects are linked. Hearing a parent read aloud encourages language exploration.

will reach their arms up while making pleading noises, so that there is no mistaking what they want.

FIRST WORDS

At around 10–15 months, the first meaningful words appear. These words may be any sounds that are used consistently to refer to something, but not necessarily a word used by adults. For example, a baby may say 'egg' when it is hungry because it usually has egg for breakfast. To the baby, 'egg' is a sound to use in any situation

involving food. The first meanings of these words are acquired very slowly.

By the time a toddler is 18 months old, speech-like sounds with conversational tones and emotional inflections are used during independent play. When spoken to, the child is able to stop and listen, attending to any instructions. A child of this age normally understands the meaning of the word 'no'.

At about 18 months of age,

Before they have learned to speak, babies will combine gestures and actions with sounds to make it clear what they are asking for.

toddlers use between 6 and 20 recognizable words in an appropriate setting, and demonstrate an understanding of many more. Toddlers will want to interact in conversation, joining in songs, pointing to pictures in books and naming many objects correctly.

FORMING SENTENCES

The acquisition of vocabulary from 18 months onwards is often rapid, but it varies considerably between children. An understanding of grammar and sentence structure is usually present a long time before the child applies it, and by the age of 18 months babies will start to construct simple, two-word sentences.

The ability to associate objects with their purpose – such as a cup for drinking – gives babies the foundations for successfully using language.

Developing language skills

The ability to learn a language is something that every child possesses. It is an incredibly complex process, but children essentially master language acquisition in just a few years.

Some time between the ages of 18 months and five years, children more or less master the grammar of their native language. To appreciate what an amazing feat this is, it is important to understand that learning grammar, unlike learning words in isolation, cannot be accomplished by imitation or example. Rather, as speakers of a language, we all know a finite set of rules that allows us to generate an infinite set of grammatical combinations. Even more amazing is the fact that children accomplish this in just a few years with little help from their parents. This is known from two types of studies.

PARENTAL INVOLVEMENT
First, although it is important for parents to provide an adequate language model for their children, they do not explicitly teach their children how the grammar of their language works. When parents spontaneously correct their children's utterances, such correction is typically focused on the truth or falsity of the

utterance rather than grammar.

For instance, if a child says, 'He a boy', when in fact the referent is a girl, an adult is more likely to explicitly correct the gender of the referent rather than the child's failure to use a

verb. In the cases where adults do attempt explicit correction of their child's grammar, the correction is usually not successful, at least in the short term.

INNATE LANGUAGE SKILLS
Second, children with very impoverished language input still manage to learn language. Thus, while it is important for parents in a normal language-learning situation to provide adequate input so that their children learn the conventional form of grammar, adults cannot claim credit for 'teaching' their

By the time children begin formal education at five years of age, their language development is already sophisticated. Social interaction at school will help refine their language skills.

children language: much of the ability is innately specified.

Likewise, except in rare cases of abuse or neglect, parents are not to be blamed for aberrant language development. Research in recent years has shown that there is a physiologic and even a genetic basis for many forms of speech, language and reading disorders.

Before speech as recognizable words develops, children follow adult-type patterns of behaviour. For example, they may babble into a telephone, leaving pauses for an imaginary reply.

The ability to read is usually acquired at a stage when the basic rules of grammar are already understood. However, the speed of acquisition is very variable.

Language development continues far beyond childhood. Effective communication relies on an instinctive understanding of how people interact.

COMMUNICATIVE COMPETENCE

Although children have made considerable progress in grammar and vocalization by the age of four, their conversational competence – that is, the ability to carry on an adult-like conversation – is still noticeably under-developed.

On the other hand, children do know something about conversation at an early age. For instance, even infants can make the intonation of their pre-speech vocalizations conform to what sounds like conversational interchange. (Indeed, such interchanges between infants often prompts parents of twins to believe their children have a 'secret' language.)

Furthermore, children as young as four know that they have to modify their speech for younger children to make it understandable.

However, more subtle but equally essential aspects of proper conversation are acquired later. These elements are encapsulated in the 'maxims' of communication described by the philosopher H.P. Grice:

■ **Quantity**
Give as much information as necessary for a child to understand, but do not give too much. Children frequently err on the side of giving too much information, including extraneous details and stories.

■ **Quality**
Tell the truth. Children often tell falsehoods to avoid punishment or simply to advance a conversation.

■ **Relevance**
Responses should be on the same topic as your interlocuter's and relevant to the ongoing context. Children often completely ignore the topic and instead talk about whatever strikes them.

■ **Manner**
Be clear, brief and unambiguous.

Children eventually learn these rules through two means. First, through experience with adult conversation. Second, by learning through independent channels that other people are thinking, feeling creatures. Once children can see the world from another person's perspective, many of these rules come naturally.

In reading exercises, children show remarkable expertise in higher brain function, such as concentration, visual acuity and concentration.

Word association with pictures helps children to increase their vocabulary. Even in the early stages of language development, toddlers may mimic animal sounds, for example.

The end of language learning: puberty

Some time during puberty, the ability to learn language – whether it be a first language or second – decreases. This fact has been noticed for many years with respect to learning foreign languages.

When moving to a foreign country, it is easier for children to pick up the language than their parents. People who emigrate after puberty tend to retain their foreign accent, even if they otherwise manage to become completely fluent in their adopted tongue.

Such anecdotes are backed up by studies showing that the older immigrants are, the less likely they are to achieve native-like competence.

Sign language as a first language develops in the same way as any spoken language. Hearing parents of deaf children find the acquisition more difficult than their children.

Linguistic isolation

First languages are also difficult to learn after puberty. Although the instances are fortunately rare, children are occasionally rescued from situations of severe neglect in which they do not receive adequate exposure to a language in early childhood.

When such 'linguistic isolates' are found after puberty, they never fully master language, even with extensive therapy. When they are discovered before puberty, they can make a nearly full recovery.

More commonly, linguistic isolation occurs in deaf children of hearing parents. If these children are not exposed to a manual language (such as sign language) before puberty, they have trouble mastering it. However, if they are exposed before puberty, they achieve nearly the same competence as children exposed from birth.

Developmental progress from 18 to 36 months

The period from 18 to 36 months sees many fascinating developmental changes in a young child. This is a critical time for neurological development.

A child's handling skills (fine motor skills) during the period from 18 to 36 months rapidly advance; everything is to be opened up and explored, and their imagination and curiosity know no bounds. At 36 months of age, a child will be constantly asking questions about the world in which they live.

The way a child plays with sand, for example, is typical of the way they interact with and explore their environment. They will run it through their fingers, scoop it up, add water to it, tip it from hand to hand, throw it, burrow in it, cover their feet with it, put it into a bucket, draw patterns in it, rub it into their own hair, and put it in their mouths and spit it out. This demonstrates how the child learns about the texture, volume, taste and feel of the world around them.

GROSS MOTOR SKILLS

During this period, a young child progresses from climbing stairs without the assistance of an adult, just holding a rail, to being able to take the stairs one at a time – albeit with one foot on each step on the way up and two feet per step on the way down.

Their gait develops from the shuffling, high-stepping walk of the toddler to being able to walk

Children constantly experiment with objects and textures in their environment. Playing is an important way of learning about how things work.

backwards at 21 months, being able to jump and walk on tiptoe at two-and-a-half, and to being able to stand on one foot for a few seconds by the time they are three years old.

A child's desire to explore their environment will be applied to any medium. At three years of age, children want to experiment with anything they can find in home or garden, preferably items from closed cupboards.

The development of a child's

As children get older, their hand–eye co-ordination improves. Building with blocks helps a child develop fine motor skills.

fine motor skills takes on an extra dimension with the exploration of sound. By banging on musical instruments such as toy drums and xylophones, children will explore how their actions result in certain sounds.

COGNITIVE SKILLS

It is in the area of gaining knowledge and the skills of recognition that the child makes its greatest advances. By 21 months, a child can attract attention by pulling someone's sleeve, they know four parts of the body, and can obey simple requests such as 'Take it to Mum', or 'Put it on the table'.

By three years of age, a child can climb the stairs on its own. This task is difficult for a younger child, but a three-year-old is much more balanced.

ACHIEVEMENTS

By the age of two, a child is capable of simulating a train shape using cubes, making a vertical stroke with a pencil, knows at least two common objects and can obey four simple requests. At 18 months old, they could only point correctly to one picture card when asked 'Where is this?', but by two they can name at least three objects from the cards when asked 'What is this?' and can identify five when asked 'Where is the...?'

It is usually at the age of two that parallel play starts. Up until now, a child will have played alone and shown little interest in playing with another child. By two, however, a child will watch others play and play near them, without actually playing with them.

At the age of two-and-a-half, a child will be able to write vertical and horizontal strokes and start to repeat numbers. They can name five common objects, know their own name and can help to put things away when asked. At this age, children start taking an interest in their sex organs.

Musical instruments are irresistible to children once they discover that their actions will produce sounds. They also start to learn about pitch and melody.

GENDER AWARENESS

At three years old, children can name around eight objects on a picture card when asked 'What is this?' They can draw a circle, and will know some simple nursery rhymes, and may be able to count up to 10.

At this stage, a child is aware of gender differences and knows whether they are a girl or a boy. Another development is that a child happily joins other children in play, engaging in co-operative play rather than the parallel play of earlier months.

Children will ask for food or drink or to use the toilet by the age of 21 months. Although children's speech is not very advanced at this point, they are able to understand much more than they can actually say. By the age of two, however, a child will

A young child will be able to point at pictures of objects that they recognize and name them. This demonstrates their intellectual development.

probably be talking incessantly.

Most children develop understandable speech by the age of three years. Some aspects of speech remain difficult to a three-year-old, however, including the use of tense and plurals.

PRE-SCHOOL EDUCATION

Between the ages of two-and-a-half and three, a child may start attending pre-school or play group. This often coincides with the time that the child has become dry during the day and so no longer needs nappies.

At this age, the child has developed a sufficient level of communication and is, to a certain extent, independent enough to cope with the temporary separation from their

As a child becomes more mobile, it becomes far more active in its play. Children test their skills as they become stronger and more balanced.

parents. The pre-school environment offers an opportunity for a child to interact with other children of the same age, developing co-operative and social skills.

Despite these remarkable developmental advances, a two-year-old child is, at worst, at the peak of negativity and senselessness, and is only capable of living in the present. A two-year-old can be stubborn, self-centred and antisocial, but will soon change into a more capable and thoughtful three-year-old.

Co-ordination of motor skills

At around 18 months of age, a toddler will be able to build a tower of three cubes, manage a spoon and take off their gloves and socks. By 21 months, the child can build towers of six cubes or more.

By the age of two, a child can turn the individual pages of a book, turn door knobs, open cupboard doors, unscrew a lid, put on its own pants, socks and shoes, and wash and dry its hands unaided.

By the time they are three years

old, most children can undress themselves, and some will probably be able to dress themselves as well. An average three-year-old child can also build a tower of nine cubes and carry plates, without mishap, to the dining table. It continues to learn through play and interaction with other children.

Learning to play together takes time. Playing with other children at pre-school or nursery teaches co-operation.

Potty training

Toilet timing and toilet training can only be established when a child has developed bladder and bowel control. The age for this is enormously variable and bears no predictive value for intelligence.

Toilet training is a process that can take years for a toddler and young child to master. Some children are toilet trained before their second birthday, while others may still be having lapses nearer to their third or fourth birthdays.

Toilet training depends essentially on three separate mechanisms: maturation, learning and conditioning. Only when these stages have been achieved can a young child master voluntary control of bladder and bowel.

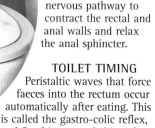

As children become aware of their bodies, they start to show great interest in toilets and potties. This indicates they are ready for toilet training.

INVOLUNTARY REFLEXES
The bladder and bowel muscles are involuntary – they contract by reflex stimulation of nervous pathways. Continuous leakage of urine and faeces is prevented by sphincters which are under voluntary nervous control. However, the ability to control contraction of the sphincters is developmentally acquired and is not present in early infancy.

Until voluntary control is acquired, the bladder will empty automatically when its capacity is reached (volume is age-dependent). Emptying the bowel occurs when peristalsis (rhythmic contractions of the intestines) forces fecal material into the rectum from the large bowel (the rectum is normally empty). The ensuing expansion of the rectal wall triggers a reflex nervous pathway to contract the rectal and anal walls and relax the anal sphincter.

TOILET TIMING
Peristaltic waves that force faeces into the rectum occur automatically after eating. This is called the gastro-colic reflex, and for this reason babies often soil their nappy after feeding. This reflex action may be exploited to assist children to associate sitting on the potty with bowel action by timing the

Potty training can take a long time. The child needs the physical maturity to control their body and to have learned what is socially appropriate.

use of the potty with meal times – this is known as toilet timing.

Once the reflex action begins, emptying the bowel often stimulates urination at the same time. However, since both outcomes result from involuntary stimuli, there is nothing to be gained by leaving the child to sit on the potty for more than five minutes (most children will not tolerate this length of time).

Furthermore, a successful outcome does not mean that an infant understands how the result was achieved, which

Children often use mimicry in their play. 'Toilet training' a doll by putting it on a potty is common and reflects the way that children learn from adults.

means that toilet timing cannot really be described as toilet training.

VOLUNTARY CONTROL
Normally, voluntary bladder control is acquired between 15 to 18 months of age. The first indication of voluntary bladder control is when a child starts showing interest in a potty, the lavatory and in their own urine and faeces. Children may also start placing a doll on a toy potty, mimicking how a parent puts them on the potty. Toilet timing can begin at this time.

There is little need to consider toilet training until the child has developed an awareness of having had an accident, and is capable of being aware of being wet. No amount of training can succeed if a child does not know whether or not they are wet. This stage is often not attained until well into their third year. This is an entirely genetic matter and nothing to do with good or bad behaviour, and children do not benefit from being reprimanded or punished for accidents.

Some parents are convinced that early mastery of toilet use is a sign of a child's intelligence and obedient nature, but this is not so. The age at which toileting is mastered and the child becomes reliable does not reflect their level of intelligence.

LEARNING AND CONDITIONING

The learning and conditioning processes are initially achieved through toilet timing. If a child is placed on to a potty as soon as it shows any sign of wanting to go, the association between urinating and defecating in the potty or toilet is strengthened. This is termed conditioning.

Some children, however, show no overt signs of understanding the need to urinate by the age of 30 months or even older. For these children, conditioning occurs by regularly sitting them on the potty until the timing coincides with a full bladder.

The child is then congratulated upon successfully using the potty, while no comment is made when they do not empty bladder or bowel. In time, a child will come to realize

Many children master bladder control at the age when they begin attending nursery school or playgroup. The social setting often assists the conditioning.

that they can earn their parents' approval and delight through using the potty. They may even claim to want to use it when they do not need to in order to claim more than their fair share of parental pride.

URINARY URGENCY

When a child begins to acquire a sense of bladder function, they often give a number of signs that they realize that they need to urinate. They may clutch their

clothes, look tense and worried or hop from one foot to another.

This urinary urgency is related to the fact that the child is not yet able to delay urination; their bladder is small and can only hold a small amount of urine at this stage. A child, therefore, may tell a parent immediately before urinating, leaving no time for preparations.

Until this urgency has lessened, and a child can anticipate needing to go to the toilet and then hold the urine in, there is little point starting potty training. Similarly, the developmental limits on bladder capacity dictate that the younger the child is out of nappies, the more often they are likely to need to visit the toilet.

A young child will probably continue to have accidents for some time before toilet training is complete. They may be caught before they can reach the potty and either wet or soil their clothes, often to their considerable distress, and may also take some time to achieve night time dryness.

DRYNESS AT NIGHT

Staying dry during the day and the night are not the same thing, and 10 per cent of five year olds and five per cent of 10 year olds

Boys often take slightly longer than girls to acquire control over their urinary sphincters. Initially, they learn to urinate in a sitting position before being able to do so standing up.

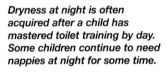

Dryness at night is often acquired after a child has mastered toilet training by day. Some children continue to need nappies at night for some time.

are wet during the night. The timing of dryness at night tends to have a familial element, particularly for boys, although other factors can influence whether a child wets the bed.

In some cases, a child is dry through the night from the age of six months, but this is unusual. It may be that the child will continue to urinate involuntarily at night until they are four or five years old.

A child who is normally dry at night may suffer lapses when ill or distressed such as during a stressful life event (the arrival of a new baby in the family or moving house, for example).

The ability to control bladder function at night is dependent on the deepness of sleep and the ability of the child to wake when neurological signals indicate a full bladder. It is not dependent on how much a child may drink before going to bed.

Bed-wetting

Bed-wetting (medically known as enuresis) can be a problem
for a child and for the family. There are, however, various ways to
treat the condition, both at home and with the help of a doctor.

Bed-wetting (enuresis) is a common complaint of childhood. It is a disorder of delayed maturation, but it is not medically diagnosed until after the age of five. Babies naturally do not have bladder control but, as they mature and become toilet-trained, they learn to control the voiding of urine.

TOILET-TRAINING
Some children become toilet-trained faster and more efficiently than others and, in general, most children are dry at night by the age of three. At the age of five, however, 10 per cent of children still wet the bed on a regular basis.

Occasional episodes of bed-wetting (often associated with exhaustion) are common in young children and, although inconvenient for parents, are not of any medical significance. However, other family members, particularly siblings who share a room with a bed-wetter, may be resentful of the 'trouble' a bed-wetting child causes. This can exacerbate the problem.

Enuresis is not medically diagnosed in children under the age of five. However, younger children can still have feelings of guilt about repeated 'accidents'.

A rubber sheet can protect a mattress from wetting. Making a child an active part of the nightly 'ritual' of laying the sheet may help to rid it of any feelings of guilt or embarrassment.

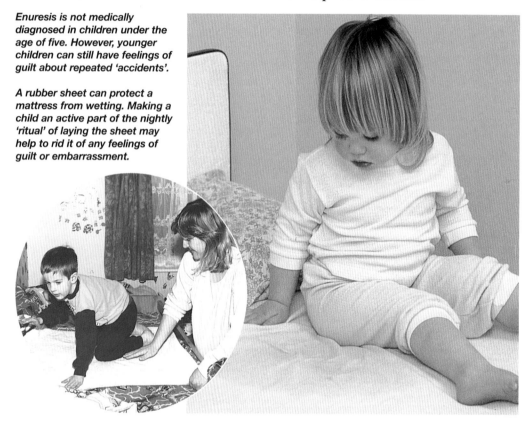

What are the causes of bed-wetting?

Enuresis may be familial in some cases: for example, it is not uncommon for one or both parents to have had problems with bed-wetting in their own childhood. The definitive underlying cause has, however, yet to be determined but it is likely to be multifactorial.

Suggested factors include deficiency of nocturnal antidiuretic hormone production, sleep apnoea, psychological problems and delay in development of control of urination. Enuresis is rarely due to an abnormality of the urinary system itself.

A full assessment of the medical history of a child and the attainment of normal developmental milestones is important. If the enuresis is part of an overall developmental delay, there may be other signs of development failure.

Analysis of urine for glucose (diabetes) and infection will rule out many obvious physical causes. Detailed urological  investigation is rarely necessary unless a child also has daytime wetting or is found to have an abnormal finding on examination or investigation.

TYPES OF ENURESIS
Enuresis may be primary or secondary. In primary enuresis (the more common type), a child has never been dry at night and is more or less continuously wet at night. In secondary enuresis, a child has been previously dry (continuously for more than one year) and begins regularly to wet the bed again.

Many causes of secondary enuresis (and some causes of primary enuresis) are due to stress. Common stressful triggers include parental disharmony, hospital admission, maternal illness, bullying at school and moving house.

Problems at school can be a contributory factor in a child's bed-wetting. Emotional stress in general is a common cause of secondary enuresis.

Treating bed-wetting

Before seeking a consultation with a doctor, parents of a bed-wetting child may try non-medical methods to improve the situation. If these do not prove successful, there are various measures that can be taken in an attempt to resolve the problem.

One non-medical method for treating bed-wetting is to lift a child from sleep to go to the toilet before the parents go to bed. This is a practical way of trying to reduce the likelihood of bed-wetting. Fluid restriction is, however, not useful, and no treatment should be started in children under the age of five.

At the doctor's surgery, the child should be talked to with its parents and on its own. Sensitive interviewing allows a child to describe its feelings about the problem and may bring to light any relevant stress factors. The interview also allows the doctor to 'empower' a child to be an important part of the management, since the co-operation of the child is important in resolving the problem.

Lifting a child from bed and taking it to the toilet may pre-empt bed-wetting. This method is often successful and avoids the need for medical treatment.

When the star chart method is used, the child is rewarded for every dry night with a star. Often, this encouragement is sufficient to resolve the problem.

STAR CHART
A star chart is helpful for some children. In this method, the child records each dry night by sticking a star on the appropriate day on the chart. Children gain praise and positive feedback when they are able to signal success, and may respond well to this method.

For other children, especially those whose attempts at being dry are unsuccessful, it can be very disheartening to have no dry nights, no stars and no success.

BUZZER TREATMENT
If the star chart is unsuccessful, a paediatrician may suggest buzzer treatment. This associates night-time bed-wetting with a buzzing noise. The bed-wetting child sleeps on its own bed on a sheet, which covers a buzzer apparatus. This consists of a wire-mesh detector, which is an electrical circuit that is only completed when urine is passed.

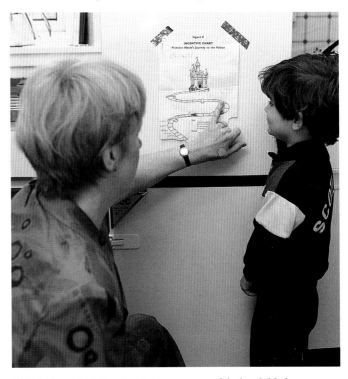

With bed-wetting, the circuit is completed and a buzzing sound is produced. This wakes the child, who turns off the noise and goes to the toilet to finish urinating.

With buzzer treatment, the amount of urine a child involuntarily passes usually decreases with time. A child will eventually wake before the alarm starts and will go to the toilet to urinate without bed-wetting. If successful, the child sleeps throughout the night and remains dry.

Around 80 per cent of children become dry within four months, and most within the first two months; 10 per cent of children who do become dry using this technique may have a later recurrence of bed-wetting but they respond quickly to the re-introduction of the buzzer.

Drinking and bed-wetting

If your child has a tendency to wet the bed at night (known as enuresis), you may be tempted to reduce the amount of fluids that he or she is drinking. However, drinking plenty of water each day is vital for general health, especially in a growing child.

Liquid intake
Although some adults and children find that avoiding drinks for the hour or two before bedtime can help, every child should drink plenty of water during the day. There are no specific guidelines as to how much, but a minimum of one litre (2 pints) of water every 24 hours is recommended. Older children (over the age of 9) should aim for around 1500 mls to two litres (3–4 pints).

Remember that you can never drink too much water but, if possible, avoid fizzy or sugary drinks, as these can lead to weight gain and cause damage to teeth.

The benefits of water
Over half of the human body is water – in fact, without water we would not be able to live. It has many functions, including transporting important nutrients to where they are needed and taking part in the millions of chemical reactions that enable the body to function.

If we fail to drink enough water, we become dehydrated and these vital processes slow down. Children are more prone to dehydration than adults because they have a higher surface area to body mass and

therefore lose more water through their skin. Their thirst response is also less well developed so their bodies do not "tell" them to drink as promptly.

During the day, children are usually very active and need to increase their water intake. Advising children to take a bottle of water to school and drink at regular intervals during the day rather than wait until they feel thirsty, can avoid dehydration.

Some schools have an active hydration policy that encourages children to drink water during classes, and teachers in these schools have seen a significant improvement in concentration levels among pupils. So water can have educational benefits.

Dehydration
There are a number of side effects of dehydration, some so mild that they may not even be noticed by the lay observer. Children may show a lack of concentration, and may be unable to memorise facts.

Regular headaches can be a sign of not drinking enough water, as can lethargy and a dry mouth. Dehydration can also contribute to the development of a urinary tract infection or constipation, both causes of bedwetting.

In addition, if a child with enuresis does not drink enough during the day, his or her bladder size may – over time – become smaller and unable to hold urine through the night, thereby exacerbating the problem.

Entering childhood

By the age of 18 months, a baby enters a new stage – childhood.
Unlike a baby, a child is self-aware and this, combined with social
influences and developmental progress, will prepare it for adulthood.

The transition from toddler to child comprises many complex changes in every area of development, from motor skills and the acquisition of language, to perception and the struggle for independence from parents.

The chief characteristics of toddlers at this age are living in the moment, living for oneself, total free will with few innate constraints, and absolute dependence upon parents and carers. These characteristics make for some interesting push-pull power struggles between a developing child and those around it.

THE BID FOR INDEPENDENCE

In learning to become an individual, a growing child must rely on its genetics, its constitution and its parenting. These are the three factors that largely determine a child's temperament, personality and the development of a free will which is combined with social and moral conscience.

Temperament can be defined as the individual's emotional reactivity or behavioural style in interacting with the environment – in other words, how a child relates to others and responds to the world around it. Personality can be described as one's inborn style of response.

Children's development towards maturity and independence is strongly affected by how they 'fit' with their parents. A volatile and impulsive child, for example, can alarm and distress a placid

parent who is not used to coping with this type of personality. Equally, dynamic, high-achieving parents may be disappointed in an 'easy' child who sleeps a lot, takes change in their stride and reacts slowly to external stimuli.

IDENTITY AND SELF-ESTEEM

How parents act with and react to their child has considerable bearing on the child's growing identity and self-esteem. For example, a very young child will sooner or later show signs of wanting to feed itself. Children may be very slow and messy doing this, but the time at which they show interest in doing so is the right time for that individual to be allowed to try.

If the parent habitually takes over, because it is quicker and cleaner to feed the child, the child may eventually not want to try and may develop food fads and food refusal. It is easy

Some children will sit quietly and draw or try to write from an early age. Others will need more encouragement or supervision to work in this way.

to see, therefore, how a child's emerging independence can be misunderstood and may create problems where none need have existed.

A toddler's difficulties eventually resolve between the ages of three-and-a-half and four-and-a-half. A child is then able to consider the repercussions of their actions and develops common sense.

THE VITAL ELEMENTS

Important elements of development in childhood, and later adolescence, include attachment, sense of worth and a child's individual temperament.

Playing with other toddlers helps a child to develop motor skills and assert independence. It is also a time for taking the feelings of others into account.

ATTACHMENT

It is known that the emotional development of children is determined long before they are born. Much depends on whether or not a child is wanted and whether or not the parental relationship is secure. Infants respond in various ways to parental attitude, and in so doing influence the behaviour of those looking after them. The strength of attachment and the affection shown to an infant by its parents has a bearing on a growing child's ability to make successful relationships, both as a child and as an adult.

Acceptance of individuality on the part of the parents is vital to a child's psychological well-being. A sense of personal worth is critical to small children and remains of central importance for human beings throughout their lives. A diminished sense of worth is responsible for emotional disturbances of many kinds and to a number of psychiatric conditions.

STIMULATION

A child needs mental and physical stimulation of many sorts in order to thrive. During play, children use all five senses in order to understand an object. Physical play is also necessary

When children play a game of make-believe, they are often copying adult behaviour. This helps them to learn more about the adult world.

for a child's healthy physical growth and maturity. In play, a child learns many useful skills, including taking turns and learning to play co-operatively.

Play school, and later school, offer a growing child an opportunity to expand their skills and knowledge. This is an important time for a child to interact with other children of their own age and develop the social skills that will be used for the rest of their life.

ACADEMIC EXCELLENCE AND LEADERSHIP

As a child's motor skills and understanding of how they fit in to their environment develop, they may exhibit particular talents or abilities. An exceptional child, a prodigy in other words, will excel at one or more of these skills. An intellectually gifted child may show an aptitude in a particular field, for example, a specific academic aptitude – often in maths or science. Other children show that they are talented creative or productive thinkers, excelling in art or music.

A child may demonstrate leadership ability and organizational skills which may,

Playing with friends helps a child to assume different roles. During play, children often take turns, and this enables them to expand their social skills.

in turn, be teamed with particular athletic skills, such as demonstrated in dance or team sports. These abilities are known as psychomotor skills.

The journey from childhood to sexual maturity comprises physical, mental and emotional changes. Children take their cues from what their parents do rather than what they say. To become independent, a child must achieve cognitive development, perception and an awareness of morality.

Temperamental differences

Potty training may cause distress at first, but it is one of the most important basic skills a toddler can learn.

There are many factors that may contribute to a child's overall temperament. These so-called 'defining characteristics' include:

■ General activity level
■ Regularity of biological function (routines of sleeping and eating, for example)
■ Ability to adapt to change
■ Tendency to approach or withdraw when confronted with new situations
■ Intensity of emotional reaction to pleasant and unpleasant situations
■ Reactions threshold (ability to cope with change)
■ General quality of mood
■ Distractibility and attention persistence when involved with a specific task.

Development of vision

Visual development is closely linked to brain growth. There is constant interaction between eye and brain, and many important functions rely on the ability to interpret correctly what is seen.

An enormous amount of visual development has taken place by the time a child is three years of age. Most children have fine enough vision by this age to be able to spot very small specks of dust on a carpet and aeroplanes in the sky at quite a distance.

However, one way in which pre-school vision is not adult-like is in visual crowding. Four-year-olds find it harder to identify a letter shape when it is surrounded by other letters which 'mask' it or distract the attention of the child away from the target letter.

LEARNING TO READ

For reading, children have to learn to overcome this 'masking effect' so that they can identify individual letters, combine them into a word and separate them from the next word. A persistent crowding effect could be one factor in slowing a child learning to read, and may be one of the initial problems in dyslexia (reading difficulties).

Other visual factors can be involved in reading problems. Some dyslexic children have particular difficulties with tasks such as judging the relative movement of objects and carrying out tasks that need visual and motor co-ordination.

Such actions depend on the correct functioning of a part of the brain called the dorsal

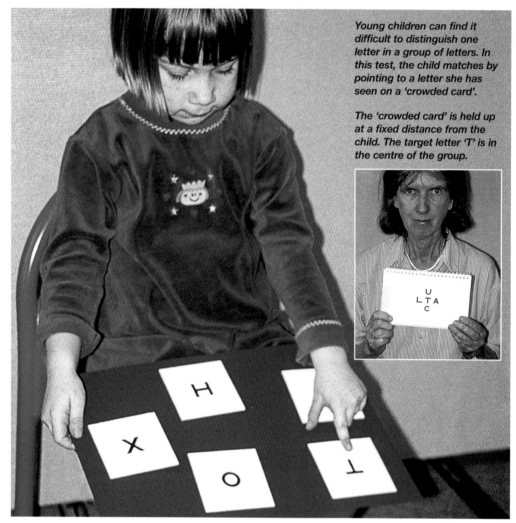

Young children can find it difficult to distinguish one letter in a group of letters. In this test, the child matches by pointing to a letter she has seen on a 'crowded card'.

The 'crowded card' is held up at a fixed distance from the child. The target letter 'T' is in the centre of the group.

pathway. This pathway contains a special brain area called V5, which is important for detecting movement, and further specialized areas that are needed for carrying out visuomotor tasks. If this pathway does not develop normally in early childhood, children may have difficulty with sequential eye movements (needed for reading) and everyday tasks, such as safely crossing a busy road.

OBJECT AND ACTION PATHWAYS

A second major system in the brain used in object and face recognition is called the ventral pathway. These ventral and dorsal pathways are sometimes called the 'what?' and 'where?' or 'who?' and 'how?' pathways. One helps us understand 'what' we are looking at and the other helps us act upon objects by, for example reaching out to pick them up. New tests can measure brain development in these 'object' and 'action' pathways in children.

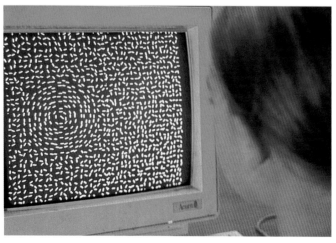

A random dot pattern, containing a circular array of dots (on left side of screen) is used to test the 'object' pathway in the child's brain.

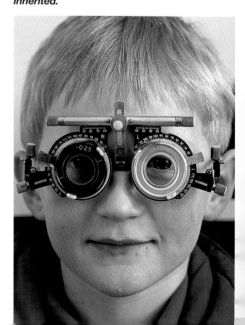

Children's eyesight should be checked regularly so that any problems can be rectified. Some visual problems are inherited.

Visuomotor and visuospatial tasks rely on normal object and action pathway development. This girl shows good skills acquisition in these areas.

Growing children need to learn how objects relate to each other in terms of relative orientation, size and shape.

Young children have problems with visual reasoning. In this case, the child thinks that there are more bricks in the 'spread out' row than in the 'closed up' row.

treated early, are likely to have poor vision in the squinting eye and a lack of binocular vision in using the two eyes together. Permanent poor vision in one eye is often called 'amblyopia' or 'lazy eye' and is present in two to five per cent of school-age children in Europe.

BRAIN DEVELOPMENT

Children progress a long way between three and 11 years in visual understanding and reasoning; this development is related to maturation of the brain, and particularly the frontal lobes.

By the time children are 11 years old, their visual competence is in many respects adult-like for many everyday tasks. However, their visuomotor skills and powers of selective visual attention are still improving, so the best footballers and chess and computer games players are still likely to be teenagers or adults.

In normal children, the 'object' system develops relatively early with the result that faces and objects can be crudely recognized from the first few months of life. The 'action' system takes considerably longer to become mature, and abnormal development of this pathway can hold a child up in many school activities. The challenge is to help these children (from normal children, who are a little clumsy, to those with severe disabilities) to develop compensating strategies to overcome their problems for everyday life.

PHYSICAL PROBLEMS

Some events very early in life can affect children's vision for the rest of their lives. For example, it is known that children with cross-eyes (called 'strabismus' or 'squint'), if not

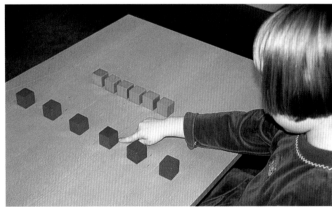

Risk factors for squint

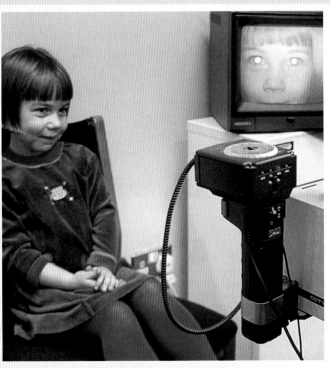

This special monitoring equipment, the videorefractor, is used to measure squint and refractive errors in babies and young children. It permits very high diagnostic accuracy.

It is known that the incidence of squint is much higher if a child has a mother, father or sibling with a squint. The incidence is also much higher in children with other problems, such as Down's syndrome and cerebral palsy. It is also known that certain refractive errors (in particular hypermetropia, or long-sightedness, in one or both eyes), are commonly linked to strabismus and amblyopia. In many cases, these problems may be prevented by the child's wearing spectacles.

Around 20 per cent of adults in the UK need to wear spectacles or contact lenses or have laser treatment to correct short-sightedness (myopia). Around a third of all myopic adults first become short-sighted in the primary school years. This means that regular eye checks for all young children are advisable, and are particularly important if a child has short-sighted parents.

Problems with eyesight can be hard to detect in younger children. The spectacles worn by this child are to reduce the likelihood of squint developing.

Stimulation and play

Through play, children learn about the world and themselves. Play develops strength and co-ordination, creativity and intellect, and teaches children valuable lessons about social rules and behaviour.

By choice, a child spends almost all its time playing. Only when it is distracted by adults in order to be fed, bathed or to sleep does it stop playing – it has to be encouraged to engage in other activities. A child learns to make sense of the world around it through this play process.

LEARNING THROUGH PLAY

Through playing, a child learns to control the movements of its body, and develops balance and co-ordination of brain, eyes and limbs. A child is naturally curious, and enjoys exploring the textures of grass, earth, leaves and rain, collecting facts about the world and how it works. All of this experimental play leads a child to become a social person. Play, therefore, is a child's natural way of learning.

A child needs stimulation and a variety of games and toys in order to be able to learn. It will benefit greatly and learn quickly through talk and play with an adult, usually its parents. Stimulation is vital to prevent boredom, destructiveness and irritability. Children who are deprived of stimulation and contact can become withdrawn and disturbed and show delayed development. Therefore, it is better for a child to be presented with challenges that are too difficult rather than too easy.

Many theories have been advanced as to why children play, but most experts now agree that play is a fundamental means of learning for a child. It has also been suggested that play is a way of using up surplus energy and a means of rehearsing skills for later life.

Types of play can be divided into a number of categories. Each type of play serves an important function in a child's learning and development.

Construction toys appeal to almost all children. These types of toys encourage imagination and problem solving, colour recognition and fine motor skills.

VIGOROUS PHYSICAL PLAY

Climbing, throwing, catching, kicking balls and dancing, for example, help in learning to control the body by co-ordinating actions. Physical, energetic play also helps to achieve hand–eye co-ordination and balance.

EXPERIMENTAL PLAY

This includes putting objects into containers, stacking objects of different sizes and shapes, sorting and classifying, and playing with jigsaws, peg boards and magnets.

Play is essential for a child's normal physical and intellectual development. While they play, children learn about their environment and how things work by constantly experimenting and exploring.

Stages of play

Children start learning about the world through play by exploring with all of their five senses: sound, smell, touch, vision and taste.

Up until about the age of two, children engage in solitary play, from two they progress to looking-on play (watching others play) to parallel play (using same materials but not relating to their

It is not until a child is about four years old that they will begin to play co-operatively with another child.

play companion). From the age of two or three to about four, they progress to associative play (interacting with but not actually helping one another) and soon to co-operative play, when children play with one another.

Play helps children to release aggression and anxiety and enables them to exhibit their independence. In play, they are empowered. This is why it is most important that adults do not intervene or help a child too much during play.

Experimental play helps a child learn how objects relate to one another, and how to solve problems while developing powers of concentration. In this way, a child learns to distinguish through careful examination and experimentation, between, for example, a rattle and a bunch of keys.

CREATIVE PLAY

Children become absorbed in creating things with household objects, for example, margarine cartons, lavatory rolls and paint. This aspect of play also includes making music. Creative play enables the development of creative skills in music and in art and builds a sense of confidence and spatial awareness.

IMAGINATIVE PLAY

Children actively use their imagination when acting, dressing up, playing with toys or having an imaginary friend. Imaginative play gives a child an insight into the role of others, enabling them to rehearse adult roles and learn how to do tasks for themselves. All the things that adults take for granted are entirely novel skills and experiences when first acquired by a child.

Painting is an activity that children readily take to. Mixing colours and painting on different surfaces encourages creative thinking and self-confidence.

MESSY PLAY

Playing with sand, water, clay and play dough helps co-ordination. Messy play also helps a child to learn about the properties, texture, volume and behaviour of materials.

PLAYING WITH FRIENDS

This is important in developing social skills, learning about fair play, keeping rules, sharing and retaining a sense of humour in games. These types of activities include marbles and role playing, such as 'cowboys and

Imaginative play allows a child to slip into another role, often acting out the role of an adult. A common example of this is a child playing 'mother' to dolls.

Indians'. Sociable play helps to modify the egocentrism of the toddler and very young child.

The beginnings of altruistic behaviour, one of the unique elements of being human, will be seen in co-operative play. However, all forms of play are important for the development of a child's intelligence and social relationships.

The very young child finds out about the world by touching it, tasting it (everything is put to the mouth), looking at it and experimenting with it. Children discover the properties of materials (hard/soft or warm/cold), learning that some

Learning to play music is a creative skill that children often enjoy. Young children seem to be fascinated by the fact that their actions produce sounds.

things can be bent or squeezed and some not. This expanding knowledge is learned through experimentation and then experience: a child finds that sand behaves differently from water: sand can be pushed into a heap, but water can't.

PLAY GROUPS AND PLAY SCHOOL

By the time a child goes to school, they will have accumulated an enormous amount of information, some of it in context and some not.

A child from the ages of one to three collects more information than at any other time in their life. The value of play groups and play school lies in catching the child in these years, and providing the stimulation and challenges they need before they go into formal education at the age of four or five.

Brightly coloured construction toys are a perfect tool for a child to learn about shapes and develop spatial awareness. Co-ordination is also developed.

Temperament and personality

Children's personalities are influenced by a combination of environmental and genetic influences. Each child's personality is unique to the individual and will remain with it through life.

Personality can be defined as the collection of individual and relatively enduring patterns of reacting to and interacting with others that distinguishes one child from another. Temperament and personality characteristics vary as much as physical characteristics and these are what makes a person unique. Even identical twins will display differences in disposition and personality.

Genetic inheritance is known to influence temperament and personality. However, a child's genetic make-up is not the only

The differences in temperament between children is what make them unique. Social factors may influence these traits.

influential factor. Context, or the environment in which a child is brought up in, is also significant.

Infants are very dependent on their environment for the opportunity to develop and thrive. A child's environment, the characteristics of a child's parents, their education and schooling, and the way a child interacts with its parents all influence the child's personality as it grows older.

TEMPERAMENTAL VARIATIONS

All of the following factors can be regarded as inborn character traits: independence of character, determination, obsessional thoroughness, placidity and social responsiveness. Studies by researchers have shown that temperamental differences in babies and children can be measured within certain fundamental categories. These are:

■ **Level of activity**
The proportion of time per day that a baby is active and inactive

■ **Rhythmicity (regularity)**
How predictable or regular a child is in any biological function (eating, sleeping and bladder and bowel functions)

■ **Approach or withdrawal**
How a child initially responds to a new stimulus (a toy, food, a stranger). Approach responses are positive and shown by smiling, gurgling and reaching out, for example.

Some traits in an infant will be carried into childhood and possibly adulthood. An energetic child may be able to harness its energy into constructive and creative areas once it has started school.

Types of personality

An infant's basic temperamental differences are apparent in the first weeks of life. This has led to children being broadly categorized as 'easy', 'difficult' and 'slow to warm up'.

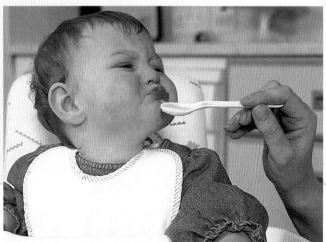

'Easy' children
About 40 per cent of children fall into this category. It is characterized by regularity in body functions, such as feeding and sleeping, positive responses to

new stimuli, swift adaptability to change and mild or moderate intensity of mood which is predominantly positive.

'Difficult' children
These represent about 10 per cent of children and they will have irregular bodily functions, negative responses to new stimuli, slow adaptability to change and intense moods which are often negative. They may prove difficult to feed, reluctant to go to sleep and negative and prone to anger at frustration. This category does not

Some children find it hard to adapt to new stimuli and may be classed as difficult. This type of child may be difficult to feed.

include minor and often transient upsets of temper, sleep, feeding and movements of bladder and bowel.

'Slow to warm up' children
Some 15 per cent of children are not necessarily difficult but they take longer than the 'easy' child to adapt to new stimuli and change. They may show negative responses to new stimuli with slow adaptability, and generally a mild intensity of reactions, but with more regular biological functioning than 'difficult' children.

The remaining 35 per cent of children cannot be so easily classified and will show a combination of various temperamental traits.

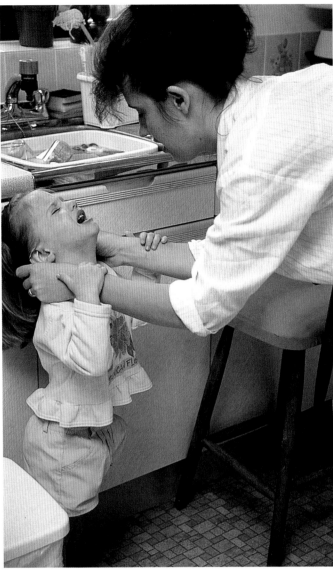

out, for example. Withdrawal responses are negative and are displayed by crying or turning the face away

■ **Adaptability**
How quickly and easily a child responds and adapts to new situations

■ **Threshold of responsiveness**
The degree of stimulation a child requires to produce any discernible response

■ **Intensity of reaction**
The energy level of a child's response

■ **Quality of mood**
The amount of pleasant, joyful and friendly behaviour of a child, contrasted with unpleasant and unfriendly behaviour

■ **Distractability**
How effective other extraneous environmental stimuli are in altering a child's current behaviour

■ **Attention span and persistence**
How long a child pursues an activity and to what degree it will continue with that activity despite being faced with obstacles.

INFLUENCES ON PERSONALITY

While basic personality patterns may remain unaltered, suggesting a permanent or inherited aspect to personality, studies have shown that a child's temperament may change somewhat as it grows older.

The home and school environment, and, to a degree, a child's genetic make-up, has a significant effect on its temperament.

Studies of twins have

Families are an important influence on a child's developing personality. Supportive parents and siblings will encourage confidence in a child.

suggested that a link does seem to exist between genetics and temperament. However, determining which of genetics and environment has the greatest influence on a child's personality and disposition is the subject of much debate.

ENVIRONMENTAL FACTORS

The way a parent interacts with their child is influenced by the culture they have been raised in and by their preconceived ideas of gender. From birth, parents have been shown to treat girls and boys differently. This stereotyping (for example, boys being aggressive and active and girls being quiet and easily upset) can encourage certain temperamental characteristics in a child and discourage others.

The relationship between parent and child is a matter of each continually reacting to the other. If a parent believes a child to be 'difficult', they will treat this child differently from an 'easy-going' child, and therefore elicit a different response.

The way a parent treats a child has an effect on its personality. A happy and stimulating environment is essential to the development of a well-balanced child. Insufficient affection at an infant's highly vulnerable stage of development is significant. A child who grows up feeling confident will find it easier to take steps towards independence, an essential part of maturing.

A child's personality is unique and is a defining part of who it is. Although a baby will be born with certain temperamental characteristics, how it is raised remains crucial to how its personality develops.

▲ *The way a parent responds to a child's behaviour will either discourage or encourage certain temperament traits. However, this is not the only influential factor.*

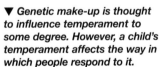
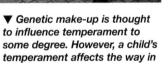

▼ *Genetic make-up is thought to influence temperament to some degree. However, a child's temperament affects the way in which people respond to it.*

▲ *An outgoing child can find adjusting to school and making friends easier than a shy child. Given time, however, a shy child can become more confident.*

Temper tantrums

Tantrums are common as toddlers start to challenge their parents' decisions. Without the language skills of an older child, toddlers can become overwhelmed with frustration, resulting in a tantrum.

Although each child is born with its own unique personality, it will, for the first year or so, act in ways that are usually a response to changes in its environment or its physical needs. If a baby is hungry, it will cry until it is fed; if it is put down, it may cry until it is picked up and cuddled.

A baby has little control over its environment, merely the ability to respond to it. It will respond to smiles with more smiles; it will try to talk back to those who speak to it; and try to please those who care for it. This will, in turn, help it to get the feelings of love and security it needs.

STRIVING FOR INDEPENDENCE

As a baby develops into a toddler, a new way of thinking arises, along with the more obvious physical changes. A child begins to realize that its actions affect the world around it and it can therefore control its environment in some way. A toddler can make choices, even if the choice is simply to say 'no' when told to do something.

As a toddler begins to feel its independence, it will challenge decisions in order to try to gain control over all aspects of its life. At this stage, a child may feel passionately about its right to do things its own way. Although it wants to be in charge, it is still very young and so under the constant care and supervision of adults. Decisions will be made for it about what to eat and when and where to play, it will be dressed and undressed, and it will be taken away from its toys.

EXPRESSING EMOTIONS

Such parental control inevitably leads to feelings of disappointment, anger and frustration and these feelings may be intense and literally overwhelming.

At this early stage, while language skills are still developing, children have trouble

Tantrums can erupt over seemingly minor issues. They are a sign of a dependent young child trying to gain some control over its life.

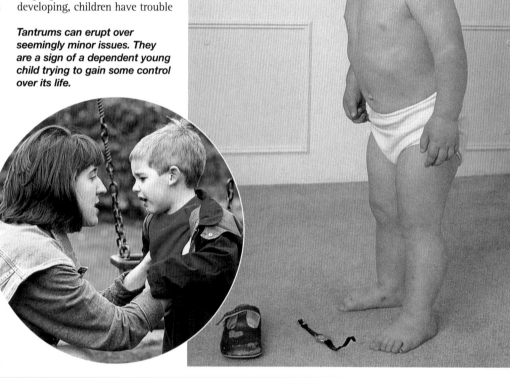

<hr>

What is a tantrum?

In a tantrum, a child's emotions take control of body and mind and the child may cry, scream, kick and dramatically throw itself to the floor. It is not open to reason or threats. After the tantrum has finished, a child may be in need of comfort as it may well have been scared by the overwhelming feelings it has just experienced.

Tantrums generally occur only when there is an audience and usually only in the presence of trusted adults. It is as if the child is trying to communicate its strong emotions, but is only free to 'give in' to them in a safe and loving environment.

Young children do not have the language skills to express what they want. Unable to argue verbally with a parent, a child may have a tantrum in order to vent its frustration and anger.

Tantrums are a normal part of toddler development. At this age, a child starts to feel its independence and will often challenge its parents' decisions.

expressing these strong emotions verbally, and the outburst of frustrated energy that we know as a tantrum results.

This period of a child's life, often called the 'terrible twos', usually occurs between the ages of one-and-a-half and three. By about the age of four, a child's communication and language skills have usually developed sufficiently well for it to be able to express its feelings verbally and negotiate with its carers.

Toddlers often have spectacular tantrums, screaming and falling to the floor. Little can be done to appease the child until the tantrum has finished.

Children require routine in their lives to make sense of their world. Routines at bedtime in particular are important in avoiding conflict before bed.

Other features of the mindset of a child during this challenging stage are feelings of intense possessiveness, and the love of and need for ritual and routine in its life.

■ **Possessiveness**
A child will feel that it owns everything, and in particular toys and other familiar household objects. Children are told to share in vain – the concept of sharing is alien to them until they are a few years older and have firmer ideas of identity and boundaries. A child may become aggressive towards others who try to take its things. Probably the most that can be hoped for is that children will learn to 'take turns' under adult supervision.

■ **Ritual and routine**
Children of this age benefit from, and sometimes demand, fixed routines. For example, a child may request the same flavour of yoghurt every day and the use of a special spoon with a particular coloured handle, or that the same book is read every night and a favourite toy is tucked up in the same place.

A rigid routine in a child's life allows it to exercise its passionate need for control and will give it the comfort and safety of an ordered life. Bedtime rituals are particularly important in allowing a child to prepare for the change of pace that comes with the end of the day.

NORMAL OR NAUGHTY?
Tantrums are a normal and indeed vital phase of a child's development. A child is not 'bad'

Conflicts arise between what a child is capable of doing for itself and what it wants to do. As it matures, it learns what behaviour is acceptable.

because it has tantrums or will not share its toys – it is acting in a normal way for a child its age. A child needs help to cope with its strong feelings and learn to express them in a socially acceptable way.

Children cope best when they are used to daily routines. However, although children need the comfort of predictable routines, they also like to make their own choices. Allowing a child to make some decisions for itself can satisfy its urge for independence. As a toddler's language skills improve, it becomes more able to discuss its feelings and less likely to have a tantrum because it cannot express its needs.

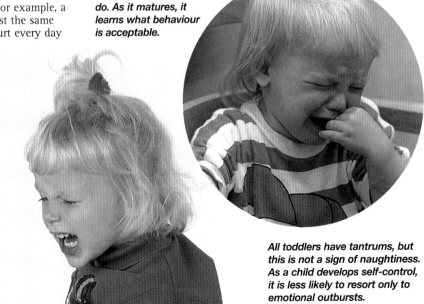

All toddlers have tantrums, but this is not a sign of naughtiness. As a child develops self-control, it is less likely to resort only to emotional outbursts.

Good eating habits

Children need a balanced and healthy diet to supply the nutrients required for their rapid growth and development. Childhood is also the time when children learn many of the eating habits that they will carry into adulthood.

Children need an adequate quantity and balance of food to provide the nutrients essential for normal growth, maintenance and repair of the body. A child's nutritional requirements are substantial because its brain and body grow rapidly. A young baby, for example, uses 25 per cent of the energy supplied by

Foods such as chocolate are high in sugar and fats. Excessive amounts should be avoided, as a balance between carbohydrate, protein and fat is essential.

food for growth alone. Bone and tissue formation requires a lot of energy. Adequate growth only takes place when there is a surplus of energy, after the other essential processes of the body have been undertaken.

During infancy and childhood, malnutrition, either due to insufficient quantities of food or deficits in the diet, will affect the normal development of body and brain.

Children, like adults, need a balanced, healthy diet free from too much sugar, fat, salt, additives and preservatives, colourings and flavourings. A balanced diet is especially important for children as they lack the reserves of fats and proteins that an adult's body has stored.

Without a diet that supplies enough essential nutrients, a child's health suffers and it may not gain weight or height (appearing stunted for its age) or may lose weight.

Many of the eating habits that are carried into adulthood are formed in childhood. Foods that are high in sugar can cause tooth decay and may also curb

a child's appetite for healthy foods later. Therefore, the key factors in a balanced diet include the content, the amount of food, and the frequency of meals.

Children carry many of their eating habits into their adult life. It is important that school lunches provide children with a balance between what they want to eat and what is nutritional.

What a healthy diet contains

Family meals are important in maintaining good eating habits. Here, the children are given well-balanced meals, in small portions, so as not to overwhelm them.

All foods comprise one or more of the major nutrient groups: carbohydrates, proteins and fats. Food may also contain vitamins, minerals and fibre. A healthy diet will contain all of these.

■ **Protein**
Proteins are essential for growth and are found in meat, fish, milk, cheese, eggs, pulses, flour and some root vegetables.

■ **Carbohydrate**
This food group provides energy and is found in cereal grains, beans, potatoes, bread and pasta. Carbohydrates can be broken down by the body into glucose and cellulose (which is indigestible and makes up roughage in the diet).

■ **Fats**
Fats are found in meat, vegetable and fish oils, butter, cheeses, margarine and in many other foods. Fats are essential for the absorption of some fat-soluble vitamins, and provide easily stored energy.

Saturated fat intake, although essential to the diet, should be halved by most people.

■ **Vitamins and minerals**
Vitamins A, B, C, D, E and K and numerous minerals are all essential for good nutrition in the right amounts, especially in growing children.

Regular consumption of fruit is important in providing fibre, vitamins and minerals. Gentle encouragement will foster healthy eating in later life.

MAIN FOOD GROUPS

People who eat a normal, healthy, balanced diet do not need to take additional vitamin and mineral supplements. A person needs to eat selectively from the following main food groups every day:

■ Protein in the form of meat, poultry and fish
■ Smaller amounts of protein and calcium from dairy products
■ Protein from nuts and pulses, such as beans, lentils and soya
■ Carbohydrate and fibre from grains and pulses in the form of barley, bran and beans
■ Fruit and vegetables.

Vegetarians and vegans obviously have a reduced selection of choice from the above food groups, but are still able to satisfy their nutritional requirements.

FOOD INTAKE FREQUENCY

Most paediatricians and nutritionists are agreed on these basic guidelines for a healthy diet:

■ Children and adults should eat breakfast; children, in particular, benefit from protein in the form of an egg, for example, at breakfast
■ It is more healthy to 'graze' (eat six small meals a day) than to eat one or two big meals, particularly for growing children
■ If eating three meals a day, it is preferable for healthy growth and development to eat a large breakfast, a good lunch and a smaller tea or supper.

HEALTHY SNACKS

Foods such as fizzy drinks, sugary and salty snacks, highly processed convenience foods, fried food and foods high in salt have little nutritional value.

To ward off hunger pangs and provide maximum boosts of energy, a child should be encouraged to eat foods such as bananas, apples, tuna mix sandwiches on wholemeal bread and baked potatoes.

Vitamins, minerals and fibre

Vitamin	Source	Essential for
A	Liver, milk, butter, eggs	Night vision; health of skin
B complex vitamins	Liver, meat, fish, some in yeast, green vegetables, cereals and wheatgerm	Growth, health of skin, nervous system, blood hair and nails
C	Oranges, tomatoes and other fresh fruit (not cooked)	Growth of blood vessels; prevention of scurvy; reduces likelihood of minor infections
D	Butter, milk, meat, action of sunlight on skin	Absorption of calcium from intestine and for deposition of calcium in bones and teeth
E	Green leafy vegetables, nuts and seed oils	Neuromuscular function
K	Made by bacteria in intestines	Blood clotting

Minerals Essential for health, these include calcium, phosphorus, magnesium, potassium, chloride, iron, zinc, copper, selenium and iodine.

Fibre An essential element of our diet and the one most neglected food groups in the developed world. Nutritionists believe that the majority of people should eat at least double the usual amount of fibre; this applies particularly to children. Many children need to halve their fat intake and double their fibre intake.

Calorie requirements

A calorie is a unit of energy. When a food is said to contain 500 calories, that means that it will provide 200 calories' worth of energy to the body.

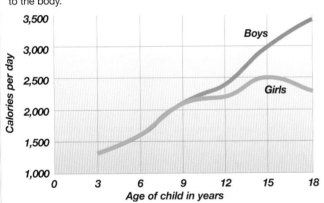

Graph: Calories per day vs Age of child in years (0 to 18), showing **Boys** and **Girls** curves.

Obesity tends to run in families – this is largely due to availability of high calorie foods. A home where food has a high emotional value is also a factor.

It is not unhealthy to eat so-called junk food occasionally. However, regular consumption can lead to poor eating habits and obesity.

Eating problems in children

Appetite is controlled by the hypothalamus in the brain. Genuine eating problems are very rare and such problems that do exist are often caused by the parents, rather than by any innate disorder in the child. Problems include dawdling over food, refusing food, deliberate vomiting and food fads.

The solution to all these problems is to ignore them until the child grows out of them. Food forcing by the parent may lead to a child dawdling or playing with its food.

Parents often believe that their child is not eating enough without taking into account the child's build, the child's likes and dislikes, the child's need for independence, their desire to feed themselves (however slow and messy a process that may be) and children's phase of negativism from the age of about two to the age of three.

Many children become fussy eaters in childhood. This can be dealt with by gentle persistence and repeated exposure to foods.

Pre-school children

Between the ages of three and four, children develop rapidly in all areas. By the time they are ready for nursery school, they are agile, using language confidently and are starting to become independent.

From the age of three to four-and-a-half, children change dramatically from energetic, quick tempered two-year-olds to more reasonable and rational pre-school children. The major change in this time period is the acquisition of reason.

A child of three may not yet be ready for deductive logic, but it is capable of listening and acting with reason. This is a very substantial developmental change from a two- to two-and-a-half year old. This is the age when a child starts to look outward from the immediate family to the world outside.

Some of the troubling events for the growing two-year-old are now behind them. Teething is more or less complete and

Three- and four-year-old children will happily join in groups to play. They will form groups of friends and their peers' attitudes will start to exert an influence.

bladder and bowel control is often a source of pride; a child may show considerable distress in the event of an accident.

CHANGING NEEDS
Three-year-old children require a great deal of attention, outlets for their physical energy and materials to express their creativity – such as paint, dough, paper and brushes.

The fourth year is the start of a developing empathy for other people. A child will become sad if its mother is sad, angry if its playmate is angry. A child starts

to learn that other children are happy to play with it if it is co-operative and friendly. In essence, it is becoming simultaneously more independent and less egocentric. The concept of taking turns during play starts to have an impact on how three-year-old children think and act.

A three-year-old child is about ready to start nursery school, as it is now more companionable and more reasonable than a two-year-old, and eager to learn. Children of this age welcome approval by adults, but by the age of four, they will be showing that they no longer need the proximity of an adult for their security. They will form into groups – which often break up and reform in different

By the time a child is old enough to socialize with other children and has sufficient language skills, it can benefit from the stimulation of nursery school.

configurations – and will start to have a 'best' friend.

Key features of a pre-school child are:
■ The acquisition of a sense of initiative in which the child is excited and challenged by new things, rather than frightened or overwhelmed
■ A rich fantasy life, which manifests itself in play
■ The acquisition of many more skills of socialization

■ The development of a sense of self and a unique identity
■ Development of intellectual functions and cognitive skills
■ A sense of responsibility and conscience
■ The development of a child's sexual identity
■ The use of increasingly complex language
■ The emergence of identifiable and consistent behaviour patterns.

Children have very stylized ways of representing people and objects. In the early stages they are not concerned about realism, but become more so later.

Children make many significant advances in their development during this important period of their lifespan.

GROWTH AND CO-ORDINATION

Physically, a child's co-ordination is continuously improving. At three, children can climb the stairs one at a time and can walk along a narrow, straight line. They will practise their co-ordination skills and balance by climbing on a climbing frame, and by the age of four, children will be walking, running and climbing confidently. They are now physically agile.

Children display an ever-increasing sense of independence and desire to do things for themselves. During their fourth year, they learn to dress and undress themselves, with some help, and will brush their own teeth. They are also able to manipulate a fork and spoon. At four, they are more confident with fine motor skills.

A three-year-old will be strong enough and balanced enough to master riding a tricycle. These small milestones are a source of great pride for a child.

Co-operative play among children is well established by the age of four. This is an essential social skill once a child goes to nursery school.

UNDERSTANDING

By the time that a child is three, it will know whether it is female or male and can give its name and age when asked, and will recognize its name in written form.

At this age, children enjoy drawing and will be able to draw a circle and copy a cross and a square. The way they represent objects is not realistic, but this continues to improve with their fine motor skills. Objects are classified by shape, size or colour. By four-and-a-half, they may be able to count up to 10 but as yet do not have a fully developed concept of quantity.

SOCIAL DEVELOPMENT

As a child develops, their social and language skills continue to improve. A four-year-old appreciates rules and criticizes those who do not adhere. They can obey simple requests, such as 'put the ball outside'. A three-year-old has greater reserves of patience than a two-year-old but is still very attached to its mother,

As balance and co-ordination improve, a child will be better at catching and kicking a ball, for example. Play helps children to develop their motor skills.

especially if under stress. At this age, children start to imitate parental behaviour and attitudes, especially temperamental traits.

They start to join other children in co-operative play, with rough and tumble play predominating, and begin to recognize feelings such as joy and sadness. By four, a child develops a sense of responsibility and will turn to an adult for advice or help when necessary.

At this stage, children are much more self-confident and boisterous. They are energetic and friendly, but have greater control of their emotions. Soon they may become bored and need the extra stimulation of school.

Most three-year-old children talk incessantly and question the world around them. They are starting to gain an understanding of the rules of grammar and will practise forming sentences. By the age of four, children use language quite competently, and by four-and-a-half they start to use the past tense and plurals.

Children will practise using their expanding language skills at any opportunity. They are becoming more confident and will readily talk on the telephone.

Developmental progress up to five years

By the age of five, children are energetic and imaginative. They are far more independent than younger children and their language skills enable them to communicate easily with other people.

The period between the ages of four and five is a time of exploration, advance, reinforcement and consolidation for pre-school children. A child of five is very much a person in its own right now, and only reverts to a 'baby' state when tired or upset.

The developmental period between four and six years is one of steady maturation towards the stage of formal schooling and the middle childhood years (six to 12). A typical five-year-old child is energetic, friendly, active and resourceful.

REALITY AND FANTASY

At this age, a child still believes that objects that move are animate; for example, that a marble is alive because it rolls, or that the sun is alive because it changes position in the sky.

Although a five-year-old's fine motor skills have developed very rapidly since early childhood, he will still need help with some delicate or complex tasks.

Reality and fantasy are not yet firmly distinguished and five-year-olds enjoy embellishing and embroidering their exploits and the distinctive merits of their families.

A child at this age does know the difference between right and wrong in the context of simple issues, but it does not see an imaginary fantasy world as lying.

GROWTH

A child's growth slows down after the age of four. Between the ages of one and two years, it would have grown some 10–12 cm (4–5 inches), but in the period between four and five years of age, it is unlikely to grow more than 5 cm (2 inches). A child's body shape continues to change from a babyish form to that of a child, with longer legs and a face that has lost the typically plump look of a baby.

By now, a child will be able to run with increasing speed, jump with skill, hop on one foot, climb with increasing agility and skip using alternate feet. It will

By the age of five, children show considerable energy and initiative. Their play is often fantasy-based, with imaginative role-playing.

have the ability to use a bat and a ball and will generally be energetic and lively.

A child's fine motor skills are still developing – at this age, it is unlikely to be able to tie shoelaces, for example, but it is becoming more adept with pencil, crayon and brush.

PERSONALITY AND SOCIAL AWARENESS

A child's social skills, intellectual functions and cognitive abilities continue developing rapidly. The beginnings of conscience formation and the process of identification with family members is continuing.

Although a five-year-old has grown out of the earlier tantrum phase, he may lapse into seemingly babyish behaviour when overtired or stressed.

The use of reason and logical thought now has some impact on a child, and it will start to use logic as a means of getting what it wants, rather than simply crying or shouting.

KEY FEATURES

Five-year-old children are more reasonable and less demanding than younger children. They can frame their questions and wishes in a socially acceptable fashion. They are rapidly learning how to play with other children of their own age, but have not yet progressed to the stage where team games hold an attraction.

A group of playing five-year-olds spend a lot of time running and jumping, but they are not operating as a group. In reality, each child is performing for itself. Five-year-olds are, however, usually rather conventional and believe in 'sticking to the rules'. At this age, they can find it distressing not to know exactly how to behave.

A rapid increase in the complexity of language used and understood can be seen. A child of this age has been fluent for some time, although it still makes grammatical errors. Gradually, it incorporates more tenses in its use of language, and its vocabulary increases almost daily.

No child develops consistently and without lapses to an earlier stage. A four-and-a-half to five-year-old child is no different.

Play is an important part of childhood and is necessary for children to learn to co-operate and share with one another. It is also an outlet for their energy.

Although a five-year-old shows an increasing interest in her independence and autonomy, she also needs the security and love of her parents.

When it is tired or distressed it may well revert to babyish behaviour, such as clinging to one of its parents, sucking its thumb or crying.

However, a five-year-old's initiative develops each day. It will want to cross roads by itself, although it is not yet sufficiently aware of traffic. Its rich fantasy life may be peopled by imaginary friends.

It is rapidly identifying with its parents, and developing motivation and an identifiable personality. Its behaviour patterns are becoming recognizable and consistent.

A five-year-old child needs a lot of stimulation in every area of life. At this age, children enjoy playing with others but are not yet ready for the organized team games of older children.

The impact of siblings

First-born children are often treated very differently from subsequent children. First-borns are often expected to achieve more, and will be talked to with more complex language. A first-born's rearing is often more restrictive and disciplinarian, parental anxiety will be greater and family activities will centre around the one child rather than all offspring. The subsequent

Younger children can benefit from the attention of older siblings. Older children often take great pleasure in teaching younger children the 'right' way to do things.

children may be slower to acquire speech, but they benefit from the eldest helping them, showing them how to do certain activities and looking after them.

Starting school

Going to school is a vital part of child development, not just because of the formal education, but also because it allows children to interact with their peers as part of a wider community.

Many children are ready for some form of schooling by the time that they are three or four years old. They have often exhausted the possibilities for exploration and learning within their immediate environment and they are ready for new challenges and stimulation. However, in the UK, children are not legally obliged to attend school until the age of five.

PRE-SCHOOL EDUCATION

Some children will already have attended playschool, nursery school or kindergarten before they start their formal schooling, and it is believed that this will help prepare them for 'proper' school at the age of five. They will have experienced leaving their parents for a day or a half-day, will have learned how to function in a group with other children and will understand certain necessities, such as finding out where the lavatory is located.

Five-year-old children are often very eager for the opportunity to learn. By now they have the creative powers, intellectual and cognitive skills, the physical strength, the fine motor skills and the language skills and sociability needed in order to benefit from formal education.

COPING AT SCHOOL

Once at school, five-year-olds are introduced to the subjects of the curriculum. At the same time, they have to master rising to the challenge, overcoming shyness, developing perseverance and dealing with any anxieties that they may have about being at school or

As well as being the beginning of their formal education, starting school gives children the opportunity to associate with many others of their age.

about leaving their mother.

Of course, the school day is not just about reading and writing, but also about taking turns when responding to a question, alternating play and education, waiting to fulfil bodily functions, being part of a collective taking responsibility for own belongings, appreciating structure and order, listening and concentrating. These are all examples of learnt behaviours.

The best foundation for any child benefiting from education and being happy and willing to learn is stability and happiness in the home background. Paediatricians recognize, and have done so for many years, that this is what is vital in order for a child to develop normally.

OTHER INFLUENCES

Children receive their education in a number of ways, chiefly through formal schooling but also from their parents and siblings at home, through asking questions of increasing complexity, through their friends and relatives in a social setting, through reading and through the medium of television.

Lessons provide children with the mental stimulation that their developing brains need. Teaching is structured to encourage a child's natural curiosity.

The first day at school is often a time of great apprehension for a child. It may be the first time that it is separated from its mother for a whole day.

Television programming can be of great educational benefit to children, and its potential value should not therefore be underestimated. However, reading and creative play in the home are invaluable for children's education in the broad sense, but these activities can be eclipsed by television, which is an entirely passive experience.

Once children are old enough to start school, they are able to begin to learn about similarities and dissimilarities, relationships and cause and effect. They have an increasing ability, which needs to be encouraged, to think around a subject, and especially to look for explanations other than the immediately obvious.

THINKING LOGICALLY
Rather than accepting what they are told at face value, children now seek the evidence for what their parents tell them or what they read and what they see on television. Children of this age are also able to reason in a

School encourages children's physical development by giving them the opportunity to participate in organized games, and especially team sports.

logical manner by asking and answering their own questions; for example, 'Do I need to wear a coat? Is it cold? Yes it is, therefore I do'.

Perseverance, accuracy and thoroughness do not come naturally to a five-year-old child, but these are some of the skills and qualities that formal schooling is designed to impart.

It is clear that children not only do not know as many facts

Children do not only learn at school; the process is a continuous one, requiring parental participation as well.

as adults, but that they also think quite differently from adults; consequently, they learn differently.

Children develop in gradual and overlapping stages, and because each of these stages represents quite different modes of learning, information has to be repeated and reinforced at successive stages for a child to make the full use of the information. With a child's increasing maturity, information takes on deeper and deeper levels of meaning and nuance.

In terms of practical education issues, children do better in

School encourages a whole range of skills in children, including fine motor ability, as demonstrated by using scissors.

small rather than large classes, and better in smaller rather than larger schools. Girls do better at maths and science in single-sex classes rather than mixed sex classes. Self-esteem and self-confidence are integral and invaluable in a child's ability to fully benefit from the different kinds of education to which it is exposed: for these, home life is the key.

Non-curricular learning at school

The advent of formal education around the age of five leads to a sense of curiosity which continues at home. Children of this age are naturally curious about the world about them and are entering an age of rapid information absorption; the brain of a five-year-old is able to assimilate large amounts of knowledge.

The value of school lies not only in the learning of specific skills, such as reading and writing, but also in more general social development. Thus, children come to realize that they are part of a wider community, consisting of other children of differing ages, as well as influential adults other than parents and relatives.

Learning about time
Children begin to understand the 'cyclicity' of events that happen to them; this realization is reinforced by the ordering of the school day, with lessons, playtimes, lunch and home-time at fixed times each day, and by the weekly repetition of the timetable, so that the same activities occur at the same time on the same day each week. This leads on to an understanding of the concept of the days of the week and the calendar as a whole.

Social development takes place in the classroom both under the supervision of the teacher and spontaneously between the children themselves.

Losing the first set of teeth

An important stage in a child's development is the gradual loss of the first – or milk – teeth and their replacement with the second, permanent teeth, which will last for the rest of their life.

Two sets of teeth develop in the growing child. The first set are the primary, deciduous or 'milk' teeth, which begin to erupt at about the age of six months. There are 20 milk teeth in all and they are usually all present by the age of two-and-a-half.

At about the age of six, shedding of the milk teeth begins, with the incisors at the front usually being the first to go. At the same time the secondary, or permanent, teeth begin to erupt. A new permanent molar at the back of the jaw is usually the first to appear, followed by the permanent incisors.

A child then enters the period of 'mixed dentition' which is so familiar to parents as the milk teeth are lost one by one to be replaced by the larger, often yellower, permanent teeth.

The last of the milk teeth to be shed are usually the upper canines, which go by about the age of 12. By the time a child is 13, 28 permanent teeth are usually in place. The final four teeth, the wisdom teeth or third molars, may not appear at all, but if they do it is usually several years later in the late teens or early 20s.

SHEDDING MILK TEETH

The shedding of a milk tooth is connected to the growth and development of the permanent tooth which lies under it in the jaw. Where no permanent tooth is present the shedding of the milk tooth is delayed.

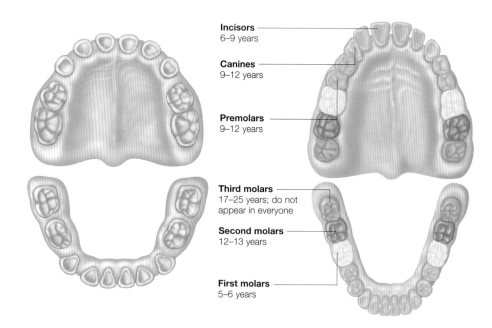

Ages at which permanent teeth appear

Incisors
6–9 years

Canines
9–12 years

Premolars
9–12 years

Third molars
17–25 years; do not appear in everyone

Second molars
12–13 years

First molars
5–6 years

The illustration on the left shows the full set of 20 milk teeth, which emerge by the end of the third year. On the right, the order of emergence of the 32 permanent teeth is shown.

The permanent tooth bud, which has been lying dormant within the jaw, becomes active and begins to develop around the child's fifth year. The relatively large crown of the permanent tooth is formed and, when ready, begins to move towards the surface of the gum. The overlying bone is resorbed (that is, broken down and the constituents reabsorbed) by the action of osteoclasts – cells specialized for that function. As the root of the overlying milk tooth is reached, that is resorbed as well.

As the crown continues on its way to the surface, its root develops and becomes firmly attached to the underlying bone of the jaw.

The entire root of the milk tooth is eventually resorbed as the permanent tooth comes to lie just beneath it. The crown of the milk tooth is now attached to the mouth only by the soft tissues of the gum. It soon drops out either of its own accord or as a result of the minor trauma involved in biting and chewing.

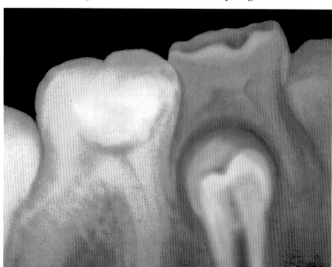

A permanent tooth can be seen erupting below the milk teeth in this coloured X-ray. As the roots of the milk tooth are resorbed, it loosens and then falls out.

The appearance of the permanent teeth is often a source of great pride for children. It is a visible sign of growing up.

ERUPTION OF PERMANENT TEETH

The permanent tooth will continue to erupt until it takes the place of the lost milk tooth in the mouth. The permanent teeth that have no milk tooth precursors (the premolars and third molars) will erupt into their places at the back of the mouth without the need for resorption of an overlying tooth.

This pattern of shedding and eruption of teeth is usually symmetrical between the right and left sides. Girls generally shed their milk teeth and gain their permanent teeth before boys, although in both sexes the permanent teeth (apart from the wisdom teeth) have all usually appeared by the age of 12.

This seven-year-old girl has both milk teeth and permanent teeth. This temporary state is termed 'mixed dentition', and continues until all the milk teeth are lost.

THE IMPORTANCE OF MILK TEETH

Although the milk teeth are only temporary, it would be incorrect to believe that it does not matter what happens to them. It is important for a number of reasons that they should develop properly and that they are kept until they are lost naturally:

■ Good nutrition – healthy milk teeth are needed to allow young children to eat a wide range of foods, so allowing them to grow and develop properly; poor nutrition in early life may lead to poorly developed adult teeth

■ Speech – good dentition is important in the correct development of speech and pronunciation in young children

■ Appearance – the effect of the appearance of the teeth on the happiness and psychological well-being of the child should not be underestimated.

A balanced, nutritious diet is as important for the growth of strong and healthy teeth as it is for all other areas of child development.

Children often 'encourage' their milk teeth to come out by wobbling them once the teeth are loose. They may gain great satisfaction from this.

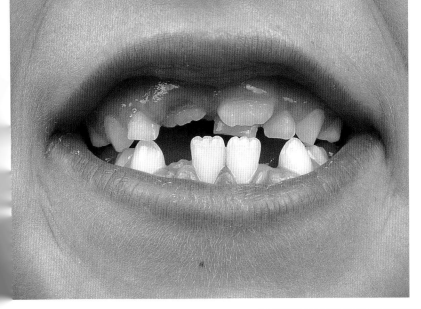

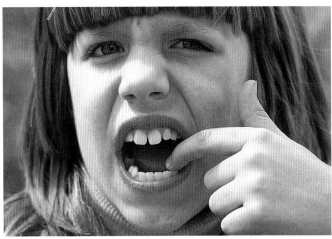

Thumb-sucking

Sucking the thumb or the fingers is a normal way for a young child to gain feelings of comfort and security and usually comes to an end naturally by about the age of five.

However, if the habit persists after the age of six or seven when the permanent teeth are coming in, then problems with the alignment of teeth may develop, such as:■

Thumb-sucking is very common in young children and rarely causes any dental development problems. If the habit persists, however, the teeth may become misaligned.

Protrusive upper teeth – this is usually simply a case of the upper teeth sticking out as a result of the constant pressure of the thumb upon them, but occasionally the maxilla (bone of the upper jaw) may be involved

■ Tipped back lower incisors – this is a common finding with prolonged thumb-sucking where the pressure of the thumb forces the lower incisors backwards towards the tongue

■ Open bite – when the molars are together the front teeth do not come together in the normal bite action; instead, they overlap with a gap between them – this gap may match the shape of the child's thumb, and this makes it

hard for the child to bite food properly, which can lead to problems with nutrition

■ Distortion of nasal growth – rarely, in a severe long-term situation, the constant pressure of the thumb on the underside of the upper jaw and nasal bones can lead to the nose appearing 'tipped up'.

Treating thumb-sucking

The most effective way to stop thumb-sucking is by persuading a child that it wishes to do so and then rewarding their achievements. Orthodontic work may be necessary to correct the misalignment of the teeth once thumb-sucking has been stopped.

Growth rates in childhood

The body does not grow at a uniform rate throughout childhood.
After an initial period of rapid growth up until about the
age of four, growth slows until a child enters adolescence.

During the months of pregnancy, a fetus grows at an enormous rate, developing from a tiny fertilized cell into a newborn baby. After birth, a baby continues to grow rapidly in height and weight, although the rate of that growth decreases progressively as the child gets older. The rate of growth increases again for a few years in the final growth spurt at puberty.

■ **Height.** Children grow very quickly in the first few years of life, doubling in length by the age of four. On average, the height of a child at three years is roughly 55 per cent of the final adult height. The rapid growth rate tails off at around the age of four and a period of slower growth ensues.

However, when the child enters puberty it enters a new period of rapid growth which will take the child to its final adult height. The age at which this final height is achieved will vary from child to child but will generally be earlier in girls than in boys by an average of two years.

■ **Weight.** A newborn baby loses weight just after birth but will usually have regained its

Height, like age, can be a source of great pride to many children. Between the ages of four and 12 a child's growth is slow and continuous.

birth weight by the age of two weeks. By five months, the birth weight has doubled, and by the end of the first year it has tripled. This phase of rapid increase in weight leads into the more gradual increase in weight seen in the prepubertal child. At puberty there is an increase in the rate of weight gain to match the rapid increase in height.

ASSESSING GROWTH

The normal patterns of growth are affected by the genetic make-up of the child, its health and the level of care, both physical and emotional, that it has received. In particular, body weight is the most sensitive indicator of nutritional status and general health. Therefore, the growth of young children should be routinely monitored by measuring the height, weight and head circumference at regular intervals and the results compared with the normal range for that age group by plotting the measurements on a growth chart (or centile chart).

Babies are measured and weighed regularly in the first year of life. These are good indicators of the overall health of the child; poor growth may indicate underlying problems.

Newborn babies have very different facial proportions from those of an adult. This is due in part to the fetal skull growing more rapidly than the face.

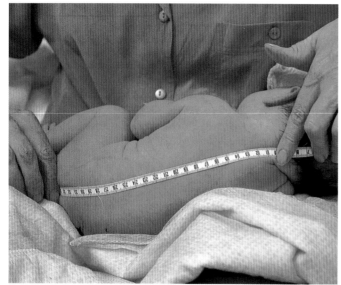

Changing body proportions

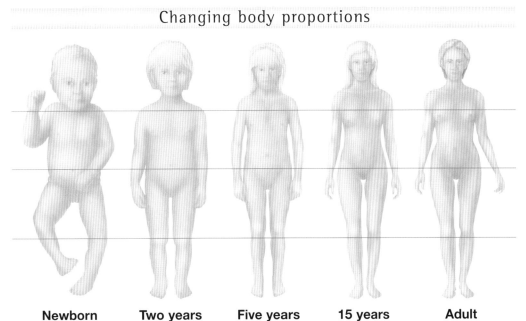

| Newborn | Two years | Five years | 15 years | Adult |

An infant's head is roughly one quarter of the total body length. As a child ages, its body proportions change until by the end of puberty it has the physique of an adult.

GROWTH ABNORMALITIES

After monitoring the growth of a child over time, particular attention should be paid to the children who are shorter or lighter than expected. This will include those children whose height and/or weight falls below the third percentile (97 per cent of children of the same age will have greater measurements), especially if the parents are of average or above average height, and those children whose measurements are falling away from their original percentile curve.

Causes of growth abnormalities include:

■ Inheritance – being short or very thin may run in the family

■ Poor fetal growth during pregnancy – due perhaps to extreme prematurity, maternal drugs, infection or genetic disorders

■ Social deprivation – poor care and nutrition will hinder normal growth

■ Other illnesses – for example kidney failure, coeliac disease, immune deficiencies

■ Endocrine (glandular) disorders – uncommonly there may be a deficiency in growth hormone production by the pituitary gland in the brain. Children whose weight is much greater than others of their own age may be simply obese or may, uncommonly, be suffering from a disorder of the endocrine system, such as hypothyroidism.

BODY GROWTH

During childhood, not only does the body grow in height and weight but the proportions of the body change as well. At birth, the head and the trunk are approximately one-and-a-half times as long as the lower limbs while the head makes up one quarter of the total length of the body. During childhood, the lower limbs grow more rapidly than the head and trunk until about the age of 10.

At birth, the baby's cranium (dome of skull) is large relative to its face, which appears small and flattened. The cranium is large to accommodate the well-developed brain and, in fact, at birth the head circumference is already three quarters that of its adult value. However, between the ages of six and 11, the head appears to get much bigger as the face develops and grows; the nose and cheekbones become more prominent and the jaw increases in size.

▲ *On average, girls reach their final, adult height around two years before boys. Differences in height can be a cause of awkwardness among teenagers.*

▼ *There is a large degree of variability between similarly aged children. This variation is due to both genetic and environmental factors.*

The size of the head in relation to the rest of the body decreases as a child develops. A baby's cranium is very large compared to the rest of its body.

Inherited characteristics

A child inherits its genetic material from both parents. Genes exert an influence on a child's physical traits and personality, but predicting inheritance is complex as environment also plays a role.

Although we think of a developing child as being a unique person, it does, in fact, share over 99 per cent of its genes with all other humans. The differences in the last one per cent is what helps to make each person a unique individual. In some cases, it can be predicted what form these differences are likely to take by looking at the inheritable characteristics of the parents and wider family.

A child is expected to look somewhat like its parents, to be generally of the same height and build and, in many cases, to have similar hair colour or pattern. There are many characteristics of the parents that the child may inherit to some extent, including talents, aptitudes and physical traits.

PATTERNS OF INHERITANCE

Some characteristics have a simple pattern of inheritance due to the fact that only one gene is involved. The end result seen in the body depends on the combination of dominant or recessive alleles (gene alternatives) of that one gene and so there are limited options.

Examples of this type of inherited characteristic include blood group, the ability to roll the tongue, the presence of freckles and whether the child's ear lobes are attached directly to the side of the head.

Short-sightedness may be influenced by genes. In some families both of the parents and will have poor eyesight, and so will their children.

Some physical traits, such as freckles, are determined by only one inherited gene. If the gene responsible is dominant it will be expressed in the child.

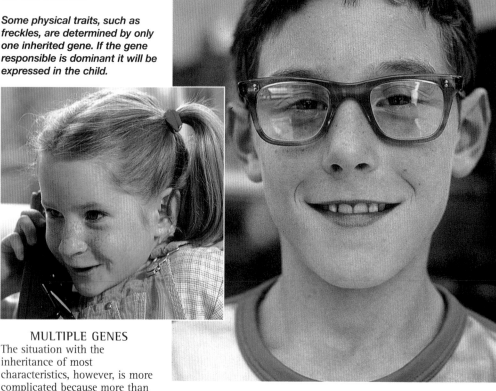

MULTIPLE GENES

The situation with the inheritance of most characteristics, however, is more complicated because more than one gene is involved, often many more. The child can inherit from its mother and father any of the possible combinations of alleles for each gene.

This means that instead of the relatively few possible combinations that we see with a single gene involvement, with these multiple gene (or polygenic) characteristics there is a wide spectrum of possible results. This makes it much harder to predict in what form a child will inherit these characteristics from its parents.

Polygenic inheritance is the method of inheritance of such characteristics as skin colour, eye colour, hair pattern and height.

GENES AND ENVIRONMENT

A child may also inherit a 'tendency' towards a characteristic which, given the right environment, will appear. In this case, the term 'environment' includes everything that the child experiences both before and after birth.

It is believed that an inherited tendency to gain weight is the

As all human beings share 99 per cent of their genes, it is the one per cent which is variable that helps to make each child a unique individual.

situation in many cases of obesity. It is well known that being overweight 'runs in families' but it is not simply the inheritance of a gene or set of genes, that makes the family members obese.

The eating habits of the family and the amount of exercise that is taken will have a major impact upon the weight of the child. However, it does seem that the genetic make-up of the child is a factor in determining fat accumulation and distribution, and so inheritance plays a part.

It is also thought that intelligence, sexuality and

Obesity is not due to inheritance alone. Family eating and exercising habits may result in obesity but inherited genes will influence fat accumulation.

perhaps personality are determined, to some extent, by a combination of the child's genetic make-up and the environment in which the child is raised.

GENOTYPE AND PHENOTYPE

A child has two copies of each gene; one from the mother and one from the father. These copies may be the same or may differ in some small but significant way. Differing copies

A number of genes affect skin colour. This is not a simple pattern of inheritance and a range of shades of skin colour may be seen in mixed race families.

of the same genes are known as 'alleles' and which alleles a child has for each gene is termed its 'genotype'. If a child has identical alleles for a gene, it is said to have a 'homozygous genotype'; if differing alleles then it has a 'heterozygous genotype'.

One of the reasons this is important is that some alleles will only have an effect if there are two of them acting together (recessive), while other genes

Being able to roll one's tongue is an inherited characteristic that is determined by a simple inheritance pattern of one gene.

will be dominant and produce an effect by over-riding the other gene. The final effect that the genotype determines in the body is known as the 'phenotype'.

Inheritance of blood groups

The inheritance of an ABO blood group is one of the most clear-cut and predictable characteristics of a child, illustrating the difference between genotype and phenotype. The gene for the important ABO system of blood groups can be in one of three forms, A, B or O, and a child will inherit one gene from each parent. The actual blood group, the phenotype, of the child will be one of four: A, AB, B or O.

The reason that there are four groups is that the A and B alleles will not mask each other (they are both dominant) while the O will be masked by both of them (it is recessive). So the child will be said to have blood group A if it has the genotype AA or AO; blood group B if it has the genotype BB or BO. If the genotype is AB then the blood

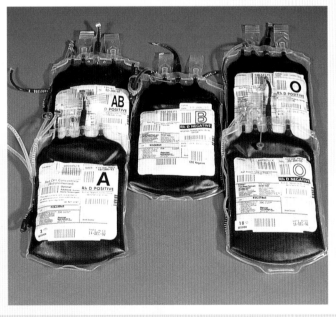

group is also AB as both A and B are equally dominant. Finally, if both the inherited alleles are O then the blood group is O.

Each child's parents have two alleles; however, they can only pass on one allele to their child in the random splitting of their genes when the egg or sperm is formed. If the blood groups of the parents are known then a prediction can be made about what proportion of their children are likely to have which blood group, although each child born may have any of the possible combinations of the four blood group alleles they carry.

A child's inherited blood group can be predicted if the parents' blood groups are known. There are four possible blood types: A, B, AB or O.

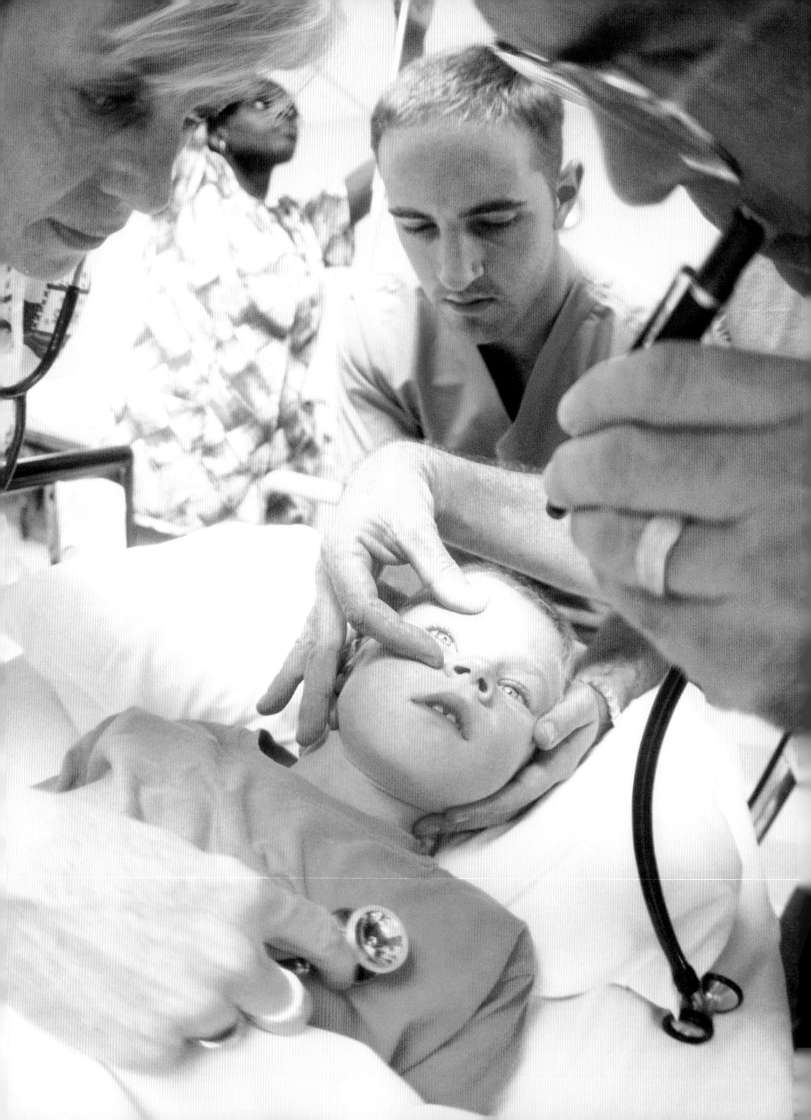

Chapter Three

Common Problems with Children

Most children have daily contact with other children of all ages, and they will inevitably pass around infections and even head lice! Suffering coughs and colds are an important part of growing up as they help to strengthen the immune system and create life-long resistance to numerous bacteria and viruses. In this section, you can check the symptoms of these common infections and find out how to deal with them. In addition, there is helpful information about problems such as constipation and bed-wetting, which can be distressing for both parents and children. Dyslexia and dyspraxia are also included in this section – they are learning disabilities that can be mild or more severe, but are now much more readily recognised and easily treatable.

Sticky eyes in children

There are three main causes of sticky eyes in early childhood.
The condition usually resolves without treatment, although very
occasionally antibiotics may be needed to treat an infection.

Many babies suffer from a sticky eye at some time during infancy. After sleep, the eye may become crusted or the lids may be stuck together. Although symptoms can be distressing, in most cases this is a mild, self-limiting problem and is not always a sign of infection. However, if there is redness of the eyes or a worsening discharge, treatment may be needed.

CAUSES OF STICKY EYES
There are three main causes are:
■ Conjunctivitis
■ Blocked tear ducts
■ Ophthalmia neonatorum (infection acquired at birth).
With the exception of infections acquired at birth, sticky eyes usually clear without treatment.

Sticky eyes are quite common among babies and young children. Although the condition can cause distress, it does not usually indicate an infection.

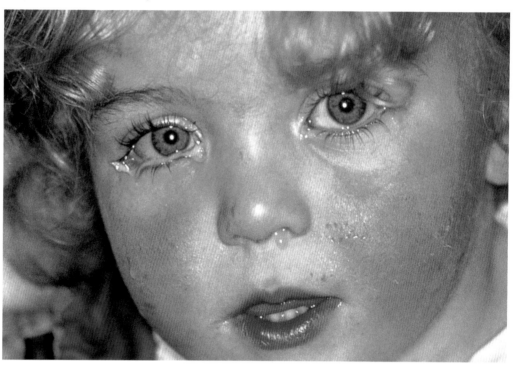

Conjunctivitis

Conjunctivitis is inflammation of the conjunctiva, the delicate membrane covering the sclera (white of the eye) and the inside of the eyelids. Conjunctivitis may be caused by a viral or bacterial infection or by an allergy or irritation.

Viral conjunctivitis often occurs in association with a cold, usually affects both eyes, and may persist for several weeks. Viral conjunctivitis does not respond to antibiotic eye drops.

ALLERGIC CONJUNCTIVITIS
Allergic conjunctivitis usually causes mild redness and itching and arises from a reaction to an allergen such as pollen, house dust mites or cosmetics. It mostly affects older children and adults. Irritant conjunctivitis can be caused by chlorine in swimming pools, for example, or by cigarette smoke.

BACTERIAL CONJUNCTIVITIS
Bacterial conjunctivitis is caused by several different bacteria, including *Staphylococcus*, *Streptococcus* and *Haemophilus*. Acute bacterial conjunctivitis tends to produce more severe symptoms than viral or allergic conjunctivitis, with marked redness, profuse mucous discharge and the sticking together of the eyelids during sleep.

Bacterial conjunctivitis is highly infectious and is easily spread from eye to eye. Hygiene is important after cleaning a baby's eyes or putting in eye drops to prevent further spread of the infection.

TREATMENT
The treatment for conjunctivitis depends upon the cause. Allergic conjunctivitis responds to sodium cromoglycate eye drops or oral antihistamines. Antibiotic eye drops, such as chloramphenicol and fusidic acid, are only helpful in treating bacterial conjunctivitis. Antibiotic ointment preparations are available, which need to be used less frequently. Eye drops and ointment should be disposed of after the course is complete.

If conjunctivitis persists after treatment, a swab may be taken to identify any bacterial organism, and so indicate which antibiotics will be effective.

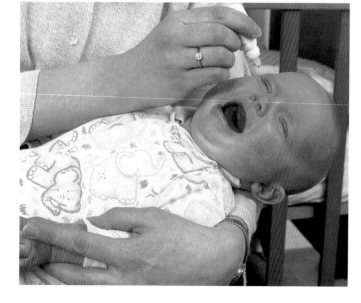

Antibiotic eye drops are helpful in treating bacterial conjunctivitis. They are not always easy to administer, which can affect treatment success.

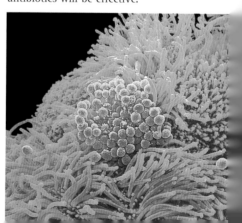

Bacterial conjunctivitis can be caused by the Staphylococcus bacteria, seen here (yellow). The condition can be treated with antibiotic eye drops or ointment.

Blocked tear ducts

It is very common for babies to have a blockage of their tear ducts in the first year of life. As a result, it is difficult for tears to drain away from the eye to the nose and the eye may become watery. After a while, a discharge from the eye may appear, which may become sticky.

PREVENTION
To prevent infection, it is important to bathe the eye regularly using cooled boiled water and clean cotton wool, starting at the inner corner of the eye and wiping outwards.

A doctor may advise parents to massage the tear duct in the inner corner of the eye, using gentle sweeping movements with the little finger underneath the eye.

SECONDARY INFECTION
If the eye becomes reddened or the discharge becomes more profuse or green in colour, it may be a sign of secondary infection. In this situation, antibiotic eye drops or ointment may be prescribed.

Fortunately, blocked tear ducts usually clear spontaneously, without any treatment, by around one year of age.

SURGERY
If the problem persists, the advice of an ophthalmologist should be sought, who may decide to open the blocked tear duct with a small probe. This is a quick and simple procedure, but must be performed under a general anaesthetic in order to keep the baby perfectly still.

It is important not to delay treatment for too long, because probing may be less effective at curing the problem in older children.

Blocked tear ducts in infancy usually resolve by the end of the child's first year. Sometimes, however, an operation to open the ducts may be necessary.

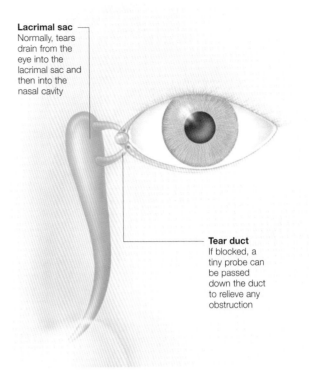

Lacrimal sac
Normally, tears drain from the eye into the lacrimal sac and then into the nasal cavity

Tear duct
If blocked, a tiny probe can be passed down the duct to relieve any obstruction

Ophthalmia neonatorum

A rare but serious eye infection, ophthalmia neonatorum, occasionally occurs in newborn babies. This is caused by infection transmitted from the birth canal during delivery.

Ophthalmia neonatorum usually appears 5–14 days after birth as an intense conjunctivitis affecting both eyes, with lid swelling and profuse redness and mucous discharge. A swab will be taken for analysis, to ensure that the correct treatment is given. This infection is usually caused by chlamydia, gonorrhoea or herpes simplex viruses, which are sexually transmitted. The mother and her sexual partner will also need treatment.

CHLAMYDIA
Nowadays, chlamydia is an increasingly common infection in young women. The infection often goes undiagnosed and may lie dormant in the genital tract. If untreated, ophthalmia neonatorum can cause scarring and visual impairment. Babies with a chlamydial eye infection are also at risk of developing pneumonia. Urgent treatment with oral or intravenous antibiotics is therefore essential.

HERPES SIMPLEX
Herpes simplex infection can be transmitted via the birth canal from a mother who has active genital herpes at the time of vaginal delivery.

Neonatal herpes simplex infection can occasionally present as conjunctivitis or as blisters of the skin and mouth. However, it sometimes occurs without these early warning signs, as a more widespread infection of the central nervous system and other organs, and can be life-threatening.

It is important for herpes not to be overlooked as a cause of conjunctivitis in the first two weeks of life, as urgent intensive treatment with anti-viral drugs will be needed to stop the infection from becoming more generalized.

The rash on this child's face is the result of herpes simplex virus infection. Transmitted from mother to child at birth, the virus can cause ophthalmia neonatorum.

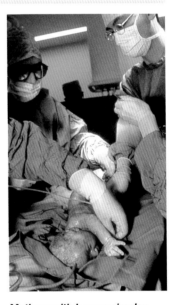

Mothers with herpes simplex may have active genital ulcers at the time of delivery. If so, a Caesarean section will be advised in order to prevent transmission of the virus.

CLOSE MONITORING
To prevent this serious neonatal infection, mothers with a history of genital herpes simplex are monitored in the last weeks of pregnancy and after delivery.

If a woman has active genital ulcers when she is due to give birth, a Caesarean section is recommended to prevent transmission of the virus to the baby during birth.

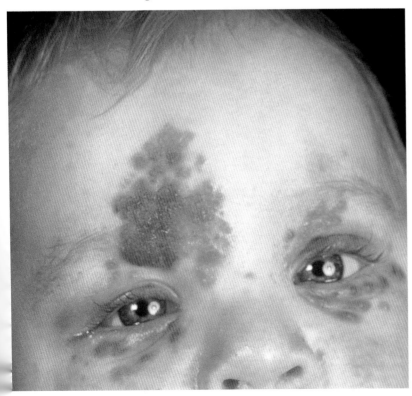

Squints in children

Squint – non-alignment of the eyes – can develop at any age, but is especially common in children. The ophthalmologist will decide how to treat the condition once the cause has been identified.

It is important to appreciate the difference between what the medical profession mean by 'squint', which is the non-alignment of the eyes, as opposed to what lay people often understand from 'squint', which is focusing on an object through half-closed eyes.

For this reason, many ophthalmologists prefer to use the word 'strabismus' rather than squint.

TYPES OF SQUINT
Children with a squint are unable to focus the image of an object onto the fovea (the central patch of the retina which contains the highest density of light-sensitive photoreceptors) of both eyes simultaneously. If one eye is not looking at the target, then that eye is considered to be squinting.

If the affected eye turns inward (toward the nose), it is termed a convergent squint; if it does not turn in sufficiently, it is called a divergent squint. Convergent squints are much more common than divergent squints.

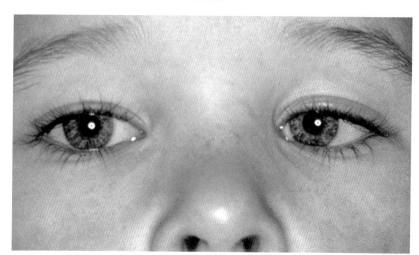

This boy's left eye has a convergent squint. As the right eye focuses on an object, the left eye deviates inwards.

How normal eyes focus

When an object is brought close to a child with normal vision, three processes occur which act to focus the image of the object onto the back of the retina: the eyes are turned in (this is known as 'convergence'); the power of the lens inside the eye is increased (this is known as 'accommodation'); and the pupil becomes smaller.

SYNCHRONIZED MOVEMENTS
The turning in of the eyes and the accommodation are two synchronized movements which both increase as the target gets closer. If a normal individual looks at an object more than six metres away, the target should be clearly seen without the need to either converge or accommodate the eyes.

However, some children are unable to disassociate the two movements; once they start to accommodate they also start turning their eyes in. The brain of these children will 'decide' to keep one eye fixated on the target object, while the other eye points in (converges) to a greater degree than it would normally. This is called a convergent squint.

Viewing a distant object

Viewing a close object

When a child looks at an object far away, the eyes point straight ahead and the lens is relaxed (thin). This is demonstrated in the first illustration (far left).

When a child looks at a close object, the eyes point inwards and the lens becomes thicker – this is illustrated in the picture on the left. These two actions act to focus the image of the object onto the fovea, located at the back of the eye.

Types of squints

Ophthalmologists classify squints into two groups: concomitant and inconcomitant squints.

Concomitant squint
The majority of children who squint, when each eye is tested separately, are found to have a full range of eye movement. However, they do have an imbalance between the axis of the two eyes. In a large proportion of children, it is found that the reason they have a convergent squint is that they accommodate too much.

Inconcomitant squint
This condition is seen less frequently in children. It can be caused by a limitation in the movement of one of the eye muscles, resulting in the child being unable to move the eye in a particular direction. The severity of the squint varies, depending on the direction of the gaze.

It is important to diagnose and treat squint as early as possible. Quite often, even the parents will be unaware that their child is affected.

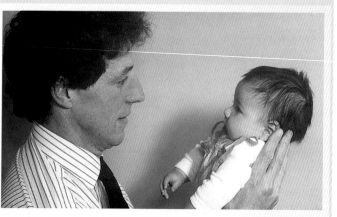

Diagnosing a squint

A child's squint will probably be diagnosed by an ophthalmologist using a 'cover test'. This test consists of asking the child to look at a target at varying distances while the ophthalmologist covers one eye at a time. If, when one eye is covered, the other eye does not move, it means that it is looking at the target properly. If the same happens when the other eye is covered, then the child does not have a squint for that particular distance.

MANIFEST SQUINTS
However, if the eye that is not covered has to move to look at the target, it means that it was not aiming at the target properly, and so the child has what is known as a 'manifest squint'.

LATENT SQUINTS
Latent squints are discovered by a test called the cover/uncover test. After establishing that the child does not have a manifest squint, one eye is covered and then uncovered; children who have a tendency for a squint will not, once the eye is covered, make the effort to keep the eye straight. Thus the eye will drift inwards behind the cover if they have a latent convergent squint, or outwards if they have a latent divergent squint. Latent squints may become manifest later on.

Squints in children are diagnosed by covering one eye at a time and looking at the movement of the uncovered eye.

A squint can be diagnosed by covering and uncovering each eye in turn. If the uncovered eye has to move to look at the target, it was previously squinting.

Manifest squint

 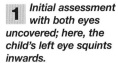

1 *Initial assessment with both eyes uncovered; here, the child's left eye squints inwards.*

2 *When the right eye is covered it squints inwards, and the left eye moves outwards so that it can focus on the target.*

3 *The right eye straightens when it is uncovered and the left eye points inwards as before.*

Latent squint

1 *Initial assessment shows that both eyes point straight ahead.*

2 *When the left eye is covered it squints inwards, and the right eye continues to look straight ahead.*

3 *The left eye straightens when it is uncovered, showing that the child has a latent squint.*

Determining the cause of a squint

Having established that a child has a squint, a test called 'refraction' is carried out to determine whether an eye is long-sighted or short-sighted. This differentiates between those children who have a convergent squint because they are long-sighted and those who appear to squint for no obvious reason. Those who are long-sighted will be given glasses; the others may need surgery.

SECONDARY SQUINT
During an examination, the back of the eye is also

examined to diagnose the very small number of children who have a squint because the affected eye has another disease that prevents it from seeing properly.

For example, a child with a scar in the retina or a tumour at the back of the eye would not have normal vision and therefore would have a secondary squint.

An ophthalmologist uses a slit-lamp to examine the eyes of a girl. A small number of squints are due to clinical disease.

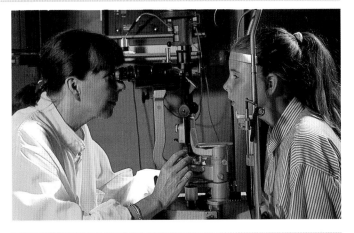

Lazy eye

Amblyopia or 'lazy eye' is often confused with squint, but it is a separate condition. However, in some cases, lazy eye may develop due to a squint as one eye is favoured over the other. The eye that is not used becomes weak and may develop amblyopia.

Amblyopia may also occur if an eye is deprived of light in the critical early months of life or if the eyesight in each eye is poorly matched; for example, if only one eye is short-sighted.

A lazy eye can be treated by 'patching' the good eye, thus strengthening the weak eye.

Treatment

Patients who have an inconcomitant squint may have a muscular or neurological cause which is treated accordingly. If the squint causes double-vision (diplopia), or if it is cosmetically unacceptable, then surgery can be offered once the squint is stable.

Children with a concomitant squint due to long-sightedness are treated by giving them the appropriate glasses. Those who do not appear to have an identifiable cause for their squint can have surgery.

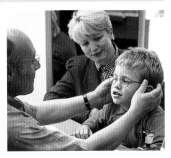

If a child is found to be long-sighted, the squint is treated by prescribing the child appropriate glasses.

Upper airway problems

Children are prone to infections of the upper airways. These may
be caused by viruses or bacteria. Many are simple conditions such
as the common cold but others can have serious complications.

Minor upper airway diseases are the commonest of all paediatric problems. The average pre-school child has between six and 10 upper respiratory tract infections per year. The majority of these are trivial and self-limiting, but occasionally acute upper airway problems can be life-threatening.

SYMPTOMS
There are two major symptoms of upper airway problems:
■ **Stridor**
A rasping sound heard on inspiration (breathing in). This indicates poor airflow through narrowed upper airways.
■ **Stertor**
A low-pitched snoring sound in inspiration and expiration indicative of a lesser degree of obstruction.

This cross-section shows the structures of the upper respiratory tract. The upper airways are a common site for infection.

Anatomy of a child's upper respiratory tract

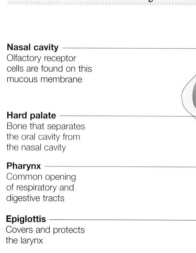

Nasal cavity
Olfactory receptor cells are found on this mucous membrane

Hard palate
Bone that separates the oral cavity from the nasal cavity

Pharynx
Common opening of respiratory and digestive tracts

Epiglottis
Covers and protects the larynx

Oesophagus
Part of digestive tract which links the pharynx and the stomach

Trachea
Partial obstruction of the windpipe causes 'stridor' on inspiration

Simple upper respiratory tract infections

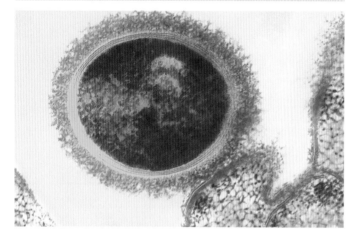

Viruses are the most common cause of infection in the upper airway. The manifestations vary from simple coryza (the common cold) to pharyngitis, causing a sore throat or otitis media (acute infection of the middle ear).

The most common pathogens are rhinovirus, para-influenza, influenza, adenovirus and respiratory syncytial virus (RSV). Most of these infections are short-lived and self-limiting but serious complications are possible, such as:

A streptococcal bacterium is seen attached to a human tonsil cell in this electron micrograph. Streptococcus is the most common cause of tonsillitis.

■ Serious involvement of the lower respiratory tract, as in RSV bronchiolitis
■ Secondary bacterial pneumonia
■ Asthma attacks in susceptible children; minor upper respiratory tract infections commonly exacerbate childhood asthma.

Congenital upper airway problems

■ Pierre Robin sequence – this is the combination of a small jaw, a cleft palate and a tendency for the tongue to prolapse (fall back) and block the airway; treatment in the short term is to place the child in the prone position to move the tongue forward and away from the airway
■ Vascular ring – rare abnormalities of the great blood vessels can cause an artery to pass very close to the trachea and indent it, causing an obstruction to breathing
■ Oesophageal atresia and tracheo-oesophageal fistula – in this condition the oesophagus ends blindly in a pouch and the trachea and oesophagus are joined; if a newborn with this condition is fed, milk will enter the lungs.

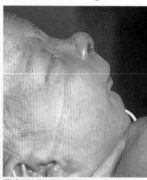

This baby has Pierre Robin sequence. This condition involves a series of congenital features which cause a hazard to adequate breathing.

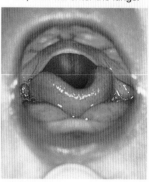

Infants with Pierre Robin sequence have a small jawbone and a cleft palate – when the two halves of the palate do not fuse properly.

Tonsillitis

The tonsils, which are an aggregation of lymphoid tissue (special tissue which is involved in the body's immune defences) are relatively large in children and minor infections are common. The organisms that most often cause infection are viruses, particularly the Epstein–Barr virus (EBV) and parainfluenza, but bacteria, especially Group A haemolytic streptococcus, must also be considered.

Contrary to widespread belief, the appearance of pus on the tonsils does not make the cause any more likely to be bacterial than viral, although in practice a course of penicillin is often prescribed if this is apparent.

COMPLICATIONS

Rare but serious complications of tonsillitis can occur, particularly para-tonsillar and retro-pharyngeal abscess, which require surgical attention.

Tonsillitis is a common condition in childhood which may be caused by bacteria or viruses. Often there is a white exudate overlying the tonsils.

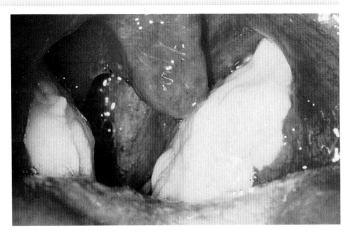

Enlarged adenoids and otitis media

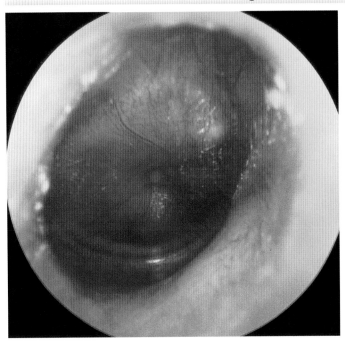

Adenoids, like tonsils, are enlarged in childhood and sometimes cause troublesome symptoms. They sit at the back of the nasal space at the end of the auditory (Eustachian) tube. If chronically enlarged they both obstruct breathing and interfere with the ventilation of the middle ear, contributing to chronic inflammation (otitis media) and fluid build-up (glue ear).

Acute infections of the middle ear cause the tympanic membrane (eardrum) to appear red and bulging and it may rupture. The causative agents are respiratory viruses, as well as bacteria such as *Streptococcus, Haemophilus*

Chronic middle ear infections may be caused by enlarged adenoids. If fluid builds up behind the eardrum, it will appear to bulge and may perforate.

and *Moraxella catarrhalis*. The distinction between viral and bacterial infections on clinical grounds is unreliable and antibiotics are often prescribed.

SURGICAL TREATMENT

Chronically enlarged adenoids and tonsils may cause sleep apnoea, which occurs when obstruction to airflow during sleep causes a fall in oxygenation. Characteristically, an affected child will snore very loudly.

Operations such as tonsillectomy, adenoidectomy and the insertion of grommets (placing a ventilation tube into the eardrum) may be necessary in certain cases, such as:
- Para-tonsillar abscess
- Obstructive sleep apnoea
- Severe glue ear, causing hearing loss
- Recurrent severe tonsillitis.

Foreign bodies

The sudden onset of respiratory distress in a young child should raise the possibility of an inhaled foreign body. The object may be lodged at any point and the required treatment (which may be undertaken on suspicion) is bronchoscopy to remove it. Typical inhaled objects include toys and foods, such as nuts.

This child has inhaled a small screw, which is clearly visible on X-ray. Bronchoscopy will be used to remove it.

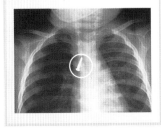

Epiglottitis

The epiglottis sits above the vocal cords and is another anatomical feature which is relatively larger in children than in adults. In acute epiglottitis it becomes greatly enlarged and blocks the whole of the inferior larynx.

The hallmark of epiglottitis is that, unlike with croup, there is also obstruction to the oesophagus causing the child to drool saliva as well as having stridor. The child must be kept calm until specialists can obtain control of the airway under sedation. The main cause of this condition is *Haemophilus influenzae* type B, which has dramatically declined in the UK due to routine immunization.

The epiglottis – seen here through a laryngoscope as the white flap – protects the larynx. In epiglottitis, the flap becomes enlarged and blocks the airway.

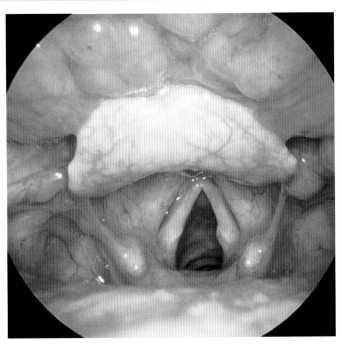

Tonsillitis

Symptoms

Tonsillitis – inflammation of the tonsils – is usually due to a viral or bacterial infection of the tonsils. It generally lasts for about five days.

CLINICAL FEATURES

Symptoms may be severe in bacterial tonsillitis and the patient will complain of a sore throat often accompanied by:
- Malaise (a general feeling of being unwell)
- Pyrexia (fever)
- Cervical lymphadenopathy (swelling of glands in the neck).

There may be pain referred to the ear – this may be confused with otitis media (middle ear infection) in young children. Very commonly tonsillitis causes halitosis (bad breath).

NECK SWELLINGS

The oropharynx (between the soft palate and the epiglottis) is generally red and congested and there may be exudate over the tonsils. There will always be enlarged lymph nodes in the side of the neck, which will be palpable and often tender.

Gross in the neck and exudate on the tonsil also occurs in glandular fever. Rarely the enlarged tonsils may cause airway obstruction – again this is more likely in glandular fever.

It is necessary to distinguish between the bacterial sore throat of tonsillitis and viral pharyngitis (inflammation of the pharynx).

Bacterial infection will cause redness of the tonsils and fauces (the opening from the mouth into the pharynx), crypts full of pus in the tonsils, bad breath and 'plummy' speech.

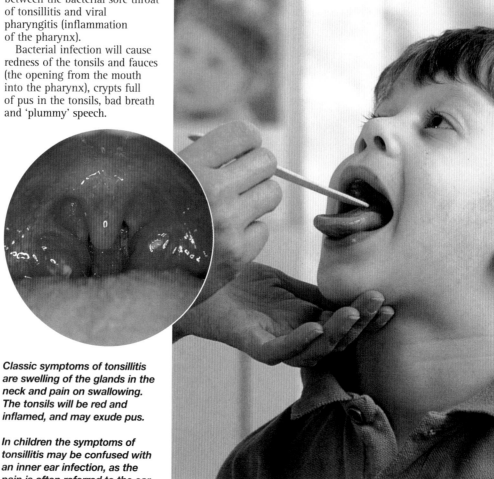

Classic symptoms of tonsillitis are swelling of the glands in the neck and pain on swallowing. The tonsils will be red and inflamed, and may exude pus.

In children the symptoms of tonsillitis may be confused with an inner ear infection, as the pain is often referred to the ear.

Diagnosis

It may not be possible to distinguish between viral infection and bacterial infection initially, and throat swabs may give misleading results.

The diagnosis of tonsillitis must be based on the clinical picture, primarily the swelling in the neck glands and the inflamed tonsils, and the patient's symptoms.

If glandular fever (infectious mononucleosis) is the cause of the inflamed tonsils, a monospot test on a sample of venous blood will confirm this.

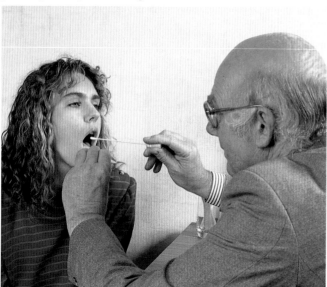

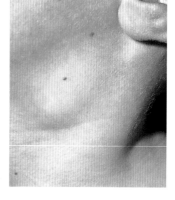

Swollen neck glands are an indication of tonsillitis, and will be tender to the touch. Such swellings rarely cause obstruction of the airways.

A throat swab may be taken to help identify the causative agent in a case of bacterial tonsillitis. However, this is not necessarily an accurate diagnostic test.

Incidence

Sore throat is one of the commonest reasons for a patient going to see the GP, and tonsillitis is probably the cause of up to 30 per cent of all sore throats.

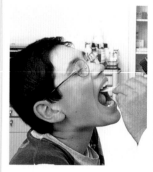

Sore throats are extremely common, although tonsillitis is only responsible for a minority of cases. An oral examination will determine the cause of the discomfort.

Treatment

Bacterial tonsillitis requires antibiotics, preferably oral penicillin or erythromycin if the patient is allergic to penicillin. Amoxicillin is not recommended as this may produce a rash if the case is one of glandular fever.

SURGICAL TREATMENT
Tonsillectomy is now rarely performed as a routine procedure, but is necessary in cases of frequent and recurrent tonsillitis. Sleep apnoea (difficulty in breathing) due to large tonsils, and quinsy (abscess of tonsil) if preceded by recurrent tonsillitis, are other indications for removal of the tonsils.

In adults, gargling with soluble aspirin may help to relieve a sore throat. Paracetamol is the best treatment for pyrexia (fever).

Children under 12 should not be given aspirin, but gargling with cool water may help relieve the symptoms of tonsillitis.

Causes

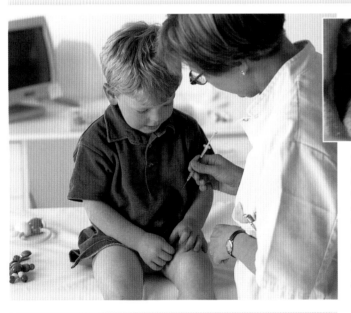

Often, a white or yellow exudate, consisting of protein and white cells, will form over the tonsils. This is a result of the body's normal defence against infection.

Immunization against diphtheria means that it is now a rare condition in developed countries. It was once a common cause of throat inflammation.

Tonsillitis principally affects children and young adults and is spread by droplet and dust infection. Usually tonsillitis starts as a viral infection, a secondary bacterial infection then developing, usually with the beta-haemolytic streptococcus, which may chronically infect the tonsils.

QUINSY
A quinsy (peritonsillar abscess – collection of pus) is usually unilateral (one-sided) and is due to streptococcal organisms.

Diphtheria used to be a significant cause of a membranous exudate affecting the tonsils and constricting the throat. However, routine immunization has virtually eliminated diphtheria in the UK.

Prognosis

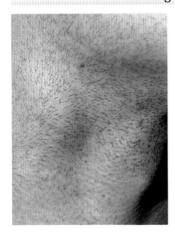

Almost invariably, tonsillitis resolves after about five days. The condition is nearly always self-limiting, although persistently recurring infections may be may be a cause of debility in some patients.

Unilaterally enlarged cervical lymph nodes may be suggestive of neoplasia (formation of a new, abnormal tissue) and should not be ignored.

Enlarged glands on one side may be suggestive of a form of cancer called lymphoma, and should be investigated.

Prevention

Tonsillitis is very common in childhood due to hypertrophy (excessive growth) of the tonsils and repeated infections. Good oral and dental hygiene measures may help to reduce its occurrence. Children with tonsillitis should be excluded from school as the infection is easily spread in crowded classrooms and public places.

Although tonsillitis is rarely serious, affected children should be kept away from contact with other children until the infection passes.

Croup

Croup is inflammation and obstruction of the respiratory tract
as a result of infection, and the symptoms can be alarming. It occurs
most often in children aged between three months and five years.

Croup is characterized by a loud, harsh, brassy cough. It is not a single illness but a disease entity covering a number of conditions which can produce this effect. It is therefore quite common.

CAUSES

Most croup is caused by viruses, including parainfluenza viruses, adenovirus, respiratory syncytial virus (RSV), measles and influenza. It can also have an allergic basis. Some children therefore can get recurrent problems. Very rarely bacteria can be involved.

There is, as a result of this infection, an inflammation of part of the upper air passages, especially of the area which influences the production of sound.

The clinical name for croup is laryngotracheo-

The term croup is used to describe a number of respiratory conditions affecting the upper air passages in children. The majority of cases are viral.

bronchitis because many structures within the airways may be involved in the infection at some stage, particularly, of course, the larynx and the vocal cords.

Croup is an infection of structures within the airway, often affecting the larynx and vocal cords. It is characterized by a harsh-sounding cough.

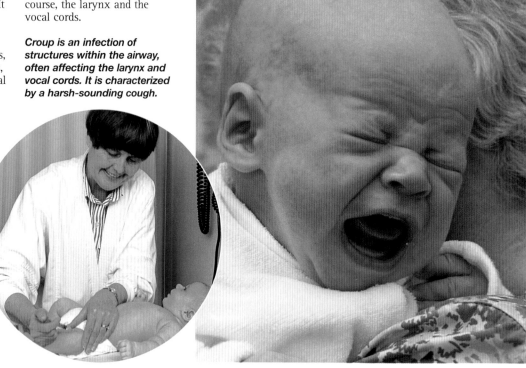

How is the airway affected?

The epiglottis is a fold of tissue which covers the airway when we swallow food or drink. Just below the epiglottis in the larynx are the vocal cords (which vibrate in order to allow speech).

The soft tissue lining of these structures becomes inflamed and swollen and therefore narrowed; there is also a mucous secretion which makes the narrowing worse. The result is that it is more difficult for air to pass through, causing harsh, difficult breathing. Rarely the airway can become

obstructed by an inhaled foreign body.

The epiglottis can be involved in bacterial infection with *Haemophilus influenza* B, a serious condition that is now rare as a result of HiB immunization; affected children look extremely ill and require admission to hospital.

As the soft tissue lining of the larynx and vocal cords becomes inflamed, the airway becomes swollen and narrows.

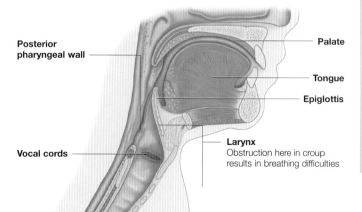

Posterior
pharyngeal wall

Palate

Tongue

Epiglottis

Vocal cords

Larynx
Obstruction here in croup
results in breathing difficulties

How croup starts

Most children who develop viral croup are between three months and five years of age. Symptoms are most severe in pre-school children. Viral croup tends to occur between October and March.

Typically the child has had a cold for a day or two. Indeed other members of the family may also have had colds. Gradually the child becomes hoarse. The problem often seems to get suddenly worse during the night. The child awakes (and so disturbs the parents) with a loud, brassy cough.

Between coughs the child seems to have difficulty getting air into the lungs. There is a harsh sound coming from the windpipe when the child breathes in (termed 'inspiratory stridor'). The child may be using the abdominal muscles during breathing – a sign of breathing distress. There may or may not be an associated fever.

Children aged between three months and five years are particularly susceptible to viral croup. The condition commonly arises after a cold.

Treating croup

An attack of croup can be quite alarming both for the parent and the child.
Fortunately most cases resolve spontaneously and quickly without medical intervention.
Parents can take a number of simple measures to help the child's breathing.

The first rule is not to panic. If children sense a parent is frightened they in turn get even more frightened, which can itself cause spasm and further narrowing of the air tubes.

A parent should take the child into the bathroom, close the door and turn on a shower or a bath in order to run hot water. This creates a beneficial steamy atmosphere.

REASSURANCE

The child should be cuddled for reassurance and encouraged to breathe in the warm humid air for 20–30 minutes. Reading the child a story can be helpful. The symptoms often improve after just a few minutes.

If there is no improvement, taking the child outside to breathe in the cold night air may well prove effective. Indeed, some parents take children with recurrent problems for a drive with the car window open.

The symptoms of croup often become worse at night, and the child may find it more difficult to breathe. It is important that parents remain calm.

Creating a warm and humid atmosphere by running a steamy bath, should help to ease breathing. Fresh air may also help relieve symptoms.

Helping the child to breathe

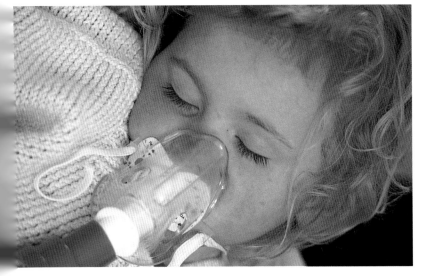

A vaporizer or a humidifier can be placed in the child's room and a 'croup tent' can be made by placing a blanket over the cot over the child's head. An umbrella may provide a useful frame for older children. The child should not be left alone in the tent. The parent should stay in the same room. Smoking should not be allowed in the house while the child is ill.

Children may be more comfortable sitting or sleeping in a propped-up position. Crying is a good sign as it means the

Parents can take action to ease their child's breathing, however a doctor must be called if the condition deteriorates.

child is breathing well enough to actually do this.

MEDICAL INTERVENTION

Medical help will be needed if the breathing difficulties do not resolve. Tugging in of the ribs during breathing (paradoxical respiration) may be present. Medical advice should be sought if there is continuous stridor (heavy wheezing), drooling or difficulty swallowing, decreased consciousness or if the child seems particularly sick or has blue lips and nails (caused by a lack of oxygen).

Hospital treatment includes humidified air supplemented with oxygen, and vaporized adrenaline and steroids.

Complications of croup

In most cases medical attention is not needed. The condition cannot be treated with antibiotics if it is viral in origin.

The croup may last up to five days. A vaporizer or humidifier should be placed in the child's bedroom until the condition settles down.

About 15 per cent of children with croup develop complications in other parts of the lower respiratory tract and middle ear infections. This will show itself by the croup settling,

but not the child. There may be a complaint of earache or a continuing cough. The family doctor should be consulted about this and also about any child who seems to be having recurrent problems.

In the event of recurrent attacks of croup there may be a family history of allergy.

In most cases the croup will clear up in a few days. If the condition does not improve, further medical advice should be sought.

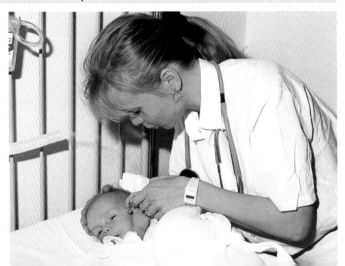

Asthma in children

Asthma is a chronic respiratory disease affecting about 10 per cent
of children. Symptoms are caused by inflammation and constriction
of the muscles of the airways, reducing airflow to the lungs.

Asthma is the most common chronic disease in childhood. It affects the airways in the lungs (the trachea and bronchi) causing a reversible obstruction to the flow of air. The hallmark of asthma is inflammation and hypersensitivity of the airways affecting the whole tracheo-bronchial tree, with the greatest effect on small and medium-sized airways.

Inflammation leads to the swelling of the lining of the trachea and bronchi and increased production of mucus, causing the airways to narrow.

Asthma symptoms are caused by inflammation of the airways, resulting in mucus production, swelling of the airway lining and smooth muscle contraction.

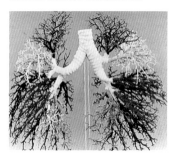

Hypersensitivity is defined as an exaggeration of the tendency for the trachea and bronchi to narrow in response to a variety of stimuli, including non-specific irritants, such as cold air, as well as infection or specific allergens.

Asthma is not a directly inherited disease but has a strong genetic component, such that if there is a family history of asthma, or related allergic conditions such as eczema and hay fever, then the chances of the child being similarly affected are greatly increased.

EFFECTS ON CHILDREN
Asthma causes considerable anxiety in children, including the fear of acute attacks, limitations on normal activities, feeling different from peers and the need to take medication on a long-term basis. Although the disease is chronic, long-term management can control the disease and reduce the frequency and severity of symptoms.

The external intercostal muscles between the ribs are drawn inward with the effort of inspiration. This produces a characteristic appearance.

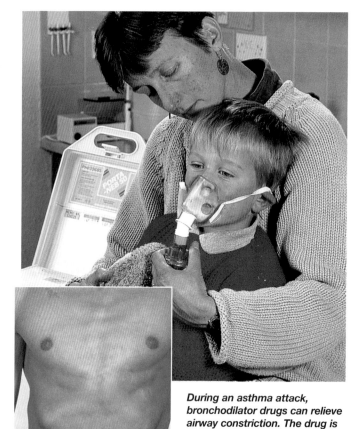

During an asthma attack, bronchodilator drugs can relieve airway constriction. The drug is inhaled as a mist through a mask attached to a nebulizer.

Clinical symptoms

The symptoms of asthma are due to the marked narrowing of the airways. This has a huge effect on the movement of air – if the size of the airway lumen (within the airway tube) is reduced by half, there is a 16-fold reduction in airflow.

Airways are obstructed in two ways: inflammation leads to fluid accumulating, which results in swelling of the airway lining and

excess mucus secretion; and also due to the contraction of the smooth muscles in the bronchi.

A history of typical symptoms includes:
■ Wheezing – a high-pitched, predominantly expiratory sound due to flow of air through partially obstructed airways
■ Shortness of breath – may be triggered by exercise
■ Cough – may not produce

sputum and is low pitched. Coughing attacks are persistent and often occur at night
■ Deformity of chest shape – a sign of chronically increased work of breathing
■ Airflow obstruction – may be evident on lung function testing.

Not all children have all of the typical symptoms; in some children, a chronic night cough may be the only symptom.

Incidence

Asthma is the commonest disease causing chronic symptoms in childhood. Between one and two million children in the UK have repeated episodes of wheezing. With 2 million at the top of this range, this corresponds to a total child population of 20 million. The prevalence of childhood asthma has increased greatly in the last 30 years for reasons which are not readily apparent.

There has been a decline in hospital admissions for asthma during the 1990s, which possibly reflects the benefit of national treatment guidelines leading to better control of symptoms. However, 30–50 children in Britain die annually as a result of acute asthma, a figure which has yet to show a significant decrease.

Normally, the airways are unobstructed by inflammation or smooth muscle contraction.

Hypersensitivity of the lungs causes the smooth muscles of the airways to contract.

The size of the airway is further reduced by swelling of the airway lining and mucus production.

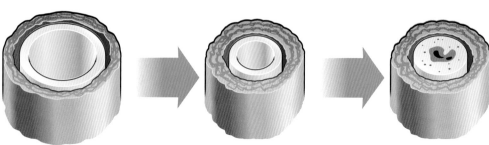

Investigating childhood asthma

A diagnosis of asthma can be confirmed by lung function tests. Monitoring of lung function with peak flow meters is part of the long-term management.

Although asthma is very common in children, lung infections and other diseases can lead to similar symptoms and will need to be excluded. The key features of asthma include an episodic course of the disease, with exacerbation of the symptoms characterized by shortness of breath and decreased exercise tolerance.

The typical causes of exacerbation are viral respiratory tract infections, exercise, cold air and exposure to cigarette smoke, house dust and dander (small scales of skin and hair) from pets. A persistent cough, particularly occurring during the night, is an important indicator.

CLINICAL EXAMINATION
An initial examination by a doctor may not reveal the symptoms brought on by an asthma attack, but may reveal deformity of the chest as a result of persistent airway obstruction. The diagnosis can be confirmed by physical examination and testing the child's lung function.

Chest X-rays are often normal but if there is severe airflow obstruction, hyperinflation of the lungs may be apparent. An X-ray can show the presence of any congenital abnormalities in an infant previously suspected of having asthma, therefore excluding asthma as a cause.

Metered dose inhalers are used in conjunction with a nebuhaler. The plastic spacer device increases the amount of the drug reaching a child's airways.

ALLERGY TESTING
Allergies are a common cause of asthma, and allergy testing can confirm a child's sensitivity to air-borne or other allergens. A skin-prick test involves pricking the skin with a drop of allergen, such as pollens, house dust mites and animal dander. This may help to determine which specific allergens are causing the inflammation of the airways.

TESTING LUNG FUNCTION
The pattern of airflow at different degrees of lung inflation can be helpful in the diagnosis of asthma, and can assist in monitoring the course of the disease and response to therapy. Spirometry, for example, is a method of diagnosing and measuring the degree of impairment of lung function.

The house dust mite, shown above on a coloured electron micrograph, commonly causes allergic reactions. Allergy tests can confirm sensitivity to mites.

A child performs spirometry by taking in a breath and then exhaling as quickly and as completely as possible. Expiration is rapid and should be continued until no more air can be exhaled. This test is repeated in order to obtain three similar results. The child is then given a bronchodilator drug to open the airways, and the spirometer test is repeated. A significant improvement in the result after giving the bronchodilator will establish the diagnosis. This test is limited to children aged over five as younger children cannot provide reproducible results.

Monitoring asthma

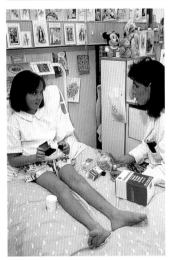

Asthma inhalers can be awkward for children to hold and use. Unless they are shown the correct way to use an inhaler, they will not gain the full benefit from the device.

One way to monitor asthma is to use a maximum peak expiratory flow rate (PEFR) meter. This measures the force at which air is exhaled from the lungs. The devices are cheap and robust and the results are very reproducible.

The regular monitoring of peak flow can give an indication of how well drugs are controlling symptoms, and may give early warning of an asthma attack. Children are given charts so that they can fill in peak flow measurements at home for review on clinic visits. There are charts which provide normal values for PEFR for boys and girls, but there is a wide 'normal' range.

It is important to note that the value of taking peak flow measurements is dependent on consistent daily readings. For this reason, parents may need to encourage the child to regularly use the peak flow meter.

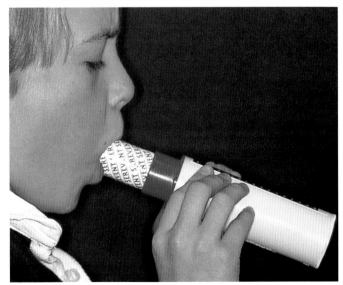

This child is using a peak flow meter to monitor the level of airway obstruction. Peak flow measurements are valuable for monitoring asthma in children, but spirometry is the preferred diagnostic method.

Treating childhood asthma

Asthma management relies on the use of drugs aimed at preventing or reducing symptoms. Delivering these drugs directly to the lungs can present problems in children and so various methods are used.

Asthma is a chronic disease of the respiratory tract which restricts airflow. Treatment of asthma is drug-based.

DRUG DELIVERY
As asthma is an airway disease, inhalation of medication offers the best chance of delivering the drug to where it is needed. There are a few oral drugs used in asthma but the mainstay of therapy is the inhaled route.

The preferred approach to asthma therapy involves the patient receiving medication based on an escalating or reducing scale of severity. Types of drug and methods of drug administration include:
■ Bronchodilator as required
■ Bronchodilator plus mild preventer (sodium cromoglycate or low-dose steroid)
■ Bronchodilator plus mild preventer plus long-acting bronchodilator
■ Bronchodilator plus high-dose preventer plus long-acting bronchodilator.

There is a wide variety of devices to maximize delivery of drug to its site of action in the lining of the small airways.

METERED-DOSE INHALER
A metered-dose inhaler delivers a fixed dose of drug as an aerosol, which is inhaled. The main weaknesses of this method are the tendency for the drug to impact on the throat and the need to co-ordinate use of the device with inhalation correctly.

A metered-dose inhaler used with a spacer delivers the drug effectively and is easy for a child to use. One drawback, however, is the size of the device.

With a metered-dose inhaler and spacer, the drug is delivered into the chamber and then inhaled via a valve and mouthpiece or, in very young children, a mask. This removes the problem of co-ordination and is a highly effective method of drug delivery.

Dry powder inhalers can also be used. This allows the drug to be inhaled directly by suction into the airway. They are suitable for children of school-age and older.

NEBULIZER
Nebulizers deliver a mist of drug and can be driven by air or pure oxygen. They require little effort to use and are the main route of administration of drugs in acute asthma cases in hospital and GP surgeries.

Nebulizers are often used in severe attacks of asthma to administer both drugs and oxygen. The drugs are inhaled easily as a fine mist.

Life-threatening asthma

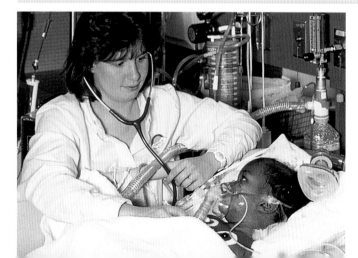

In the most severe cases of asthma, intravenous administration of bronchodilator drugs may be required to open the airways. The drug most frequently used is aminophylline, but some evidence supports the use of salbutamol instead.

Some children may not respond quickly to bronchodilators. Thus, drugs may need to be delivered intravenously and mechanical ventilation may be required.

If a patient with very severe asthma does not begin to improve with maximum therapy, they may become exhausted and will require mechanical ventilation. In patients with the severest symptoms, pneumothorax (collapsed lung due to air in the pleural cavity) must be excluded by chest X-ray.

Children with life-threatening asthma require transfer to a paediatric intensive care unit.

How asthma drugs work

Effective management of asthma requires several types of medication. Bronchodilators can provide symptomatic relief by relaxing the smooth muscle of the airways; corticosteroids are used as preventatives by reducing the inflammatory response.

Complex cellular interactions are triggered in an asthma attack. Of central importance in the disease process is a white blood cell called a T-lymphocyte. Once stimulated, these cells produce proteins called cytokines, which act on other cells, particularly a type of white blood cell called an eosinophil. This is the direct cause of the airway hyper-responsiveness of asthma.

In addition, a 'mast' cell is activated, releasing chemicals such as histamine which cause airway inflammation.

RELAXING MUSCLE

Contraction of the smooth muscle of the airway is controlled by receptors in the membranes of the muscle cells – β_2 adrenergic receptors and acetylcholine receptors are the two most important.

Stimulation of β_2 receptors relaxes the muscles and stimulation of the acetylcholine receptors causes them to contract. Drugs to stimulate β_2 receptors (β_2 agonists) and those to block the acetylcholine receptor (acetylcholine antagonists) act to relax smooth muscle in the airway, thus relieving asthma symptoms. The β_2 agonists (such as salbutamol) are the most important.

REDUCING INFLAMMATION

Simple airway muscle relaxation alone is not sufficient to deal with the problem, as narrowing of the airway by inflammation of its lining is unrelieved.

Corticosteroids act on a variety of the cell processes involved in asthma and generally damp down inflammation. They act as preventers of the symptoms rather than relievers, as their onset of action is only over a matter of hours and they have to be taken regularly, irrespective of symptoms.

Relaxed and asthmatic airways

Relaxed airway

Smooth muscle
Smooth muscle is relaxed in a normal airway

Mucus secreting cell
Mucus traps small particles to prevent damage to the lower regions of the lung

Vein
Carries waste products (such as carbon dioxide) away

Artery
Supplies the bronchiole's cells with oxygen and nutrients

Asthmatic airway

Smooth muscle
Contracts as a result of inflammatory mediators

Mucus
Secretion of mucus increases as a result of the inflammatory process

Vein
Inflammatory substances cause dilatation (widening) of the veins

Artery
Inflammatory substances cause dilatation of the arteries

During asthma, inflammatory chemicals are released from cells lining the airways; these cause constriction of the airway and excess secretion of mucus.

A micrograph of the airways in asthma shows constriction (A) due to increased responsiveness of the smooth muscle; and clogging of the airway, due to overproduction of mucus (B).

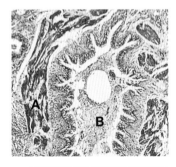

Can asthma be prevented?

Smoking is known to worsen asthma symptoms. Children who are exposed to passive smoking may show increased bronchial responsiveness.

It is doubtful whether the most intensive efforts in susceptible individuals can truly prevent asthma. The symptoms can be reduced by eliminating some of the known precipitating factors from the environment, including:

■ House dust

The house dust mite is the most significant identifiable precipitant of the symptoms in most children. In practice, real reductions in levels are hard to achieve but measures include removing carpets and soft toys, intensive vacuuming and regular dusting.

■ Passive smoking

Cigarette smoke contains high concentrations of chemicals that irritate the respiratory tract. Studies have also linked parental smoking with increased bronchial hyperirritability in their children.

■ Pets

Some asthmatic children are hypersensitive to the dander from pets, particularly cats and dogs. Removal of these pets may be an unpopular intervention and requires sensitive negotiation.

■ Foods

Certain foods that trigger asthma may be identified.

Glue ear and grommets

Glue ear – when fluid collects in the cavity in the middle ear – is the most common cause of deafness in children. Although it may resolve spontaneously, the condition can be treated by the insertion of a grommet.

Secretory otitis media (glue ear) develops when fluid collects in the usually air-filled middle ear cavity. A child with glue ear has muffled hearing because the sound is moving through fluid rather than air. It is a transitory disorder which, if not treated surgically, normally disappears by the age of 12, by which time the child's resistance to infection has increased.

BLOCKED TUBE

In its healthy state, the middle ear is an air-filled cavity connected to the back of the nose by the Eustachian tube. This tube enables air to enter the middle ear, which equalizes the pressure inside and outside the middle ear.

If the tube becomes partially or totally blocked – perhaps due to a chemical inflammation, allergy, or respiratory infection – the mucosa in the nasopharynx will swell. As a result, the air in the middle ear becomes absorbed by the mucous lining of the Eustachian tube. A vacuum is created and fluid is drawn from the mucosa into the middle ear cavity.

Watery at first, this fluid gradually thickens to a thin jelly that causes hearing to diminish progressively.

An otoscope, comprising a funnel, light source and magnifying lens, is used to closely examine the eardrum.

When healthy, the middle ear is a cavity filled with air. If the connecting Eustachian tube becomes blocked due to infection, the middle ear can then become filled with fluid that gradually thickens to a jelly and distorts hearing.

Eustachian tube
Connects the back of the nose to the middle ear; the tube opens during swallowing playing an important role in equalizing pressure inside and outside the middle ear

Tympanic membrane
An elastic membrane, commonly called the eardrum; vibrates when hit by sound waves

External auditory canal
Directs sounds to the ear drum; normally contains dark wax

Tympanic cavity (middle ear)
Normally filled with air; in glue ear, the cavity fills with fluid which muffles sound

INCIDENCE

By age 10, 20 per cent of children will have been affected by glue ear. For the first three years of life, mild to moderate hearing loss due to glue ear is common. Deprived of normal sound stimulation, the problem may result in delayed speech development.

Generally, the infection clears within three to four weeks. If the condition does not clear up, the child may need surgery.

If antibiotics fail to resolve glue ear, surgical treatment may be required. An incision is made in the tympanic membrane (eardrum) and a grommet is inserted to ventilate the middle ear. Without the grommet, the incision would seal over and the middle ear cavity would fill again with fluid.

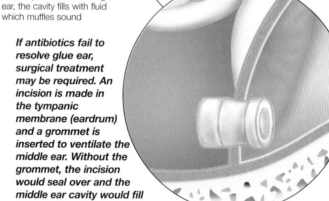

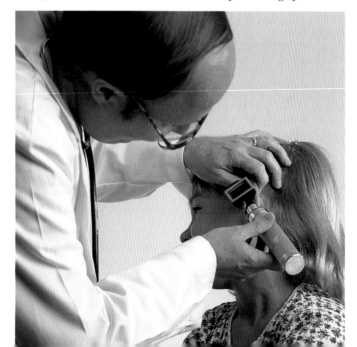

Surgical use of grommets

A child with a history of middle ear infections, delayed speech development and social difficulties due to their hearing problem should be recommended for surgery. If glue ear is left untreated, the eardrum may be retracted, leading to chronic ear infection.

Surgical treatment involves implanting a small tube called a grommet into the eardrum. The aim is to drain fluid from the cavity and restore hearing.

To relieve glue ear, the tympanic membrane (eardrum) is punctured and the fluid is sucked out. A grommet is then inserted into the tympanic membrane to act as a ventilation tube, normally the function of the Eustachian tube, allowing air to enter the middle ear.

A grommet is necessary as the incision in the tympanic membrane closes very quickly, causing glue ear to return. It enables the fluid, which could not be removed from the ear by aspiration, to dry up.

Grommets are used to restore hearing in children with transmission deafness. A grommet can be as small as 3 mm long, although others are much longer.

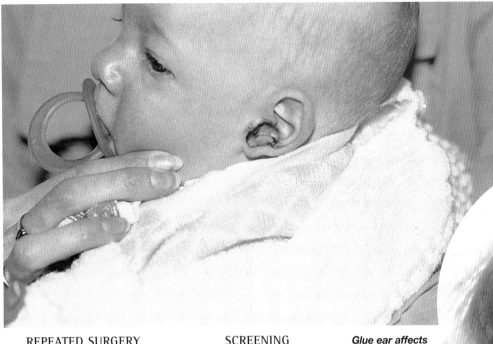

Moderate loss of hearing due to glue ear is common during the first three years of life. It can be difficult to diagnose when it occurs in very young children. There may be no visible symptoms, or a dark or yellowish glaze may be apparent in the ear canal. Occasionally, bubbles or fluid levels can be seen through the drum membrane.

REPEATED SURGERY

Some children affected by glue ear will require two or even three operations over a period of time to maintain their hearing. This is because as the child gets older, the anatomy of the head changes and the grommet may be pushed out of the eardrum.

There has been criticism about the use of grommets because of this need to repeat the procedure, which conflicts with the government aim to try to cut the cost of surgery.

However, they fulfil the purpose of aerating the middle ear cavity and restoring normal hearing until the problem resolves itself by around the age of 12.

SCREENING

The incidence of glue ear is quite high under the age of four years old, but it often remains undiagnosed for a long time. Many children with the problem are noticed during routine screening at school.

Glue ear eventually rectifies itself. Grommets do not cure the problem itself, but treat the symptoms, rather like someone taking aspirin for a headache.

GROMMET SURGERY

A child's ear canal is quite small and narrow, which presents difficulties for a doctor trying to insert a grommet into the eardrum. A grommet operation is often considered minor

Glue ear affects the hearing as the soundwaves have to travel through fluid instead of air. This can have implications for the child's ability to learn speech and their later progress at school.

surgery, and is sometimes left to junior doctors to perform.

Difficulties can arise if the grommet has not been correctly placed, however. There might be bleeding at the time of the operation and the incision might be too large so that the grommet falls out soon afterwards. For these reasons, the operation should always be performed by

an experienced surgeon.

The grommet operation takes 10-15 minutes and requires the child to have a general anaesthetic. A child may have their adenoids and tonsils removed at the same time if the surgeon thinks this is necessary. If only grommets are to be inserted, the child may be admitted as a day case.

Tools for grommet insertion

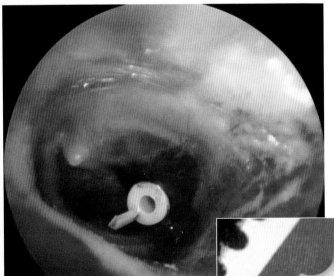

As the opening into the ear is so small, the operation is carried out using a microscope and a strong source of illumination.

Fine surgical instruments are used. A sickle knife is used to make the tiny incision in the tympanic membrane (the eardrum), then a fine suction tube is used to aspirate (remove by

Once the grommet has been placed in the eardrum, normal hearing is restored. When the condition corrects itself, around age 12, it may be removed.

suction) the fluid. Very small forceps are then used to hold the grommet and insert it into the incision in the tympanic membrane. Specialized forceps, shaped with handles at almost 45 degrees to the gripping stems, can be used without obstructing the view down the microscope.

Sometimes there is bleeding during the operation. Bleeding must be controlled as it makes it difficult for the surgeon to see what they're doing, and when the blood dries it can dislodge the grommet.

The tiny grommet, seen here on a postage stamp for scale, is inserted into the eardrum to ventilate the middle ear. Some grommets are as small as 3 mm and need to be replaced as the child grows and the grommet is pushed out of place.

Dental problems in children

Children have two sets of teeth: the deciduous or 'baby' teeth,
and their permanent teeth. Both sets can be damaged through decay,
disease, trauma or genetically-inherited syndromes.

Teeth form an integral part of the mouth and play a vital role in eating, chewing, speaking and in a person's appearance.

TWO SETS OF TEETH
Children have two sets of teeth:
■ Deciduous teeth – these form during fetal development, erupt from six months of age and are lost by the age of 12
■ Permanent teeth – these start developing at birth, appear at around six years of age and are usually present until old age.

DENTAL PROBLEMS
Children may experience problems with their teeth failing to develop or they may lose teeth. Teeth are extracted or lost for many reasons including:
■ Decay
■ Gum disease
■ Trauma
■ Anomalies and abnormalities

Children have only 20 deciduous teeth, which are replaced by 32 permanent teeth (shown below). Incisors, premolars and wisdom teeth may be missing.

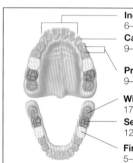

Incisors
6–9 years
Canines
9–12 years
Premolars
9–12 years
Wisdom teeth
17–25 years
Second molars
12–13 years
First molars
5–6 years

of eruption or exfoliation (shedding teeth) – these may be genetically determined, brought about by systemic (whole body) or localized changes, or be due to a combination of reasons.

Many dental problems start in childhood, and unless they are treated they will cause problems into adulthood. Good oral care and hygiene as a child promote healthy practice later in life.

Dental problems can begin surprisingly early. Children should start making regular visits to the dentist from around 2–3 years of age.

Form, shape and number of teeth

There are 20 deciduous and 32 permanent teeth. The form and shape of both sets depends on the individual.

ABNORMALITIES
Less than one per cent of children have a missing baby tooth, and three to six per cent of children do not have a full set of permanent teeth.
The teeth most often missing are the incisors, the second

premolars and the wisdom teeth.
The reasons for missing, abnormally-shaped or additional teeth are uncertain. Dental anomalies are associated with:
■ Genetic determinants
■ Certain syndromes, such as Down's syndrome
■ Trauma or infection while the fetus is in the uterus
■ Developmental problems – for example, children with cleft lip and palate may have missing or

The deciduous teeth begin to fall out at around the age of six. In some cases they have become badly eroded by this time and could be causing pain.

small lateral incisors.
Abnormalities in the shape of the crown (the visible part of the tooth) may result from an infectious disease in early childhood or infancy. The extent of the damage is determined by the age of the child at the time of the illness.

ERUPTION OF TEETH
Baby teeth generally have a finite lifespan. They are lost in succession, starting with the incisors at around six years of age and ending with the molars at around twelve years of age.
Loss of baby teeth may be accelerated or delayed by trauma or disease. Delay in the permanent teeth appearing can also occur if the tooth becomes 'submerged', fused or stuck in the jawbone.
Permanent teeth have a much longer lifespan and are not lost

unless there are signs of dental decay, gum disease or trauma.
The pattern of eruption is influenced by:
■ Gender (girls' teeth erupt earlier than boys')
■ Diet
■ Chronic illness.
Delayed eruption can happen; this is associated with certain syndromes, the position of the teeth and extra teeth (which may impede the eruption of the tooth in question).
Occasionally teeth can erupt too early; 1 in 2–3,000 children have one or more teeth at birth. As these have no root formation (making them mobile) and they interfere with the baby's feeding, they are usually extracted.

TREATMENT
Disturbances in form, size, shape and number of teeth can usually be treated by a general dentist, but specialist care may be needed to restore form and function. A useful tool is the X-ray, as it can diagnose anomalies in teeth that have not yet erupted and detect tooth decay.

Dental decay

Dental decay is a disease of the hard tissues in the mouth. It is caused by the action of bacteria on fermentable carbohydrates in the diet, and is characterized by alternating periods of destruction and repair of the hard tooth tissue (enamel, dentine and cement).

Bacteria in the mouth may also be responsible for causing gum disease.

DENTAL DISEASE

Most children experience some dental disease. While levels have improved over the last 30 years, around 20 per cent of toddlers, half of five-year-olds, and a third of 16-year-olds still suffer some tooth decay.

Unless dental decay is treated, children will suffer from toothache and may ultimately need to have the tooth extracted. This can be avoided in developed countries, where simple measures are widely available to prevent decay and disease.

Tooth decay needs rapid treatment to prevent further spread. If bacteria are allowed to invade the living centre of the tooth, it may become infected.

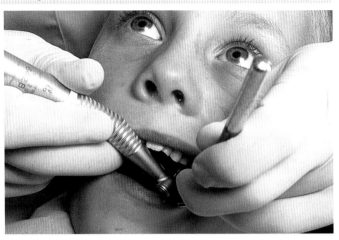

Diet

Dental caries (decay) are inextricably linked to diet, especially carbohydrate and sugar intake. Increased sugar consumption leads to dental decay from infancy through childhood, adolescence and into adulthood.

BALANCED DIET

The Scientific Basis of Dental Health Education recommends limiting the amount of sugary food and drink consumed, both in terms of quantity and frequency. Infants and children who are fed sugar-containing juices or squashes frequently or at night often develop dental caries that can be devastating.

A balanced diet including fresh fruit and vegetables eaten at regular meal times is the best way to prevent decay. However, maintaining this diet in children can be difficult, given factors directing them in the opposite direction, such as advertisements and peer pressure. Many processed foods contain high levels of sugar, and yet these may be the cheapest, quickest or most easily available forms of food for some families.

EARLY FEEDING

A recent government infant feeding report reinforced dietary guidelines set out by dentists:
■ Breast-feeding is important as it provides the best infant nutrition
■ Weaning should start at four months of age and certainly by six months
■ Bottle feeding should be discouraged by one year
■ Sugar should be limited to 10 per cent of a child's energy intake
■ Water should constitute the majority of a child's drink intake, especially outside meal times and at bedtime.

Children often follow a diet that is too high in sugar, leading to dental problems. Regular intake of squash and fizzy drinks can cause erosion of tooth surfaces.

Cleaning teeth

Another important factor in helping to reduce dental decay in children is cleaning teeth twice a day with fluoride toothpaste.

Parents need to take every opportunity to drum home the message that teeth can only remain healthy with effective, regular brushing.

Fluoride

Fluoride is an important adjunct to oral health and can be delivered in a number of ways: in water, toothpaste, drops, tablets, rinses or varnish (applied in the dental surgery). Fluoride strengthens tooth enamel by making it more resistant to decay. It may be incorporated during tooth development, after tooth eruption, during maturation of the tooth surface and later.

Fluoride works to establish an equilibrium in the daily cycle of destruction and repair that occurs within the tooth surfaces (enamel) of the mouth. It also halves dental decay.

If used in excess, fluoride may cause flecking of the tooth enamel surface. While unsightly, this is not a serious problem, and does not constitute a reason for avoiding fluoride toothpaste.

National dental surveys of children aged 5–15 years old show a decline in dental decay over the past 30 years. This has been attributed to the now established and widespread use of fluoride.

Tongue-tie

Tongue-tie is a minor defect of the mouth that limits the movement of the tongue. A simple operation can help correct feeding problems and speech defects in children affected by tongue-tie.

Tongue-tie (ankyloglossia) is a disorder in which the strip of tissue (frenulum) between the tongue and the floor of the mouth is too short, and prevents the tongue protruding below the lower lip. The tongue itself will be stumpy and broad-ended, and it may have a central dimple. In extremely rare cases, the tongue may be fused to the floor of the mouth.

INCIDENCE

Tongue-tie is three times more common in boys than in girls. Up to 50 per cent of people affected have a close relation who has tongue-tie. Although most children are otherwise normal, in some it may be part of a major congenital abnormality.

The incidence is not known exactly, but one study has indicated that one in 110 newborn babies had tongue-tie.

In tongue-tie, the frenulum – the strip of tissue attaching the tongue to the lower part of the mouth – is too short. The strip may be thin or quite thick.

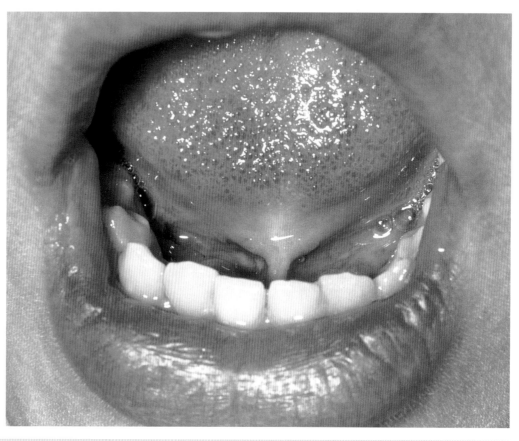

Feeding problems

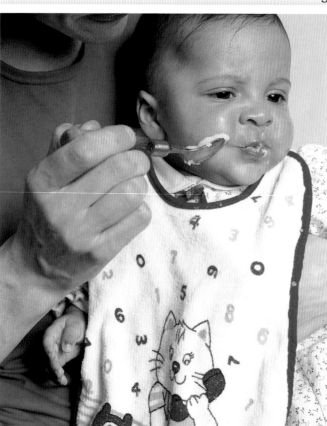

Some babies with tongue-tie cannot transfer food from the front to the back of their mouth. These children have problems when eating solids and may push the food out.

Successful breast-feeding requires the mother's nipple to be massaged by the baby's tongue to stimulate the lactiferous lobules in the breast which secrete milk. Some babies with tongue-tie cannot do this and instead chomp on the nipple. This is painful for the mother and inefficient.

These babies become tired after feeding and fall asleep, but as they have not fed sufficiently, they wake early, needing more milk. Some feed almost continuously, exhausting both themselves and their mothers.

BOTTLE-FEEDING

Historically, the frenulum of all babies with tongue-tie was cut by a midwife at birth as it was known to affect breast-feeding. However, in some cases the introduction of bottle-feeding has made it easier for children with tongue-tie to feed, as they can chomp on the bottle teat. Hence, some babies with tongue-tie are now transferred from breast-feeding to bottle-feeding.

SOLIDS

Some babies with tongue-tie who feed well on breast or bottle, have problems with solids. Solids have to be placed on the back of their tongue in order for them to eat successfully.

OTHER LIMITATIONS

Some children with tongue-tie cannot clean the inside of the mouth. Thus, solid particles – rice, for example – can become stuck under the tongue. Tongue-tie also makes licking the lips, licking an ice cream and sticking the tongue out impossible.

Speech problems

It is generally agreed that tongue-tie does not delay speech acquisition. However, a child whose tongue is tethered by the disorder often learns to make certain incorrect sounds while attempting to produce the correct ones.

CORRECTING SPEECH PROBLEMS

Children with tongue-tie may have problems with the letters 'd', 'l', 'n' and 't', and with the sound 'th'. By the time these children are referred to a speech therapist they will usually be four years old and may not be able to re-learn the correct sounds after the tongue-tie is divided. This reinforces the view that division of the tongue-tie is unnecessary. Only surgical division before the development of speech may prevent speech problems.

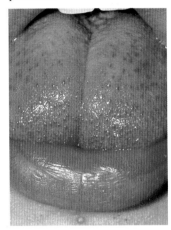

Children with tongue-tie may have difficulty in making certain speech sounds. These children will most likely need an operation and referral to a speech or language therapist.

Some children with tongue-tie may have a groove that runs the full length of the tongue. The tongue may also be forked.

Correcting tongue-tie surgically

In previous times midwives used a sharpened fingernail to divide the tongue-tie. Nowadays, the treatment depends on the age of the child as well as the seriousness of the condition and whether it is associated with a forked tongue. If the tongue-tie is not too short or thick, reassurance may be all that is necessary. Both the operations mentioned below are notable for being relatively painless.

TREATMENT OF BABIES

Nowadays, a baby aged under nine months who has tongue-tie will be treated under local anaesthetic by dividing the frenulum quickly and carefully using scissors. The baby is then put on the breast or given a bottle. He or she will normally stop crying within a minute. There is virtually no blood loss.

TREATMENT OF CHILDREN

Children who are older than nine months and have teeth or a thick tongue-tie, should have the frenulum divided across its width under general anaesthetic. This allows the division to be performed with diathermy scissors, which use an electric current (electrocoagulation) to prevent any bleeding.

A minor operation to cut the tongue-tie may need to be performed. This operation is relatively painless and may be carried out under anaesthetic as a day case.

Results of the operation

Both the above-mentioned operations to cut the tongue-tie are straightforward, and the floor of the patient's mouth usually heals well within 24 hours.

Most small babies with tongue-tie feed better after tongue-tie division. Indeed, the division can be of immediate benefit to breast-fed babies, who may be able to suck on the breast better than before and thus receive the milk they need. The operation, in which the frenulum is cut, enables all babies to protrude their tongue and lick their lips.

After the operation, most children with tongue-tie become better feeders. However, a few older children, who have already learned one way of feeding to cope with a tethered tongue, may not improve.

A child's speech may also improve after the operation, although this will take a while if the tongue-tie is divided late, as the child will have to re-learn the correct sounds.

In most cases, division of the tongue-tie is a successful operation. Activities that previously were hard to carry out – such as licking an ice cream – become possible.

Constipation in children

Constipation is the infrequent and forceful passage of hard faeces.
It is a common complaint in childhood and may need to be treated
either by changing the child's diet or by administering laxatives.

Constipation refers to the infrequent, forceful passage of hard faeces. Many children are incorrectly labelled as suffering from constipation, however, because of common misconceptions about what is 'normal defecation'.

There is such a great variation in the frequency of bowel motion within the individual (and within members of the same family) that it is an understandable subject of confusion. For example, normal bowel frequency can vary from four faeces per day to one every three to four days. The consistency of the faeces is also very important: the infrequent passage of soft faeces is not likely to indicate a significant medical problem.

The large intestine is made up of the colon (ascending, transverse and descending), rectum and anal canal.

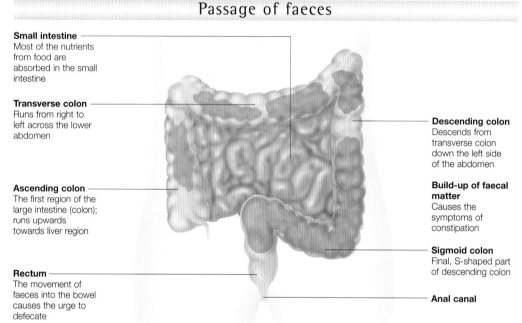

Passage of faeces

Small intestine
Most of the nutrients from food are absorbed in the small intestine

Transverse colon
Runs from right to left across the lower abdomen

Ascending colon
The first region of the large intestine (colon); runs upwards towards liver region

Rectum
The movement of faeces into the bowel causes the urge to defecate

Descending colon
Descends from transverse colon down the left side of the abdomen

Build-up of faecal matter
Causes the symptoms of constipation

Sigmoid colon
Final, S-shaped part of descending colon

Anal canal

Constipation in newborns and infants

In a newborn child, the first bowel motion produces what is known as meconium. This is generally passed within 24 hours of birth. If this neonatal bowel residue is not passed within this time, it may raise suspicions of an anatomical or congenital problem. Beyond the

If artificial milk is too concentrated, there may be insufficient water available to maintain soft faeces; constipation may result.

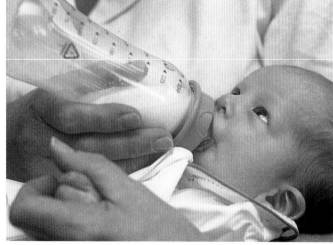

neonatal period, the cause of constipation in around 95 per cent of cases is not due to significant disease.

Once feeding is established, an infant settles into its own pattern of defecation. The amount, consistency and frequency of bowel movements may differ widely in the same child from time to time. These differences are often due to diet and, with breast-feeding, to maternal diet.

The passage of faeces in infants (as in adults) is

dependent upon the amount of food and liquid consumed. Properly constituted artificial milk feed contains a similar ratio of water to solid as breast milk; if it is too concentrated, the baby may have problems forming soft faeces, leading to constipation. In addition, many young infants have a minor degree of anal stenosis (narrowing), which may cause them to strain and pass small faeces. This condition is treated by mild dilatation of the anus.

When a child is introduced to cows' milk (usually between the age of nine months and a year), faeces tend to become smaller, harder and less frequent. These changes in faecal consistency can make it difficult for children to have a bowel motion. The hard stool can irritate the anus. If a painful anal fissure develops, the child may prefer not to defecate and may withhold the faeces. This withholding may lead to constipation.

The first movement passed by a newborn baby is the meconium. Meconium is composed of cells lining the fetal bowel, bowel mucus and bile from the liver.

Children will establish their own routine for going to the toilet. If constipation is a serious problem, however, medical help should be sought.

Constipation in older children

In older children, most causes of constipation are functional or related to diet.
In rare cases, however, constipation can be due to organic disease (such as short
segment Hirschsprung's disease) or a side effect of drug treatment.

There are two main categories of constipation in older children: acute (sudden onset) constipation and chronic (long-standing) constipation. The causes of each may be different but children with acute constipation may go on to develop chronic constipation if not treated correctly.

ACUTE CONSTIPATION

The commonest cause of acute constipation is a reaction to childhood fever. Febrile illnesses are common in children and are usually viral in origin. During such illnesses, children often

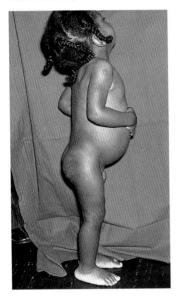

In Hirschsprung's disease, the nerves supplying the colon fail to develop, resulting in abdominal swelling and pain.

Fever can sometimes cause acute constipation in children; a febrile illness may cause the development of hard faeces.

develop hard faeces, which can lead to tears of the skin around the anus. These fissures cause pain during defecation and children will often try to retain their faeces to prevent the pain.

However, withholding further increases faecal hardness, making defecation yet more painful. This can lead to chronic constipation, which may persist well after the viral illness has passed. This is one reason why it is important to encourage children to drink plenty of fluid when they are feverish.

CHRONIC CONSTIPATION

Chronic constipation in children can be apparent in several ways. A child with chronic constipation may, for example, complain of abdominal pain, lack of appetite or vomiting. Such children may also fail to grow satisfactorily and are often prone to urinary infection. And, since children with chronic constipation can also develop diarrhoea, it can often be difficult for parents to accept a doctor's diagnosis.

General measures when treating constipation include encouraging a high fluid intake and a diet that is high in fibre.

Treating constipation in children

Constipated

Hard faeces
During constipation water is absorbed from the colon causing hard faeces to form

Wall of the large intestine

After laxative

Lactulose
Lactulose passes through the gastro-intestinal tract undigested

Soft faeces
Following administration of lactulose, the faeces become softer and easier to pass

Water movement
Lactulose attracts water molecules into the large intestine

The treatment of chronic constipation is relatively straightforward, but success depends upon understanding and patience. Treatment involves removing the constipated faeces, encouraging the child not to withhold and reassuring the child that defecation is painless and easy. Oral therapy is the preferred route of treatment. However, suppositories or enemas may be needed in cases which are resistant to such treatment.

The most common approach to removing the constipated faeces is to use a liquid laxative, usually lactulose. This complex

Lactulose (a complex sugar) is a laxative which acts by attracting water into the lumen of the large intestine, so softening the faeces.

sugar molecule is not absorbed after ingestion and remains in the intestine unchanged. It attracts water around it by a process called osmosis. This leads to the production of softer faeces, which are easier to pass.

It may also be necessary to prescribe a bowel stimulant. These drugs work by stimulating the muscle tone of the bowel. This promotes easier passage of faeces by increasing the power of the gastrocolic reflex, which is the means whereby food entering the stomach stimulates the bowel to expel faeces. This reflex is the main reason why people commonly defecate soon after meals.

Successful treatment will lead to an improvement in both the child's physical and emotional symptoms.

Urinary tract infections in children

Urinary infections are fairly common in children, and most of them can be successfully treated with antibiotics. In rare cases, infection is due to an underlying disorder known as vesicoureteric reflux.

Urinary tract infections are common in young children, affecting about three per cent of girls and one per cent of boys.

They are generally caused by bacteria from around the anus travelling up the urethra (the tube from the bladder to the body's exterior) and infecting the bladder.

UNDERLYING DISORDERS

In many cases, there is no cause for concern and the infections can be treated easily. However, in some children, the infection may indicate an underlying problem in the urinary tract and this requires early investigation and diagnosis.

Any child suspected of having a urinary tract infection should be seen by a doctor as soon as possible, so that the appropriate tests and treatment can be instigated.

Particular concerns include:
■ Checking that the child does not have a disorder known as vesicoureteric reflux, which predisposes an affected child to kidney damage as a result of urinary tract infections
■ Ensuring that kidney damage does not occur as a complication of infections.

Urinary tract infections occur fairly commonly in young children. Children tend to have non-specific symptoms, such as fever and loss of appetite.

Vesicoureteric reflux

The urinary tract

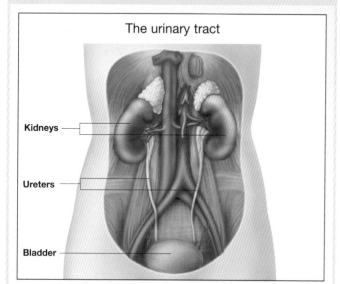

Kidneys

Ureters

Bladder

Normally, when a child urinates, valves prevent urine in the bladder from flowing back up the ureters (the two tubes connecting the kidneys to the bladder) to the kidneys. If these valves do not work properly, backflow occurs in a condition known as vesicoureteric reflux.

If infections travel up the ureters, the kidneys may become scarred. This can result in high blood pressure and, rarely, kidney failure. It also

Normally urine is unable to flow back up from the bladder to the kidneys due to valve control. In vesicoureteric reflux, the valves fail to control flow.

increases the risk of infections developing.

Vesicoureteric reflux alone does not produce any symptoms; it is only diagnosed when children are being investigated for urinary tract infections.

Causes and symptoms

Urinary tract infections are caused by bacteria. The most common is *Escherichia coli,* which is usually present in the large intestine. Girls are more at risk of urinary tract infections than boys because their urethra is shorter, making it easier for bacteria to pass up the urethra to the bladder.

SYMPTOMS

In very young children, the symptoms are likely to be non-specific, such as fever, poor appetite, vomiting and diarrhoea.

Older children may exhibit symptoms more suggestive of a urinary tract infection, such as:
■ Pain on passing urine
■ Bed-wetting
■ Pain in the small of the back
■ Frequent need to urinate.

Babies can also be affected; they are likely to be fractious and reluctant to feed.

This micrograph shows a bladder infected by Escherichia coli *(seen here in yellow). This bacterium is the commonest cause of urinary tract infections.*

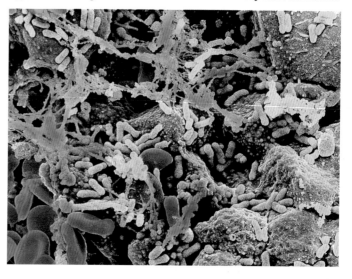

Treating urinary tract infections

Initial diagnosis is made by a doctor and confirmed by laboratory tests.
Further tests, such as ultrasound and radioisotope scanning, may be required to
exclude underlying disorders, in particular vesicoureteric reflux.

Initial diagnosis of urinary tract infections can be made by a doctor using a special test dipstick. This is able to detect certain substances in the urine, the presence of which suggests an infection.

If this test is positive, the GP will immediately prescribe antibiotics, while also sending a urine sample to a laboratory for testing. This will confirm:
■ Whether a bacterial infection is present
■ Which type of bacteria is involved. Determining the exact bacterium involved will allow the doctor to check that the antibiotic already prescribed is correct, or to change it if necessary.

URINE SAMPLES
The urine sample must be taken in as sterile a way as possible, avoiding contamination by bacteria on the skin. There are a number of methods for doing this, which vary with the age of the child. Ideally, the sample should come from the middle of the urine stream. If it is not possible to take a sample without contamination, a suprapubic aspirate may be taken. This involves insertion of a small needle into the bladder through the skin of the lower abdomen and the withdrawal of a sample.

TREATMENT
Oral antibiotics are normally taken for seven days, continuing for longer if investigations are still in progress. Antibiotics may initially be given intravenously to infants or those who are very ill, before transferring to oral treatment as the condition improves.

A further sample of urine should be tested a few days after the antibiotic course has been completed to ensure that the urine is clear of infection. In addition to antibiotics, the affected child will need plenty of fluids and possibly a simple analgesic such as paracetamol to reduce fever.

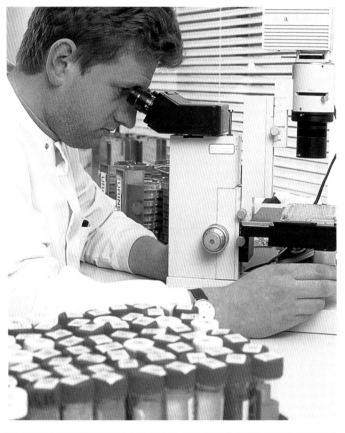

Urinary tract infections can be diagnosed by the analysis of a urine sample. The presence of any bacteria will be determined by simple laboratory tests.

Further investigations and treatment

When a urinary tract infection has been diagnosed in a child for the first time, further investigations will be necessary to check the urinary tract for evidence of abnormalities, in particular vesicoureteric reflux and scarring of the kidneys.

Investigations might include:
■ An ultrasound scan
■ A DMSA (dimercaptosuccinic acid) radioisotope scan to check for kidney scarring
■ A micturating cystourethrogram, in which a radio-opaque dye is introduced into the bladder and a series of X-ray pictures is then taken to look for backflow up the ureters as the child passes urine.

DMSA scanning
DMSA scanning is used to look for kidney scarring. A small

Liquid paracetamol may be given to children with urinary tract infection. This helps to reduce fever, which may be a symptom of the condition.

amount of DMSA (a harmless radioactive substance) is injected into a vein in the arm. After about two hours, this collects in the kidneys, allowing pictures taken with a gamma camera to show the size of the kidneys and any scarring. Children with proven vesicoureteric reflux will require:
■ Long-term antibiotics to prevent further infections
■ Regular monitoring for high blood pressure and signs of kidney scarring
■ Surgery (in severe cases), in which the ureters are detached from the bladder and then re-attached to form valves.

The outlook
Urinary tract infections often recur in children; up to 50 per cent will have a recurrence within a year.

Infants, in particular, are at risk of kidney scarring from infection, even if they do not have vesicoureteric reflux. Vesicoureteric reflux tends to resolve with age. Children with severe reflux are at significant risk of kidney scarring and require close monitoring. If infections continue despite the child taking long-term antibiotics, surgery may be necessary.

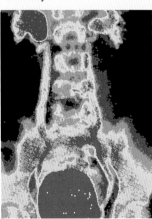

Vesicoureteric reflux occurs when urine (shown here in red) passes back from the bladder to the kidneys. This can be a cause of recurrent infection.

Treating eczema

Eczema is a common skin condition affecting about one in six children and anything up to one in ten adults. Although there is no cure as such, various treatments can be used to help alleviate the unpleasant symptoms.

The word eczema comes from the Greek for 'boiling', which refers to the blisters that may be present in the early stages of this itchy skin disease. Many factors can cause or worsen eczema, including climate changes, central heating, dust mites, emotional stress and food allergies. Because of this, eczema is very common, particularly in children.

TREATING THE SUFFERER
Eczema can affect many people, and the disease will affect all areas of the sufferer's life, including friendships, work and sleep. Therefore, dermatologists consider it important to treat the whole person and give support and understanding. It is usually a great reassurance to people when they are told that eczema will often resolve completely, or at least improve with time.

Types of eczema

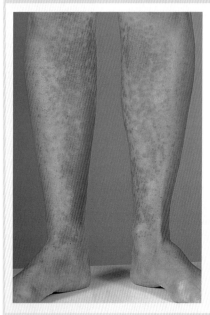

There are two main types of eczema:

Exogenous eczema is caused by factors originating outside the body, such as allergies and irritants. Allergy testing in the dermatology clinic is worthwhile if allergy is suspected. If it is confirmed, contact should be avoided with the culprit substances to enable the eczema to improve.

This woman's red eczema rash has been caused by a reaction to a particular brand of shaving foam. This condition is also called contact dermatitis.

Endogenous eczema means that it 'comes from within' and implies a genetic cause. Seventy per cent of people with eczema have a positive family history of eczema, asthma or hay fever. These three conditions are classified as 'atopy'. Atopy occurs when the body over-reacts to allergens in the air, such as house dust mites, grass pollen and cat or dog fur, and produces too many antibodies. **Atopic eczema** is the main type of **endogenous eczema**. Other forms include **pompholyx, discoid, seborrhoeic** and **asteatotic eczema** (see overleaf).

Atopic eczema

SYMPTOMS
The main symptom is itching, but other features include scaling, redness, dryness, skin thickening and sometimes small blister formation. Atopic eczema typically appears under the age of two years, mainly between two and six months old, but can occur at any age. In infants, it usually affects the scalp and face.

As the child reaches 18 months, the eczema alters its main site and appears in the bend of the elbow and behind the knees. Most children see a significant improvement in their eczema by the age of five years, and the majority are clear by their teens. Some people continue to have eczema into adult life, though it may become less severe with increasing age.

Atopic eczema occasionally develops for the first time in adulthood. The causes are unknown.

The itchy red rash of infant eczema is often treated with soothing cream to reduce the temptation to scratch.

INFECTIONS
Reducing infection is an important part of treating of eczema. People with atopic eczema tend to have more bacteria growing on their skin than unaffected people. The common bacterial infections are staphylococcus and streptococcus, and such infections can worsen the eczema. The herpes simplex virus, which often causes cold sores, can also worsen eczema.

TREATMENT
Treatment advice for eczema includes avoiding the use of soap. An emollient, which moisturizes and softens the skin, may be used instead, and can be applied to dry skin three or four times a day. An antiseptic, oil-based bath lotion is helpful, and bathing once or twice a day will reduce the number of bacteria growing on the skin.

Antihistamines can help to lessen the itch, and for about one third of people with eczema, evening primrose oil is found to be helpful.

For more active eczema, a steroid or anti-inflammatory ointment or cream should be applied evenly over the affected areas of skin to leave a fine film on the surface. The minimum strength of steroid is used, especially in treating eczema on the face. The use of the strongest steroids on the skin can lead to it thinning in the long term, but this is not a problem when milder steroids are used. These treatments can be used at home, and also if some time is spent in hospital.

If scratched, eczema is likely to become infected and scabbed, which in turn worsens the condition.

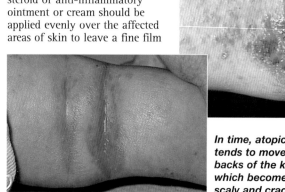

In time, atopic eczema tends to move to the backs of the knees, which become red, scaly and cracked.

Pompholyx eczema

SYMPTOMS
Pompholyx eczema (named after the Greek for 'bubble', after the bulbous eruptions that appear in sufferers) normally occurs in adults in their 20s or 30s and is characterized by very itchy blisters on the palms, and often on the soles of the feet.

Pompholyx eczema often causes anxiety and loss of confidence in sufferers because of the unpleasant look and feel of the symptoms.

TREATMENT
This form of eczema (also known as chieropompholyx) tends to be worse in hot weather, and requires the application of quite potent steroids to the affected areas.

As the eczema settles, the steroids can be used less frequently and eventually stopped. This can be a recurrent problem, and there is not yet a permanent cure, so repeated treatment is generally needed.

Discoid eczema

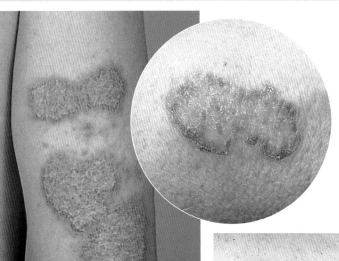

SYMPTOMS
This type of eczema is characterized by discs of red, scaly skin with a well-defined border, which may be quite widespread and rapid in their progression. It usually affects the arms, legs, chest and back, and tends to clear up after a matter of months, although it may persist for years.

◀ *Discoid eczema usually appears as symmetrical, coin-sized lesions. These most often appear on the skin over muscles that extend the limbs.*

TREATMENT
Treatment consists of emollients and powerful steroids applied to the skin. As the rash comes under control, the strength and frequency of use of the steroid applied can be reduced.

As with the other types of eczema, there is not yet a permanent cure.

▼ *In serious cases of discoid eczema, the lesions can weep fluid. This form of eczema often occurs in patients with no prior history of skin problems.*

Discoid eczema takes its name from its small, well-defined disc-shaped (or oval) appearance. This form of eczema only occurs in adults, and can spread to many parts of the body.

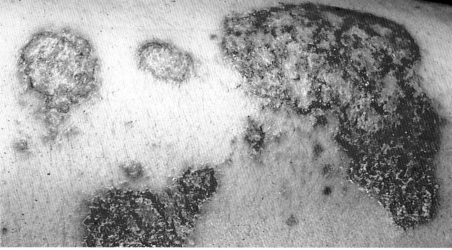

Seborrhoeic eczema

SYMPTOMS
This form of eczema is rarely encountered before adolescence, but affects between three and five per cent of all adults, and about a third of adults with HIV infection.

It affects the face (especially around the eyebrows and hairline, and near the nose and mouth), the scalp and the upper chest. On the scalp, dandruff occurs and may gradually progress to give the typical redness, scaling and itching of the scalp.

TREATMENT
Seborrhoeic eczema is associated with *Pityrosporum ovale*, a yeast infection, and is successfully treated by the use of an anti-yeast shampoo on the scalp. Affected areas on the face and chest are treated with an anti-yeast cream, often in a combined formulation with a mild steroid cream.

The condition is helped by these treatments, but there is not yet a permanent cure, so regular treatment is required for many years.

Asteatotic eczema

SYMPTOMS
This is characterized by dry, scaly skin, which tends to be worse in colder weather. Asteatotic eczema is typically a skin condition of older people, or those with a recent illness.

TREATMENT
The use of an emollient is recommended, and a mild steroid application is usually sufficient to control the eczema. Air humidifiers can also help by increasing the moisture content of the air.

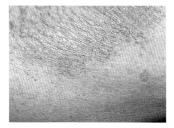

Asteatotic eczema commonly appears in the elderly, such as in this 69-year-old male patient. It is characterized by dry, cracked skin, and can be caused by malnutrition.

Measles

Measles is a highly infectious disease that usually affects children.
In most cases, recovery is straightforward but there can be
complications. Childhood vaccination provides effective immunity.

Measles is a highly contagious
viral illness of childhood
associated with fever and a
characteristic rash. Although
very common a generation ago,
measles is an uncommon disease
today. Indeed, in developed
countries many young doctors
may never have seen a case.

Measles occurs throughout
the world, and in developing
nations it is an illness of winter
and spring.

HOW MEASLES
IS TRANSMITTED

Measles is spread by droplets of
fluid from the respiratory tract
which are expelled from an
infected person during coughing
or sneezing. The droplets
penetrate an uninfected person
via the mouth or possibly via
the conjunctiva, the transparent
covering layer of the eye.

There are two phases to the
illness: a prodromal or
introductory phase with cold-
like symptoms, fever, cough, and
conjunctivitis; and the
characteristic rash phase.

Measles is most contagious
during the prodromal phase
before the rash has appeared.
Full recovery is the rule after
measles infection.

EASING SYMPTOMS

As with most viral diseases,
there is no specific treatment for
measles. General measures
include a high fluid intake and
paracetamol for reducing a fever.

*Measles is characterized by a
maculopapular rash that begins
around the hairline, and then
spreads to cover the entire body.*

*In the prodromal (introductory)
stage of the infection, the child
will have a fever, conjunctivitis
and cold-like symptoms.*

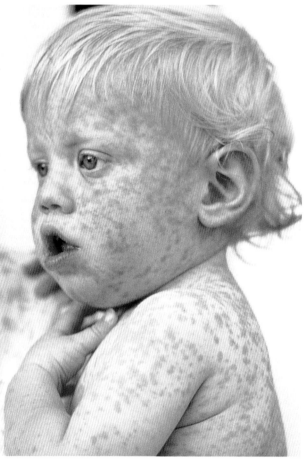

Diagnosing measles

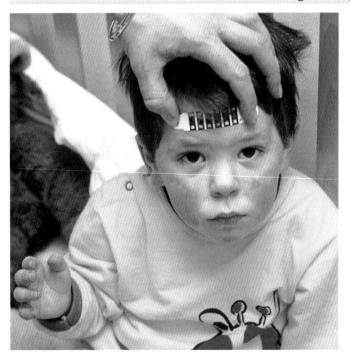

Measles is difficult to diagnose in
the prodromal stage. However, a
doctor may become suspicious
that the child is suffering more
than a simple cold if the fever
and illness are prolonged. The
presence of marked conjunctivitis
may also suggest measles.

A characteristic feature of
measles is the presence of Koplik
spots in the mouth. These small,
pinpoint, white spots are initially
found on the cheek opposite the
lower back teeth but eventually
spread throughout the mouth.
Koplik spots precede the measles
rash by 24 to 48 hours.

The rash is quite characteristic.
It is maculopapular, meaning
that it has flat areas flush with the
skin and also raised patches. The

rash begins behind the ears and
on the hairline at the back of the
head, spreading downwards to the
body and limbs. The individual
patches begin to join together to
become larger, blotchy red lesions.

The rash lasts for around five
days and it heals by darkening to
a brown colour with peeling of
the overlying skin. As with the
development of the rash, healing
begins on the head and spreads
towards the body and limbs.

*Koplik spots – small spots with
a whitish centre on the mucous
membranes of the mouth – are
diagnostic of measles.*

*Prolonged cold-like symptoms
and fever, indicated by a high
temperature, may suggest measles
infection. These symptoms occur
before the appearance of the rash.*

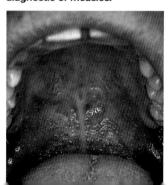

Possible complications of measles

Most children with measles will make a full recovery; however, complications of the infection may be associated with both short-term and long-term side effects.

Complications of measles can be classified into two groups:

NON-NEUROLOGICAL

Non-neurological complications tend to be mild and predictable:
■ Middle ear infection (otitis media) is very common, as are other upper respiratory complications such as laryngitis
■ Secondary bacterial pneumonia may occur; it is usually treatable with antibiotics
■ Other complications include corneal ulceration and hepatitis.

NEUROLOGICAL

Neurological complications involve the nervous system:
■ Febrile convulsions are the most common type of convulsion and occur in some children in response to the high temperature associated with measles; they are very common and, though distressing for parents, are rarely a significant problem; they settle as the body temperature lowers and usually have no long-term implications
■ Much more alarming complications include encephalitis and SSPE (subacute sclerosing panencephalitis).

Earache is a symptom of middle ear infection. This is a common non-neurological complication of measles which can be easily treated with antibiotics.

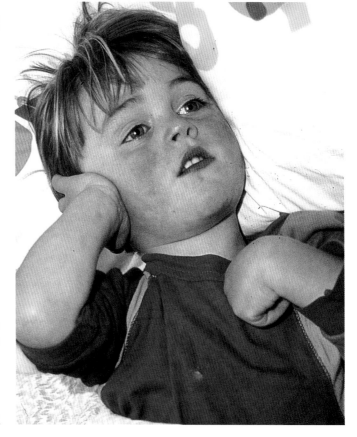

Encephalitis

Encephalitis means inflammation of the brain. In measles, it occurs in around one in 5,000 cases. It usually occurs about one week after the beginning of the illness. Affected children begin to complain of headache. Although headache is common in measles, as it is with any feverish viral illness, in encephalitis it is associated with lethargy and irritability.

SYMPTOMS OF MEASLES ENCEPHALITIS

Children with encephalitis will look quite unwell and will be both tired and sleepy but also restless and agitated. With encephalitis, the child may become more unwell and may have fits. Eventually, the child may fall into a coma.

There is a 15 per cent mortality rate with measles encephalitis, which means that one in seven affected children will die. Equally devastating is that 25–40 per cent of those who do not die will be left with long-term neurological complications, including deafness, epilepsy, limb paralysis and learning difficulties.

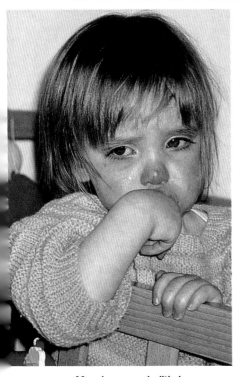

Measles encephalitis is a very serious complication and urgent treatment is necessary. The child may have a headache and appear quite agitated.

Subacute sclerosing panencephalitis

Subacute sclerosing panencephalitis (SSPE) is a rare but devastating long-term complication of measles. It occurs in one in 100,000 cases, but is not apparent as a medical problem until around seven years after the measles illness.

Patients have unusual neurological symptoms, including unco-ordinated body movement, and speech or visual problems. The disease is progressive and becomes more severe over several years. In time, patients become demented and develop rigid paralysis of the whole body.

The diagnosis of SSPE is often not made immediately, but may be suspected on clinical grounds. The diagnosis is confirmed by finding antibodies to measles in the blood and cerebrospinal fluid and by recognition of characteristic changes in the brain tracings of the electroencephalogram (EEG).

Immunocompromised patients

Children with reduced immunity usually have a more serious and more prolonged form of measles. They are typically more unwell than non-immunocompromised patients, they are prone to more side effects and the mortality rate is greater. Giant-cell pneumonia is a relatively common complication in immunocompromised patients (including those with cancer) and it may be fatal.

There is no effective treatment available for measles, although the antiviral agent ribavarin in aerosol form may be of some benefit in measles pneumonia.

Vaccination

The decline in the incidence of measles is due to the introduction of an effective measles vaccine in the 1960s. Prior to this, there were up to 800,000 cases per year in England and Wales.

In 1993, there were less than 10,000 cases. The number has fallen further since the introduction of immunization with the MMR (measles, mumps, rubella) vaccine, given around the first birthday.

Routine MMR vaccination has greatly reduced the number of measles cases in developed countries.

Mumps

Mumps is a viral infection that causes inflammation of the salivary glands on either side of the jaw. This illness mostly occurs among children, but immunization has made it less common.

Mainly a disease of childhood, mumps is a viral illness, caused by the paramyxovirus.

This virus can infect almost any organ in the body, but typically causes swelling of the parotid glands, a pair of salivary glands located just below and in front of the ears.

CONTRACTING MUMPS

Although mumps tends to be a mild illness, it can cause discomfort or even pain in particular parts of the body and, in a few cases, results in serious complications. Having an attack of the disease gives immunity, preventing further attacks of mumps in the future.

TRANSMISSION OF THE DISEASE

Mumps most commonly occurs in late winter and early spring. The illness is transmitted in droplets from an infected person's nose or throat when coughing or sneezing.

Mumps is infectious for up to a week prior to the onset of the parotid gland swelling and for about two weeks afterwards; it is most infectious from two to three days before and up to a few days after the swelling first appears.

AFFECTED PEOPLE

Mumps can occur at any age, but mainly affects school-age children; it is uncommon before the age of two years. The disease may also affect young adults.

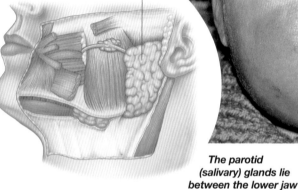

Parotid gland

The parotid (salivary) glands lie between the lower jaw and the ear. In mumps, these glands become swollen.

Children with mumps often have severely enlarged parotid glands. Swelling occurs on one or both sides of the face and is a typical sign of mumps.

Symptoms of mumps

In many cases, possibly up to 40 per cent, the disease does not cause any symptoms and passes unnoticed.

PAROTID SWELLING

If symptoms do occur, swelling of the parotid glands tends to be the first feature to develop, often appearing first on one side, followed a few days later by swelling on the other side. When both a child's glands are affected the cheeks usually appear overly round. If the parotid swelling is severe, a child's ear lobes may be pushed upwards and outwards and there may be difficulty in opening the mouth.

The skin overlying the swollen parotid glands may be reddened and warm to the touch. In addition, the mouth is often dry as a result of blockage of the normal flow of saliva from the affected glands into the mouth.

The inflammation in the parotid glands, known as parotitis, typically causes tenderness or pain. Affected children often complain of earache and possibly pain when eating or drinking.

OTHER SYMPTOMS

Children with mumps tend to feel generally unwell and to have a fever, which usually disappears within three to four days. Other common symptoms include headache and a reduction in appetite.

The salivary glands just below the jawline, known as the submandibular glands, may also become swollen, but this is much less common than parotid swelling. A particular gland tends to remain swollen for a few days and may be followed by swelling of a different gland.

Children with mumps may develop a high temperature and feel ill. However, in most cases the fever is not serious and resolves within a few days.

Mumps may cause earache in some children. The parotid swelling can cause pressure around the ear, resulting in severe discomfort.

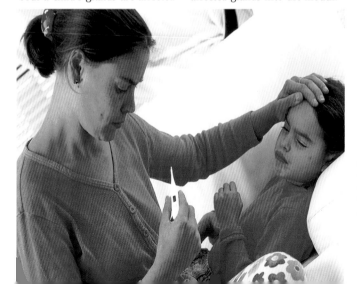

Complications of mumps

Mumps is usually characterized by a mild infection and parotid swelling,
but occasionally children develop complications. Other organs, such as the brain and
testes, may become inflamed, with potentially serious consequences.

Although mumps is normally a mild infection, in some cases complications may arise.

MENINGITIS

Meningitis (inflammation of the membranes surrounding the brain and spinal cord) occurs in up to five per cent of children with mumps. These symptoms may develop up to five days after the onset of the parotitis.

However, in some cases there is no preceding parotid swelling and the symptoms of meningitis are the first feature of the illness. Mumps meningitis tends to be mild, the nature of the symptoms varying according to the age of the child and the severity of the condition.

Symptoms may include fever, headache, vomiting, an aversion to bright light and neck stiffness. Occasionally, mumps meningitis results in temporary impairment of function in a particular part of the body; for example there may be temporary difficulty moving limbs.

ENCEPHALITIS

Encephalitis (inflammation of the tissue of the brain) is an uncommon feature of mumps, occurring in only about 1 in 5,000 affected people, but in rare cases it may be fatal. Like meningitis, encephalitis can cause a variety of symptoms, which may include a headache and drowsiness.

If either meningitis or encephalitis is suspected, urgent medical attention is required.

ORCHITIS

Orchitis (inflammation of one or both testes) is uncommon in young children but affects up to one third of males who develop mumps after puberty.

Orchitis causes testicular pain, which can be severe, together with swelling and redness of the scrotum. The swelling usually starts to disappear after three to four days. If both testes become inflamed, infertility may result.

Fortunately, the inflammation usually only affects one side and infertility is a rare and usually temporary complication.

OTHER COMPLICATIONS

In some cases, mumps causes inflammation in other parts of the body, such as the liver or joints. Inflammation of the pancreas is quite common and can cause pain or discomfort in the upper abdomen.

Inflammation of the ovaries can also develop and may cause abdominal pain. There is no evidence that fertility is affected.

The tissue of the breasts may become inflamed. This condition, known as mastitis, can develop in girls or boys, resulting in tender breasts. The condition is usually mild and short-lived.

Hearing loss can follow mumps, but this tends to affect only one side and is usually transient.

If a woman has mumps in early pregnancy, there is a risk of a miscarriage occurring.

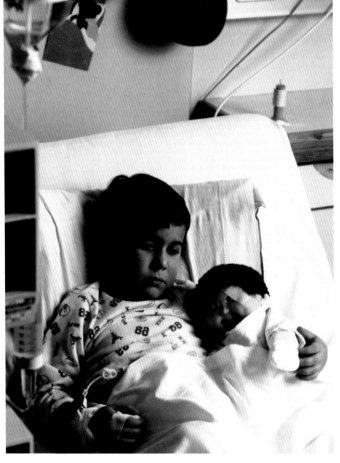

Some children with mumps develop viral meningitis. Most cases of mumps meningitis are mild, but usually require hospital admission for monitoring.

Diagnosing and treating mumps

In most children with mumps, the diagnosis is clear from the symptoms, particularly the swelling of the parotid glands. If confirmation is required, a blood sample can be tested for the presence of specific antibodies.

Alternatively, a sample of saliva or urine may be tested for the presence of the virus itself.

TREATMENT FOR MUMPS

Treatment aims to relieve the symptoms; a mild painkiller may help relieve discomfort and bring down a raised temperature.

Drinking plenty of fluids is important to ensure a child remains well hydrated.

A short course of steroid tablets may help to relieve the pain of orchitis. Although pain in the testes is reduced, it may not reduce the swelling.

There is no specific treatment for mumps. However, the symptoms of pain and fever can be relieved by taking a mild painkiller, such as paracetamol.

MMR vaccine

Normally, maternal antibodies are transferred from mother to fetus during pregnancy and these protect against mumps for the first year of a child's life.

Immunization with the MMR vaccine, the combined vaccine against measles, mumps and rubella, is recommended at the age of 12 to 15 months and again before a child starts school. The vaccination gives life-long protection against contracting mumps in the future.

The MMR vaccine aims to eliminate mumps, as well as measles and rubella. Children receive two injections before they are school-age.

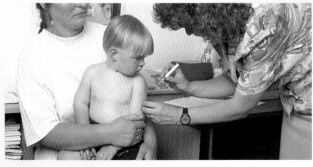

Rubella

Rubella – also known as German measles – is a viral infection
that is common in childhood. It is associated with fever, rash and
lymph node swelling, but tends to be mild and resolves quickly.

Rubella is usually a mild disease; infection passes unnoticed without any symptoms in around 25 per cent of cases. For most children, the infection is of no significance. The main concern with rubella, however, is infection of pregnant women. This is because in pregnancy, the virus can pass to the fetus via the placenta and cause abnormalities.

DISEASE SPREAD
The virus that causes rubella is found throughout the world. In developed countries, infection usually occurs in winter and spring. Today, thanks to vaccination, rubella is fairly uncommon. However, before the introduction of the vaccine, there were large outbreaks of rubella every six to nine years.

When an infected person coughs or sneezes, the virus is expelled from the body, carried on droplets of sputum or saliva. A child is usually infected by breathing in droplets from an infected person. The infected child may, in some cases, appear normal and may not have yet developed symptoms.

INCUBATION PERIOD
After picking up the virus, there is a period of 2–3 weeks before the infection becomes apparent. Infected children begin to feel unwell with a mild fever, runny nose, watery red eyes, a cough and swollen glands. The glands

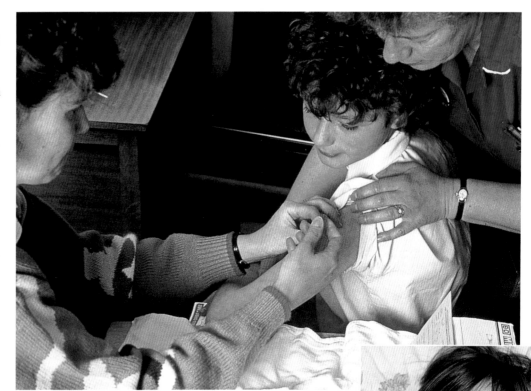

become larger and more tender as the illness progresses, reaching a peak as the rash appears.

The pink-red rash begins on the face and quickly spreads to the body, arms and legs. The rash, which is usually not itchy in children, lasts for about three days. The child has a mild fever (usually 38 °C or below) and swollen glands.

The main risk of rubella infection is damage to the unborn fetus. Therefore for many years only pre-pubescent females were immunized.

Early symptoms of rubella may include a mild fever, runny nose and swollen glands. These will be apparent before the appearance of the rash.

Diagnosing rubella

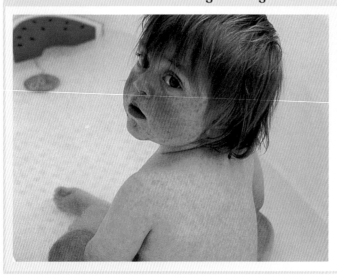

Rubella is difficult to diagnose with certainty without blood tests. However, blood analysis is rarely needed unless the diagnosis is strongly suspected and the infected child has come into contact with a pregnant woman.

Blood tests detect antibodies produced by the body in response to the rubella infection. Repeat blood tests at 10- to 14-day intervals can confirm a recent infection in a patient.

Complications are rare in childhood rubella. Most affected children and infants suffer from a mild fever and a rash (visible here) only.

Complications

Rarely, rubella is associated with certain complications:
■ **Arthritis**
This usually affects adolescent females; its diagnosis may indicate the possibility of the development of rheumatoid arthritis in adulthood.
■ **Encephalitis (inflammation of the brain)**
This affects about one in 6,000 cases. A child with encephalitis is lethargic and restless and may lapse into coma. Unlike measles encephalitis, rubella encephalitis is not fatal and the vast majority recover with no neurological after-effects.

Other complications include a reduction in the level of blood platelets and myocarditis.

Congenital rubella

Congenital rubella syndrome is a serious condition associated with low birth weight, developmental delay, blindness, deafness and heart defects. The later in the pregnancy that a mother is infected, the lower the risk of the baby suffering abnormalities.

The reason why rubella is such an important disease is that the infection of pregnant women by the rubella virus can lead to the development of congenital abnormalities in their unborn children.

Three main groups of congenital abnormalities are associated with rubella infection:
■ Cataract – can cause reduced sight or even blindness
■ Heart defects – especially pulmonary stenosis and patent ductus arteriosus
■ Low birth weight.

Reduced hearing is also a common accompaniment of congenital rubella.

RISKS TO THE FETUS

The greatest risk to the fetus is when the mother is infected before the eighth week of

Babies affected by congenital rubella syndrome often have a low birth weight. They will require close monitoring in the neonatal period.

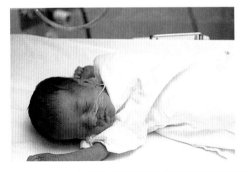

Congenital rubella results when the mother is infected in the early stages of pregnancy. The extent to which the baby may be affected is variable.

pregnancy, particularly in the first month. Around a half of fetuses infected at this time will develop congenital abnormalities. The risk of fetal infection and rubella-associated abnormalities declines after this period.

Hearing loss, eye changes and developmental delay can sometimes occur when children are infected later in pregnancy. For example, between the 13th and 16th week of pregnancy, infants have a 30 per cent chance of a congenital abnormality (usually reduced hearing). However, after the 18th week of pregnancy, there is little or no risk of a congenital abnormality developing.

CHECKING IMMUNITY

If a pregnant woman is infected, her immune status must be checked as soon as possible. If she is known to be immune or if blood analysis confirms immunity, she can be assured that there is no risk of congenital rubella in the unborn child.

If a woman is not immune and infection is confirmed by blood analysis, then she must be counselled appropriately. She should be informed of the degree of risk to her unborn

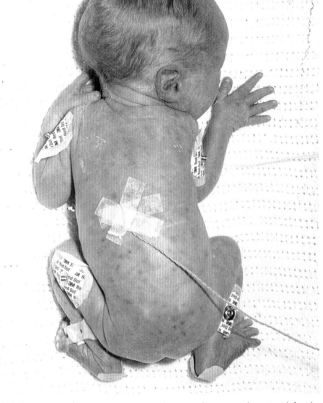

child. In some cultures, non-immune pregnant women with evidence of infection in early pregnancy may be counselled with regard to termination of pregnancy.

Immunoglobulin injection (antibody-rich injection used to

'mop up' excess virus particles in the blood) is not recommended in pregnancy. This is because although it may prevent or reduce the severity of the infection in the mother, it does not appear to prevent congenital rubella in the infected child.

Preventing rubella

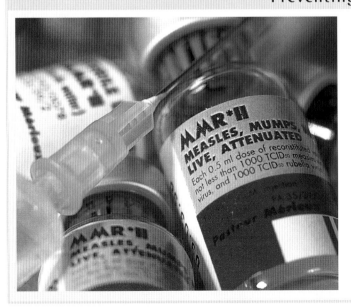

Immunization against rubella began in the UK and most developed countries around 1970. At that time, the vaccine was only offered to schoolgirls and susceptible adult females. Rubella vaccination is now given to all children as part of the MMR (measles, mumps and rubella) vaccine. The rubella vaccine is a live vaccine which has had its disease-producing potential scientifically reduced to almost zero.

Immunization is effective in over 98 per cent of cases and it

In the UK, the combined MMR vaccine is given to nearly all children at 12–15 months of age. Since 1996, a second dose at age 3–5 has also been given.

usually confers lifelong immunity. It is given at 12 to 15 months of age and, in some countries, a second vaccination with MMR is recommended either at primary school or secondary school entry.

The vaccine is usually free from any problems or side effects, but a rash with fever and enlarged glands can appear seven to 10 days after vaccination. In post-pubertal females, temporary arthritis can occur two to three weeks after immunization.

Contra-indications to vaccination include immune system deficiency due to illness or drug treatment. HIV-positive children can, however, safely be given rubella vaccine. Pregnancy and recent blood transfusion are other contra-indications.

Chickenpox

Chickenpox is a common, highly infectious illness in childhood, characterized by an itchy rash of crops of tiny blisters. The disease is caused by the varicella-zoster virus, a type of herpes virus.

Chickenpox mainly affects children; most people have had it by the time they reach adulthood.

CHILDREN AT RISK
Fortunately, in young children the illness tends to be mild. However, in babies it can be severe and even life-threatening. Children with impaired immunity are particularly at risk of severe and, in some cases, fatal complications. This group includes those taking corticosteroids and those having chemotherapy for cancer.

DISEASE TRANSMISSION
The varicella-zoster infection can be transmitted in airborne droplets when a person coughs or sneezes. It can also be passed on by touching the lesions of the rash, or clothes that have come into contact with the lesions. Less often, it is passed on from a person with shingles.

INFECTIOUS PERIOD
Chickenpox is infectious from 1–2 days before the rash appears until the lesions have scabbed over (usually 5–6 days). The rash can last for up to two weeks.

Chickenpox is a highly infectious disease that usually affects children. It causes an itchy rash of red spots that may cover the trunk, scalp, face and limbs.

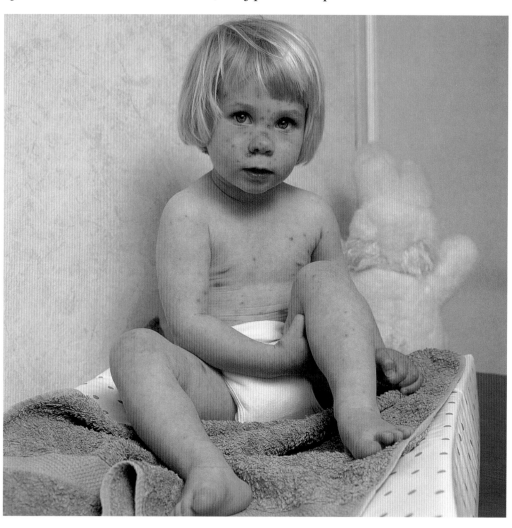

Symptoms of chickenpox

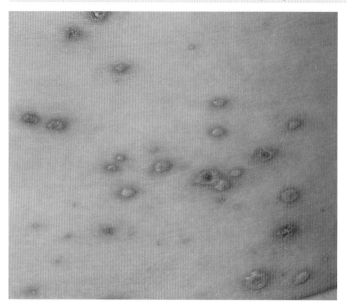

The main feature of chickenpox is the rash of tiny blisters, which begins to appear up to three weeks after contact with an infected person.

COMMON SYMPTOMS
Other symptoms, such as a mild fever, lethargy, headache, and poor appetite, may start a day or two before the rash develops. Swollen glands may also be a feature. Although usually mild or even absent in children, the flu-like symptoms of chickenpox are often severe in adults and may be debilitating.

Chickenpox is characterized by a distinctive rash. The lesions pass through several stages: red spots which then become blisters, before crusting over.

CHICKENPOX RASH
The rash appears in the form of small red spots, which are at first flat and then become raised. These spots rapidly develop into tiny blisters within a matter of hours. The rash may affect any area of the body, although the lesions mainly tend to develop on the face, scalp, and trunk. The number of lesions varies from a few to several hundred.

Within five to six days the blisters dry and then scab over. Red spots and scabs can be seen at the same time in an area of skin. The rash is very itchy, which can be distressing for children and may lead to problems with sleeping. Shallow ulcers may develop in the lining of the mouth, causing discomfort when eating.

Complications of chickenpox

Repeated scratching of the itchy lesions can lead to scarring. Scratching also increases the risk of the lesions becoming infected with bacteria. If lesions are not scratched or infected, they usually heal well without the problem of residual scarring.

LIFE-THREATENING RISKS
The other complications, including pneumonia and encephalitis (inflammation of the brain) are uncommon in healthy children, but are major life-threatening risks for children with impaired immunity.

Scratching chickenpox blisters can leave scars after the rash has disappeared. Keeping a child's fingernails short can prevent this happening.

Treating chickenpox

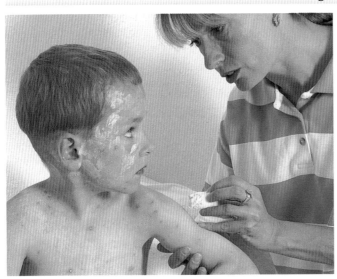

The diagnosis can be made easily from the appearance of the rash. Healthy children usually need only simple treatment to relieve symptoms. This includes taking paracetamol to bring down a fever, and applying calamine lotion and having cool baths every few hours to relieve itching. Taking promethazine (antihistamine) syrup may help to calm children who are distressed by the itching.

Aspirin should not be given to children under 12 years of age,

Applying calamine lotion can relieve itching caused by the chickenpox rash. Regular applications soothe the skin and reduce the desire to scratch.

as it is implicated in the development of Reye's syndrome, a rare but serious disorder that causes inflammation of the brain and the liver.

An affected child's fingernails should be kept short and clean to avoid scratching and minimize the risk of bacterial infection and scarring.

Pregnancy

If contracted during pregnancy, chickenpox can cause fetal abnormalities. Fortunately most women have become immune before reaching child-bearing age. However, if there is any uncertainty, medical advice should be sought immediately.

The varicella-zoster virus, responsible for chickenpox, can be passed from mother to fetus. However, most pregnant women are immune to the disease.

Severe cases

For children with impaired immunity, urgent medical attention is required. If there is any possibility of contact with chickenpox, an injection of immunoglobulin may be recommended. This is a preparation of antibodies against the varicella-zoster virus, which may prevent or reduce the severity of the illness.

HOSPITAL TREATMENT
For children with reduced immunity who have contracted the illness, urgent treatment in hospital with an intravenous antiviral drug is required. This

Babies who contract chickenpox are at risk of developing serious complications. They may need intensive nursing and require intravenous antiviral drugs.

needs to be commenced as soon as possible to give the best chance of it being effective.

Small babies in whom chickenpox is suspected also require early medical review.

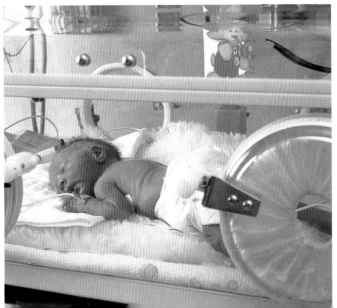

They are also at increased risk of developing severe complications and may need intravenous antiviral therapy. There is currently no vaccine licensed for chickenpox in the UK.

Hand, foot and mouth disease

Hand, foot and mouth disease is a viral infection which generally affects children of pre-school age. The virus tends to occur in summer and early autumn and produces distinctive symptoms.

Hand, foot and mouth disease (so called because these are the parts of the body affected) is a viral infection of childhood. It occurs more commonly in children under four years of age.

VIRAL DISEASE
Hand, foot and mouth disease is one of many childhood viral diseases that are associated with fever and a rash.

Most of these illnesses cannot be specifically diagnosed, nor is the virus that causes them known. The reason for this is that there are many thousands of viruses that cause non-specific viral illnesses and it is therefore not possible to diagnose each viral illness with any degree of certainty.

DISTINCTIVE SYMPTOMS
Hand, foot and mouth disease, however, can usually be diagnosed because of the distinctive symptoms suffered. The illness is caused by a particular virus, known as the Coxsackie virus.

INFECTIVITY
Hand, foot and mouth disease is mildly contagious, although not as contagious as other viral diseases. In chickenpox, for example, there is a 90 per cent chance that non-immune people in contact with an infected person will contract the disease.

The infection is spread by droplets of mucus in the atmosphere. These droplets contain virus particles and are expelled into the air after an infected child coughs or sneezes. The infection can also be spread by close personal contact, such as kissing. It normally occurs during the summer months and early autumn.

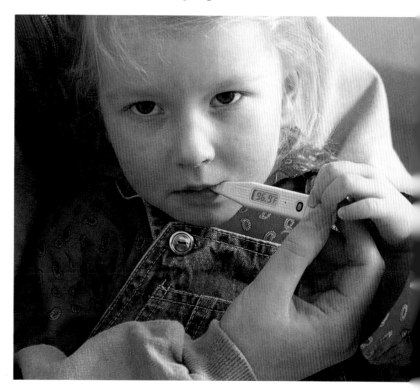

Hand, foot and mouth disease is a viral infection that tends to occur in younger children. One of the early symptoms of the infection is a mild fever.

Signs and symptoms of hand, foot and mouth disease

Children usually appear to be quite well immediately after infection with the Coxsackie virus. It takes around four days before affected children begin to show symptoms.

The four days following infection but prior to development of the illness are known as the incubation period. During this time the virus multiplies in the body until it produces symptoms.

FEVER
Initially, children appear only mildly unwell, with a fever. Almost all viral illnesses begin this way, and parents may suspect that their child has contracted a cold.

However, about two days after the onset of initial symptoms, a characteristic rash in the mouth and on the skin begins to appear. The rash usually takes the following form:
1 First, small vesicular (fluid-filled) spots appear in the mouth
2 The vesicles in the mouth may then burst and turn into ulcers. The mouth ulcers that result in hand, foot and mouth disease are usually quite small – around 3 mm in diameter. They are white with a red rim
3 Spots appear on the hands and feet. Initially, the spots are red and may be slightly raised.

The disease is characterized by a rash on the hands and/or feet. At first, the spots are red and may be raised – they then become blistered.

Oral blisters are common in children suffering from hand, foot and mouth disease. These blisters may burst and develop into small, painful, ulcers.

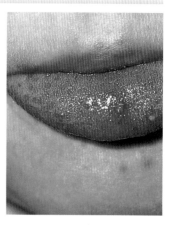

They then turn into small blisters similar to chickenpox.

Although the condition is referred to as hand, foot and mouth disease, the rash is not always found in all of these areas. In most cases, however, there will be mouth ulcers.

Affected children tend to be unwell for about one week. They then go on to make a complete recovery.

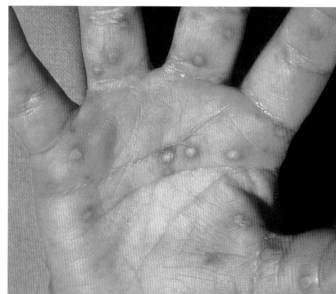

Treating hand, foot and mouth disease

There are no specific treatments for hand, foot and mouth disease or another
condition that is closely related to it – herpangina; neither responds to antibiotics.
However, there are a number of ways to ease discomfort in affected children.

Because hand, foot and mouth disease is a viral illness, there is no specific treatment that will cure the disease or shorten its duration – antibiotics are of no help in viral infections.

General measures can, however, help to make affected children feel more comfortable.

FEVER
There are several practical ways to reduce a child's fever. These include:
■ Giving regular doses of paracetamol syrup (such as Calpol or Disprol)
■ Removing heavy bedclothes, ventilating the room and using a portable fan
■ Tepid sponging – ice-cold water is best avoided since it can actually cause the internal body temperature to rise.

SOOTHING THE RASH
Although not as intensely itchy as a chickenpox rash, the rash that appears with hand, foot and mouth disease can be very uncomfortable. If itching is a problem, calamine lotion can be applied to the affected areas several times a day to soothe the skin.

MOUTH DISCOMFORT
One of the main problems in hand, foot and mouth disease is mouth ulcers. These are usually extremely painful and can make children reluctant to eat or drink. Over-the-counter gels containing local anaesthetic can help to reduce the discomfort in the mouth. A medicated mouthwash can soothe ulcers and also help to prevent bacterial infection.

FOOD AND DRINK
Whether or not these treatments are helpful, it is very important to encourage children to eat and, particularly, to drink. Cold liquids, such as milk or diluted juice, can be soothing, although orange juice and other citrus juices can irritate mouth ulcers.

Soft, bland foods, such as bread, scrambled eggs, ice-cream and jelly are easier for children to take than chewy and spicy foods.

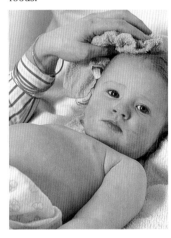

Tepid sponging is an effective way of bringing down a child's high temperature. Other methods include ventilating the room and using paracetamol.

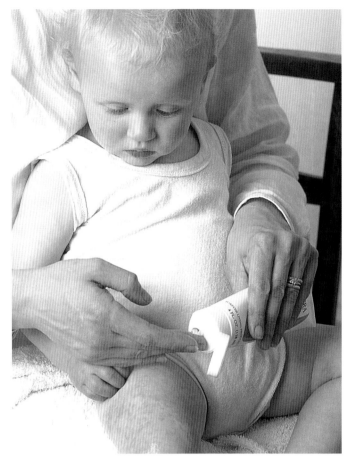

The rash occurring in hand, foot and mouth disease can cause itchiness and irritation. Calamine lotion often helps to relieve symptoms of itching.

Herpangina

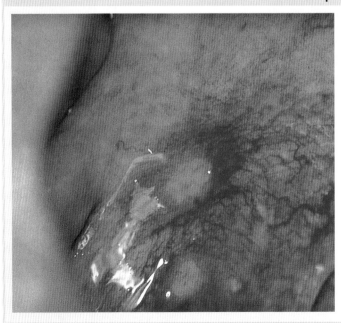

In herpangina, only the mouth is affected. A small number of mouth ulcers normally appear, commonly around the palate, tonsils or uvula.

Herpangina is a condition very closely related to hand, foot and mouth disease. It is also caused by a Coxsackie virus, and is usually spread by droplets of saliva in the atmosphere after an infected child coughs or sneezes.

Symptoms
Herpangina differs from hand, foot and mouth disease in that it is an acute infection confined to the mouth. It can produce 2–14 ulcers, the usual number being 5 or 6.

The ulcers are about 1–2 mm in diameter and can be seen at the back of the palate, around the tonsils and on the uvula (small extension of the soft palate which hangs from the roof of the mouth).

In its very early stages, herpangina may be mistaken for tonsillitis. This is because, initially, white spots may be confined to the tonsil area alone.

As with hand, foot and mouth disease, affected children will have a fever and will look and feel unwell; the main problem, however, is that it is very painful for a child to eat or drink.

Treating herpangina
Herpangina is treated in the same way as hand, foot and mouth disease. As herpangina is caused by the same virus, antibiotics are again of no use.

Children with herpangina are usually unwell for around two to five days.

Head lice

Familiar to parents with young children, head lice can in fact be a problem at any age. Although an infestation with these parasites is not pleasant, it rarely has serious effects and can be readily treated.

Head lice (*Pediculus capitis*) are tiny, wingless, parasitical insects that depend on humans for their survival. They are 2–3 mm long, live close to the skin for warmth and feed by sucking tiny amounts of blood from the scalp. Despite the common belief that they can be caught from animals, head lice only live on humans. In fact, they are so specialized to living on humans that lice in Africa prefer oval hair shafts, while those in North America prefer round shafts.

Lice rarely, if ever, cause physical health problems other than itching of the scalp. They do not carry or transmit disease, nor are they an indicator of poor hygiene.

The females lay their whitish, oval eggs (nits) on individual hairs within a centimetre of the scalp. Nits found much further down the shaft of hair are old and will have already hatched. The female can lay up to 10 eggs a day and will lay 50–100 eggs before she dies. They take about 7 to 10 days to hatch.

WHO GETS LICE?

People of any age can suffer a head lice infestation, but children of school age are most susceptible. Head lice can walk from head to head if they are in direct contact – which often happens when children play together – but they cannot swim, fly, hop or jump.

Life cycle of a head louse

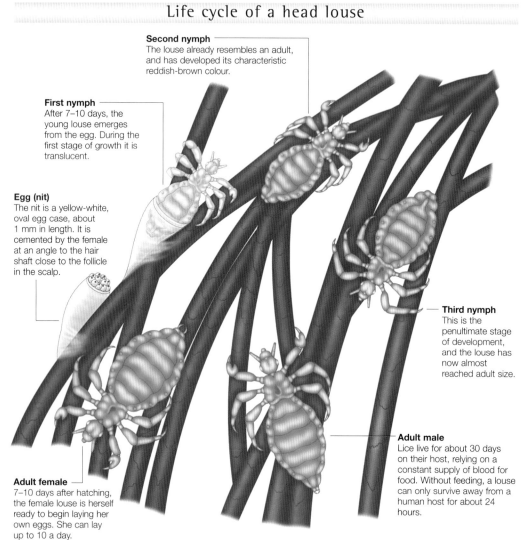

Second nymph
The louse already resembles an adult, and has developed its characteristic reddish-brown colour.

First nymph
After 7–10 days, the young louse emerges from the egg. During the first stage of growth it is translucent.

Egg (nit)
The nit is a yellow-white, oval egg case, about 1 mm in length. It is cemented by the female at an angle to the hair shaft close to the follicle in the scalp.

Third nymph
This is the penultimate stage of development, and the louse has now almost reached adult size.

Adult male
Lice live for about 30 days on their host, relying on a constant supply of blood for food. Without feeding, a louse can only survive away from a human host for about 24 hours.

Adult female
7–10 days after hatching, the female louse is herself ready to begin laying her own eggs. She can lay up to 10 a day.

Lice detection

Adult lice are difficult to see in hair, but they will obviously be present before eggs are laid. The main symptom in the affected person is an itchy scalp, but this can take up to three months to develop after the initial infestation. Lice droppings may fall onto the pillow at night, and this is a good indicator of their presence.

Combing is the most effective way of checking for head lice if an infestation is suspected. The procedure is sometimes referred to as the 'detection ritual'.
■ A plastic detection comb (available from the chemist), good lighting and an ordinary comb are necessary for detection.

■ The hair should be washed as normal with ordinary shampoo, and then conditioned. Some authorities advise using oil rather than conditioner.
■ A white towel or sheet is then placed around the base of the head and the wet hair is combed with the ordinary comb.
■ The hair is combed outwards from the scalp with the detection comb; the comb is wiped on the towel after each stroke.
■ The conditioner or oil makes the hair slippery so that lice have difficulty gripping and will be more easily combed out.
■ It takes about 15 minutes to perform the detection process.

A special nit comb is the simplest method for detecting any lice in the hair.

Treatment options

Infestation with head lice can be irritating and embarrassing for the sufferer. Fortunately, there is a range of treatments available to combat the problem.

Combing & chemicals

Recently, there has been some concern about various lice treatments available over the counter as they are insecticides and may damage the hair and cause skin irritation.

As a result, some doctors have advocated regular and methodical wet combing with conditioner or oil (described on the previous page) as a safe means of treatment. Although this is an excellent way to detect lice, there has been no evidence to suggest that it is effective for treating the problem. However, if this method is used, the routine has to be repeated every three days for two weeks. This will remove lice emerging from the eggs between treatments.

The definitive treatment is by using chemical lotions. There are three main groups: pyrethroids, malathion and carbaryl. They are all effective, although there have been reports of resistance. In the past, it was advised that if one member of a household was found to have lice the rest of the household should be treated, but this is unnecessary. Instead, the advice is to inform all household members, friends and close contacts so that they can each perform the detection ritual. Only those with live, active lice need to be chemically treated.

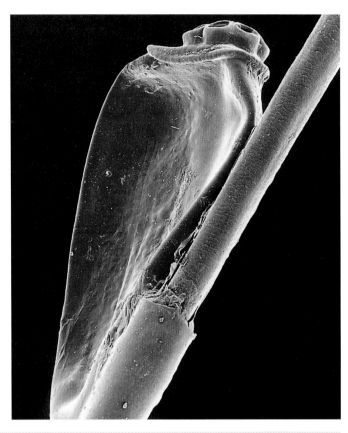

Female head lice cement their egg cases directly onto hair shafts, here magnified 130 times.

Preventing the spread of head lice

A number of simple steps will stop the infestation spreading:
■ Combing regularly leads to early detection.
■ Vacuum the house thoroughly to remove any hairs which may have nits attached to them.
■ Wash all clothes – especially headgear – and bedding, at 50 °C for at least 10 minutes to ensure the eggs have been destroyed. Adult lice die after 5 minutes at this temperature.
■ Anything that cannot be

laundered (such as soft toys) should be sealed in a plastic bag for three weeks. This gives time for lice to hatch and starve.

REINFESTATION OR TREATMENT FAILURE
Many supposed cases of infestation are in fact due to imagined lice, misdiagnosis or inadequate or inappropriate treatment. Reinfestation may result when young lice which had not hatched at the time of

An exceptionally bad infestation is shown here. This causes intense itching and can lead to an infection of the scalp.

Head lice have adapted successfully to living solely on humans, relying on us for food and habitation.

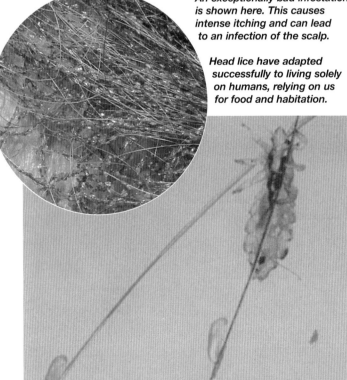

Parents should regularly examine their children's heads for signs of head lice. Close inspection of the scalp and careful combing are advised.

the first treatment emerge before the second application several days later. True reinfestation is usually from a close contact in the family or community. If the first course of treatment has failed then a second course using a different preparation should be considered. It may be advisable to do this with appropriate medical supervision.

HEAD LICE IN CHILDREN
The 'nit nurse' routines that used to be commonplace in schools were shown to be ineffective and are now rarely done. The sending out of 'lice alert' notices by schools is also unproductive as most schools will have pupils with lice at any one time. Parents can be convinced that

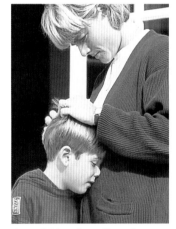

their children have lice when in fact they do not.

Health authorities leave the prime responsibility for detection to parents. The GP may ask for proof of infestation before initiating a course of treatment. The proof, such as a louse found after combing, may be stuck to a piece of paper with clear tape.

Applying chemicals

■ Hair dryers should not be used after applying lotions.
■ A contact time of 12 hours, or overnight, is recommended for lotions and liquids. A two hour treatment is probably insufficient.
■ Aqueous (water-based) preparations are thought to be better for asthmatic patients

than those which are solvent-based; small children should not be exposed to the alcohol fumes from some lotions.
■ It is advised that treatment is repeated after seven days to ensure that all newly hatched lice are destroyed.
■ Products claiming to 'repel' lice are not recommended.

Dyspraxia

Dyspraxia refers to the inability of a child to perform and co-ordinate movements with accuracy. Therapy and support from parents and teachers can do much to improve the condition.

Dyspraxia is a common disorder of child development in which the child's ability to carry out and co-ordinate movements is significantly impaired. The condition is also known as developmental co-ordination disorder or, sometimes, persistent clumsiness.

PERSISTENT CLUMSINESS

Dyspraxia affects up to 10 per cent of schoolchildren, most of whom are boys.

Many normal children go through a clumsy phase during development, but most grow out of it. In children with dyspraxia, however, the tendency towards clumsiness persists and interferes with everyday life and/or with progress at school. Behavioural problems are common in children with the condition.

EARLY DIAGNOSIS

Early identification and treatment of dyspraxia is important in reducing the chances of educational and behavioural difficulties occurring.

Around one schoolchild in 10 suffers from dyspraxia. Affected children can have difficulty with schoolwork and experience behavioural problems.

Identifying children with dyspraxia

The symptoms and severity of the condition are very variable in affected children, who may:
■ Frequently fall down
■ Knock things over
■ Spill drinks and eat messily
■ Have difficulty in performing physical activities such as riding a bicycle or playing ball games
■ Have problems using their hands accurately for tasks such as doing up buttons, tying shoelaces or using cutlery
■ Have difficulties with eye and hand co-ordination
■ Seem generally disorganized, often lose things and become muddled about orders of sequence
■ Have problems in interpreting what they see and in understanding how objects are arranged. For example, they often put their clothes on back to front and their shoes on the wrong feet
■ Be overactive, with short concentration spans and may not be able to cope with more than one or two instructions at a time
■ Have speech difficulties.

EDUCATIONAL PROBLEMS

Children with dyspraxia are otherwise bright and intelligent, but tend to have problems with their schoolwork. They often:
■ Find it difficult to write neatly and legibly
■ Have problems with reading
■ Are slow in their work
■ Tire easily
■ Become frustrated and discouraged, especially if they are repeatedly rebuked or punished by parents or teachers who do not recognize that they have genuine difficulties
■ Develop a fear of demanding activities such as sport and games

Some children with dyspraxia have difficulty carrying out specific tasks such as putting shoes on. Their ability to carry out other activities is normal.

Frequent tumbles, such as falling off a bicycle, are common in children with dyspraxia. Frustration can cause affected children to become withdrawn.

■ Suffer from a lack of confidence and self-esteem
■ Have difficulty in making friends and may be left out or bullied by peers
■ Become anxious, withdrawn, depressed or aggressive, and may start to avoid school
■ Develop aches and pains due to anxiety about their abilities.

POSSIBLE CAUSES

The underlying cause of dyspraxia is unknown. Studies have shown links between dyspraxia and premature delivery, very low birth weight and lack of oxygen at birth.

Possible explanations include faulty co-ordination between different areas of the brain, slow development in parts of the brain, or a very slight degree of brain damage. Genetic factors are probably important in many cases.

Assessment and diagnosis

Dyspraxia is often identified when a child encounters problems at school. The child is then referred to a paediatrician or school doctor for assessment.

OBSERVATION

The doctor will test the child's movement and co-ordination by observing the performance of tasks such as hopping, walking heel-to-toe, building bricks, threading beads and copying shapes. A careful physical examination is important to rule out any neurological disorder, such as mild cerebral palsy.

Children with speech problems are usually referred to a speech and language therapist. Significant educational problems should be assessed by an educational psychologist. Vision tests may also be necessary to check for any associated visual problems.

If problems are encountered at school, a child may be referred to a paediatrician. The doctor will set the child a variety of tasks to check co-ordination.

Treating dyspraxia

There is no cure for dyspraxia but children can be helped if their symptoms are spotted at an early stage and their difficulties explained. Treatment can improve self-confidence and performance; it may involve input from occupational therapists, physiotherapists, speech and language therapists, teachers and parents. Child guidance can help to reduce anxiety or other emotional difficulties in the child and family if needed.

THERAPY

Occupational therapy and/or physiotherapy are important aspects of treatment. The aim is to gradually learn motor tasks and to practise them until competent. Various methods may be used, including:
■ involvement in movement and gym groups to help improve balance, co-ordination and control of body movements
■ the use of techniques such as drawing around the body, identifying different textures and singing-with-action games
■ the encouragement of activities such as dancing and swimming to instil an awareness of rhythm
■ exercises that improve self-help skills in tasks such as eating and dressing, thus increasing independence.

IN SCHOOL

Careful teaching at school can make a huge difference. Teachers should be made aware that the child has specific problems and is not being lazy or careless. Children should be taught in gradual stages and allowed extra time for classwork.

Writing can be made easier if the child's table and chair are at the correct height and the table-top is slanted. Special easy-grip pencils can be useful.

A Statement of Special Educational Needs from the local education authority may be required, entitling the child to additional help at school.

AT HOME

Parents should encourage their children to pursue activities for which they show an aptitude and which will help them to develop skills. For example, joining in at a leisure centre, gym club or adventure playground can help to improve physical skills, as can helping with gardening and housework at home.

Hand and visual skills and eye–hand co-ordination can be improved by activities such as drawing, tracing, model-making, sewing, cutting and sticking, and playing musical instruments.

Children with dyspraxia can often be helped with music therapy. Playing musical instruments encourages co-ordination and self-confidence.

Outlook

Most children with dyspraxia show improvement with time, but are likely to remain more unco-ordinated than other children. With practice, they may appear not to have obvious difficulty with particular tasks, but problems may re-emerge when they are challenged by new tasks.

Clumsy children who are not given additional support early on are more likely to continue to have movement, learning and emotional problems during their teenage years. Individuals, however, differ in the extent to which they learn to cope with their continuing difficulties.

Dyslexia

Dyslexia is a developmental disorder that affects a child's ability to learn how to read and write. Early recognition of the condition can help affected children to achieve their full potential.

Dyslexia is a chronic neurological disorder that manifests as a specific learning disability. Affected children have great difficulty in learning to read and spell despite being of normal or above-normal intelligence.

Dyslexia affects the individual's ability to recognize how words (and sometimes numbers) appear on the page. Affected individuals have difficulty in recognizing word sounds (phonemes) and placing these and whole words in the correct order when reading or writing.

POSSIBLE CAUSES

There is no universally accepted single cause of dyslexia. Most experts accept that it is due to specific anomalies within the brain, the underlying cause of which is unknown. Faulty interaction between the right and left halves of the brain is suspected and it is believed that dyslexia is a problem of the left hemisphere. Dysfunction of brain areas involved with language association (Wernicke's area) and speech production (Broca's area) is implicated.

There is a marked hereditary tendency and a strong genetic link – dyslexia tends to run in families.

Dyslexic children have difficulty in placing whole words in the correct order while reading or writing. This causes problems in acquiring language skills.

Characteristics of dyslexia

Dyslexia is a varied problem; although all dyslexics have difficulty in acquiring reading and writing skills (usually out of proportion to their overall intelligence), they may exhibit other traits. The characteristic clues are:
■ Difficulty in sorting out sounds within words
■ Difficulty in remembering names of letters, numbers and colours

The difficulties that children with dyslexia face with written language may lead to feelings of hopelessness and isolation from their peers.

■ Difficulty in blending sounds or rhyming words
■ Confusing letters and words with similar structures: thus 'd' becomes 'b', 'h' becomes 'n', 'm' becomes 'w', 'was' becomes 'saw', and 'on' becomes 'no'
■ Clumsiness or lack of coordination
■ Confusing left and right
■ Limited attention span and concentration
■ Becoming easily frustrated
■ Tendency to be disorganized
■ Inability to plan ahead; confusion between tomorrow, today and yesterday
■ Problems in learning basic mathematical concepts.

Effects of dyslexia

Although dyslexia is present from birth, problems arise in the educational setting when affected children first encounter written language, and it is here that dyslexia is first identified. However, dyslexia should be suspected in pre-school children who show delayed language production, especially when there is a family history of dyslexia.

LEARNING DISABILITIES

Lessons are very difficult for dyslexic children, who may try hard and spend more time on work than their peers, but to no avail. Untreated dyslexics simply do not possess the required skills; even if they recognize that their work is wrong, they cannot put it right. They become frustrated and bored, and find it hard to concentrate. They may even avoid doing school-work because they know that it is impossible for them to do well. Doing badly at school often undermines self-confidence, which may isolate affected children still further.

An angry, frustrated, bored and misunderstood child usually develops behavioural problems at school and at home. Worse still, if dyslexia is not recognized early, the condition can have devastating effects not only on a child's school life but beyond.

Parents, teachers and others often fail to recognize that there is a problem and fall into the trap of believing the 'dyslexia myths'.

Dyslexia is a development disorder that affects a child's ability to read and write. The condition can create serious emotional problems.

Early identification of dyslexia is vital in an affected child. If the problem goes unnoticed, it can lead to severe learning and communication problems.

Misconceptions about dyslexia

There are several common myths or misunderstandings about dyslexia:
- Dyslexics are not 'stupid' – individuals with any level of intellectual ability can be affected
- Dyslexics are not 'lazy', 'making silly mistakes', 'careless' or 'not trying hard enough' – it is a real problem for them to process information
- Dyslexics are not untalented
- Dyslexics are not insensitive
- Dyslexics do not end up in dead-end jobs – once the problem has been recognized and managed effectively, there is no barrier to choosing from a wide range of careers.

Perpetuating such myths only delays early identification of the condition, causing more problems.

Dyslexia need not prevent academic success: Albert Einstein, one of the world's greatest thinkers, was dyslexic.

Incidence

Since the nature of dyslexia is so variable, the exact incidence is undetermined, but it is thought that four to five per cent of the UK population is affected.
- 375,000 British pupils (at all levels of education) are affected
- About two million people in the UK are severely affected
- Boys are more often affected than girls, by a ratio of three to one.

With 4–5 per cent of the population believed to be affected by dyslexia, on average one child in every class will need appropriate specialist teaching in school.

Diagnosing dyslexia

Dyslexia can be diagnosed by a series of tests. An early identification of the disorder, along with special teaching aids, can help in the overall development of affected children.

Children who do not progress at the expected rate, even when teaching is specifically targeted to improve any identified area of weakness, should be evaluated for dyslexia (or other specific learning difficulty). This evaluation is particularly important if a bright child appears to be progressing normally in spoken language.

ASSESSMENT

Any struggling child who faces difficulty in understanding reading, writing or arithmetic or in following instructions and remembering what they have been told, should be assessed.

Dyslexia is not purely concerned with reading difficulties, and a child must be assessed not only from a reading point of view, but also with a view to their language skills, level of intellect and physical state (hearing, sight and neurological).

TESTING FOR DYSLEXIA

■ Physical tests are rarely diagnostic for dyslexia, but they may exclude other unsuspected causes of the child's problems; for example, undiagnosed epilepsy
■ Social and emotional or behavioural tests are often of use in planning treatment and gauging the child's progress
■ Reading evaluation should look for patterns in the child's errors. The test includes word recognition and analysis; fluency (accuracy and rate of recognition in passage reading); and reading and listening comprehension
■ The child's understanding of vocabulary and the reading process, along with their thinking and reasoning skills should also be included in diagnosing dyslexia
■ Decoding skills are tested by checking the child's ability to name letter sounds, to split words into pronounceable segments and to integrate these sounds into recognizable words
■ Language skill tests involve assessing the understanding and use of language by the child
■ 'Intelligence' (cognitive ability) testing of memory, attention and reasoning is essential for a specific diagnosis
■ Psychological assessment is necessary since behavioural problems can complicate dyslexia.

A child struggling with writing or reading should be tested for dyslexia. A missed diagnosis can have the damaging consequence of life-long learning disability.

Making the diagnosis

Dyslexia is a medical matter in origin, but an educational matter in recognition and treatment.

Parents may have their suspicions, but teachers are best placed to identify children with learning difficulties. Any child with learning difficulties must have their educational needs assessed by their school.

All UK schools and government-funded providers of pre-school education must abide by the Special Educational Needs (SEN) Code of Practice, as part of the 1996 Education Act. The Code gives practical advice in helping schools and education authorities meet their responsibilities towards children with learning disabilities. One of its core themes is to promote early identification and assessment of such children in order to help them achieve their full potential.

SPECIAL LEARNING PLANS

Parents, carers, teachers and health professionals all play a part in picking up any diagnostic clue that would highlight the need for an assessment.

Each school has an SEN co-ordinator who will carry out

In this test, a dyslexic boy listens to tones and makes his choices, which are recorded by a computer. Such tests help to gauge the level of dyslexia.

a school-based assessment of a child with difficulties. However, information from additional professionals, including an educational psychologist and possibly the child's GP or health visitor, may well be considered.

The assessment delivers a profile of the child's strengths and weaknesses and allows an individual education plan to be drawn up. In the majority of children, both the assessment and the plan can be handled within the school without the need to take the child out of mainstream classes.

A few children have special needs which cannot be met from within the school's resources. The local education authority would issue an official 'Statement of special educational needs' to meet the needs of these children.

Treating dyslexia

The goal of diagnosis is not a cure as such, but to allow the required skilled, specialist teaching programme to be put in place. This is because the cause is most often congenital and undetermined, with no available drug treatment.

Dyslexic children need flexible teaching arrangements and help with the following:
■ Direct teaching of phonic skills (recognition of word sounds and their order within words) and word decoding and analysis
■ Help with acquiring language and literacy skills
■ Help in organizing and co-ordinating written language
■ Help in using different forms of communication.

Dyslexic people learn to accommodate their condition to a greater or lesser degree, depending on their own personality and the support they receive from home and school. Some individuals experience difficulties throughout their lives, especially in conditions of stress, but the majority learn to develop strategies to enable them to cope most of the time.

Close working between teachers and parents will help the overall development of a dyslexic child. Flexible teaching arrangements can be tailored to meet the needs of affected children.

Prognosis for children with dyslexia

Despite dyslexia being a life-long problem, many dyslexics develop functional reading skills, if not full literacy. With early recognition and provision of the extra teaching they require, dyslexic children can learn to read, spell and write to a level equivalent to that of their peers, but these skills will always be difficult.

If an early diagnosis is made within the first two years of starting school (between the ages of five and seven), over 80 per cent of dyslexic children can be brought up to normal classroom standards by a structured individual educational plan and appropriate specialist teaching.

Any delay in diagnosis makes such an improvement both more difficult to deliver in a mainstream setting and less likely to be achieved in the long run.

Many dyslexic children succeed academically and go on to higher education. Some have special talents in, for instance, architecture or engineering.

Chapter Four

Diseases, Conditions and their Treatment

This section describes a number of childhood conditions that are uncommon, but which – when they occur – have more serious consequences. They include congenital conditions (those that a baby is born with), such as some heart defects, muscular dystrophy and cystic fibrosis, severe infections such as meningitis and surgical emergencies, like appendicitis. You can also read about illnesses that affect children from different parts of the world and which involve long-term treatment; these include thalassaemia, Reye's syndrome and rickets. Some childhood cancers are described, as is the specialized care that children who are terminally ill and their families receive.

Gastroenteritis

This condition is characterized by bouts of diarrhoea, which can be severe and lead to serious dehydration. It is caused by bacterial infection, and it is particularly common in childhood.

Gastroenteritis is a disease characterized by inflammation of the stomach and intestines. The commonest presentation is diarrhoea with or without vomiting. It is particularly common in childhood and, although usually a mild disease, it can be severe and sometimes fatal. In older children, abdominal pain may be a prominent feature.

CAUSES OF INFECTION
Gastroenteritis is an infectious disease. It can be caused by bacteria (*Salmonella*, *Shigella*), protozoa (*Giardia*) or yeasts. The most common type of causative organism, however, is a virus – in particular, the rotavirus. This accounts for around 60 per cent of all severe diarrhoeal disease. After an incubation period of around one to three days, it produces a self-limiting diarrhoeal illness, which may last up to six days.

NATURAL PROTECTION
Infants under six months of age usually have some degree of natural protection against rotavirus gastroenteritis but maternity hospitals may harbour virulent strains which can overcome this natural immunity. Rotavirus gastroenteritis has a worldwide distribution. It typically causes winter epidemics in developed countries. In developing countries, however, it can produce a year-round threat with a summer peak.

The virus can be detected in the faeces by electron microscopy or by immunological procedures such as enzyme-linked immunosorbent assay (ELISA) or latex agglutination. There is no vaccine currently available to counter rotavirus infection but several candidate vaccines are being evaluated.

The symptoms of gastroenteritis include fever, diarrhoea and abdominal pain. Dehydration can cause serious complications.

This micrograph shows rotaviruses, which can cause gastroenteritis. They are so named because of their wheel-like appearance.

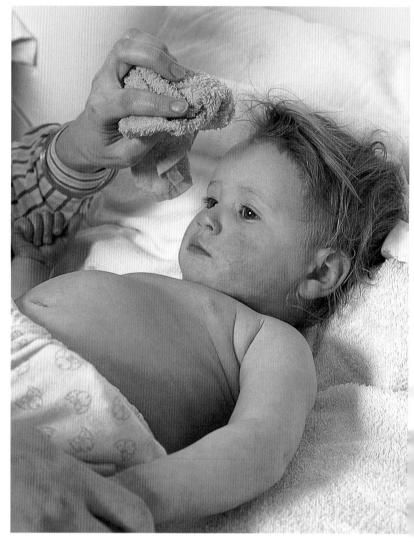

Symptoms of gastroenteritis

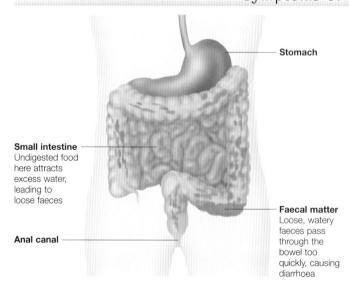

Stomach

Small intestine
Undigested food here attracts excess water, leading to loose faeces

Anal canal

Faecal matter
Loose, watery faeces pass through the bowel too quickly, causing diarrhoea

The main problem encountered with gastroenteritis is not the infection itself but the potential for an affected child to become dehydrated because the bowel is not functioning normally.

DIGESTIVE PROBLEMS
The small bowel is the main site of digestion and reabsorption of broken-down protein, fat and carbohydrate. Dysfunction of the small intestine leads to incomplete digestion and absorption of food. The undigested food

Diarrhoea is the main symptom associated with gastroenteritis. It develops because food cannot be properly digested by the small intestine.

attracts excess water around it, leading to loose faeces.

The large bowel is responsible for the reabsorption of water from faecal material as it passes from the small intestine to the rectum. In gastroenteritis, there is an increased speed of transport of watery faecal material through the bowel with impaired water reabsorption, which further contributes to the development of diarrhoea.

It is unusual, though not rare, in developed countries for an affected child to become seriously dehydrated. In developing countries, however, dehydration due to gastroenteritis is the commonest cause of death in infants and young children.

Treating dehydration

Dehydration can occur as a result of gastroenteritis, and in rare, severe cases this can be fatal. Children suffering from the condition are encouraged to drink plenty of fluids, and a temporarily restricted diet may be recommended.

Dehydration is more likely to develop in infants than in older children. This is because young infants are small, with a large percentage of body water: in a newborn, body water accounts for 80 per cent of body weight, compared to 60 per cent at the age of one.

TYPES OF DEHYDRATION

Dehydration may be classified as mild, moderate or severe:

■ Mild dehydration is defined as being a loss of less than five per cent of body weight as water. Affected infants may have loss of normal skin elasticity and the child may appear lethargic and have sunken eyes

■ Moderately or severely dehydrated children (more than five per cent body water loss) are clearly unwell. The skin loses even more of its elasticity and it can have a mottled appearance, indicating poor circulation. The child will be very lethargic or comatose, and there will be detectable changes in the circulation. The pulse rate is increased and the volume of the pulse will be reduced.

Children with gastroenteritis should be encouraged to drink as much fluid as possible. Some doctors will prescribe oral rehydration products – electrolyte powders which are reconstituted with water and replenish water, salts and sugar lost during a diarrhoeal illness. Cows' milk and solids should be withheld for 24 hours. Following this rest period, fruit and vegetable puree and half-strength milk feeds may be re-introduced.

Some experts advocate the removal of milk and dairy products from the diet for up to one week. However, breast-fed children should continue breast-feeding during an episode of gastroenteritis.

MANAGEMENT

■ **Mild dehydration**
Infants with gastroenteritis and mild dehydration can be managed at home but should be assessed daily.

■ **Moderate or severe dehydration**
These children will require urgent hospital treatment, including intravenous fluid replacement

Daily weighing by a paediatrician is an important and practical method for gauging fluid loss or gain during a diarrhoeal illness such as gastroenteritis.

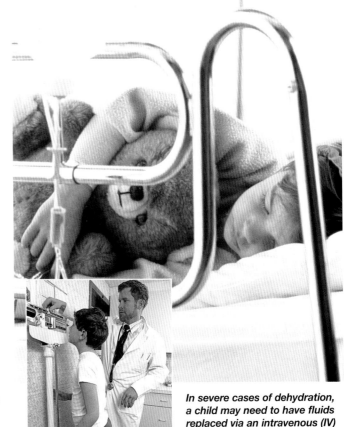

In severe cases of dehydration, a child may need to have fluids replaced via an intravenous (IV) drip. The IV fluid consists of a solution of saline and sugar.

Lactose intolerance

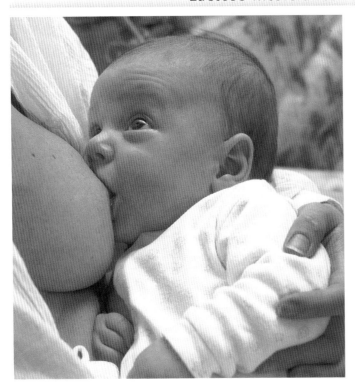

Diarrhoea may persist for up to six weeks after an episode of gastroenteritis. Providing the child is not dehydrated, no treatment is necessary. However, there may be persistent diarrhoea due to lactose intolerance.

Lactose is the predominant sugar in human and animal milk. It is broken down into absorbable sugar units (galactose and glucose) in the intestine by the enzyme lactase. In gastroenteritis, there is a temporary deficiency of lactase and the undigested lactose molecules attract water, making diarrhoea more prolonged.

In some infants, a deficiency of lactase enzyme may persist for several weeks and such babies may need to switch to a lactose-free soya-based milk.

Lactose is found in all milk, including breast milk. The inability to absorb this type of sugar can cause persistent bouts of diarrhoea in young babies.

Antibiotics

Use of antibiotics is rarely necessary in gastroenteritis. This is because antibiotics have not been shown to speed recovery from illness and they may worsen diarrhoea. Their use should be reserved for cases where the gastroenteritis has spread throughout the body. Antidiarrhoeal agents should also be generally avoided.

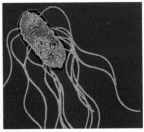

Salmonella bacteria live in the gut and can cause gastroenteritis. However, antibiotics may not be an effective form of treatment.

149

Appendicitis

Acute appendicitis is the most common condition requiring abdominal surgery in childhood, and appendix removal is a routine procedure. However, if diagnosis is missed, complications can arise.

Appendicitis is the most common surgical disease of the abdomen in childhood. The incidence peaks in the early teens, but it is very low in infancy. If appendicitis occurs in the under two age group it can be fatal without early diagnosis.

Appendicitis occurs when the neck of the appendix becomes blocked. This results in secretions from the inner lining of the appendix accumulating in the lumen (central space) of the appendix and impairing the blood supply from the appendicular artery. Once the blood supply is impaired, bacteria from the intestine infects this weak site. The sequence of events that ensues if treatment is not instituted is illustrated (right).

COMPLICATIONS

The disease runs a much more rapid course in children than it does in adults. If appendicitis is not treated by surgical removal, the condition can become much more serious, sometimes leading to an abscess. If perforation takes place at the site of the abscess, infected material can spill out into the abdominal cavity, leading to generalized peritonitis (inflammation of the abdominal lining).

Progression of appendicitis without treatment

1 Normal appendix – a healthy appendix may lie in an unusual position, causing pain and the suspicion of appendicitis.

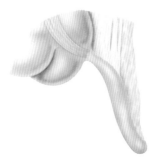

2 Inflamed appendix – at this first stage, the inflammation is confined to the mucous membrane.

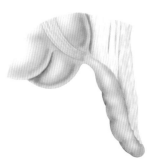

3 Infected appendix – the appendix now appears enlarged and thickened and is bright or dark red.

4 Gangrenous appendix – the formation of abscesses in the wall of the appendix results in a build up of pressure.

5 Perforated appendix – this can lead to peritonitis (inflammation of the peritoneum), which can be fatal.

6 Appendiceal abscess – localized pus in the abdominal cavity can spread and cause generalized peritonitis.

Structure and position of the appendix

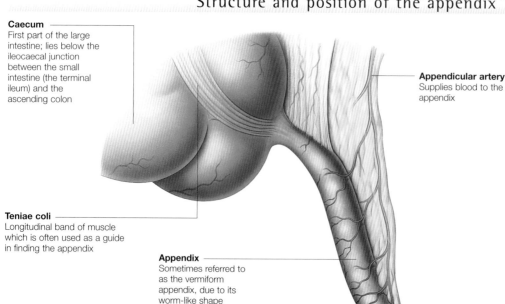

Caecum
First part of the large intestine; lies below the ileocaecal junction between the small intestine (the terminal ileum) and the ascending colon

Teniae coli
Longitudinal band of muscle which is often used as a guide in finding the appendix

Appendix
Sometimes referred to as the vermiform appendix, due to its worm-like shape

Appendicular artery
Supplies blood to the appendix

The appendix is a finger-like structure located at the beginning of the large intestine. To date, the function of the appendix is not understood, and it is regarded as a vestigial (redundant) structure from our evolutionary past. Some surgeons routinely remove the appendix during other abdominal operations.

Appendicitis is the term given to inflammation of the appendix, and the operation to surgically remove it is called an appendicectomy. This is a relatively quick and straightforward procedure.

The appendix lies in the lower right of the abdominal cavity. It is attached at its upper end to the caecum, at the beginning of the large intestine.

Symptoms of appendicitis

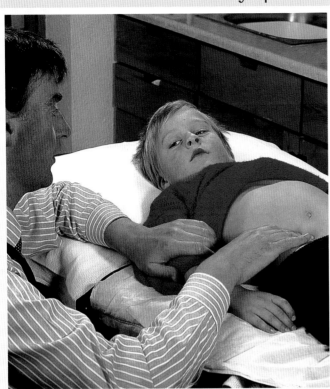

Pain is the first and most important feature of appendicitis. Initially, the pain is felt around the navel and slowly migrates to the right lower part of the abdomen. Nausea and vomiting occur shortly after, and loss of appetite invariably occurs.

An examination will reveal that the child is suddenly unwell with a slight flush of the cheeks, walks slowly and is bent over. They may prefer to bend their legs when lying down. The tongue may be dry from lack of fluids.

Other symptoms include:
■ A low-grade fever (this is usually present)
■ The right lower part of the abdomen is painful to the touch
■ The child tenses the abdominal muscles when touched in the right lower abdomen.

When appendicitis is suspected, the doctor will carefully examine the child's abdomen. A physical examination reveals tenderness when the right lower abdomen is palpated.

However, there are other conditions that have symptoms similar to those of appendicitis, which include:
■ Gastro-enteritis – abdominal pain
■ Urine infection – fever, lower abdominal pain
■ Constipation – loss of appetite, abdominal pain
■ Pelvic infection – fever, right-sided abdominal pain, loss of appetite.

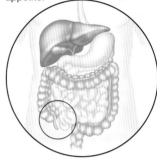

The appendix (circled) is situated about 4 cm beneath the navel and to the right. Its function is not understood.

Surgical procedure

Once appendicitis is suspected, the child is admitted to a hospital. Local anaesthetic cream is applied to enable the pain-free insertion of a drip to improve hydration. Blood samples are taken to help with the diagnosis, and if there is doubt about the diagnosis, X-rays and ultrasound may be performed. A urine sample may be taken to exclude the possibility of a urinary tract infection.

PRE-OPERATIVE
Once the decision to operate has been made, the operative procedure is explained to the child and parents, and the parents are given a consent form to sign which gives the doctors permission to go ahead with operative treatment. The consent form explains the legal rights of the parents. The child then changes into a theatre gown and the nurse will check their temperature, pulse, blood pressure and breathing rhythm.

Questions are asked about allergies, previous operations, illnesses and the timing of the last food intake. An anaesthetist will assess the child and ask more questions. The parents accompany the child into the anaesthetic room in the theatre complex. The child may be given a choice of anaesthesia – either by gas inhalation or via injection through a drip –

and a video may be played to distract the child while the appropriate anaesthesia is introduced. Once the child is asleep, the parents return to the ward and the anaesthetic team further manage the child and prepare for pain relief.

INTRA-OPERATIVE
The patient is wheeled into the operating room. The operation site on the abdomen is prepared with antiseptic solutions, and a 4–6 cm incision is made. The abdomen is entered and the appendix identified. The appendix is then mobilized (freed from the surrounding structures), tied off from the large bowel and removed. The area is then washed with warm solutions and the incision in the abdomen is closed.

The skin is sutured so that no stitches are visible. Antibiotics and pain relief are given in theatre, and the patient is then taken to the recovery room.

POST-OPERATIVE
After surgery, an oxygen mask is placed over the patient's mouth and nose. Once the patient is fully awake, the ward nurse comes to the recovery room to accompany the child back to the ward. Monitoring and pain relief continues, and feeding can commence after 12–24 hours.

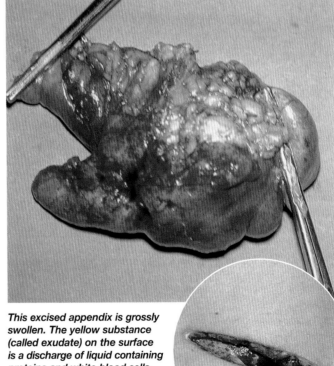

This excised appendix is grossly swollen. The yellow substance (called exudate) on the surface is a discharge of liquid containing proteins and white blood cells.

COMPLICATIONS
Post-operative complications after appendicectomy are rare, but include:
■ Collection of pus in the abdomen
■ Intestines stuck together (adhesions)
■ Wound infection
■ Wound hernia.

There are three possible sites for the appendicectomy incision, usually on or around an area of the abdomen called McBurney's point.

151

Intussusception

Intussusception is a rare but serious condition in which one part of the intestine slides into another. Diagnosis can be confirmed by X-ray or ultrasound and most children make a good recovery.

Intussusception is an uncommon, but potentially fatal, condition in which a segment of intestine telescopes into the segment immediately beyond, forming a tube within a tube. The condition causes obstruction or blockage of the intestine.

Left untreated, the blood supply to the affected part of the intestine may be cut off due to pressure on its blood vessels. The intestine may then become gangrenous and can perforate (burst) or cause peritonitis (inflammation within the abdominal cavity).

In most cases, intussusception starts at the junction between the ileum (the last part of the small intestine) and the caecum (the first and widest part of the large intestine). The last part of the ileum slides into the caecum or the ascending colon beyond.

WHO IS AFFECTED?
Intussusception occurs most often during infancy, particularly between the ages of five and nine months. It affects approximately two in 1,000 babies, with males being affected more frequently than females. Newborn babies, older children and adults are rarely affected by the condition.

POSSIBLE CAUSES
In 90 per cent of cases, the exact cause is not known. It may, however, be linked to:

This illustration shows how intussusception occurs. In most cases, the final section of the small intestine slides up into the large intestine.

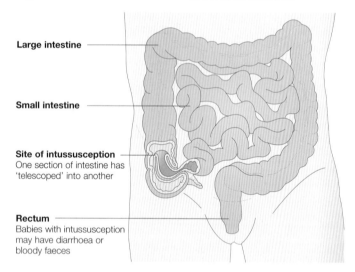

Large intestine

Small intestine

Site of intussusception
One section of intestine has 'telescoped' into another

Rectum
Babies with intussusception may have diarrhoea or bloody faeces

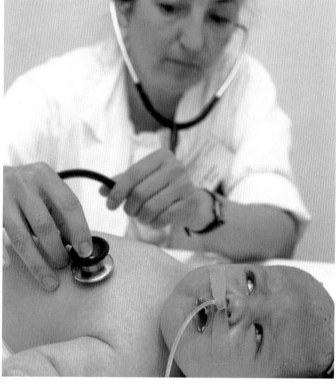

■ Enlargement of the lymph nodes in the lining of the intestine due to a viral infection such as viral gastro-enteritis or an upper respiratory infection
■ Immunization against rotavirus (a virus that causes gastro-enteritis) – the rotavirus vaccine has now been withdrawn in the US
■ A pre-existing abnormality in the bowel, such as a polyp or tumour. This is more likely in newborn babies and in children

If a baby with intussusception is vomiting, a tube may be passed through the nose and down into the stomach. Gastric juices can then be removed via the tube.

over three years, the intussusception tending to occur at the site of the abnormality
■ Cystic fibrosis – children with this condition have abnormally thick and sticky secretions in the respiratory and gastro-intestinal tracts.

Symptoms of intussusception

Intermittent inconsolable crying is often the first sign that a baby has intussusception. This distress is due to episodes of spasmodic pain in the abdomen.

Babies with intussusception appear to develop sudden bouts of severe abdominal pain, when they may draw their legs up and scream inconsolably. They may become pale and sweaty during bouts of pain, but may seem more or less normal in between.

TYPICAL SIGNS
Vomiting is also typical, usually of food material at first but, later, green bile is brought up as the intestine becomes more blocked. The baby may become dehydrated as a result of frequent vomiting. At a late stage, the baby typically passes

faeces containing a mixture of mucus and blood, and resembling redcurrant jelly.

OTHER SYMPTOMS
Many babies do not show the characteristic symptoms of abdominal pain, vomiting and bloody faeces. They may instead be irritable and lethargic, which may be overlooked. Diarrhoea and fever may also occur.

Sometimes, a swelling can be felt in the abdomen. As the condition progresses, a child may gradually develop shock, becoming very quiet, pale, floppy and unresponsive.

Diagnosing and treating intussusception

Intussusception can be diagnosed by X-ray examination following a barium enema, or by ultrasound scanning of the abdomen. The enema itself often successfully relieves the condition, although in severe cases surgery is carried out.

A child with suspected intussusception will be admitted to hospital immediately. Fluids are given intravenously to treat dehydration and a narrow tube is usually passed through the nose into the stomach so that digestive juices can be aspirated from the stomach to control vomiting.

BLOOD SAMPLES

There are no specific laboratory tests for the diagnosis of intussusception, but blood samples are taken for full blood count, chemical levels and cross-matching (in case a blood transfusion is required during surgery). The child is usually given painkilling medication and intravenous antibiotics.

INVESTIGATIONS

The diagnosis of intussusception can be confirmed in two ways:

■ X-ray examination of the abdomen – the child is usually given an enema of compressed air, barium solution or saline (salt solution). This allows the outline of the intestine to be identified more easily
■ Ultrasound scanning of the abdomen. An important advantage of ultrasound over X-ray is that the risk of radiation is reduced.

TREATMENT

In about three quarters of cases, the enema used to diagnose intussusception successfully treats the condition. The gentle pressure applied when the liquid or compressed air is introduced into the intestine forces the prolapsed segment back into its correct position. Provided the child's condition remains stable, enema treatment is occasionally repeated if not successful at first.

SEVERE SYMPTOMS

Enema treatment is not used at all if the child has signs of peritonitis (inflammation of the lining of the abdomen) or intestinal perforation, is in a severe state of shock or is otherwise extremely unwell.

In these cases, or if enema treatment fails, emergency surgery is

Diagnosis of intussusception can be confirmed by X-ray. Barium solution allows the intestine to be clearly visible on the monitor.

necessary. A laparotomy – an operation in which the abdomen is cut open – is performed and the intestine gently squeezed to push the inner segment back into its correct position. Any damaged intestine, or abnormalities such as polyps, may be removed.

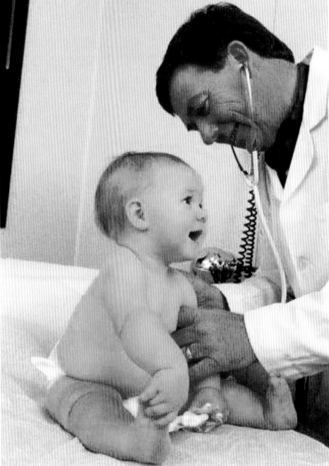

If the doctor suspects that a baby has intussusception, he will examine the abdomen. In some children, a sausage-shaped swelling can be felt.

Occasionally, intussusception can be treated by laparoscopic (keyhole) surgery.

Recovery and outlook

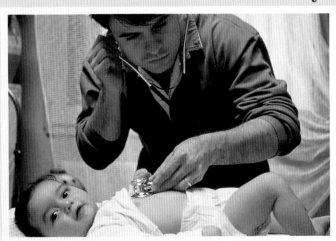

After enema treatment, the child is usually kept in hospital for an observation period of 24–48 hours. Hospital follow-up is not usually required after discharge.

Following surgical treatment, the child will have to remain in hospital for a longer period, depending on the general condition and the exact nature of the surgery performed. A child is usually seen again for a hospital

Most children recover quickly from intussusception. Once doctors are certain that the intestine is functioning normally, a baby can go home.

check-up four to six weeks after discharge.

Recovery rates
Most children make an excellent recovery, with no ill effects on subsequent health, growth or development.

However, the risk of recurrence is 5–10 per cent and is more common after enema treatment than after surgery. Unfortunately, a few children (approximately 1–3 per cent of cases) die as a result of intussusception, mainly because the condition is not diagnosed and treated at an early enough stage.

Hirschsprung's disease

Hirschsprung's disease affects the nerves of the large bowel, impairing normal bowel movement. Affected babies and children have symptoms that range from mild to life-threatening.

Hirschsprung's disease is a rare condition of the large bowel that affects children, particularly small babies.

MUSCLES OF THE BOWEL
The muscles of a healthy bowel contract and relax rhythmically to propel food along its length. Known as peristalsis, this process is under the control of a network of autonomic nerves supplying the bowel wall.

In Hirschsprung's disease, however, a segment of the large bowel (the colon) lacks the necessary nerves to enable it to contract and relax. The affected bowel segment becomes narrowed and the normal movement of stool along the bowel is prevented. The part of the bowel above the affected area, which has a normal nerve supply, becomes greatly dilated (widened).

The affected segment of bowel always includes the rectum (the lowest part of the bowel above the anus) and can extend for a variable distance up the bowel. In five per cent of cases the whole of the large bowel is affected.

CONGENITAL DISORDER
The underlying abnormality is congenital (meaning that it is present at birth) and is the result of a failure of the nerves supplying the large bowel to

▶ *Hirschsprung's disease sometimes develops later in childhood. The main symptoms are then abdominal bloating and constipation.*

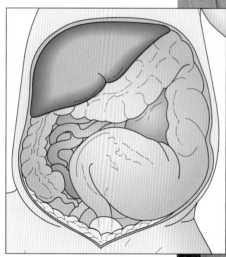

▲ *In Hirschsprung's disease, the nerves supplying part of the bowel have failed to develop. As a result, the bowel above this area becomes greatly dilated.*

form normally during early embryonic development. Usually, nerves continue to develop up to the 12th week of pregnancy.

The cause of the condition remains unknown, but it seems to run in families, which suggests that there may be a genetic factor involved.

Boys are affected much more commonly than girls – they are four times more likely to have the disease.

ONSET OF SYMPTOMS
The symptoms of Hirschsprung's disease may develop rapidly or gradually and the disease may

be life-threatening or may be a long-term condition.

The symptoms of the disease may manifest in babies in the first few days or weeks of life, or may not appear until later in infancy, when severe constipation often prompts parents to seek medical advice.

Symptoms of Hirschsprung's disease

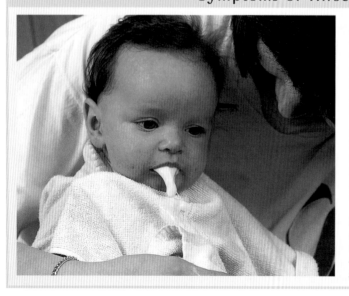

If Hirschsprung's disease develops soon after birth, nurses will notice that the baby has failed to pass meconium (first stools of a newborn) in its first 24 hours. An affected baby may also have a distended abdomen and may refuse to feed.

Symptoms in children
Less commonly, milder cases may present later in infancy or in childhood. In these children, usually only a short section of the bowel is affected and the first

Babies with Hirschsprung's disease often vomit after a feed. Other symptoms include a poor appetite and a failure to gain weight.

symptom is often persistent constipation.

The symptoms tend to develop more slowly than in babies, and may include abdominal bloating, a poor appetite accompanied by a failure to put on weight, impaired growth and anaemia.

Complications
If the affected bowel becomes inflamed (enterocolitis), more serious additional symptoms may develop, such as watery diarrhoea and fever. This condition can be life-threatening, as there is a risk of the bowel perforating and leaking its contents into the abdomen. Urgent medical help is needed if these symptoms arise.

Diagnosis

A definitive diagnosis of Hirschsprung's disease is usually made on microscopic examination of a sample of bowel wall. In most cases, treatment for the condition involves surgery.

The diagnosis may be apparent from the description of the symptoms and following a careful examination of the child's abdomen. However, tests are usually required to confirm the diagnosis.

CONTRAST X-RAY

A routine X-ray of the abdomen may be arranged, which may show dilated loops of bowel if Hirschsprung's disease is present. As hollow structures, such as the bowel, are not well visualized on normal X-rays, a barium enema may be performed.

In this test, barium, a contrast medium that shows up well on X-rays, is introduced into the bowel via the anus. A series of X-rays are then taken, which will identify any narrowed area of bowel caused by Hirschsprung's disease.

A barium enema is not absolutely reliable for making the diagnosis of Hirschsprung's, but it will allow the doctor to determine the length of the affected section of bowel.

BOWEL BIOPSY

A definitive investigation for Hirschsprung's disease is a biopsy, in which a small sample of bowel tissue is removed to confirm that the nerve supply to

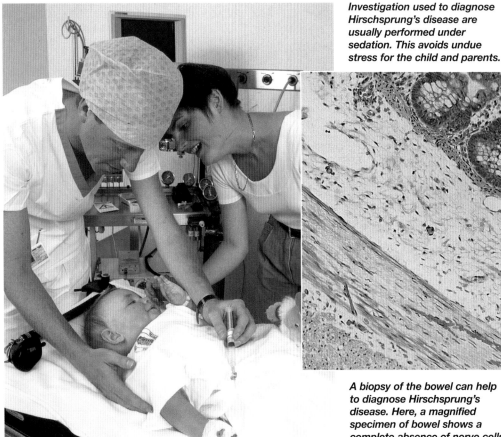

Investigation used to diagnose Hirschsprung's disease are usually performed under sedation. This avoids undue stress for the child and parents.

A biopsy of the bowel can help to diagnose Hirschsprung's disease. Here, a magnified specimen of bowel shows a complete absence of nerve cells.

the bowel wall is abnormal. This procedure is carried out during a colonoscopy.

During this test, a flexible viewing tube, called a colonoscope, is passed up into the large bowel via the rectum. A light source allows the bowel wall to be viewed clearly and

instruments attached to the colonoscope can be used to take biopsies.

In children, colonoscopy is performed under a general anaesthetic or with sedative medication. This has two advantages: it avoids distress and discomfort and it prevents

undue movement on the part of the child.

MICROSCOPY

The samples of tissue are sent to the laboratory, and microscopic examination may reveal the absence of nerve cells in the wall of the bowel.

Treatment for Hirschsprung's disease

Specialist stoma nurses provide after care for children who have undergone a colostomy. They can offer advice on how to cope with a stoma.

There are a number of ways of treating Hirschsprung's disease, all involving surgical procedures.

Surgical procedures

In many affected children, the treatment of the disease involves two operations.

In the first, a colostomy is formed, in which the normal bowel above the affected segment is cut and brought onto the surface of the abdomen; the opening of the bowel at the skin surface is called a stoma. This is a temporary arrangement, in which faeces pass through the stoma into a specially designed and fitted bag, enabling the dilated bowel to return to its

normal diameter. It also enables the child to gain some weight before the second operation, in which the affected segment is resected and normal bowel is joined to the anal canal.

Support and advice

Stoma nurses are specially trained nurses, who are available to help affected children and their parents cope following the formation of a colostomy. As well as giving general advice on stoma care, they provide ongoing support.

Some parents may find the presence of the stoma upsetting at first but it will not cause the child any distress and is a temporary situation.

Following the operation, some children continue to have problems with constipation for some time. Others, however, have loose, frequent stools.

Inguinoscrotal disorders

The embryology and anatomy of the testes within the scrotum
are such that the inguinoscrotal region is liable be affected by three
main disorders: inguinal hernia, hydrocoele and torsion.

A hernia is defined as the protrusion of an organ from the cavity in which it normally resides. Most inguinal hernias in children are indirect in nature. A hernia of this type emerges through the internal inguinal ring within the innermost of the three layers of the abdominal wall, extending down the inguinal canal for various distances. Direct inguinal hernias are rare in children.
Approximately 60 per cent of indirect inguinal hernias are right-sided and 25 per cent left-sided. Around 15 per cent are bilateral. Inguinal hernias most frequently come to notice in the first year of life, particularly during the first three months.

SYMPTOMS

An inguinal hernia is a painless groin mass which appears intermittently, especially with straining, coughing and standing up; it is usually noted by the infant's mother. Other symptoms related to this type of hernia are feeding problems, irritability or infant colic.

COMPLICATIONS

Inguinal hernias require surgical treatment because there is a risk of strangulation of the testis and obstruction in the scrotum.

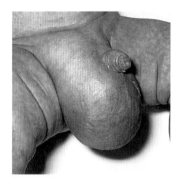

This newborn's scrotum is distended by bilateral inguinal herniae. Loops of small intestine have followed behind the descending testes through the inguinal canal into the scrotum.

Inguinal hernia

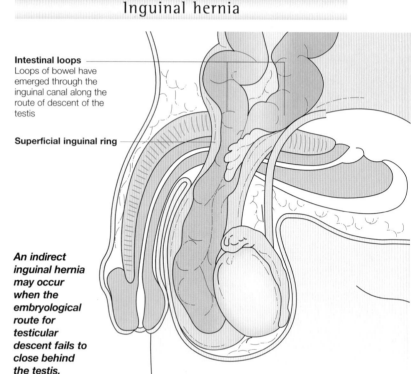

Intestinal loops
Loops of bowel have emerged through the inguinal canal along the route of descent of the testis

Superficial inguinal ring

An indirect inguinal hernia may occur when the embryological route for testicular descent fails to close behind the testis.

Surgical treatment: herniotomy

Since there is a high incidence of complications associated with inguinal hernia, it is normal for an operation to be performed as soon as possible to correct the defect.

The operation is usually performed under a general anaesthetic. After the induction of anaesthesia, the lower abdomen and scrotal region are washed with an antiseptic in preparation for the first incision.

A transverse incision is made through the skin above the external inguinal ring, and the outermost of the three layers covering the spermatic cord is separated.

Once the hernia sac has been identified and separated from the vas deferens and spermatic vessels the contents of the sac (that is, intestine) are pushed back up inside the abdomen. The sac is then twisted by the surgeon to ensure that all the contents have been returned to the abdomen. The base of the sac is then transfixed with a non-absorbable suture.

When the infant wakes up from the anaesthetic, normal feeding may resume. Normal activity is allowed and baths may be given a few days after the operation.

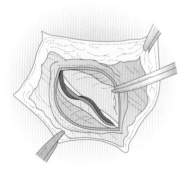

After an incision has been made through the skin, the inguinal sac is located and subsequently isolated from the spermatic vessels and vas deferens.

The sac is emptied of its intestinal contents and then removed. It is important that the vas deferens is not grasped with forceps as damage could result.

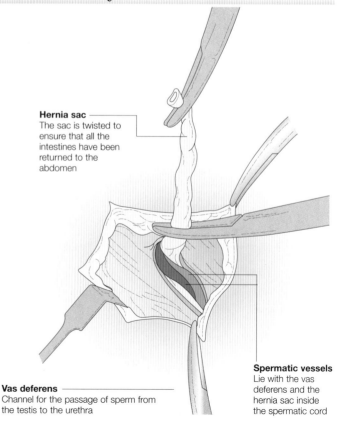

Hernia sac
The sac is twisted to ensure that all the intestines have been returned to the abdomen

Vas deferens
Channel for the passage of sperm from the testis to the urethra

Spermatic vessels
Lie with the vas deferens and the hernia sac inside the spermatic cord

Hydrocoele

Hydrocoele is when the fluid formed by the serosa (lining) of the peritoneal cavity trickles down a narrow patent (open) processus vaginalis and collects in the tunica vaginalis around the testes.

The infant's mother will usually give a history of a painless, soft swelling in the scrotum. On lying down the swelling may disappear and on standing it fills the scrotal sac.

On examination a hydrocoele can be seen as a non-tender soft swelling. One of the tests that a doctor uses is to hold a pen torch against the skin of the scrotum. In hydrocoele, the fluid in the swollen scrotum will be lit up (transilluminate).

TREATMENT
Treatment involves ligation of the patent processus vaginalis when the child is about 18 months of age. The reason for waiting until this time is that the hydrocoele may resolve naturally within the first 18 months of life.

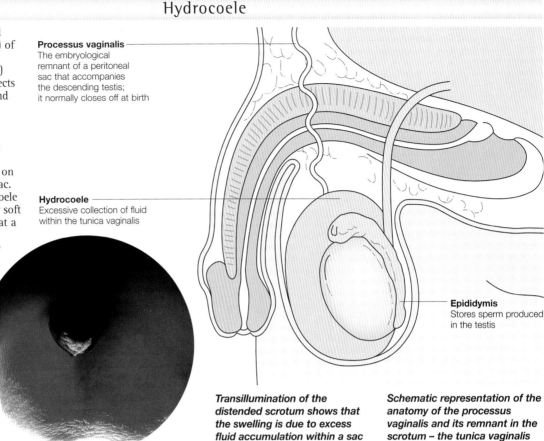

Processus vaginalis
The embryological remnant of a peritoneal sac that accompanies the descending testis; it normally closes off at birth

Hydrocoele
Excessive collection of fluid within the tunica vaginalis

Epididymis
Stores sperm produced in the testis

Transillumination of the distended scrotum shows that the swelling is due to excess fluid accumulation within a sac in front of the testis.

Schematic representation of the anatomy of the processus vaginalis and its remnant in the scrotum – the tunica vaginalis that surrounds the testis.

Torsion of the testis

Torsion of the testis is a surgical emergency. The testis twists on its axis causing occlusion of the blood supply and testicular infarction (cell death) in just a few hours. Early recognition and an immediate emergency operation are necessary if the testis is to survive.

There are two major forms of torsion of the testis: intravaginal and extravaginal. Intravaginal torsion takes place within the tunica vaginalis and results from an abnormally high envelopment by the tunica of the spermatic cord within the scrotum. It is the most common abnormality associated with torsion. Extravaginal torsion results when the testis and the cord twist because of the non-fixation of the testis, cord and processus vaginalis, noted in newborns and patients with undescended testes.

SYMPTOMS
Younger boys are more susceptible to torsion of the testis, although it can occur at any age. A history of trauma is present in 20 per cent of patients, but in most there is no precipitating event.

About one-third of patients have had prior episodes of testicular pain, usually of short duration. Pain is almost always the first symptom: it may begin suddenly and increase with time. Erythema (redness) and swelling of the scrotum develop rapidly, sometimes involving the opposite side. The testis is exquisitely tender, often so much so that accurate palpation is impossible. A high-riding testis may be noted.

INVESTIGATIONS
Since testicular salvage can be achieved in patients with torsion of the testis only if the diagnosis is promptly made, no time

Torsion of the testis is treated surgically by delivering the testis from the scrotum and untwisting it. When the surgeon is sure that blood flow has returned, the wound is stitched.

Torsion of the testis on its axis obstructs blood flow through the testicular vessels. The testis becomes darkly discoloured.

should be wasted in unnecessary tests. The main problem is differentiating torsion of the testis from a non-surgical scrotal affliction such as epididymitis (inflammation of the epididymis).

TREATMENT
Surgical treatment involves de-torsion by delivering the testis from the tunica vaginalis in the scrotum, untwisting the spermatic cord and fixing the testis to the scrotum. The other testis will be fixed to prevent torsion recurring.

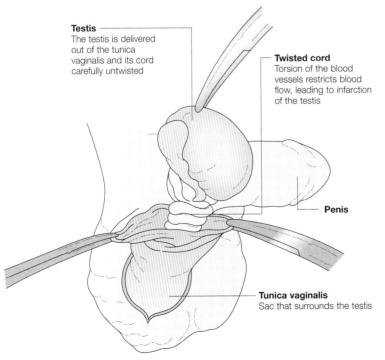

Testis
The testis is delivered out of the tunica vaginalis and its cord carefully untwisted

Twisted cord
Torsion of the blood vessels restricts blood flow, leading to infarction of the testis

Penis

Tunica vaginalis
Sac that surrounds the testis

Congenital dislocation of the hip

Congenital dislocation of the hip (CDH) is one end of a spectrum of conditions collectively termed 'developmental dysplasia of the hip'. These range from hip instability to a true dislocation of the hip's ball and socket joint.

SCREENING

Since the 1960s, all children in the UK have been checked at birth for CDH under a national screening programme, and the incidence is found to be about one in 700 newborns. CDH is more common in girls than in boys by a factor of about seven to one, and is found more often on the left side than on the right – the reason for this is unknown.

CDH is not painful, nor will it prevent the child from crawling or walking. The child develops normally, with the usual developmental milestones, and crawls and walks at the expected age. However, if left undiagnosed or untreated, CDH can lead to a limp, or one leg being shorter than the other, which becomes noticeable when the child begins to walk.

The clinical tests to screen for CDH are usually carried out by the paediatric unit (rather than by a paediatric surgeon), at birth and again at the first checkup at around six to eight weeks by the GP. Thanks to developments in ultrasound in the last 10 years, the results of the clinical tests can now be confirmed much earlier.

ULTRASOUND

Ultrasound is used because in a young baby X-rays do not show developing bone that has not calcified. The earliest time that progress can be checked with X-ray is after four to six months. By then, the bone has enough calcium in it to see the relationship between the ball and the socket. Ultrasound will show up the cartilaginous parts before this time.

If every child were to be screened by ultrasound, the incidence of abnormality would go up to between 60 and 70 per 1,000, because the ultrasound is so sensitive. But if they were retested eight or nine weeks later, 90 per cent of these would turn out to be normal.

If all those with an initially abnormal ultrasound were treated, doctors would end up treating a much higher percentage than necessary. Therefore, paediatricians tend to focus their efforts on certain 'at risk' groups. These include children with:

■ **A family history of CDH** Some 10 per cent of affected children have a close relative with the condition. Because of this genetic factor, if a parent

had CDH, the doctors will ensure that the child is carefully screened.

■ **Breech presentation at birth** (that is, rump-first rather than head-first in the uterus). For this reason, many breech babies are delivered by Caesarean section.

Breech births make up only four per cent of all births, but around 17 per cent of CDH babies are breech births.

■ **Other physical conditions** associated with CDH, such as spinal, foot or skeletal abnormalities.

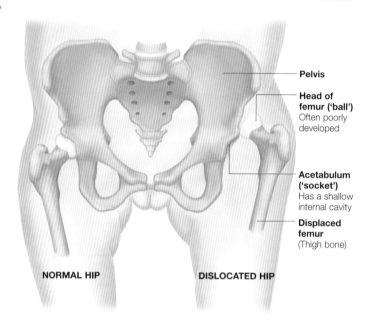

Comparison of normal & dislocated hip

Pelvis

Head of femur ('ball') Often poorly developed

Acetabulum ('socket') Has a shallow internal cavity

Displaced femur (Thigh bone)

NORMAL HIP

DISLOCATED HIP

Clinical tests for CDH

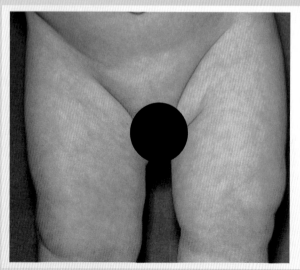

The way this baby boy leans slightly to the right is the only visual indication that his left hip is dislocated. Ortolani's manoeuvre or Barlow's test should confirm the initial diagnosis.

There are two tests performed by paediatricians for the diagnosis of CDH, neither of which is painful for the baby:

Ortolani's manoeuvre
(named after an Italian paediatrician) The child lies in a relaxed and comfortable position, and the doctor supports the pelvis with one hand, gently bringing the knees towards the belly. The doctor then gently pushes the knees outwards so that

the child's legs are moved apart. If the hip is dislocated, it cannot be moved in this way due to a restriction of movement. It will, however, relocate in the socket with an obvious 'clunk' and the doctor will be alerted to the abnormality.

Barlow's test
(named after a British doctor) This is another clinical test to see whether the hip is unstable and can be readily dislocated. The hip is flexed up to 90 degrees, and then the doctor holds the femur, manoeuvring the hip to see if it is dislocatable. If the head of the femur is dislocated, it will usually relocate with the same clunk felt in the Ortolani test.

Treatment

Traction may look unpleasant, but it is noninvasive and causes no pain to the baby, and gradually encourages the hip ball to slip into its socket.

This baby girl is wearing a Pavlick harness. She can remain at home while wearing it, and the hip should be trained into its correct position within three months.

USING A SPLINT
If a child has an unstable hip at birth, the standard treatment is to stabilize the hip in a comfortable position, by applying a Pavlick harness. The child's hip is kept flexed over 90 degrees and the hips are splayed apart at about 40–50 degrees. There is some room for the child to move within that range of positions. The Pavlick harness maintains the hip in the optimum position for keeping the ball in the socket joint. Although the splint looks uncomfortable, the child soon gets used to it. If necessary, the paediatric surgeon can put an affected baby in such a splint shortly after birth.

The harness needs regular adjusting every week or so to make sure it does not become too tight as the baby grows. It is usually worn for between six and twelve weeks in total. The child can be removed from the splint for bathing, but is dressed over the splint.

If CDH babies are diagnosed early, the majority of them can be treated with the splint, with a success rate of over 70 per cent. Splints can cause temporary damage to the ball and socket joint, but the risk of this is minimal.

CLOSED REDUCTION
If the problem presents later (after six months or so, but before the age of two), or if splint treatment fails, then other measures may be required. Often it is possible to put the ball and socket back together with 'closed reduction' under anaesthetic. Reduction means restoring the displaced femur into the correct position in the acetabulum.

Prior to closed reduction, traction is sometimes used. This keeps the baby's body in a straight line, with the bed inclined and the head back. At the start, the child's legs are raised straight up in the air. They are then gradually abducted (held apart). The aim is to overcome the contracture of the muscles, release the tension, and bring the ball towards the socket.

Before the plaster is applied, the doctor examines the hip under anaesthetic. If the hip is nearly reducible, then soft tissue releases might be performed through a small incision in the groin to encourage the hip into place.

The aim is to try to keep the ball located in the socket. Once this is done, he puts the child in a plaster-cast in what is termed the 'human' position (the legs are bent and splayed).

Six weeks later, the doctor examines the hip again. If the joint is firm and beginning to stabilize, then the plaster treatment is continued for another three months until the ball and socket are beginning to develop. After this stage, the plaster comes off, and the child can move and exercise the joint.

Surgical solutions

If the hip joint is not stable, then the paediatric orthopaedic surgeon may elect to do an open reduction. This involves surgically opening up the capsule of the hip joint, taking out tissue inside the acetabulum, releasing all the contractures around the hip, and putting the ball in the acetabulum (socket). Further surgery either above or below the hip may be required to help stabilize the joint. Once again, the patient will be followed up on a regular basis.

Children diagnosed with CDH will need to have follow-up checks until the age of skeletal maturity. The surgeon will check them regularly until about the age of four, and then see them every year or two until 9 or 10 years old, before the start of pubescent growth. From this time, they will be seen again more regularly to make sure that the hip remains stable.

If the hip joint is still not developing correctly, the surgeon may intervene. The hip could become problematic during puberty, when one area grows faster than the other. By the time the child reaches their late teens, and has stopped growing, it will be clear what the final outcome is likely to be.

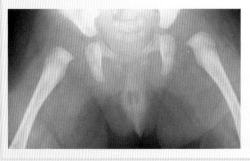

This X-ray reveals CDH on the left side in an infant of six months. Before this age, the bones would not contain enough calcium to show up on an X-ray.

Talipes

Talipes, or club-foot, is a deformity of the foot and ankle seen
in newborns. The condition affects the bones, ligaments and muscles
of the feet and ankles, and is classified into four main types.

Talipes is a congenital condition (present from birth) of the lower leg, and the foot in particular. This condition used to be called 'club-foot' but is now more correctly called talipes. It is more common in boys than girls (2:1), and in about 50 per cent of cases both feet are involved.

CAUSES OF TALIPES

In most cases, the cause is not known: this is called primary or idiopathic talipes. It is known that twin births are more likely to have a postural talipes.

Research has shown that in true structural talipes, called equinovarus, the problem is not confined to the foot. The muscles of the lower leg are often weak and underdeveloped, the bones of the hindfoot are often abnormally shaped and the blood supply to the lower leg may be abnormal. It is clear therefore, that all of the tissues

Postural talipes is a deformity caused by compression of the foot while in the uterus. Twins (shown on this ultrasound image) are often affected.

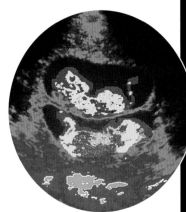

A child with talipes is not able to place the sole of the affected foot flat on the ground. This child has talipes equinovarus of the right foot.

(bone, muscle, nerve, blood vessels and skin) are abnormal to a greater or lesser extent.

Much less often, the talipes deformity may be secondary to other conditions such as a congenital vertical talus, spina bifida, arthrogryposis (contractures of soft tissues) and other neuromuscular disorders.

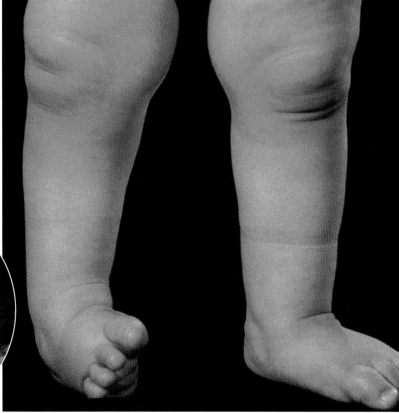

Types of foot deformity

The foot is considered to consist of two parts: the hindfoot, which is below the tibia and includes the heel, ankle and sub-talar joints; and the forefoot, the rest of the foot extending in front.

Talipes (from the Latin: *talus* = ankle; *pes* = foot) is the name of the foot deformity. The direction of the deformity is then indicated by two words that follow: one word for the hindfoot deformity and one word for the forefoot deformity:

■ Hindfoot: equinus (heel high), calcaneus (heel low)
■ Forefoot: varus (forefoot twisted inwards), valgus (forefoot twisted outwards).

These four words can be combined to describe four different deformities, all of which are types of talipes.

■ Talipes equinovarus

This is the most common type of deformity and often requires surgery to correct it. The heel is high and the foot points down and is twisted in.

■ Talipes calcaneovalgus

This is the second most common type of deformity. It is almost always postural (see below) and is due to the baby being too confined within the mother's uterus. This type of talipes rarely requires surgery.

■ Talipes equinovalgus/calcaneovarus

These two types of talipes are exceptionally rare and may require surgery for correction of the deformity.

Postural and structural talipes

As well as determining the type of talipes that the baby has, an assessment is also made of the 'rigidity' or 'stiffness' of the deformity. When the baby has been confined in too small a uterus, the deformity is often less severe and may be corrected with gentle manipulation. This less severe type is called 'postural' talipes and rarely requires surgery.

In more severe cases, the deformity may be much more rigid and cannot be corrected at all. This type is called 'structural' and will almost certainly require surgery at some time.

In general, talipes calcaneovalgus is postural and talipes equinovarus is often structural, but early in life it may be difficult to determine whether the deformity is postural or structural.

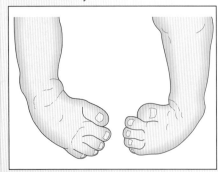

Talipes equinovarus, when the toes point down and the ankle is twisted in, is the commonest foot deformity. It is a complex abnormality and often requires surgery.

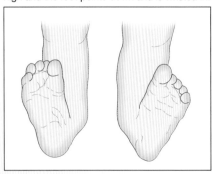

Talipes calcaneovalgus is often the result of the feet being compressed in the uterus. It may be corrected with physiotherapy, but can be associated with other abnormalities.

Diagnosing and treating talipes

A baby with talipes will first be carefully examined for any other associated abnormalities. Once the type of talipes has been determined, the appropriate treatment will be started. Treatment may take the form of physiotherapy, strapping or surgery.

When a baby is born with talipes, it will be thoroughly examined and the deformity assessed. A paediatrician will perform this assessment, but it is also important that physiotherapists see the baby to start treatment. Often, an orthopaedic surgeon will see the baby and its parents, particularly if the talipes is thought to be structural.

ASSESSING TALIPES

Assessment includes determining the type of talipes, and whether it is postural or structural. The baby will also be examined for other anomalies; the hips should be examined for developmental dysplasia of the hip (DDH) and the spine examined for evidence of spina bifida.

The baby's parents can be reassured that in postural cases, the results are excellent and a normal foot can be expected. In structural cases, the foot will never be completely normal, but will work very well even if both feet are affected.

A paediatrician will examine the baby's feet in order to assess the extent of the deformity. This will help to determine the type of treatment to undertake.

Infants with talipes may have other abnormalities, such as developmental dysplasia of the hip. This baby is wearing a Pavlik harness to correct the condition.

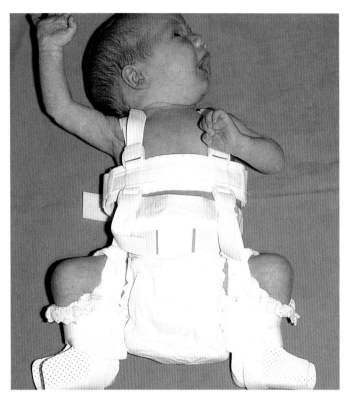

Treating talipes

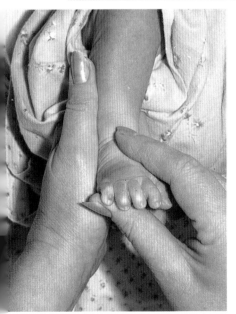

Physiotherapy may be sufficient to correct mild postural cases of talipes. Manipulation of the baby's foot should be started as soon as possible.

Surgery is needed in many cases of structural talipes, and further operations may be necessary as the child grows older.

Treatment should start as soon as possible after birth:

■ **Physiotherapy**
Initial treatment is most often by physiotherapists who will start a programme of stretching exercises, which will be shown to the parents and must be performed every day. Postural talipes is usually successfully treated by such exercises alone.

■ **Strapping or plastering**
In more resistant cases, strapping or possibly plaster casts will be necessary. It is important that the foot is treated with great care and manipulation is gentle. The strapping or casts are frequently changed as the deformity is gently corrected.

After a month or two of treatment, it is usually clear if the foot is being corrected. If not, surgery will be considered and the baby will be referred to an orthopaedic surgeon.

■ **Surgery**
Surgical treatment is tailored to the residual deformity and is directed at releasing tight soft tissues and tendons around the back of the heel (posterior release) and sometimes along the medial side of the foot as well (postero-medial release). At the end of the surgery, the deformity will be corrected and a plaster cast applied.

Strapping of the foot and ankle will stretch the tissues tightly on the inner side of the leg. This must be done when the baby is still young and supple.

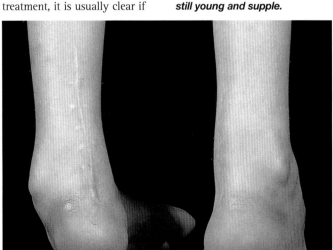

RESULTS

In general, most children have a good prognosis with a supple, pain-free foot that allows them to run about. The affected foot will never be completely 'normal', and it will often be one or two shoe sizes smaller than the normal foot. The calf on the affected side also tends to be thinner, and the whole leg may be a little shorter than the unaffected limb.

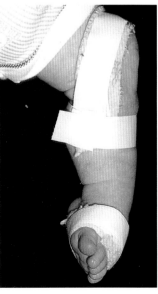

Juvenile idiopathic arthritis

Arthritis (defined as an inflammation of the joints) is very rare in children. Once the condition has been diagnosed, juvenile idiopathic arthritis usually responds well to drugs and physiotherapy.

Juvenile idiopathic arthritis is a specific arthritis (inflammation of the joints) that develops during childhood. The incidence in the UK is thought to be approximately 1:10,000. The cause of the condition remains unclear – hence the term 'idiopathic' which means cause unknown – but it is thought that an abnormal immune response may be involved.

CRITERIA

Arthritis in children presents as swelling in a joint or limitation in joint movement. This is usually accompanied by pain and tenderness, which is not due to a mechanical or physical problem. A child can only be defined as having arthritis if the following criteria are met:
- The symptoms have been present for more than six weeks
- The onset of arthritis occurred before the age of 16
- Other diseases that cause similar symptoms have been excluded.

Conditions that need to be excluded include osteomyelitis (infection of the bone) or septic arthritis (infection of the joint). Other possibilities are a reaction to infections, cancers such as leukaemia and lymphoma, connective tissue problems or overuse injuries. An injury of any kind is important to exclude, and non-accidental injury should not be forgotten.

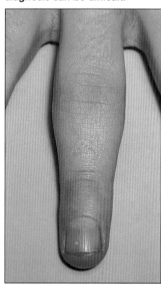

Arthritis is inflammation of one or more joints, for example those in the fingers. Juvenile idiopathic arthritis is rare, and diagnosis can be difficult.

A diagnosis of arthritis may not be easy to make as there is no single test which confirms diagnosis. The child may not complain of pain, stiffness and swelling. Rather, they may simply start to limp, not wish to take part in games at school or have non-specific symptoms such as fever or lethargy.

DEVELOPMENT

Any long-standing, systemic illness can cause disruption of a child's normal growth and development. A thorough examination is therefore vital to give any clues as to any other potential causes for the problem.

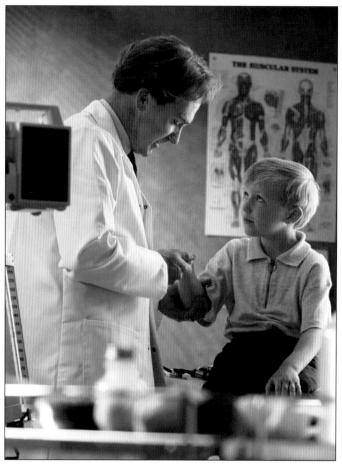

Diagnosing arthritis in a child can be difficult. It is important to find out about all the different aspects of the child's life when making a diagnosis.

Classifying juvenile idiopathic arthritis

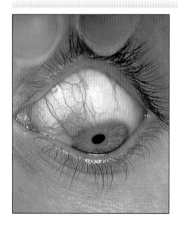

Uveitis (inflammation in front of the eye) is found in 20 per cent of children with oligoarthritis. This is the most common type of JIA and affects girls under four.

Once arthritis has been diagnosed, it can be further categorized. Types of juvenile idiopathic arthritis include:
- Oligoarthritis – this is the most common type. It affects girls of pre-school age and is associated with specific antibodies in the blood. A fifth of affected children develop anterior uveitis or inflammation in the front of the eye. They may not have any symptoms, but can develop blindness
- Polyarthritis – affects up to 40 per cent of children with juvenile idiopathic arthritis. It is more symmetrical and affects many joints
- Psoriatic – psoriasis can occur before, during or long after the onset of arthritis. Sometimes a family history, nail changes in the absence of skin problems or even joint involvement such as dactylitis (a single 'sausage'-shaped digit) may be sufficient to diagnose psoriatic arthritis
- Enthesitis related – this involves inflammation of an enthesis (the point at which a tendon inserts into a bone. Areas affected are the feet, plantar fascia and Achilles tendon. It affects boys predisposed to ankylosing spondylitis
- Systemic is the rarest type of arthritis in children. There are extra-articular (non-joint) problems such as a rash, fever, large liver and spleen, and enlarged lymph nodes.

Caring for a child with arthritis

Finding out that a child has arthritis can have consequences for other children in the family. Apart from looking at different treatments and supportive measures, it is important that the whole family are well-informed about the disease.

Tests should be performed carefully to avoid undue distress. Smaller blood tubes that require less blood for analysis are available for children.

TESTS

There is no one test that will diagnose the condition, but the following tests may help to exclude other disorders:
■ Inflammatory markers – these confirm that an inflammatory process is taking place and include looking for a particular protein in the blood (C reactive protein) and erythrocyte sedimentation rate, which measures the rate at which red cells settle in a test-tube
■ Checking for anti-nuclear antibodies in the blood – the presence of these can indicate that eye problems may develop.
■ Full blood count and iron levels to check for anaemia
■ X-rays and scans
■ Bone marrow biopsy – this might be done if leukaemia or lymphoma is suspected.

IMPACT ON THE FAMILY

A multi-disciplinary approach is very important in the management of childhood arthritis. Nurses, psychologists,

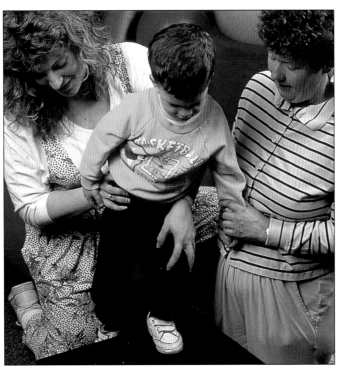

teachers, physiotherapists and occupational therapists as well as doctors and dentists will work together to devise effective strategies. The disease has a major impact on the family unit and it is therefore important to

educate the entire family about the condition. Children who are ill often have to attend hospital on a regular basis. This can have consequences for other children in the family, who may feel neglected by their parents.

Arthritis can make a child's joints extremely swollen and painful. The skill of a physiotherapist will help to maintain and improve mobility.

One blood test measures the erythrocyte sedimentation rate (the rate at which blood cells settle in a tube). This can detect inflammation in the body.

Physiotherapy

It is very important to keep a child with arthritis as active and mobile as possible. It is essential that deformities, such as contractures are prevented, and

in some cases this may mean aggressive physiotherapy. The spine, hips, knees and ankles are particularly susceptible to problems because they are

weight-bearing joints.
Although some children with the condition may need physiotherapy regularly, it is important that they continue

If a child has arthritis, progress must be watched closely. Height and weight should be monitored to see if developmental milestones are reached.

their education with the minimum amount of disruption if possible.

SUPPORT GROUPS

For children suffering from arthritis, practical help is also available, both for them and their families, through a number of different organizations and support groups.

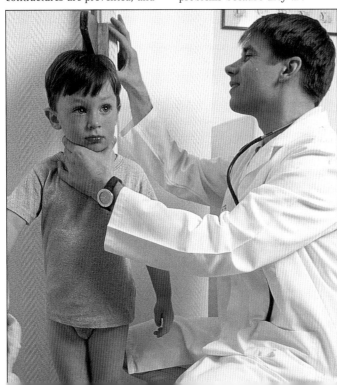

Drug treatment

NSAIDs can be helpful in these children to reduce pain and inflammation. The dose depends on the child's weight. Steroids are also used in some cases and severely swollen joints can be injected, usually with a corticosteroid such as triamcinolone. In children, this can be a frightening and painful experience, so the procedure usually takes place under a general anaesthetic.
An alternative is immuno-suppressive treatment which

lowers the activity of the immune system. However, long-term use of these drugs can reduce a child's inability to fight infection, so careful monitoring is necessary.

New developments

More recently, new highly effective immunosuppressants, such as etanercept, have been used with some success in children with polyarthritis who have not responded to other drug therapies.

Rickets

Rickets is a disease of childhood which causes deformity of the bones, with the most obvious sign being bowing of the legs. It is due to a deficiency of vitamin D and is thus often related to diet.

Rickets is a bone-deforming disease of childhood due to a deficiency of vitamin D. (In adults, the same condition is known as osteomalacia.) More precisely, however, rickets is a syndrome rather than a disease. In other words, it describes a group of recognizable abnormalities that can be produced by several different diseases or causes.

BONE STRUCTURE

Rickets is due to reduced mineralization of growing bone. Bone is composed of a fibrous, non-bony latticework (matrix) which is turned into hard, mature bone by the laying down of minerals such as calcium and phosphorus within this matrix.

In rickets, the bone is neither hard nor calcified; on the contrary, it is soft and spongy. These soft bones take on a deformed, twisted appearance.

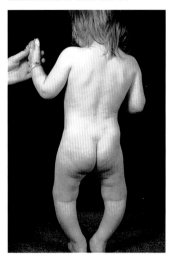

Bowing of the legs is the classic sign of rickets. The condition is caused by vitamin D deficiency, due to lack of exposure to sunlight or poor diet.

Children whose diet is deficient in vitamin D are more likely to develop rickets, even if they are exposed to adequate amounts of sunlight.

Clinical signs

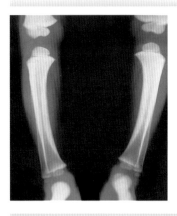

The illness is usually not detected until a child begins to walk. However, it may be recognized earlier in infancy, as it is one of the many causes of 'failure to thrive'. The most characteristic finding in rickets is the development of bent, bow-shaped leg bones. The spongy,

This false-colour X-ray of the legs of a child with rickets shows the characteristic curving of the bones. This is due to a deficiency of vitamin D.

femora (thigh bones) and the tibia and fibula of the lower leg bend under the weight of the body when children begin to walk. These children also have a prominent forehead and the soft, demineralized bones of the skull (craniotabes) can be indented by finger pressure.

Another sign is 'rickety rosary' – marked prominences at the points where the ribs meet the breastbone (sternum). These prominences look like rosary beads, hence the name.

This micrograph shows a sample of tissue taken from an infant with rickets. Cartilage is not being replaced by calcified bone, leading to the typical sponginess.

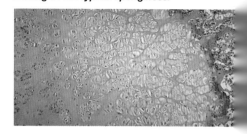

The link with vitamin D

Vitamin D, which undergoes transformation in the liver and kidneys to produce its most active form, controls the metabolism of calcium and phosphate in the human body. It does so in conjunction with parathyroid hormone (synthesized and released by the parathyroid glands).

ESSENTIAL VITAMIN

The most common source of vitamin D is the action of sunlight on skin. The ultraviolet rays in sunlight convert a precursor of vitamin D, which lies in the skin, into vitamin D proper.

Vitamin D is also found in certain foodstuffs; important dietary sources of vitamin D include liver, fish oils and fortified milk feeds.

A balanced diet should supply adequate amounts of vitamin D. Fortified milk feeds contain vitamins necessary for healthy bone development.

Causes of rickets

■ Nutritional rickets

The most frequent cause of rickets is dietary deficiency of vitamin D, usually in combination with poor exposure to sunlight. It is commoner in latitudes closer to the polar regions. In northern hemisphere countries, such as the UK, it is more common in northern regions.

Infants who are exclusively breast-fed into late infancy, with no fortified milk or other foodstuffs, and toddlers who are given a diet free of dairy products, will have intakes of calcium, phosphate, and vitamin D which are inadequate for normal bone formation.

Nutritional rickets may also occur in children who have poor absorption of food from the intestine, especially fat malabsorption.

■ Metabolic causes

Rickets can also be caused by conditions which alter the production of the medically active metabolites of vitamin D.

This may be due to liver disease or kidney disease, where key steps in vitamin D metabolism take place.

■ Other causes of rickets

There are also rare enzyme-related causes of rickets. Enzymes are naturally occurring compounds which are necessary for chemical reactions to take place. If these enzymes are absent or in short supply, the body may not be able to produce some of the biological substances necessary for normal metabolism.

This is the case in vitamin D-dependent rickets. There are two different types of this hereditary enzyme deficiency, both of which may affect vitamin D metabolism and cause rickets.

Children breast-fed into late infancy without dietary supplements may develop rickets. Breast milk will not contain adequate amounts of vitamins and minerals for bone growth.

Diagnosis and treatment

Rickets is diagnosed primarily on the appearance of the child. Blood analysis will show that the level of calcium is often normal; the level of phosphate, however, is usually low.

There is also a significant increase in the level of a bone enzyme called alkaline phosphatase. This is because of increased rickets-associated activity in growing bone.

X-rays show characteristic changes at the ends of the bones, near the joints, where bone growth occurs.

TREATMENT

Simple changes in diet and lifestyle can increase vitamin D production and prevent rickets. Supplements of vitamin D and lifestyle changes will successfully treat nutritional rickets. In kidney-associated rickets, phosphate supplements may be needed, and in cases due to enzyme deficiency, higher than normal doses of vitamin D are usually required.

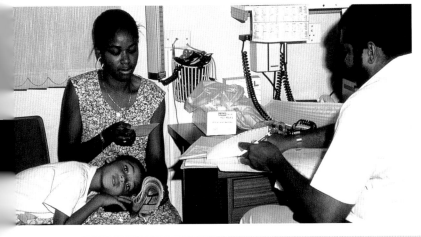

Rickets may be diagnosed by the child's characteristic appearance. Physical signs may include bowed legs, a prominent forehead and 'rickety rosary'.

Laboratory tests may be used to confirm the diagnosis of rickets. Blood tests may reveal low levels of phosphate and a high level of a certain bone enzyme.

Ethnic considerations

Rickets is very uncommon in Caucasian children in developed countries. It is, however, particularly common in Asian (Indian subcontinent) children. There are several reasons why this is so.

The deeply pigmented skin of Asian people produces less activated vitamin D than pale skin when exposed to the same amount of ultraviolet light. In some Asian cultures, custom dictates covering large parts of the body, potentially further

depriving such patients of sunlight. Some children may also have a diet that does not contain sufficient vitamin D or calcium.

Another interesting diet-related reason why Asian children are prone to rickets is that the flour used to make chapattis (Indian unleavened bread) reduces the absorption of dietary calcium.

Rickets is more common in certain ethnic groups. Cultural factors such as diet may increase the risk of rickets.

Osteogenesis imperfecta

Also known as brittle bone disease, osteogenesis imperfecta is a
rare genetic disorder resulting in fragile bones that fracture easily.
It is difficult to diagnose and can be mistaken for physical abuse.

Osteogenesis imperfecta is a rare bone condition whose main characteristic is an increased tendency towards bone fractures.

DIFFERENT TYPES
There are four recognized types of the condition, which exist on a spectrum of severity from a slightly increased risk of fractures to severe fractures. In severe cases, multiple fractures can result from everyday occurrences like sneezing and require long and painful periods of hospitalization, particularly for growing children. One form of the disease (known as type II) results in death at birth or within a very short time thereafter.

Current estimates suggest that the condition occurs in 1 in 10,000 babies, meaning that there are approximately 6,000 children with the condition at any one time in the UK.

The majority of common bone disorders, such as osteoporosis, concern the mineral deposits – calcium and phosphorus – of the bone structure. Osteogenesis imperfecta, however, is quite distinct in that there is a deficiency of the fibrous protein collagen, which forms the main framework of bones.

Osteogenesis imperfecta can be difficult to diagnose. However, the earlier a doctor makes a diagnosis, the better the outlook for the child.

DISEASE GENETICS
The great majority of cases arise from the inheritance of a dominant gene from one or both parents. Usually there is a history of the condition in one or both of the parents' families.

In a relatively small number of cases, a child may have osteogenesis imperfecta despite there being no family history of the condition. These cases are thought to result from a new dominant mutation that occurred in either the sperm or the ovum prior to conception.

As any adult with osteogenesis imperfecta will have inherited the dominant mutation, there is a 50 per cent chance of their own children having the condition. For this reason, adults with the disease are usually referred for genetic counselling if they want to start a family.

DIAGNOSING THE CONDITION
There is no definitive diagnostic test for osteogenesis imperfecta.

The most reliable diagnosis is obtained using a combination of X-ray examination and the existence of a number of distinct clinical features. The diagnosis is sometimes mistaken for non-accidental injury and vice versa.

For more severe cases where there is a family history of osteogenesis imperfecta, ultrasound scanning during pregnancy may be able to determine whether the developing baby has the disease, but cannot determine which type they may have.

Collagen deficiency

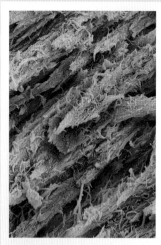

A useful analogy for the structure of bone is that of reinforced concrete. This very common construction material comprises a steel rod framework that then has concrete poured

Collagen forms the basis of bone structure. In osteogenesis imperfecta, poor quality collagen fibres result in fragile bones.

around it. In bone, the equivalent of the steel framework is the network of collagen fibres, while the minerals, mostly calcium, play the part of the concrete.

In a child with osteogenesis imperfecta, the body produces collagen of a poor or insufficient quality. This inferior-quality collagen weakens the entire bone structure, making it more susceptible to fractures.

Collagen is a fibrous protein that is vital to the structure of many body tissues, not just bone. Other tissues that rely on collagen include skin, veins, arteries, teeth and cartilage, and it is also found in the eyes.

Common symptoms

The exact symptoms displayed by a child depend on the type of osteogenesis imperfecta they have. The most common symptoms include:
- Blue–grey colouring of the whites of the eyes
- Increased range of movement of joints (hypermobility)
- Excessive sweating
- Progressive hearing impairment from early adulthood
- Skull deformities
- A triangular-shaped face
- Spinal curvature
- Short stature
- Brittle and/or discoloured teeth.

It is not unusual for a child who has a milder form of osteogenesis imperfecta to be diagnosed only when a history of fractures has been established to support a number of these clinical features.

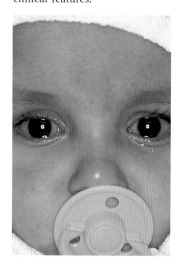

The subtle blue–grey colouring of the sclera (whites of the eyes), evident in this baby, is a characteristic feature of osteogenesis imperfecta.

Treatment and prognosis

Children may spend brief spells in hospital and in wheelchairs while
their fractures heal, but with care and support they have a normal school life. Surgical
strengthening of bones and drug therapies help to normalize life further.

All fractures are managed promptly and often take longer to heal than normal. There is currently no cure, and there are no treatments that directly address the genetics of this condition. The hope is that the decoding of the human genome may provide future gene therapies.

RODDING

For many years, children affected by osteogenesis imperfecta have had their bones artificially strengthened. Titanium alloy rods are surgically implanted into the bone. These rods are flexible enough to ensure that individual mobility is not unnecessarily impaired. In many cases, it may be necessary to replace rods after a period of years.

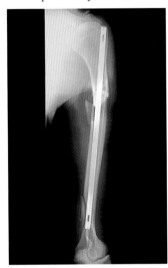

Surgeons can insert flexible titanium-alloy rods into the bones. These strengthen and stabilize them, and prevent deformity and future fractures.

DRUG THERAPY

Over the years, a number of treatments have been used but have proved of limited success, including calcium supplements and growth hormone.

Clinical trials are now ongoing using a number of drugs from the bisphosphonate family, drugs well established in the treatment of osteoporosis.

Bisphosphonates act to inhibit the natural process of bone resorption, thus allowing the bone structure to grow stronger and denser. In effect, the added strength of the minerals within the bone can compensate for the loss of strength due to the collagen deficit.

These trials have so far been quite promising. Some children with osteogenesis imperfecta have shown increased mobility, improved bone density, a marked reduction in chronic pain and a lower rate of fractures as a result of bisphosphonate therapy. It will be some time before these drugs are widely available, however, as the long-term effects are still being assessed.

OUTLOOK

With the exception of the lethal type II form of osteogenesis imperfecta, the prognosis for most people is quite positive.

Most can expect to have a normal or near normal life expectancy with successful personal and professional lives.

Because osteogenesis imperfecta is so rare, general awareness of the condition is relatively low, even among medical professionals. It is therefore vital that anyone affected by the condition learns

Many children have to spend short periods of time in wheelchairs to help heal fractures. However, only a few are wheelchair-dependent.

enough to take the role of the 'expert' when presenting to a doctor or an accident and emergency department with a possible fracture.

Osteogenesis imperfecta or non-accidental injury?

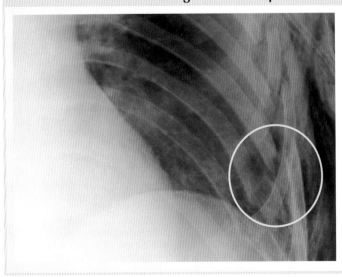

When a child arrives at hospital with fractures that cannot be explained satisfactorily, doctors must always suspect a diagnosis of non-accidental injury.

Awareness of the condition

As osteogenesis imperfecta is such a rare condition, Accident and Emergency departments may not be aware that it is an alternative diagnosis to suspected physical abuse. The fact that diagnosis relies on

It can be difficult for a doctor to diagnose osteogenesis imperfecta as the cause of fractured ribs in children, as it such a rare condition.

radiological examination and a number of clinical indicators means that a non-specialist may be unaware of the significance of such signs as blue–grey colouring of the whites of the eyes.

Difficult diagnosis

X-rays will normally be performed in all cases but may not be an effective diagnostic tool for this condition. For example, an X-ray showing a history of previous fractures may be interpreted as evidence of osteogenesis imperfecta. Equally, however, it could prove a history of physical abuse. Diagnosis can be extremely difficult and parents may be wrongly prosecuted.

Muscular dystrophy

Muscular dystrophy refers to inherited muscle disorders in which there is a slow, progressive degeneration of the muscle fibres. There is no cure, although physiotherapy has an important role to play.

The term muscular dystrophy covers a number of inherited diseases that are characterized by weakness and wasting of muscles. The symptoms and course of these diseases differ according to their severity, how they are inherited and which muscles are affected.

DISEASE TYPES
There are many types of muscular dystrophy, all of which are very rare. Four types are listed below:
■ **Duchenne muscular dystrophy (DMD)**. This is the commonest form of the disease; it affects only boys and is diagnosed in around one in 3,000 infants. Beginning in early childhood, it leads to a progressive deterioration in mobility
■ **Becker muscular dystrophy.** This is rarer than DMD, with milder symptoms, but also causes worsening disability in boys
■ **Congenital myotonic dystrophy.** This occurs in girls as well as boys. Affected babies often display breathing problems and poor muscle tone
■ **Limb-girdle muscular dystrophy.** This condition affects both girls and boys – the muscles of the shoulders and pelvis are affected.

DISEASE PROGRESSION
Boys with DMD have a poor prognosis and do not usually live beyond the age of 20.

Most boys with Becker muscular dystrophy eventually become severely disabled. They are likely to be confined to a wheelchair within 25 years of the onset of disease, although life expectancy is near normal.

Congenital myotonic dystrophy can be fatal, although children who survive beyond their first birthday are likely to live to adulthood.

Muscular dystrophy is marked by weakness and wasting of the muscles. Regular physical examinations help to monitor the progress of the disease.

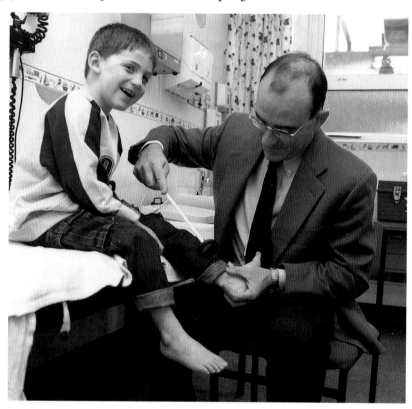

Symptoms of Duchenne and Becker muscular dystrophy

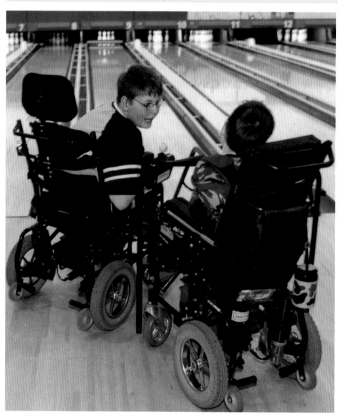

The symptoms of both DMD and Becker muscular dystrophy are similar. As the abnormality in Becker muscular dystrophy is less severe than that suffered in DMD, the onset of the disease occurs later, usually between 11 and 15 years of age.

Boys with DMD are well at birth, the symptoms first being noticed when the child begins to walk, at around the age of 18 months. A number of symptoms may then develop.

INITIAL SYMPTOMS
Early symptoms of DMD may include:
■ Weakness of the muscles of the back and around the pelvis
■ Delay in learning to walk. The affected child may appear to waddle when walking and may fall over frequently
■ Difficulty in getting to a standing position from the floor

Even though most boys with DMD will eventually need to use a wheelchair, with support and physiotherapy, a good quality of life can be maintained.

– characteristically, the child will use his hands to 'walk up' the thighs (Gower's sign)
■ The calf muscles may feel firm and appear large, but are weak.

DISEASE PROGRESSION
As the condition progresses, other symptoms may include:
■ Weakness in the arms
■ Abnormal spinal curvature
■ Walking becomes progressively more difficult; affected children are likely to need a wheelchair by around the age of 12
■ Mild learning difficulties.

COMPLICATIONS
Complications may also develop. The chest muscles gradually become involved, with the result that affected boys become susceptible to chest infections; these can be life-threatening in the latter stages of the disease.

The muscles of the heart wall may also be affected, gradually becoming thickened, but weakened, and therefore less able to pump blood around the body effectively.

Inheriting muscular dystrophy

All types of muscular dystrophy are due to a genetic abnormality. Both DMD and Becker muscular dystrophy are caused by a defect in the structure of a gene on the X chromosome (the sex chromosome present in both sexes). This particular gene is responsible for the production of dystrophin, a protein that is essential for healthy muscles. Without dystrophin, the normal structure of muscle fibres can no longer be maintained and the affected muscles are weakened.

SEX CHROMOSOME
Girls can carry the abnormal gene, but they do not usually suffer from the disease as they have two X chromosomes, and the normal version of the gene on their second X chromosome compensates for the abnormality.

If the abnormal gene is passed on to a male offspring, the disease develops, as he has only one X chromosome and no normal version of the gene to compensate.

CHILDREN OF CARRIERS
Sons of carriers have a one in two chance of inheriting the abnormal gene and having the disease; daughters of carriers have a one in two chance of being a carrier. Although this gene abnormality is often inherited, it may arise spontaneously in a boy who has no previous history of the disease in his family.

Limb-girdle muscular dystrophy is an autosomal recessive disorder; for a child to have the disease, both parents must carry the abnormal gene.

The normal magnified muscle tissue shows dystrophin (red) surrounding the muscle fibres. In muscular dystrophy, there is virtually no dystrophin, and this leads to muscle weakness.

Muscular dystrophy

Normal

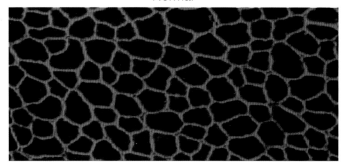

Making a diagnosis

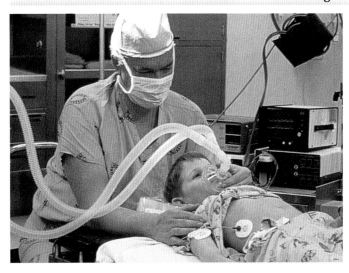

Muscular dystrophy can often be diagnosed by asking about the child's symptoms and carrying out a physical examination.

The doctor will take a blood sample, as the blood levels of creatine phosphokinase (an enzyme normally present in healthy muscles) are markedly elevated in muscular dystrophy.

ELECTROMYOGRAPHY
Electromyography assesses patterns of electrical activity in

Muscular dystrophy can be diagnosed by muscle biopsy. In children, this procedure is usually carried out using a light general anaesthetic.

a muscle; these patterns are abnormal if muscular dystrophy is present.

MUSCLE BIOPSY
In affected children, a muscle biopsy (a tiny sample of tissue removed for analysis) will show characteristic changes in muscle structure. There will be damaged muscle fibres and an abnormal deposition of fatty tissue.

ECHOCARDIOGRAM
An echocardiogram (an ultrasound scan of the heart) may also be carried out to look for evidence of heart muscle involvement.

Caring for a child with muscular dystrophy

There is currently no curative treatment for any type of muscular dystrophy. The aims of care are, therefore, to help an affected child to have a happy and active life for as long as possible.

Keeping limbs supple
Physiotherapy may be helpful in keeping limbs supple and preventing contractures (shortening of the muscles that can result in deformity of nearby joints).

The physiotherapist will also advise on using splints and other equipment to provide support for the limbs and to assist mobility.

Genetic counselling
Counselling and advice is available for the family of an affected child, both for the parents if they are considering future pregnancies and for sisters who may wish to know if they carry the abnormal gene.

DNA analysis can be performed to identify carriers. In women who are known to be carriers, pre-natal testing can be carried out to see whether the fetus is affected.

Children with muscular dystrophy should be kept as active as possible to maintain use of their muscles. This child is having playgroup therapy.

Rheumatic fever

Rheumatic fever occurs as a complication of a bacterial infection, usually of the throat. This inflammatory disease can affect the heart and joints, and tends to occur in children and young adults.

Rheumatic fever is a disease that occurs mainly in children and usually after infection with a streptococcal bacterium. It has become less prevalent since the introduction of antibiotics to treat throat infections.

Rheumatic fever, also known as acute rheumatism, is a general disorder with a tendency to spread throughout the body in an erratic manner. It involves the smooth membranes that line a variety of cavities in the body, particularly the joints and the heart, and is accompanied by feverishness, perspiration and a great deal of pain in the joints.

CAUSES

Rheumatic fever is a complication of a streptococcal infection, such as that affecting the throat or skin (erysipelas). The disease occurs because some components of the streptococcal bacteria are genetically similar to parts of the connective tissue found in the smooth membranes of the body. The bacteria stimulate the body to produce antibodies, which then attack the body's connective tissue, especially in the heart.

DEVELOPMENT

The symptoms of rheumatic fever may develop gradually or abruptly, up to six weeks after the onset of the streptococcal infection. The disease rarely develops before the age of three; the initial episode usually occurs between the ages of seven and 14, and is rare in adulthood. After the first episode, recurrent ones can continue throughout adult life and are often triggered by stress or tiredness.

The disease occurs more frequently in areas of poverty, where many streptococcal infections are left untreated. There is also some evidence that rheumatic fever occurs within families.

Rheumatic fever has declined in industrialized countries, but has increased in prevalence in the developing world. It tends to occur in areas of poverty.

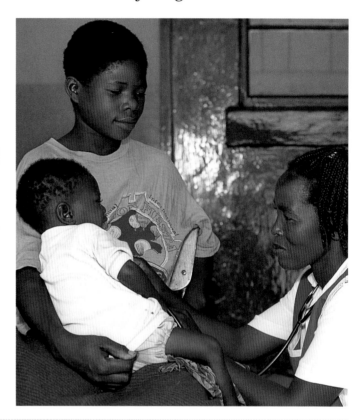

Rheumatic fever symptoms

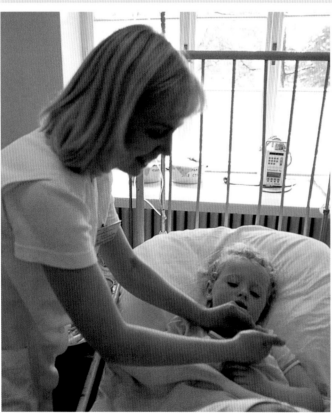

When a child is suffering from rheumatic fever, even bedclothes against the skin can feel painful. A high temperature is an early symptom of this disease.

An attack usually begins with a feeling of chilliness. This is followed by fever and stiffness or pain in one or more joints, usually the larger joints, such as those of the knee, ankle, wrist or shoulder. The pain rapidly becomes intense and the child becomes restless, while at the same time finds it uncomfortable to move or be touched.

The child's temperature soars to around 39.5°C (103°F), the face is flushed, the pulse is rapid and the whole body is bathed in perspiration that has a sour odour. The tongue becomes coated and this is accompanied by extreme thirst, loss of appetite and constipation.

JOINT PAIN

To begin with, the pain is confined to one or two joints, but this may rapidly spread to others, often moving from one joint to another in succession. The affected joints become red and swollen, hot and very tender and this may be accompanied by a skin rash. In severe cases, pea-sized nodules appear under the skin, particularly on the extensor aspect of joints, such as the outside of the elbow and the front of the knee.

Rheumatic fever attacks vary in their severity, duration and after-effects, but they usually subside within a few days, and complete recovery occurs within three weeks. Sometimes, when all other symptoms have disappeared, the joints remain stiff and swollen. This usually resolves gradually, but it can result in chronic rheumatism.

SEVERE CASES

If the child's temperature returns to normal and then rises again, or remains elevated for more than 10 days, additional complications, such as those involving the heart, may be suspected. In such cases an attack may last for many weeks, with several relapses.

Diagnosing and treating rheumatic fever

Prescribing antibiotics for a streptococcal throat infection can help to prevent
rheumatic fever from developing. If a child does go on to develop rheumatic fever,
prompt treatment is essential to prevent complications from setting in.

Prompt treatment of streptococcal infections with antibiotics, such as penicillin, can prevent rheumatic fever. Parents should therefore seek medical help if a child develops a sore throat that lasts longer than 24 hours and is accompanied by fever.

A blood test may reveal raised levels of white blood cells and other signs of inflammation. A throat swab is often taken to

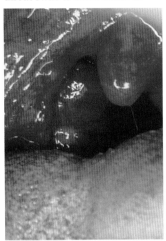

establish whether or not a streptococcal infection is present – sometimes the original infection is so mild as to cause no symptoms. If doctors do suspect rheumatic fever, electrocardiography and echocardiography may be carried out to check whether there is any heart involvement.

TREATMENT

Once rheumatic fever is diagnosed, a child is usually admitted to hospital for complete bedrest. Early treatment with antibiotics and corticosteroids resolves infection, reduces inflammation and minimizes the risk of complications.

If rheumatic fever is suspected, a throat swab will be cultured in the laboratory. The procedure may make the child 'gag', but it is over in a few seconds.

Acute streptococcal infection of the throat often precedes an attack of rheumatic fever. Treatment with antibiotics helps to avoid complications.

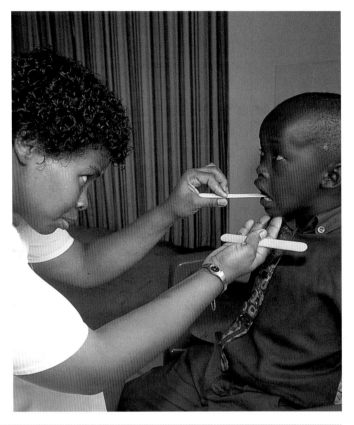

Complications

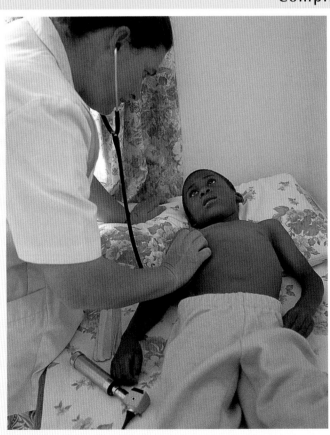

Rheumatic fever may be accompanied by complications. These include problems related to the lungs and heart, and close monitoring is essential.

Complications that arise as a result of rheumatic fever include:
■ Excessive fever (hyperpyrexia), which can develop suddenly
■ Respiratory problems, such as bronchitis and pneumonia
■ Skin conditions, such as purpura and erythema
■ Chorea (jerky movements produced by involuntary muscle movements), sometimes occurring after other symptoms have passed.

Heart disease

Apart from the risk of recurrent attacks, the most serious complication is heart disease, which develops in about half of children after the first attack. The risk of heart involvement rises from around 20 per 100,000 at the age of six to 150 per 100,000 at the age of 14. The problem is exacerbated by the fact that in young patients, the joint pains associated with rheumatic fever

are sometimes so slight as to pass unnoticed, with the result that damage to the heart may become apparent much later in life.

Inflammation

Rheumatic fever can lead to inflammation in any of the three layers of the heart:

■ Pericarditis (inflammation of the membrane that surrounds the heart) – this occurs the least often, but is the most likely to affect prospects of recovery, as it often leaves the heart weakened
■ Myocarditis (inflammation of the heart muscle) – this usually resolves after a few weeks. Only occasionally does it cause lasting damage to the heart muscle
■ Endocarditis (inflammation of the membrane that lines the cavities of the heart) – this membrane also covers the heart valves and it is these that are mostly likely to be affected. Symptoms of simple endocarditis may only present with palpitations and a slight increase in temperature. As a result, heart disease may not be diagnosed until it is at an advanced stage.

Anaemia in childhood

There are many causes of anaemia including deficiencies of production and accelerated destruction of red blood cells. Worldwide the commonest cause of anaemia in children is iron deficiency.

Anaemia is a condition in which there is a deficiency or abnormality of haemoglobin, the oxygen-carrying substance that gives red blood cells their colour.

Blood cells are produced by the bone marrow, which depends on, among other factors, a supply of iron and vitamins (folic acid and vitamin B^{12}) in order to function properly.

SYMPTOMS

Children may have no symptoms if the anaemia is mild and often the condition is found incidentally while investigating other problems such as infection or poor weight gain. When symptoms are present they include:

■ Pale skin
■ Tiredness and lethargy
■ Lack of interest in feeding
■ Fainting or breathlessness (in severe or sudden onset anaemia)
■ Susceptibility to infection
■ Rapid heart rate – a doctor may also be able to hear a heart murmur (abnormal heart sound) with a stethoscope.

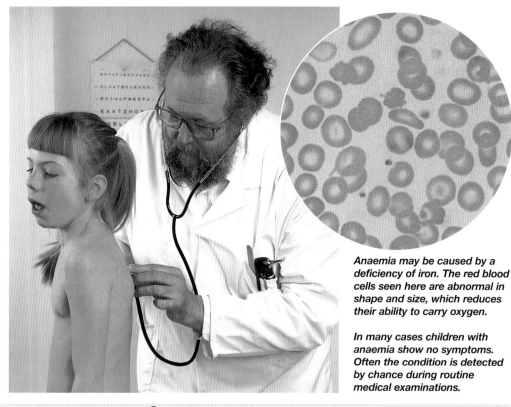

Anaemia may be caused by a deficiency of iron. The red blood cells seen here are abnormal in shape and size, which reduces their ability to carry oxygen.

In many cases children with anaemia show no symptoms. Often the condition is detected by chance during routine medical examinations.

Causes

It is useful to distinguish some of the causes of anaemia in the first few months of life from those in older children.

ANAEMIA IN NEWBORNS

A newborn baby has iron stores and a high level of circulating haemoglobin already in the bloodstream. This, combined with iron from breast milk or modified cows' milk, is usually enough to prevent anaemia. However, anaemia may develop in certain cases, such as:

■ Prematurity – a premature baby may have less stored iron and folic acid

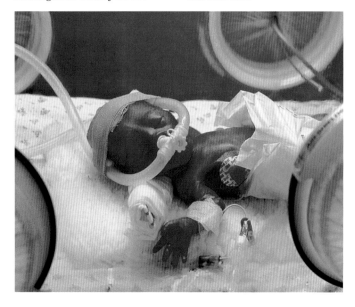

Premature babies may develop iron-deficiency anaemia. This is because they do not have the large iron stores that most babies are born with.

■ Loss of blood – during labour and delivery. Birth injury can cause severe bruises on the baby, known as haematomas. Bleeding from the placenta during pregnancy can cause blood loss from both the mother's and the baby's circulation
■ Infections – such as urine infection, chest infection and septicaemia (in which bacteria enter the bloodstream)
■ Haemolysis – the breakdown of red blood cells. This can result if the baby's blood cells are attacked by antibodies from the mother's bloodstream
■ Hereditary conditions – such as spherocytosis and G6PD deficiency – in which the red blood cells are faulty.

ANAEMIA IN CHILDREN

There are a number of causes of anaemia in older children:
■ Iron deficiency – this depends on dietary and social factors. For example, children who have a poor diet may be anaemic
■ Chronic infection or diseases such as rheumatoid arthritis, colitis (inflammation of the large bowel) or kidney failure – can reduce the body's capacity to produce blood cells
■ Lead poisoning – from dust created by old flaking paint or car exhaust fumes
■ Blood loss – regular nosebleeds or blood loss from the stomach or bowels
■ Cows' milk intolerance – the lining of the bowel becomes inflamed due to an allergic reaction, blood is lost and iron is not absorbed effectively
■ Thalassaemia and sickle cell disease – in which the production of haemoglobin itself is defective
■ Haemophilia – a deficiency of blood-clotting proteins which can cause spontaneous bleeding into joints and muscles
■ Menstrual blood loss – if menstrual blood flow is particularly heavy in adolescent girls.

Iron-deficiency anaemia

Iron-deficiency anaemia is the most common nutritional disorder in the
world, characterized by a lack of iron in the blood. This form of anaemia is corrected
by replenishing depleted stores of iron in the body with iron supplements.

If a doctor suspects that a child has iron-deficiency anaemia, a physical examination is performed taking careful note of any obvious signs such as pale mucous membranes inside the lower eyelid and the mouth. The doctor will also ask the parents about the child's general health, and whether there have been any recent infections.

BLOOD TESTS

Samples of blood are taken to diagnose the anaemia and to help determine the cause. Besides measuring the haemoglobin level, the size and number of red blood cells can also be observed. Blood tests also help doctors to detect other problems, such as kidney failure.

The level of haemoglobin varies, but in children the average level is calculated according to age:

Age	Level
0 - 2 wks	14.5-24.5 g/dl
2 - 8 wks	12.5-20.5 g/dl
2 - 6 mths	10.0-17.3 g/dl
1 - 6 yrs	9.5-14.5 g/dl
6 -16 yrs	10.3-14.9 g/dl
16 -18 yrs	11.1-15.7 g/dl

Blood tests are used to diagnose iron-deficiency anaemia. The samples are analysed for levels of haemoglobin and iron in the patient's blood.

Treatment

Iron-deficiency anaemia may be treated with iron supplements in the form of syrup. The medicine should be stored well out of reach of any children.

Iron deficiency is corrected by taking iron in the form of medicine or syrup, usually given for one month followed by a repeat blood test.

IRON SUPPLEMENTS

Over the first month of treatment with iron supplements, the level of haemoglobin should rise by about 1 g/dl. If successful, the treatment is continued until a satisfactory haemoglobin level is reached.

However, it may take a further month or two of iron treatment before the body's iron stores are fully replenished.

An overdose of iron is very dangerous, and therefore supplements should be stored away from children and should be dispensed in child-proof containers.

PREVENTION

Mothers who are breast-feeding their babies should be aware that, after six months of breast milk, other dietary sources are required. This is because breast milk alone no longer provides a sufficient amount of iron.

Children should be encouraged to eat fruit and drink natural fruit juice, as the vitamin C these contain helps the body to absorb iron.

Investigating other anaemias

Failure of iron treatment to raise haemoglobin levels should prompt further investigation into the cause of the anaemia. This will involve more specialized tests, usually performed under the guidance of a paediatrician or a paediatric haematologist.

X-rays or other scans may be performed in order to detect liver, kidney, stomach or bowel problems.

Genetic testing

There may be a family history of blood disorders such as sickle cell anaemia or thalassaemia. Genetic testing of the child and also of the parents may help to determine this.

Bone marrow aspiration

Bone marrow may be required for analysis. Samples are taken during a technique known as bone marrow aspiration: marrow is withdrawn into a needle inserted into a bone (usually the hip), usually under local anaesthesia (and sedation, especially if the child is anxious).

A pathologist then examines the bone marrow under a microscope in order to establish the cause of the anaemia.

Bone marrow aspiration is performed to find out the cause of anaemia. The marrow is withdrawn into a specialized needle and examined.

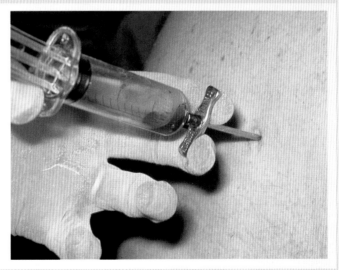

Thalassaemia

Thalassaemia refers to a group of inherited blood disorders usually diagnosed in childhood. They are caused by the abnormal production of haemoglobin, which is vital for transporting oxygen in the blood.

Haemoglobin is a complex molecule which is found in red blood cells and is essential for the delivery of oxygen to the body's tissues. If haemoglobin production is defective, as in thalassaemia, people become anaemic and their body tissues may not receive enough oxygen for their metabolic needs.

HAEMOGLOBIN DEFICIENCY
Normal haemoglobin is composed of four protein chains called globins, each of which is associated with an oxygen-carrying haem molecule. There are two types of globin, alpha and beta; they join in pairs to create haemoglobin molecules. The chains exist in roughly equal amounts and are in balance with each other.

In thalassaemia, there is defective production of either the alpha or beta chains. This results in defective haemoglobin production. It is the lack of normal haemoglobin in the circulation that leads to the development of anaemia and the symptoms of thalassaemia.

Structure of a haemoglobin molecule

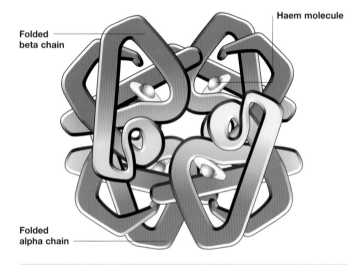

Folded beta chain

Haem molecule

Folded alpha chain

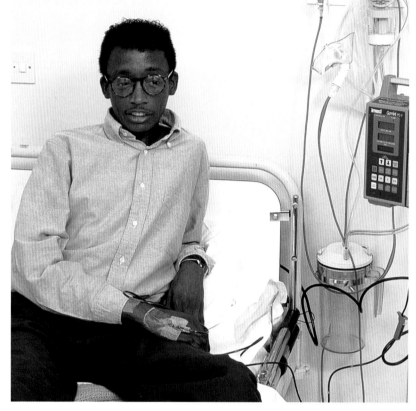

Haemoglobin is made up of four protein (globin) chains and four haem groups. The complex structure of the molecule allows it to bind oxygen.

A child with thalassaemia produces either the alpha or beta chains of haemoglobin at a reduced rate. This reduces the blood's ability to carry oxygen.

Types of thalassaemia

There are two main types of thalassaemia:
- Beta thalassaemia, in which there is defective production of beta globin chains
- Alpha thalassaemia, in which alpha globin production is defective.

Both types of thalassaemia have different sub-types with varying levels of severity. Beta thalassaemia is discussed here in more detail than alpha thalassaemia since one of its forms (beta thalassaemia major) is a very serious, life-threatening condition from childhood onwards. Alpha thalassaemia, in all its different forms, tends to affect people less seriously.

A routine blood examination may reveal the presence of previously undetected thalassaemia in a child who has mild anaemia.

Beta thalassaemia minor and major

There are three forms of beta thalassaemia: beta thalassaemia minor, intermedia
and major. The first of these has the least severe symptoms, but people with this disease
run the risk of passing the severe form (beta thalassaemia major) on to their children.

Beta thalassaemia minor

Beta thalassaemia is found all over the world, but it tends to be found in localized geographical areas. It is particularly common around the Mediterranean and in the Middle East. In fact, nearly 20 per cent of the population in these areas – over 100 million people – carry the thalassaemia gene. This localization around the Mediterranean is the reason why this disease is so named: 'thalassaemia' means 'anaemia of the sea'.

ANALYSING BLOOD
People with beta thalassaemia minor are usually fit and do not appear ill. The condition is often only detected by chance through a routine blood analysis. Affected individuals have a mild anaemia. The appearance of the blood under the microscope closely resembles that of iron deficiency anaemia, which is by far the most common type of anaemia. Further blood analysis can rule out iron deficiency, however.

More detailed analysis of the blood will reveal abnormal quantities of normal blood components.

PROGNOSIS
Children diagnosed with beta thalassaemia minor live a normal life and are not ill. They may, however, be prone to anaemia later in life, such as during pregnancy or during an infection.

The blood of a patient with beta thalassaemia has almost double the usual quantity of HbA2 (a normal type of haemoglobin).

Inheriting beta thalassaemia

People with beta thalassaemia minor can pass the severe form of the disease (beta thalassaemia major) to their children. This could easily happen if an affected individual were to have a child with another person with beta thalassaemia minor (see diagram below). Counselling of people with thalassaemia minor is thus very important in order to help prevent the birth of a child with beta thalassaemia major.

Beta thalassaemia minor may to some extent protect people with the thalassaemia trait from malaria. This may explain the high proportion of people in Middle East and in the Mediterranean area who have thalassaemia, as malaria is common in these parts of the world.

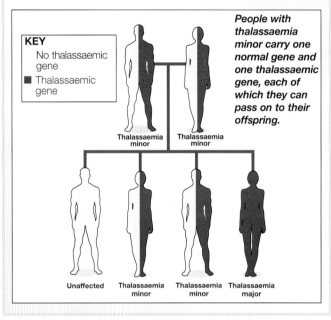

People with thalassaemia minor carry one normal gene and one thalassaemic gene, each of which they can pass on to their offspring.

KEY
☐ No thalassaemic gene
■ Thalassaemic gene

Thalassaemia minor — Thalassaemia minor

Unaffected | Thalassaemia minor | Thalassaemia minor | Thalassaemia major

Beta thalassaemia major

Beta thalassaemia major arises when a child inherits defective genes for beta globin from both parents and is consequently unable to produce normal amounts of beta globin. The excess alpha globins clump together and form insoluble lumps in red blood cells, making the cells smaller and paler. These cells do not live as long as normal and there is a marked reduction in the production of new cells. This results in a severe anaemia.

However, this anaemia does not become apparent until the patient is aged six months, as in the first few months of life most haemoglobin is fetal haemoglobin, not the adult type.

SYMPTOMS
Infants with the condition look unwell, listless and pale. They also show signs of not developing normally – in particular, they have a poor appetite and gain little weight. They are slow to begin walking but will develop normally mentally.

Affected children become severely anaemic and develop:
■ A characteristic facial appearance, known as chipmunk or Mongoloid face
■ Characteristic bone changes that are visible on X-ray, such as 'hair-on-end' skull, due to expansion of marrow
■ Bone thinning or fracturing.

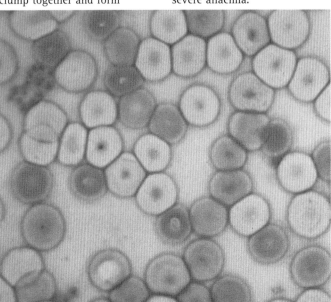

In this micrograph of a fetal blood smear, the red cells are normal oxygen-carrying red blood cells. The pale cells are abnormal thalassaemic red cells.

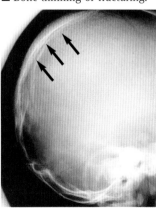

This X-ray of a child's skull shows the characteristic 'hair-on-end' bone (arrowed). The fuzzy edge of the skull is due to marrow expansion.

Treating thalassaemia

There is no cure for thalassaemia, so affected children may
suffer from the effects of the disorder throughout their lives.
However, treatment can help patients to cope with the disease.

Repeated blood transfusions are the mainstay of treatment for beta thalassaemia major. Once the diagnosis has been made, patients should have regular blood transfusions, usually every four to six weeks. The blood transfusions aim to raise the numbers of different cells in the blood (blood count), and thus correct the level of anaemia. Blood transfusion is absolutely necessary for patients with beta thalassaemia major. Without it, they would die.

Transfusions permit therapeutic adjustment of anaemia levels and allow children to grow without developing the characteristic changes to the bones.

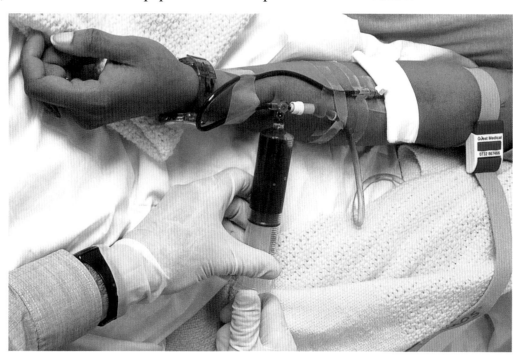

Blood transfusions are essential for the treatment of beta thalassaemia major. However, repeated transfusions introduce too much iron into the body.

Iron toxicity

The main problem with repeated blood transfusions is that they put too much iron into the body. This iron overload is toxic to the body. It can damage the liver, heart and other organs.

TREATING TOXICITY
Iron toxicity can be treated by infusion with a drug known as desferrioxamine. This drug is administered for eight hours a day five or six days a week.

In addition, oral vitamin C is given to further increase the removal of iron from the body.

The treatment regime is very demanding for patients and relatives, so it is not surprising

that people often do not conform to treatment.

Treatment undoubtedly increases the life expectancy of people with beta thalassaemia major but it is not a cure. Some children with the condition may survive into early adulthood. However, the outlook for them is still very poor. Despite treatment, it is unusual for children with this type of thalassaemia to reach the age of sexual maturity.

The drug desferrioxamine is administered to thalassaemic patients intravenously to counteract the effects on the body of iron toxicity.

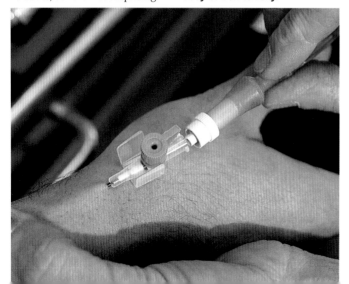

Removing the spleen

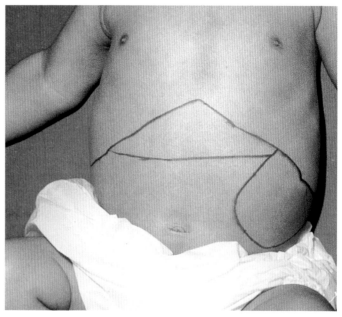

An enlarged spleen is often one of the symptoms of thalassaemia. This traps red blood cells, resulting in reduced numbers in blood vessels, increasing anaemia.

Surgical removal of the spleen can sometimes help children with thalassaemia. However, patients who have had a splenectomy (an operation to remove the spleen) are prone to

An enlarged liver and spleen (medically known as hepatosplenomegaly) can result from thalassaemia. Removal of the spleen may be necessary.

infection with pneumococcal bacteria. They should be vaccinated and given penicillin throughout their life to prevent such infection.

Other thalassaemias

As well as beta thalassaemia minor and major, there are also beta thalassaemia intermedia and alpha thalassaemias. Antenatal testing of women who have the thalassaemic trait can identify fetuses with severe forms of the disease.

Beta thalassaemia intermedia

There is a third type of beta thalassaemia, known as beta intermedia thalassaemia. This is so called because it is more serious than the minor form but less serious than the major form.

People with this thalassaemia have a haemoglobin level that is relatively low but high enough to enable them to lead a reasonably normal life. They do not need blood transfusions, thus they are at much less risk of iron overload problems.

PROGNOSIS
Children with this disease grow normally and often survive into adulthood. Diagnosis is often made because of a severe anaemia during an infection or some other stressful event.

A severe acute anaemia, which causes pale gums, is often the first indication of the presence of beta thalassaemia intermedia. The diagnosis may not be made until several years after birth.

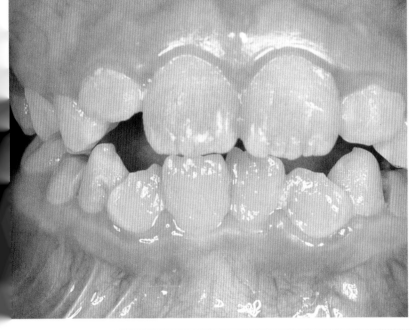

Alpha thalassaemia

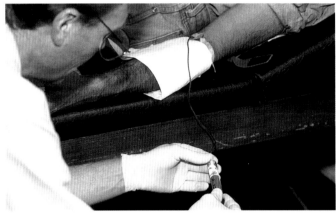

Alpha thalassaemia can produce a wide spectrum of disease and there is no clear division between a major form and a minor form. This is because there are four sets of genes which produce the alpha globin chain found in haemoglobin.

DEGREE OF SEVERITY
The severity of the disease depends on how many of these four sets of genes are affected.

If only one set is affected and three are functioning normally, the patient is essentially normal with no significant ill-health. The disease becomes progressively more serious, however, with two and three defective sets. Nevertheless, even with three defective sets, the anaemia is often mild with occasional short, sudden drops in the blood count during times

Blood analysis is essential to check for alpha thalassaemia. In this form of the disease there are increased levels of a type of haemoglobin called HbH.

of infection. When all four sets of genes are affected, no alpha globin is produced. This is incompatible with life, so the affected individual dies as a fetus before birth.

Like beta thalassaemia, alpha thalassaemia is found in localized, malarial areas in the world. It is common in southeast Asia, but not in the Middle East or around the Mediterranean.

DIAGNOSIS
Alpha thalassaemia is diagnosed by blood analysis. If it is present, anaemia will be evident. Unlike beta thalassaemia, there will be no increase in the levels of HbA2.

Antenatal diagnosis

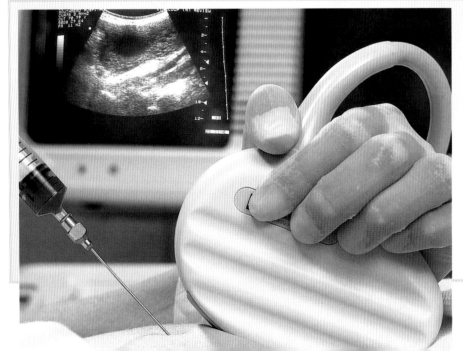

Beta thalassaemia major can be diagnosed prenatally. If a woman is known to have the thalassaemia trait, or is found to have it during a routine analysis, then the father should be screened. If both parents have the trait there is a strong possibility that the unborn child may develop the severe form of thalassaemia.

The diagnosis can be done either in the first trimester (third) of pregnancy (using a technique known as chorionic villus sampling) or in the second trimester (by directly sampling the fetal blood supply).

If the fetus is found to have beta thalassaemia major, the mother may be offered a termination. However, there may be cultural, religious or social objections to abortion.

Chorionic villus sampling involves taking a sample of the membrane surrounding the fetus. This can determine whether an unborn child has beta thalassaemia major.

Children with HIV

HIV – the virus that leads to AIDS – can be transmitted from an infected woman to her unborn child. Although not all babies acquire HIV from the mother, those that do require extensive treatment and emotional support.

CONTRACTING HIV

Virtually all new cases of human immunodeficiency virus (HIV) infection in children result from transmission of the virus around the time of birth from an infected mother to the newborn. In the past, a number of children were infected through blood products and blood transfusions, but the numbers are now very low.

Around 850 children have been identified as HIV-positive in the UK. More than 3,000 children are living in families where the father, mother or both are infected with HIV, which can greatly affect the child.

HIV IN THE FAMILY

The mother and the father may have the virus, but the child will not necessarily be infected. If the mother carries the virus, but the baby does not, the baby has an uncertain future. The health of the parents is an important issue, and infected parents will worry whether they will live to see their children grow up. The parents will want to make provision for their children when their own health deteriorates.

The children are therefore very much affected by the infection. It is estimated that by the year 2000, there will be 10 million children orphaned by HIV worldwide. There are very few

life-threatening illnesses that threaten the life of both the adult carer and the child, as is the case with HIV.

NEW CASES

Data from the antenatal screening of women and the Guthrie card test, in which a blood sample is taken from a newborn and tested for HIV, show that the numbers of infected children in the UK is not rising dramatically. However, the number of children attending clinics has risen because infected children now have a longer life expectancy.

In the early 1990s, the situation was very different. The data showed a steep rise in the number of mothers who were delivering babies exposed to HIV in Inner London. Since 1996, this appears to have levelled to about 1 in 300 women in Inner London. In Outer London, the number is less, around 1 in 1,000, and for the rest of the UK the number of HIV-infected women is around 1 in 8,500.

Discarded hypodermic syringes can be a source of HIV infection if the needle breaks the skin. Intravenous (IV) drug users – a particularly high-risk group – often discard their equipment with no thought for the public.

HIV in Europe

Children are affected by HIV across Europe in various ways, but particularly poignant are the risk factors for the mothers. For example, in southern Europe and in Scotland, a greater proportion of the women infected are intravenous drug users, whereas in northern Europe the majority of women have acquired the virus

heterosexually. These differences affect the lifestyles of the families into which these children are born.

In Romania, a particular situation arose during the Ceaucescu regime when many children were institutionalized. A large number of children became infected through blood products:

they were given immunizations and blood products as a tonic if they looked unwell.

Unfortunately, the blood supply was not screened and the needles were often reused. As a result, 5,000 children became infected with HIV. Fortunately, that has now ceased, and although there are large numbers of orphans in Romania, many of whom are still living with HIV, this problem of infection has not been repeated.

A lack of knowledge about the causes of HIV and AIDS led to many accidental infections. Tragically, many children in Romanian orphanages contracted HIV from contaminated blood products.

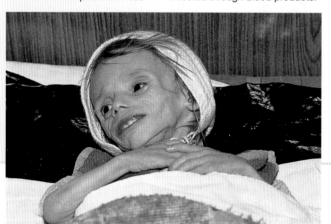

A number of haemophiliacs contracted HIV in the 1980s from contaminated blood. Today, blood is routinely screened for the virus.

Diagnosing HIV

HIV is a difficult condition to diagnose in a child, but advances in amplification techniques have meant that the virus is becoming easier to detect.

Once HIV gets into the bloodstream, it locates the cells of the immune system, and, in particular, white blood cells called T-lymphocytes. There are two types of T-lymphocyte: helper T-cells (CD4 cells) and cytotoxic T-cells (Tc-cells). Helper T-cells express CD4 receptors on their surface. The virus enters these cells by combining with CD4 receptors; they become CD4-positive cells.

Inside the CD4 cell the virus uses the cell's cellular machinery to make new copies of itself. These burst from the cell and, as a result, the cell dies. The viruses then attack other uninfected CD4 cells, and the lymphocyte population gradually declines.

The CD4 cells are destroyed at the rate of many millions each day, which must be replenished

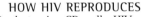

Placenta

The HIV virus can be transmitted from the placenta to the unborn baby in the womb.

in order to maintain normal immune responses to foreign organisms. After a time, the body is unable to replenish the CD4 cells as the rate at which they are being destroyed exceeds the rate at which they can be made. The CD4 cell count begins to fall, and the immune system begins to fail.

The body becomes unable to defend itself against organisms that would not normally cause infection or disease. The diseases caused by organisms that take hold while the body's immune system is weak are called opportunistic infections. These include viral infections such as *pneumocystis carinii* and fungal infections.

HOW HIV REPRODUCES
By destroying CD4 cells, HIV attacks the very cells that co-ordinate the body's own defence. Unfortunately, this is an extraordinarily good tactic for the virus as it avoids being destroyed. HIV is also able to change its outer coat by genetically varying the proteins on its surface. This makes it a difficult target for both the drugs that are used to destroy it and the body's own virus defence systems.

The immune response may be avoided by just one or two virions (virus particles) within the body that have changed their outer coat, but this is enough to set up a

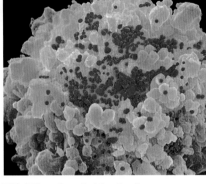

Genetic material of the cell

CD4

Viral surface protein

Uninfected CD4-cell

HIV particle

The entry point for the HIV virus is the CD4 protein, which is found in certain white blood cells. An HIV particle has surface proteins that can bind with the CD4 host and merge with it.

new round of infection with a resistant virus.

DIAGNOSING HIV
Diagnosing HIV infection in a child is complicated. The majority of infants born to HIV-positive mothers are not infected, but the mothers have special blood proteins, called antibodies, which attack specific foreign particles they encounter.

HIV-specific antibodies cross from the mother to the fetus, via the placenta, so nearly all of these babies will carry their mother's antibodies.

HIV-infection is normally

This T-lymphocyte blood cell (green) has been infected with the HIV virus (red). The virus will replicate itself, eventually causing the T-cell to die.

confirmed by an antibody test, which detects antibodies specific to HIV in the blood. This test, however, is not helpful with newborns, as a healthy baby whose mother is infected will nonetheless test positive for her HIV antibodies. The mother's antibodies will gradually disappear from the baby's circulation, but because the tests are so sensitive, tiny amounts of the antibody may still be detected up to the age of 18 months.

IDENTIFYING HIV
The HIV virus is identified using amplification techniques. These involve obtaining a small amount of the viral genetic material and amplifying it so that it becomes detectable. Immediately after birth, the technique often shows a negative result, but two weeks later, the baby can test positive. This occurs because the infant has become infected at the time of delivery, even through anti-retroviral medicines were given to prevent transmission from the mother to her child.

AIDS: a redundant term?

In the past, a number of unusual infections and complications were indicative of a severely damaged immune system in a child; they were regarded as AIDS-defining illnesses. The child's prognosis was poor, and their life expectancy was only one month from the time of diagnosis.

Today, illnesses that were once AIDS-defining, such as *Pneumocystis carinii* pneumonia, can be prevented or, with swift diagnosis, treated. With

This lung sample shows Pneumocystis carinii pneumonia. It is not fatal in its own right, but in an immunocompromised person – such as an AIDS patient – it can lead to death.

treatments becoming ever more effective, the life expectancy of infected children is being constantly extended, so the label 'AIDS' is no longer helpful.

Children who acquire the HIV virus around the time of birth fall into two groups. About a fifth of infected children have very rapid disease progression. During the first 12 months of life they may have severe opportunistic

infections or central nervous system problems, with severe developmental delay and spasticity. For the other four-fifths of infected children, their life expectancy is about nine years, but with the constant development of new drug treatments, this is always increasing. Many children can now expect to live into the second decade of their lives.

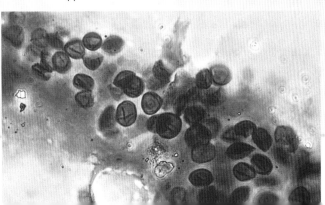

Caring for children with HIV

Advances in paediatric diagnosis and drug treatment mean that very few children infected with HIV have to be hospitalized. The vast majority are now treated as outpatients.

Children are looked after in a family clinic because for every child who is infected, there is also an adult carer who is infected, or possibly both adults who are caring for the child. As the outlook for infected children is being continually improved, the need to admit them to hospital is reduced.

Most children are now exclusively dealt with as outpatients. In a clinic of 80–100 infected children, there might only be two children who are admitted to the ward. In the past, at least 10 per cent of the infected child population would have been on the ward at any given moment.

Paediatricians are prescribing much the same combination of drugs to children as are prescribed in adult practice.

However, some drugs, called protease inhibitors, are difficult for children to swallow as they are chalky. Unfortunately, these are some of the most powerful drugs against HIV. There is only one class of protease inhibitor that is more palatable as it is a fluid, but it has a high alcohol content and tastes unpleasant.

Researchers are trying to find the best combination of drugs. This may consist of a three-drug combination that can be given once or, at most, twice daily. The combination must also be well tolerated by the child, as they have to be able to take it for the long-term. At the family clinic, time will be spent offering support to the mothers and care givers so they understand that it may take some effort to find appropriate drugs for their child.

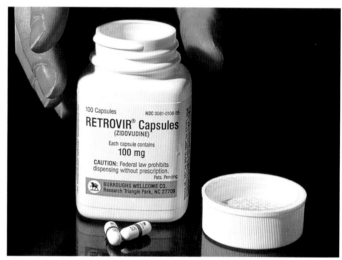

Zidovudine, or AZT, is an anti-retroviral treatment that slows the development of HIV. A woman who takes AZT during pregnancy can reduce the chances of transmitting the virus to her unborn child.

Infections in children with HIV

Conditions that are difficult to diagnose and treat include opportunist infections, unusual central nervous system disorders, pneumonias and mycobacteria infections – a class of bacteria related to tuberculosis bacteria. Normally, mycobacteria cause no disease at all, but when the

HIV-positive children may be susceptible to opportunistic infections, such as LIP, a rare form of pneumonia (below).

immune system is severely impaired they can cause illness with typically recurrent fevers and sweats, abdominal pain, weight loss, diarrhoea and abdominal distention.

Controlling such an infection is difficult and requires multiple drugs. Often, improving the child's immune system will resolve their symptoms, so tackling the virus may be the best way of tackling mycobacterial infections.

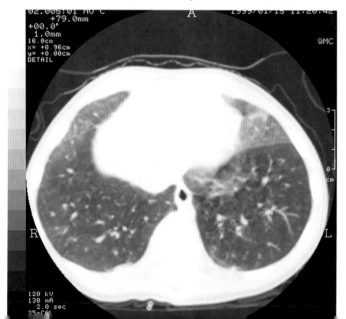

Complications with immunizations

The child with HIV may not respond well to immunizations, and there are certain immunizations, such as the influenza vaccine, which are not effective with advanced disease. The current situation may change as treatment improves.

■ Children with HIV should receive all of their routine immunizations, but administering bacille Calmette-Guérin (BCG) to prevent infection with tuberculosis (TB) is not advisable because the vaccine consists of live bacteria. If the immune system is compromised (weakened), giving such a vaccine can do similar or greater damage than TB itself.

■ Oral polio drops are also a live virus vaccine, which works by the virus replicating in the gut. If the immune system is compromised, the viral strain

of the vaccine can go on replicating in the body and is shed in the stools for weeks to months afterwards. This is not a risk to the child who receives it, but if it then infects a second person whose immune system is also weakened – such as the mother or carer who changes the baby's nappy – then the carer may develop paralytic polio disease. Inactivated injected polio vaccine is recommended for HIV-positive babies instead.

A few immunizations may cause problems for the HIV-infected child, as many consist of live bacteria that will compromise the already weakened immune system.

Prevention

HIV infection in a woman does not guarantee transmission to her baby. There are several options available to limit the spread of the virus.

Human immunodeficiency virus may be transmitted to the baby before, during or after birth. If a mother is unaware that she is HIV-infected and gives birth by vaginal delivery, and breast-feeds her child, she has a 30 per cent chance of transmitting the virus to her baby. In contrast, if a mother knows about her infection, she can take a number of precautions to reduce the risk of transmission.

Firstly, the mother can reduce her viral load to very low levels by taking anti-retroviral treatment such as AZT. Anti-retroviral treatment may also be given to the baby immediately after birth for three to six weeks, as this reduces the risk of transmission.

ROUTE OF INFECTION
Antibodies also cross the placenta and will be found in the newborn even when the viral load is low. Some types of antibody may pass to the baby without the virus and if the woman is healthy in pregnancy there is a good chance that the antibodies will not persist beyond 6 to 18 months.

Breast-feeding the baby is known to double the risk of transmitting the virus. Therefore

The unborn baby is particularly vulnerable to HIV infection during the passage down the birth canal immediately prior to birth. If the woman decides to have a Caesarean section, the risks of infection can be reduced by up to 50 per cent.

in developed countries HIV-positive mothers are counselled not to breast-feed their children. However, in developing countries, other life-threatening risks associated with bottle-feeding probably outweigh the chances of transmitting the virus in breast milk. In such cases, breast-feeding is still recommended.

REDUCED RISK
Most infections occur during the passage of the baby through the birth canal during labour. Therefore, an HIV-infected mother may be offered an elective Caesarean section. This is a planned delivery at about 38 weeks of pregnancy. Caesarean deliveries appear to halve the risk of transmission compared to vaginal delivery.

If all of these precautions are taken, the risk of HIV transmission is less than 2 per cent overall.

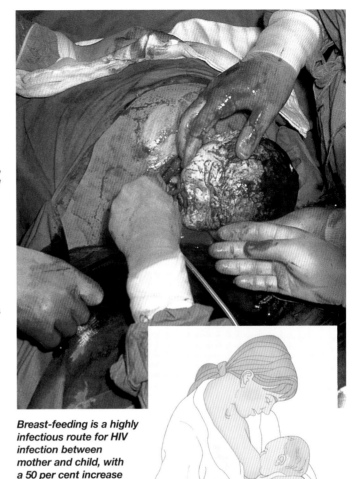

Breast-feeding is a highly infectious route for HIV infection between mother and child, with a 50 per cent increase in the likelihood of transmission. In developed countries, women who are infected with the HIV virus are advised to bottle-feed their child.

Education

The effect of HIV education on teenagers appears to be patchy, with some schools allowing more time within the curriculum for personal and social education than others. The result is that some teenagers come out of school with a very hazy understanding of HIV.

Alarmingly, many teenagers now hold the view that they are at no risk. Risk-taking behaviour increases as teenagers become sexually active so helping them to understand how they can protect themselves is an important issue. As the UK has the highest teenage pregnancy rate in Europe, this suggests that these young women are at risk of sexually transmitted infections, including HIV.

There is still a lot of ignorance

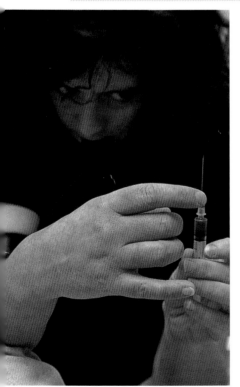

IV drug abuse is a common source of HIV infection, especially when users share needles. Teenagers need to be educated about the risks of injecting drugs and HIV.

and fear about HIV infection, and some people react irrationally towards those who are infected. Understanding how the HIV is transmitted may resolve the misunderstandings.

HIV is a difficult virus to catch: it is transmitted by unprotected sexual contact, contaminated blood products and intravenous (IV) drug use

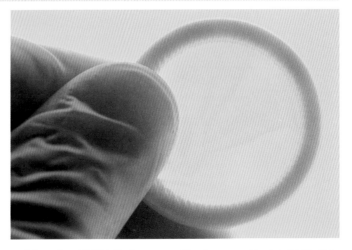

Condoms are the most effective barrier to sexually transmitted HIV infection. Both heterosexual and homosexual teenagers are encouraged to carry and use them to protect themselves.

and from mothers to their infants. Only intimate contact with an HIV-positive person can lead to transmission.

181

Diagnosing acute leukaemia

Distinguishing the subtle differences between acute myeloid leukaemia and acute lymphoid leukaemia is vital in terms of the prognosis and treatment of the condition.

Types of leukaemia

Acute leukaemia is divided into acute myeloid leukaemia (AML) and acute lymphoid – or lymphoblastic – leukaemia (ALL). There are no clinical features that can absolutely distinguish between AML and ALL.

Although the primitive blast cell is characteristic of both types, there are subtle differences in the microscopic appearances of myeloid blast cells and lymphoid blast cells. It is important to tell which type of acute leukaemia the patient has, as the treatment and prognosis differ, as shown below.

If there is uncertainty about the type of leukaemia, then special investigations may help. For example, molecules can be detected on the surface membrane of the blast cells by immuno-logical tests, characteristic of either myeloid or lymphoid cells, using highly specific antibodies.

CNS INVOLVEMENT

The blast cells of acute lymphoblastic leukaemia and, in rare cases, acute myeloid leukaemia may be hidden inside the brain and spinal cord, on the other side of the blood-brain barrier, where chemotherapy may not reach them. After the blood and bone marrow have been cleared of leukaemia cells they may be a cause of relapse. Patients with central nervous system (CNS) leukaemia may suffer from headache, vomiting, fits and a variety of nerve palsies affecting the face and eyes. In cases of acute lymphoid leukaemia, injections of chemotherapy are given into the cerebrospinal fluid by lumbar puncture to prevent CNS disease. Radiotherapy to the head is also effective.

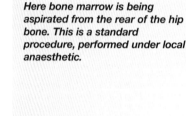

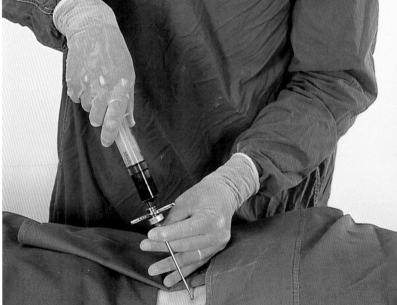

Here bone marrow is being aspirated from the rear of the hip bone. This is a standard procedure, performed under local anaesthetic.

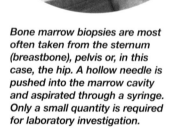

Bone marrow biopsies are most often taken from the sternum (breastbone), pelvis or, in this case, the hip. A hollow needle is pushed into the marrow cavity and aspirated through a syringe. Only a small quantity is required for laboratory investigation.

Treatments and prognoses

	Acute Myeloid	Acute Lymphoid
Cure rate	30–40% cure rate with chemotherapy	60–70% cure rate with chemotherapy
Incidence	Mainly affects adults	Mainly affects children
Central Nervous System Involvement	Rare	Common

Diagnostic tests for acute leukaemia

Primitive cells in the blood and bone marrow and changes in structure and number of chromosomes provide vital information for diagnosis and treatment.

Blood test

Blood tests will show the reduction in red cells (usually expressed as haemoglobin level), neutrophils and platelets. The leukaemia cells fill up the bone marrow and spill into the blood, often giving a high white cell count. Examination of a blood film under the microscope will show primitive blast cells.

A blood film is prepared by smearing a small quantity of blood over the length of a microscope slide – this is dried, stained and examined under the microscope. The sample shown here is taken from a patient with acute myeloid leukaemia (AML); the large, stained cells are immature blast cells.

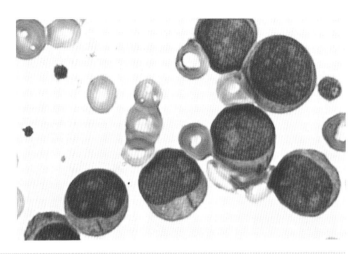

Bone marrow

Bone marrow may be examined by inserting a stout needle into the surface of the bone at sites where the bone cortex is thin, and red active marrow is normally found, for example, the breastbone or hip bone. This is usually performed under a local anaesthetic, similar to that used by a dentist before filling teeth. The bone marrow jelly may be extracted using a syringe. From this, slides are made up and examined under the microscope after staining.

In acute leukaemia many primitive leukaemia cells which are failing to mature into useful mature cells will be seen.

Bone marrow samples are taken through a hollow needle, usually from the sternum or pelvis.

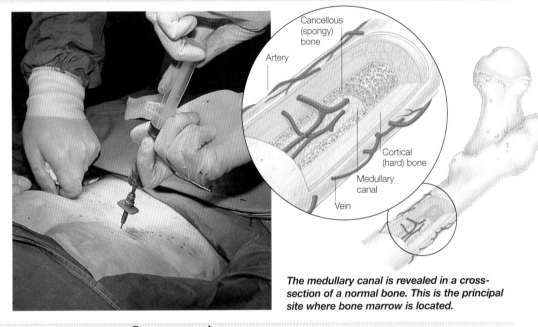

Cancellous (spongy) bone

Artery

Cortical (hard) bone

Medullary canal

Vein

The medullary canal is revealed in a cross-section of a normal bone. This is the principal site where bone marrow is located.

Cytogenetics

The activities of all cells, including leukaemia cells, are controlled by the cell's genetic code. The DNA that makes up the genetic code lies on the chromosomes within the central nucleus of the cell.

The chromosomes can be examined by culturing the cell so that it starts to go into division and then 'freezing' the chromosomes whilst they are spread out by adding a poison such as colchicine to the culture medium. The cells are then swollen by suspending them in a dilute salt solution and dropped onto glass microscope slides. The individual cells burst, releasing their chromosomes onto the slide. These are then stained and analyzed.

Using a computerized TV microscope, the chromosomes can be arranged in order of size as the cell's karyotype (the pattern of chromosomes in a particular individual). Sometimes in leukaemia the chromosomes are found to be abnormal.

Particular abnormalities may confer a better or worse prognosis than average, so that treatment may be made less or more powerful. The chromosome abnormality also provides a marker of the leukaemia cells, which should disappear when the bone marrow is restored to normal by treatment.

This karyotype shows abnormal chromosomes from leukaemic cells in a patient with AML. Here there is an extra chromosome 8, present in 13 per cent of all cases of AML.

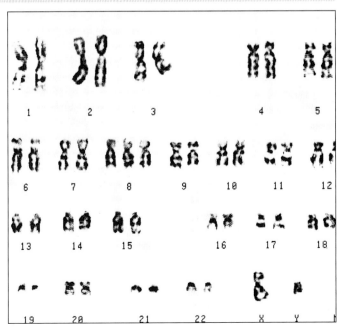

Treating acute leukaemia

Advances in bone marrow transplantation, chemotherapy, radiotherapy and supportive treatments have all improved the prognosis and survival rate both in children and adults.

Supportive treatment is required to compensate for the bone marrow failing to produce normal blood cells. Much of this is given by intravenous infusion and requires frequent monitoring of the clinical situation. It is usual to initially implant a long intravenous catheter (a Hickman line), running under the skin for a few inches before entering a large vein in the shoulder or neck. This is threaded into the largest central vein above the heart (the superior vena cava). When not in use, the end of the catheter can be sealed and filled with anticoagulant solution to prevent clotting.

This provides easy access to the patient's circulation and can be left in for more than a year if required. Chemotherapy drugs can also be administered through it.

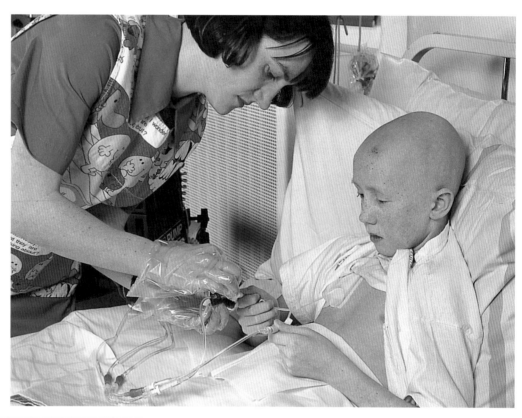

This nurse is administering intravenous chemotherapy to a young boy with leukaemia.

The causes of acute leukaemia

In most cases the cause is unknown, but possibilities include:

- Disruption to the DNA of the white cells occurs in most cases, but the cause of this damage is often unknown.
- Some children with congenital chromosome abnormalities, such as Down's syndrome, have an increased risk of developing acute leukaemia.
- Previous chemotherapy treatment for cancer may cause damage to the DNA of normal white cells and predispose to the development of acute leukaemia. This is particularly so if a class of cytotoxic drugs, known as alkylating agents, has been used and if chemotherapy has been combined with radiotherapy.
- Radiation does predispose to the development of acute leukaemia. There are increased cases in the vicinity of the Chernobyl nuclear accident, and before improved radiological safety standards, radiologists had an increased incidence of acute leukaemia.
- In dogs and cats, leukaemia may be transmitted by a virus. In humans, a very rare type of leukaemia is caused by the HTLV-I (human T-cell leukaemia/lymphoma virus), which is found in southern Japan and the Caribbean.
- Periodically clusters of leukaemia – especially ALL – are found; as in the increased incidence of acute leukaemia around the Sellafield nuclear reprocessing works, attributed to local radiation. In fact such localised collections of acute leukaemia are found throughout the world and may be caused by an unknown environmental or infective agent.

Bone marrow transplantation

Strong chemotherapy and total body radiotherapy eliminate bone marrow in preparation for transplantation from a donor. This treatment kills many residual leukaemia cells in the bone marrow. Also, the immune system transferred from the donor is often able to recognise residual leukaemia cells and destroy them – the graft-versus-leukaemia effect. The downside is that the donor's cells may fight the recipient's tissues causing graft-versus-host disease. This is centred on skin, intestine and liver, but no organ is exempt.

The donor's bone marrow is infused intravenously into the recipient. It takes 3–4 weeks for the new stem cells to grow and restore the blood counts to normal. During this period the recipient has all the problems with infection and bleeding associated with a low blood count. Sometimes the marrow fails to grow – graft failure.

Therefore, this treatment is reserved for cases which relapse after conventional chemotherapy, or when the leukaemia is unlikely to be cured by such chemotherapy. It is unusual for bone marrow transplants to be performed after the age of 50 as older patients are less able to tolerate the regime.

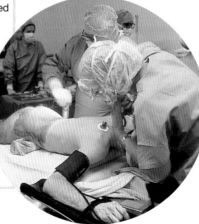

Bone marrow transplantation improves the prognosis in all patients, especially improving the outlook in children with ALL.

Chemotherapy

Chemotherapy aims to selectively kill malignant leukaemia cells, allowing normal cells to repopulate the bone marrow.

The aim of chemotherapy treatment is to kill the leukaemia cells and to allow the normal bone marrow cells to grow back. Chemotherapy treatment is divided into three phases: induction, consolidation and maintenance.

INDUCTION
The initial treatment is induction chemotherapy. After this, the bone marrow should show no evidence of leukaemia cells and the blood count will be normal. This treatment is not enough to cure acute leukaemia, as it is known from experience that residual leukaemia cells, not seen in a small bone marrow sample, will be a cause of later relapse.

CONSOLIDATION
To prevent subsequent relapse, further courses of consolidation chemotherapy are given. These treatments are usually given over a period of a few months.

MAINTENANCE
In acute lymphoid leukaemia, but not acute myeloid leukaemia, the value of maintenance chemotherapy has been proven. This is chemotherapy given in

Patients are given a number of drugs by intravenous chemotherapy. Chemotherapy for leukaemia often lasts for several months.

reduced doses, adjusted so as not to cause too much depression of the blood count, and can be administered as an outpatient. Most children with acute lymphoblastic leukaemia will have two years of chemotherapy in total, of which eighteen months is maintenance treatment.

The chemotherapy drugs used in acute leukaemia are a cocktail of anti-cancer agents similar to those used in the treatment of other malignant diseases. Multiple agents are given in order to maximize the chance of killing the leukaemia cell, as the drugs work on different areas of the cell's metabolism. Individual side effects of each drug can also be minimized by a mixture of drugs at lower doses. The recipe for each cocktail of chemotherapy drugs has been arrived at by continuing international trials, in which two similar cocktails are compared. That which produces the best results is then adopted and compared with a new drug combination.

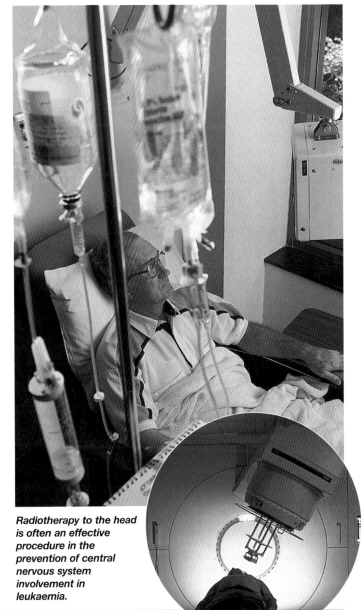

Radiotherapy to the head is often an effective procedure in the prevention of central nervous system involvement in leukaemia.

Side effects of drugs

Most commonly used cytotoxic drugs have similar side effects:

■ **Nausea and vomiting**
Fortunately the development of new anti-emetic drugs, such as ondansetron, has meant that this can be well controlled in most cases.

■ **Alopecia (hair loss) and impairment of nail growth**
Now fashion favours short hair this side-effect is better

tolerated than it used to be. Various strategies for minimizing hair loss are available, such as scalp cooling with ice packs, though they are of uncertain benefit. The hair will regrow after chemotherapy is completed and in the meantime a wig may be worn. Suspension of nail growth during the period of chemotherapy may cause ridges to form – these gradually grow down the nail.

■ **Depression of the blood count**
Often the blood count gets worse after chemotherapy before it gets better. The supportive care that is

Anti-emetic drugs are used to control the nausea and vomiting associated with chemotherapy.

necessary is outlined above. Hormones controlling the production of normal white cells from the bone marrow, particularly granulocyte colony stimulating factor (G-CSF), can be given to patients to stimulate the regrowth of normal white cells after the bone marrow has been flattened by chemotherapy. Unfortunately this is not a complete solution to the low white cell counts found after chemotherapy, as the G-CSF stimulates growth and multiplication of committed myeloid stem cells, rather than the most primitive cells which survive chemotherapy and which are the seed cells that repopulate the bone marrow.

■ **Mucositis**
All rapidly dividing tissues in the body are affected by chemotherapy, and the lining of

the gastrointestinal tract turns over rapidly as intestinal cells are continually being shed. Patients on chemotherapy may often suffer from mouth ulcers and diarrhoea and may require intravenous feeding if nutrition becomes a problem.

■ **Fertility**
Cytotoxic drugs are teratogenic – that is, they may cause fetal malformations. Patients taking them should therefore take adequate birth-control precautions. The drugs may also cause infertility, either temporary or permanent, depending on the types of drug used and the doses given. Storing of sperm may be an option for men, but for women the technology of successful freezing and subsequent thawing of unfertilized eggs has yet to be perfected.

Heart murmurs

Heart murmurs are common in infants and young children.
Most murmurs are harmless, but if a child has other symptoms,
they should be checked for structural heart defects.

In a healthy person, two sounds are distinguishable in each heartbeat. A heart murmur is an additional sound which may be heard at any point in the heartbeat cycle, although the interval between sounds one and two is the commonest point. The murmur, audible through a stethoscope, reflects abnormally fast or turbulent blood flow.

TYPICAL MURMURS

Disrupted blood flow is caused either by an abnormal connection between two chambers of the heart or by turbulent flow across a damaged heart valve. A common cause in children is a ventricular septal defect. In this condition, a hole in the septum (the inner wall dividing the heart chambers) between the high pressure left ventricle and the lower pressure right allows blood to flow from the left side to the right. Turbulent blood flow across the defect can be heard through a stethoscope as a murmur.

INNOCENT MURMURS

It is thought that up to 30 per cent of children have an audible heart murmur at some time. Most of these murmurs are harmless, or 'innocent', and are related to turbulent blood flow in the large vessels on either side of the heart, in the veins of the head and neck (this sound is referred to as the 'venous hum'), or around a valve. Innocent heart murmurs are not indicative of a structural abnormality.

Heart murmurs in children are sometimes caused by heart abnormalities. Children with heart problems may need to be admitted to hospital for surgery.

Normal heart sounds

In a healthy child, two distinctive heart sounds can be heard through a stethoscope during a normal cardiac cycle. These sounds, described as 'lub-dup', are created as the heart valves snap shut.

The first sound ('lub') occurs as the onset of contraction of the ventricles closes off both the tricuspid and mitral valves between the ventricles and atria; this is audible as a single sound.

The second sound ('dup') is heard as the emptied ventricles relax and allow the pulmonary valves to close. This second heart sound is normally heard as a split sound because closure of the aortic valve occurs slightly ahead of the pulmonary valve.

Heart valves control the direction of blood flow. Using a stethoscope, sounds made by the valves as they close may be heard.

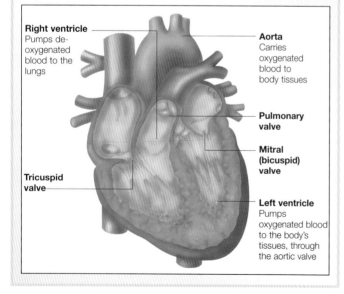

Right ventricle
Pumps de-oxygenated blood to the lungs

Tricuspid valve

Aorta
Carries oxygenated blood to body tissues

Pulmonary valve

Mitral (bicuspid) valve

Left ventricle
Pumps oxygenated blood to the body's tissues, through the aortic valve

Newborn examination

Listening to a baby's heart is an essential part of the first day examination. Eight babies per 1,000 live births have congenital heart disease.

If a baby is found to have a murmur, it is essential to check that there are no other signs of heart disease (rapid breathing, abnormal pulses or decreased levels of oxygen in the blood).

If any of these signs are present, an echocardiogram is performed to check the structure of the heart.

The majority of heart murmurs heard in newborns are transient and do not imply heart disease.

During a routine chest examination a doctor will listen to a baby's heartbeat. This is in order to detect a possible heart murmur.

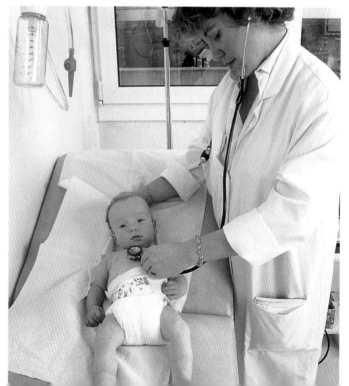

Diagnosing and assessing murmurs

Heart murmurs have certain audible characteristics, which can be heard using a stethoscope. If the doctor believes that the murmur is caused by a heart problem, further assessments and treatment will be needed.

A murmur is characterized in a number of ways:
- When it occurs during the cardiac cycle – murmurs may be heard as the ventricles empty (systolic murmurs), or as they are refilling (diastolic murmurs)
- Where it is most easily heard – murmurs due to abnormal blood flow are best heard when the stethoscope is placed on the patient's chest closest to the site of the abnormality. Traditionally, the mitral, tricuspid, aortic and pulmonary valves all have corresponding areas on the chest surface.
- Loudness – murmurs are graded for intensity from one to six. This is influenced by the presence or absence of a palpable 'thrill' when the abnormal blood flow can actually be felt through the skin.

INVESTIGATING A MURMUR
A completely well child with a typical innocent sounding murmur, who has no other symptoms or signs of heart disease, may simply be reassured that all is well by an experienced clinician.

If there are any features of concern, an echocardiogram will provide a reconstruction of the structure of the heart on screen and allow accurate diagnosis. This has now superseded all other diagnostic investigations such as chest X-ray and electrocardiogram.

BLOOD FLOW PATTERNS
In addition to the structure of the heart, blood flow patterns can also be calculated using Doppler ultrasound. This technique provides colour images of blood through the chambers of the heart and can determine the direction of any abnormal blood flow and if there is turbulence.

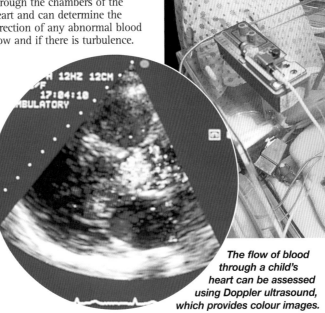

The flow of blood through a child's heart can be assessed using Doppler ultrasound, which provides colour images.

Echocardiography is a scanning technique used to detect heart defects. It enables doctors to visualize the structure of the heart and blood flow within it.

Abnormalities producing heart murmurs

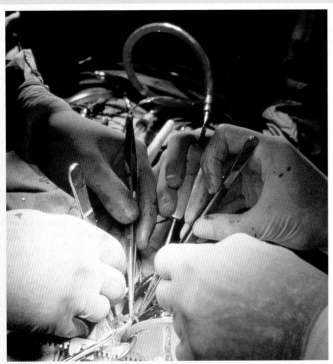

In children with ASD/VSD or patent ductus arteriosus, surgery may be necessary. The success rate of such operations is very good.

Common types of structural heart disease include:

Ventricular septal defect (VSD)
This is a condition in which there is a hole in the wall between left and right ventricles. Often the smallest holes produce the most turbulence and therefore the loudest murmurs.

Atrial septal defect (ASD)
This is associated with low pressure flow; the murmur is not due to the hole itself but the resultant increase in flow downstream across the pulmonary valve.

Patent ductus arteriosus
The ductus is present during fetal life and should close shortly after birth. If this does not happen, especially in premature babies, a loud murmur is audible. The murmur may be present only during systole or may be heard throughout the cardiac cycle.

Outlet valve stenosis
This is narrowing of one of the valves leading out of the ventricles (either the aortic or the pulmonary valve) resulting in fast turbulent flow as blood crosses it. The degree of obstruction to flow can be calculated using Doppler studies on the echocardiogram.

Treatment
Many heart defects, particularly VSDs, close spontaneously. If treatment proves necessary, it can sometimes be done via a cardiac catheter, which is threaded up to the heart through a blood vessel. Surgery is only required to treat the more complex defects.

Newborn heart disease

Developmental abnormalities of the heart and major blood vessels are relatively common in young babies. However, not all of these conditions are life-threatening.

Congenital heart disease is the most common physiological malformation in babies, affecting approximately eight in every 1,000 born in the UK. Most, however, have no symptoms, or symptoms that do not need treatment. The most common are small holes in the heart which close spontaneously.

CAUSES OF HEART DISEASE

Most heart disease is of unknown cause, but certain factors are associated with it. These include chromosome disorders and, during pregnancy, viral infections and the ingestion of toxins, such as excessive quantities of alcohol. Specific genes are associated with cardiac disease, most typically a defect of chromosome number 22.

Possible defects may occur singly or in combination:
■ Defects in the heart walls, classified as atrial, ventricular or atrioventricular septal defects (ASD, VSD and ASVD)
■ Blocked or leaking heart valves
■ Only one ventricle present – a univentricular heart
■ Abnormal connections of blood vessels
■ Heart may be abnormally placed on the right side of the chest (dextrocardia).

Dextrocardia refers to the abnormality in which the heart lies on the right side of the chest cavity (left on this X-ray image).

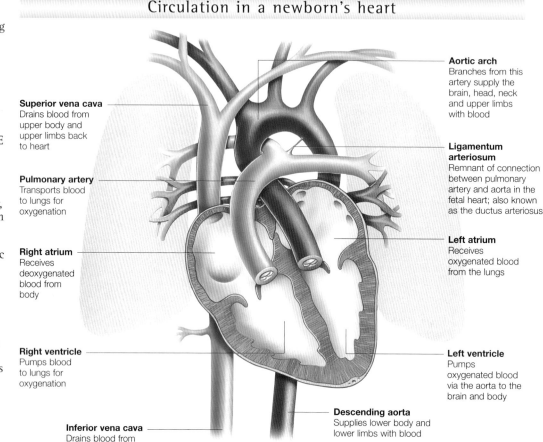

Circulation in a newborn's heart

Superior vena cava
Drains blood from upper body and upper limbs back to heart

Pulmonary artery
Transports blood to lungs for oxygenation

Right atrium
Receives deoxygenated blood from body

Right ventricle
Pumps blood to lungs for oxygenation

Inferior vena cava
Drains blood from lower body and limbs back to heart

Aortic arch
Branches from this artery supply the brain, head, neck and upper limbs with blood

Ligamentum arteriosum
Remnant of connection between pulmonary artery and aorta in the fetal heart; also known as the ductus arteriosus

Left atrium
Receives oxygenated blood from the lungs

Left ventricle
Pumps oxygenated blood via the aorta to the brain and body

Descending aorta
Supplies lower body and lower limbs with blood

The four chambers of the heart (two atria and two ventricles) are separated from each other by walls and valves, enabling blood to flow in the correct manner. Sometimes there is a defect in one of the walls, or an abnormal valve, resulting in heart disease.

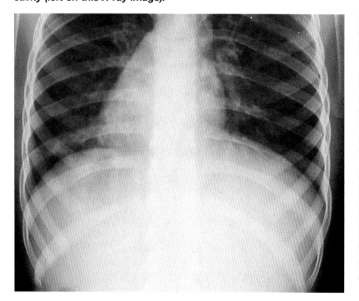

Identifying newborn heart disease

During pregnancy, a scan at 18 weeks is used to check for structural abnormalities of the fetus, as well as to monitor its size. One of the conditions that ultrasound technicians and radiographers will look for is evidence of congenital heart disease.

Some babies are born with serious heart malformations that are obvious at birth, with the baby being markedly cyanosed (skin and mucous membranes appearing blue due to inadequate oxygenation of blood). However, babies that are a normal healthy colour may still have a heart defect.

In others, there is often a delay in clinical presentation as a result of the circulatory changes in the hours immediately after birth.

The closure of the ductus arteriosus (a channel which normally closes after birth, connecting the left pulmonary artery to the aortic arch) in particular may be catastrophic in the infant with heart abnormalities, as blood may have been flowing across it to supply either the heart or the lungs. Thus, when the ductus arteriosus closes, the baby becomes cyanosed if the ductus was enhancing inadequate lung blood flow, and shocked if it had been vital for systemic flow.

Diagnosis of newborn heart disease

All newborns are examined shortly after birth to check for any irregularities of the cardiovascular system. There are specific tests that can diagnose heart problems.

The signs and symptoms of newborn heart disease include:

■ **Heart murmur**
A rushing noise which is heard with the stethoscope, indicating a turbulent flow of blood. Most murmurs in the newborn period are transient and innocent.

■ **Heart failure**
This occurs when blood supply to the tissues is inadequate. It can happen in hypoplastic left heart syndrome, when the left side of the heart is underdeveloped.

■ **Cyanosis**
A blue colour of the skin and mucous membranes due to inadequate blood oxygen. It occurs in pulmonary valve atresia (imperforation), where blood flow to the lungs is inadequate.

This newborn is cyanotic, as shown by the blue discoloration of the skin. The mucous membranes will also be affected.

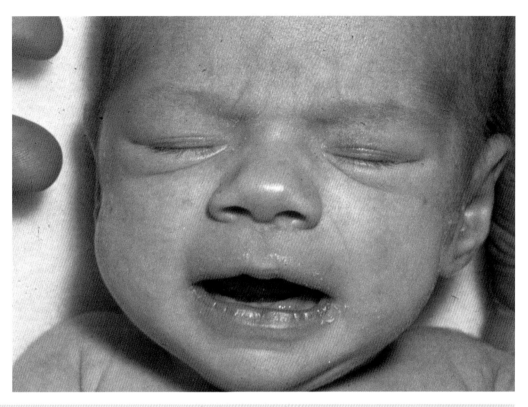

Techniques to identify heart defects

There are various methods and techniques that can be used to identify heart defects in babies. These include:

■ **Clinical examination**
Careful auscultation (listening to sounds made by gas and liquids in the body) of the heart, and feeling the pulses in all the limbs on routine examination.

Antenatal ultrasound of a fetus can help to detect a heart defect, so medical staff and parents can be prewarned of any likely sequence of events.

■ **Chest X-ray and electrocardiography (ECG)**
May help to complete the picture but are seldom diagnostic alone.

■ **Antenatal ultrasound**
This may pick up an abnormal appearance of the heart. The detection of a defect gives paediatric staff time to prepare.

■ **Cardiac ultrasound (echocardiography)**
The mainstay of diagnosis. Most lesions can be diagnosed by a skilled echocardiographer using an ultrasound machine.

■ **Cardiac catheterization**
Insertion of catheters into the heart and great vessels via a vein in the leg to inject a contrast medium. It enables direct visualization of blood flow patterns and measurement of pressures and oxygen levels in the heart. This method of diagnosis can have therapeutic potential (see below).

A doctor uses a stethoscope to listen to sounds made by the heart and lungs. Abnormalities of the heartbeart may be a sign of a heart disorder.

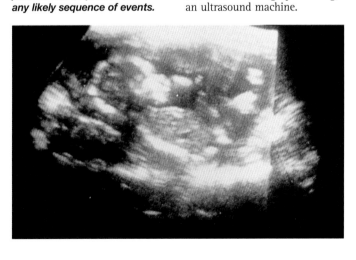

Common congenital heart defects

The ventricular septal defect (VSD) alone represents about 30 per cent of all cases. Over 80 per cent need no treatment, as the defect is in the muscular dividing wall of the heart, and closes over a period of months or years. Skilled assessment of the defect is required, as a small proportion need occlusion either by a device inserted by catheter or surgical intervention.

The classic clinical presentation is with a loud murmur in an asymptomatic child. Alternatively, the defect may cause the heart muscle to fail under the strain of the extra work of pumping blood through the defect.

All patients with VSD are at risk of infection of the heart tissue (endocarditis) and require prophylactic antibiotics when they undergo procedures that result in bacteria entering the bloodstream (such as surgery).

Treating congenital heart disease

Many congenital heart defects are detected antenatally, alerting the obstetric team that treatment may be necessary at birth. Medical intervention will then be required to stabilize the newborn.

Following a suspicion of heart disease, the infant requires transfer to a tertiary referral centre for accurate diagnosis. This will involve echocardiogram (ultrasound echo imaging) and, possibly, surgery. Before transport is arranged, the infant must be stabilized with intravenous therapy, ventilation and other measures, as required.

CORRECTING DEFECTS VIA CATHETER

If the anatomical defect requires correction, this can sometimes be achieved via a cardiac catheter without the need for open surgery. An example of this is aortic stenosis (restriction of flow through the aortic valve, which can sometimes be alleviated by stretching the valve with a balloon introduced during cardiac catheterization).

In addition, septal defects and patent ductus arteriosus can be closed with coils or umbrella-like devices deployed by catheter.

Premature babies born with suspected heart abnormalities may need to be taken in an incubator to a specialist unit by air ambulance.

If a heart defect is suspected, a doctor first uses a stethoscope to listen to the heart rhythm and breathing of a premature baby in an incubator.

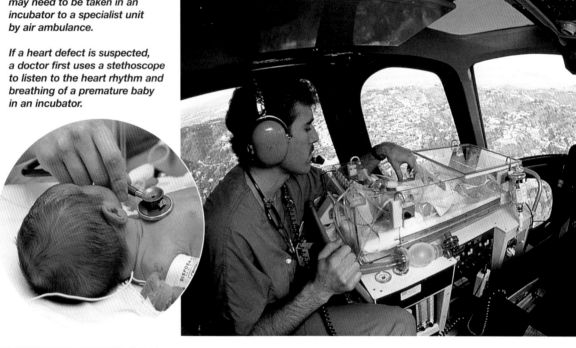

Infant cardiac surgery

Following diagnosis of a heart defect in the newborn that requires medical intervention, the cardiologist and cardiac surgeon will discuss the most appropriate course of action. If surgery is decided upon, its exact nature and timing are jointly agreed.

Detailed discussions with the parents will also occur, and this must include consideration of the benefits of any procedure and the risks involved. Some lesions require multi-stage correction, lasting into adult life, for which the family will have to be prepared.

STOPPING THE HEART

While the child is under anaesthetic, the chest is opened and, to enable the heart to be artificially stopped for surgery, blood is passed through a machine to provide oxygenation and remove waste products. This procedure is called a cardio-pulmonary bypass.

Following cardiac surgery, all children are nursed in intensive care and require a period of close observation of vital functions, sometimes lasting for several days or more. Once the patient is over the initial phase, the recovery from the operation is often rapid.

There are very rare and severe congenital disorders which cannot be surgically corrected without resorting to heart transplant surgery. This can be performed even in newborns, but it is greatly limited by a shortage of available donor organs.

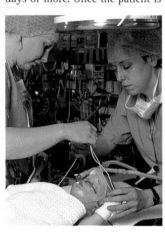

For cardiac catheterization, an infant is anaesthetized and a catheter is inserted into the groin. It is guided by X-ray imaging into a coronary artery.

Delicate surgery is required to correct a hole in the heart. However, some small holes close spontaneously and surgery is not required.

A nasal tube provides oxygen to help the baby with breathing. The doctor examines the baby with a stethoscope to monitor post-operative health.

Heart problems in older children

Heart disease in older children is usually acquired, persistent or chronic, although, occasionally, a congenital cardiac defect will not be identified until later in childhood. In most cases, the clinical picture is the same as that with adults.

INNOCENT MURMURS
The majority of healthy children with a murmur are normal, with no structural heart abnormality. An experienced clinician can recognize the sound of the so-called innocent murmur. If in doubt, an echocardiogram can be requested.

SUPRAVENTRICULAR TACHYCARDIA
Some children have an abnormal electrical pathway in their heart but the effects may not be immediately apparent. This can suddenly cause the heart to beat extremely fast (up to 300 beats per minute). At this rate, the pumping becomes inefficient and the child will develop heart failure. They are likely to become pale and sweaty and will develop shock if untreated. Placing ice on the face may restore normal rhythm, but the use of the drug adenosine may be necessary.

Occasionally, an electric shock is required to restore normal rhythm (cardioversion). Electrical mapping of the abnormal pathway may be undertaken so it can be destroyed with special radio-frequency ablation (tissue removal).

RHEUMATIC FEVER
Rheumatic fever is now rare in the UK, but is a major cause of heart disease worldwide. It occurs indirectly due to infection with the bacterium *streptococcus*, and is a result of immune mediated damage to the heart tissue. Symptoms of

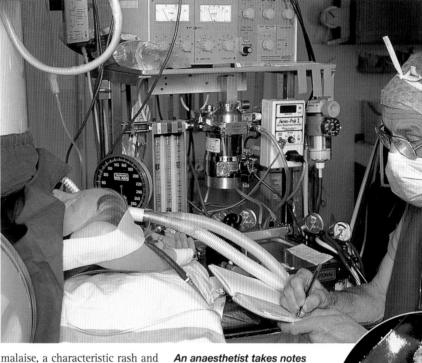

malaise, a characteristic rash and joint pain occur some weeks after the initial infection. Damage to heart valves may be considerable. Treatment consists of rest, anti-inflammatory drugs and prevention of recurrence with prophylactic penicillin. Surgery may be needed later in life.

INFECTIVE ENDOCARDITIS
This is direct infection of the heart tissue by organisms in the bloodstream. It occurs mainly in abnormal heart tissue or where there are abnormal patterns of blood flow, but it can happen in

An anaesthetist takes notes as a child undergoes cardiac catheterization. This technique is used to visualize blood flow to and from the heart.

a normal heart. Children with congenital heart lesions and those who have had rheumatic fever are at risk, and preventative antibiotics are vital.

Infective endocarditis may be hard to diagnose, although there may be tiny haemorrhages in the skin. Delayed or inadequate antibiotic treatment can have devastating consequences in terms of damage to the heart.

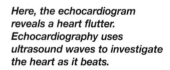

Here, the echocardiogram reveals a heart flutter. Echocardiography uses ultrasound waves to investigate the heart as it beats.

Primary disorders of heart muscle

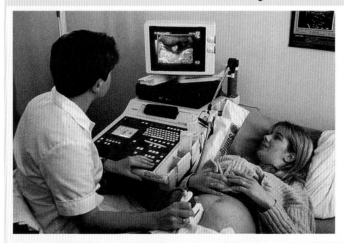

Cardiomyopathy interferes with the function of the heart even if the chambers and valves are all normal. It can be present at birth or may develop during life.

Dilated cardiomyopathy is a condition where the heart muscle becomes thin and stretched as the chambers dilate. The more the dilatation, the worse the heart function. This can occur as a consequence of viral infections

Some heart problems that become apparent later in life can be detected in pregnancy. Ultrasound scanning provides information on the fetus' heart.

either during fetal development or after birth, or a metabolic disorder may be responsible. In some cases, an underlying cause for the problem proves elusive. The condition can recover, but in many cases it progresses to the point where only a heart transplant can prevent death.

Hypertrophic cardiomyopathy is a severe overgrowth of heart muscle which blocks outflow of blood and progressively impinges on heart function. The tendency may be inherited as a dominant condition. This is one of the causes of sudden death in apparently fit, young athletes.

Chronic chest problems

Chest problems can arise from any part of the respiratory system,
from the mouth to the smallest airway in the lung. Clinical assessment
of a child with chest symptoms is vital to determine treatment.

Long-term respiratory symptoms are responsible for serious ill-health in children. They may occur in isolation, or as part of a chronic, multi-system condition. These must be distinguished from the common, acute and self - limiting coughs and colds which are part of normal childhood.

Symptoms of chronic chest problems in children include:
- Coughing or wheezing
- Shortness of breath or rapid breathing, and exercise intolerance
- Abnormal chest shape indicative of long-term problems
- Cyanosis – a blue colour of the lips suggesting low oxygen levels in the blood
- Finger clubbing – an abnormal shape of the nails which is associated with chest pathology, especially chronic infection
- Failure to thrive – if the child is falling behind their expected rate of growth an explanation must be found.

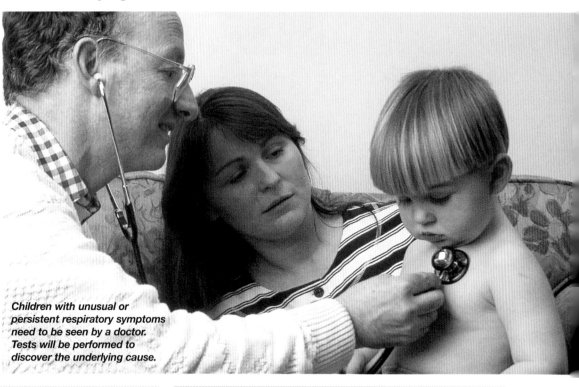

Children with unusual or persistent respiratory symptoms need to be seen by a doctor. Tests will be performed to discover the underlying cause.

Predisposing factors

Some children are predisposed to chest problems due to other conditions such as:

Neuromuscular disease
Any patient with severe muscle dysfunction or a postural deformity, particularly scoliosis (lateral curvature of the spine), is at risk of chronic under-ventilation of the lungs, difficulty in clearing infections and progressive respiratory failure. Regular physiotherapy and expert orthopaedic management are required to minimize the deformity and preserve respiratory function.

Immune deficiency
Any tendency to repeated infection may be associated with chronic chest symptoms. Clues to this diagnosis are repeated, unusually severe infections or infections with unusual organisms. Full assessment of the immune system is required in patients with severe unexplained chest symptoms.

An X-ray shows a child with thoracolumbar scoliosis, which is an abnormally curved spine. This condition is associated with serious respiratory problems.

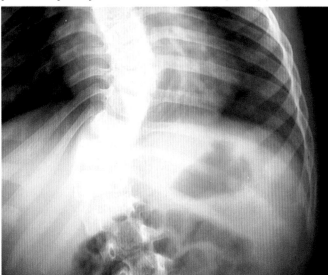

Assessing a case

A doctor presented with a child who has chest problems that have failed to respond to asthma medication should take a detailed history and perform a careful examination.

Further measures required, depending on the patient history, include:
- Measuring and plotting the height and weight on a centile chart (growth chart)
- Chest X-ray
- Detailed immune function tests
- Tests for cystic fibrosis and ciliary dyskinesia (poor movement of the fine hair-like projections on the cells lining the respiratory tract that are responsible for wafting mucus out of the airways)
- Test for gastro-oesophageal reflux
- Tests for allergies
- Tuberculin test for tuberculosis.

Asthma

The commonest cause of respiratory symptoms in childhood is asthma (which is not covered in detail in this article). It affects between 11 and 15 per cent of children. Asthma involves inflammation and constriction of the airways, which reduces airflow to the lungs.

However, a child who coughs or wheezes does not necessarily have asthma, which is a common misdiagnosis. It is important that other conditions are considered in order to provide the correct treatment.

Inhalers are used to treat children with asthma. A child must be shown how to use an inhaler correctly.

Causes of chronic respiratory problems

There are three main causes of chronic respiratory problems:

■ **Gastro-oesophageal reflux**
Gastro-oesophageal reflux (GOR) is the passive regurgitation of stomach contents from the stomach back into the oesophagus. Mild GOR is very common, causing posseting (regurgitation) of milk in young babies. Severe GOR can be a major problem with failure to thrive, severe irritability due to oesophagitis (heartburn) and severe chest problems because of inhalation of stomach contents into the airways.

This problem tends to be worse in infants and toddlers. It is investigated by measuring acidity levels with a probe in the lower oesophagus over a 24-hour period. Acid contents from the stomach should not be present in the lower oesophagus.

■ **Bronchiectasis**
Bronchiectasis is a permanent dilatation of the airways. This means that instead of tapering as they reach the peripheries of the lung, the airways run like tramlines. The condition is the result of chronic infection and inflammation in the lung.

The commonest cause is cystic fibrosis, which is associated with abnormal mucus. This mucus is viscous and encourages infection. Another important cause is primary ciliary dyskinesia in which the tiny hairs on the surface of respiratory cells do not beat properly and thereby encourage chronic infection as mucus secretions are unable to be cleared from the lungs.

Interestingly, primary ciliary dyskinesia is associated with situs inversus, a condition in which all the internal organs are arranged in a mirror image to the normal layout. The liver is on the left side of the abdomen

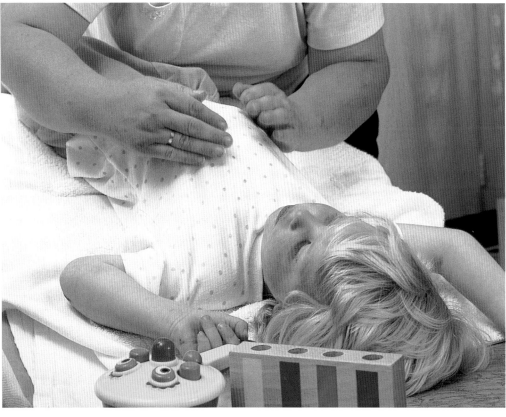

and the heart on the right side of the chest and so on. Clues to this diagnosis are chest X-ray abnormalities, the presence of finger clubbing and failure to thrive.

■ **Inhalation of a foreign body**
Inhaled objects often result in acute severe respiratory distress, but sometimes the symptoms may be more insidious. Toddlers are the highest risk group, and small objects such as nuts are typically involved.

The history of a clear time of onset of the symptom is often given. An X-ray may show up the object or there may be a discrepancy in the degree of aeration between the two sides of the chest, with air-trapping on the affected side.

Severe respiratory infections are common in cystic fibrosis. Patients often receive physiotherapy to loosen the mucus that obstructs the lungs.

The lung on the left of this X-ray is affected by bronchiectasis. The blue branching structure on the right is normal, but the left lung shows a lack of structure.

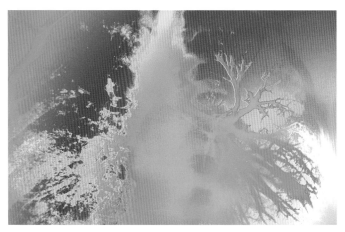

Heart failure

Heart failure causes fluid congestion in the lungs and therefore the symptoms (including breathlessness and cough) may be hard to distinguish from chest pathology. Careful cardiac examination of all patients with chest symptoms is mandatory.

Symptoms of heart failure in babies include poor feeding and recurrent chest infections. The underlying cause may be congenital heart disease.

Upper airway problems

Certain upper airway conditions (affecting the throat and nose) may be associated with chronic respiratory problems, and include:

■ **Upper airway obstruction**
Enlarged tonsils and adenoids are very common in childhood and regress with age. However, in severe cases the child may suffer from low oxygen blood levels at night which can lead to changes in the blood vessels of the lungs, which in turn causes heart failure. Loud snoring and a tendency to breathe through the mouth rather than the nose are associated symptoms.

■ **Rhinitis and post-nasal drip**
Asthma and bronchiectasis are commonly associated with conditions of the nasal (nose) and sinus linings. Symptoms include chronic inflammation (rhinitis/sinusitis) and sometimes cough due to mucus trickling down the back of the throat. There is some evidence that treating the nose and sinuses improves lung health in these cases. As with asthma, allergies may be implicated.

Acute viral bronchiolitis

Bronchiolitis is inflammation of the lower airways (bronchioles) as
a result of viral infection. In affected infants, the bronchioles become
clogged with mucus, leading to difficulty in breathing.

Acute viral bronchiolitis is inflammation of the airways due to infection with a virus. It tends to affect babies younger than six months and it is common in countries with a temperate climate.

There is typically a four- to six-day incubation period progressing to cold-like (coryzal) symptoms, dry cough and fever. The bronchioles – small airways in the lungs – become swollen and clogged with mucus and debris, and the child becomes oxygen deprived. This progresses to increased breathlessness, wet coughing and wheezing, which often necessitates paediatric review in hospital.

The causative organisms include:
■ Respiratory syncytial virus (RSV)
■ Para-influenza virus
■ Influenza virus
■ Adenovirus
■ Rhinovirus.

RSV infection is extremely common, and 10 per cent of those babies affected go on to develop lower respiratory complications. Only one per cent of all infants require in-patient hospital treatment because of RSV-related illness.

CLINICAL FEATURES

Chest X-rays during the acute stage of the illness typically show marked hyperinflation of the lungs, extensive peri-bronchial thickening and occasionally areas of collapse or consolidation of the lungs.

The presence of infecting viruses can be detected using a microscopic technique, called immunofluorescence, on nasal secretions aspirated from the upper airway.

Other conditions can have similar symptoms, and these must be ruled out.

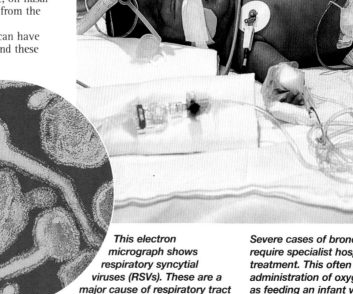

This electron micrograph shows respiratory syncytial viruses (RSVs). These are a major cause of respiratory tract infections in temperate climates.

Severe cases of bronchiolitis require specialist hospital treatment. This often includes administration of oxygen as well as feeding an infant via a nasogastric tube.

Nursing care

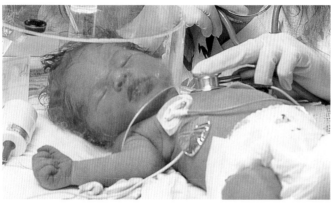

Expert nursing care is crucial in managing affected infants. Blood oxygen saturation levels can be measured with a pulse oximeter and, if low, supplemental oxygen will be given. This is most usefully administered via a head-box; concentrations of up to 80 per cent oxygen are sometimes needed.

Breathless babies may be unable to take oral feeds safely; in these cases, feeding via a nasogastric tube may be initiated. However, this additional obstruction of the upper airway can complicate matters, worsening respiratory difficulties and increasing the risk of vomiting and aspiration of the stomach contents.

Babies with bronchiolitis have difficulty breathing and so are monitored carefully. This infant's respiration is controlled and monitored through the perspex cylinder surrounding his head.

In severe cases of bronchiolitis, an infant may need to be fed via a nasogastric tube. However, this tube may make it even harder for the baby to breathe.

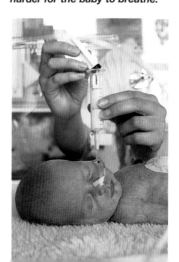

Drug therapy

Bronchodilators and respiratory stimulants are not used routinely. However, young infants with apnoea (when the baby temporarily stops breathing) or poor respiratory effort might benefit from an infusion of theophylline.

Specific bronchodilators, such as salbutamol and terbutaline, are rarely of benefit to treat the respiratory distress, cough and wheeze that are typical of a bronchiolitis episode. However, in some babies with acute, severe bronchospasm these drugs can be of benefit.

Furthermore, chest physiotherapy has been shown to have little benefit in acute viral bronchiolitis and so is usually inappropriate. Careful nursing observation, gentle upper airway suctioning and adequate hydration and oxygenation are of far greater importance in recovery.

Complications of bronchiolitis

Premature babies who suffer from periods of apnoea are at an increased risk of experiencing severe complications. Babies with congenital heart disease, immunodeficiency or pre-existing lung diseases, such as cystic fibrosis, are also at increased risk.

VENTILATION

Every year, a small number of infants require mechanical ventilation to help them breathe. This can be administered via a nasal cannula or, alternatively, after endotracheal tube intubation. Artificial ventilators allow both the rate and volume of lung inflation to be closely controlled.

In such severe cases, careful consideration should be given to the possibility of secondary bacterial sepsis and the possibility of rare complications, such as lung atelectasis or pneumothorax.

Infants suffering from recurrent apnoeas (when breathing ceases for a short period) may need to be ventilated mechanically.

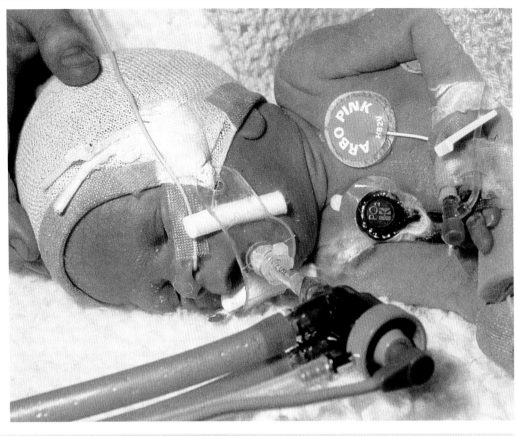

Recent advances

Ribavirin is a broad spectrum antiviral agent with activity against RSV. When given via a nebulizer, generating small particle-size aerosols for prolonged periods during the early course of illness, it might usefully impact on the natural history of the condition. However, as treatment is

Immunizing babies using injections of RSV immunoglobulins is currently being researched.

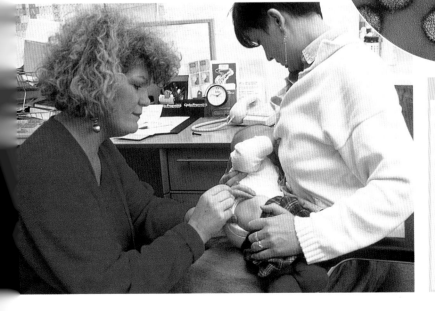

complicated and expensive and most infants have an excellent prognosis, its use is generally restricted to those considered to be at high risk of complications.

Recent research has focused on disease prevention using injections of RSV

immunoglobulin to provide passive immunity for high risk infants during the bronchiolitis season (November–February).

Future therapies might include the development of effective vaccines for widespread immunization programmes and the development of more effective antiviral agents. Improvements in the immediate future, however, depend upon high standards of nursing care to optimize the potential of infants to cope with their infections through their own immune mechanisms.

This electron micrograph shows adenoviruses. These are responsible for some cases of bronchiolitis.

Prognosis

While the usual course of bronchiolitis is gradual recovery over three to four days and cessation of all respiratory symptoms after a few weeks, there are some children who have a more prolonged illness. Up to two thirds of all patients have recurrent episodes of viral-induced wheezing for many years. In general, these are mild and do not require re-admission to hospital.

The relationship between this pattern of illness and allergic asthma is not completely understood. It is not clear whether these subsequent complications relate to susceptibility on the part of the child or airway damage following the infection.

However, the overwhelming majority of patients do not go on to have troublesome asthma and have an excellent long-term prognosis.

Pneumonia in childhood

The airways are normally completely sterile below the larynx; pneumonia is a common infection in children that affects the bronchi and supporting tissues of the lungs.

Pneumonia is a common clinical problem in childhood caused by invasion of the lungs by pathogens (disease-causing micro-organisms), resulting in inflammation.

RESPONSE TO INFECTION

The body's immune reaction to the infection results in the lung's air sacs (alveoli) filling with fluid and white blood cells. This obstructs the diffusion of gases to and from the blood, which, in turn, may result in impaired oxygenation of the body's tissues.

Pneumonia is commonly viral in nature; bacteria are often a secondary problem when there is already a viral infection.

SYMPTOMS

The classic symptoms include cough, rapid breathing and fever. Auscultation (listening with a stethoscope) may reveal reduced air entry to the area of lung affected, or that the child is wheezing.

In children, these signs of pneumonia may be very non-specific; only a chest X-ray will confirm the diagnosis.

Inflammation of the alveoli

The healthy alveoli on the left are filled with air and macrophages, which ingest inhaled irritants. The infected alveoli on the right have filled with pathogenic organisms, inflammatory fluid and neutrophils (white blood cells which fight the infection).

Infected alveolus
The yellow cells represent neutrophils, which play an essential role in the body's immune reaction by attacking the invading organism

Healthy alveolus
The blue specks represent macrophages (a type of white blood cell), which are always present in healthy alveoli to ingest inhaled irritants

Normal alveoli   **Infected alveoli**

Types of pneumonia

In bronchopneumonia, the infection is diffuse. Here, the scattered white areas show regions of inflamed lung tissue.

Three lobes of right lung
In broncho-pneumonia, inflammation may affect all the lobes of the lung

Right bronchus
One of the two main divisions of the trachea; bronchi and bronchioles become inflamed before infection spreads to the alveoli

There are two main patterns of infection in pneumonia:

■ **Bronchopneumonia**
This involves diffuse involvement of the airways; it is usually viral in origin and requires no specific treatment. In severe cases, oxygen may be required and bronchodilators may be helpful if there is an associated wheeze.

■ **Lobar pneumonia**
The infection is confined to one region of the lung. Lobar pneumonias are mainly bacterial in origin; identifying the causative organism is difficult

This X-ray shows a patient suffering from lobar pneumonia. The infection is the hazy white area of the lung (circled).

in children as they rarely cough up sputum that can be cultured.

As lobar pneumonia usually implies a bacterial infection, it will require antibiotic treatment. *Streptococcus pneumoniae* is the most common pathogen and is usually sensitive to penicillin.

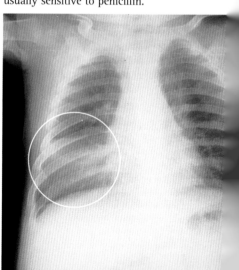

Factors predisposing to pneumonia

Most simple cases of pneumonia follow a viral upper respiratory infection and occur in otherwise healthy children. However, certain conditions make an individual or group particularly susceptible to the disease. Certain factors may put a child at risk:
■ Being immunocompromised, such as having HIV or undergoing treatment for a malignancy
■ An abnormality of the mucus, as occurs in cystic fibrosis

■ The presence of a foreign body in the airway
■ Abnormal activity of the cilia (hairs on lining cells of the respiratory system that waft mucus out of the airways)
■ Gastro-oesophageal reflux
■ Muscle weakness or structural abnormality of the chest wall.

PNEUMONIA AND HIV
HIV-positive children (and adults) are susceptible to a number of unusual pathogenic infections, including atypical pneumonias. This is because the HIV virus attacks the individual's immune system and renders them vulnerable to infection by many micro-organisms, including those that do not harm a normal host.

Lung problems associated with HIV include:
■ Lymphocytic interstitial pneumonitis – this is a non-specific inflammatory condition that may be due to viral infection by cytomegalovirus or the Epstein–Barr virus
■ *Pneumocystis carinii* – infection with this protozoan causes severe pneumonia in HIV
■ Tuberculosis.

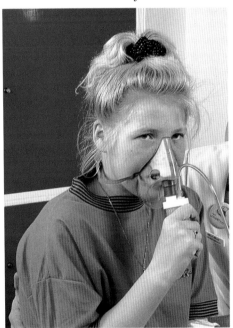

Cystic fibrosis patients often use a nebulizer to loosen abnormal mucous secretions in their lungs. This disorder will put them at greater risk of pneumonia.

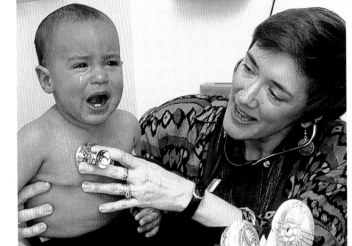

A child with simple viral pneumonia should recover with no after-effects. Recurrent attacks may prompt a doctor to look for predisposing factors.

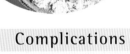

Pneumocystis carinii *is a protozoan that may infect the lungs of immunocompromised patients. It can be treated with high-dose antibiotics.*

Pneumonia in newborns

The passage of the newborn through the birth canal renders it liable to infection by organisms found in the mother's genital tract. Common bacteria that may cause pneumonia are the Group B beta-haemolytic streptococcus and organisms from the mother's bowel, such as *Escherichia coli*.

Any newborn with signs of respiratory distress must be assumed to have pneumonia until proven otherwise. The presence of infection will often inactivate surfactant (a natural chemical that helps the lungs expand) and produce a generalized collapse of the lungs which is visible on chest X-ray.

Factors which predispose newborns to infection include:
■ Prolonged rupture of fetal membranes before delivery
■ Bacterial colonization of the mother's vagina
■ Premature delivery
■ Maternal fever
■ Trauma to the baby's skin
■ Intravenous cannulae and endotracheal tubes, particularly in premature babies.

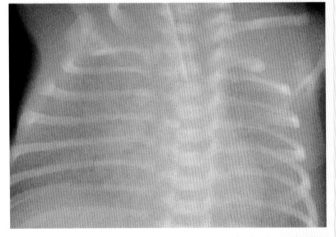

This is an X-ray of a child with Group B beta-haemolytic streptococcus pneumonia. Diffuse mottled white shadowing throughout both lungs can be seen.

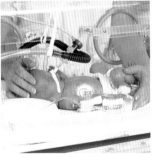

Doctors must be observant for signs of respiratory distress in children born prematurely. Those with endotracheal tubes are particularly vulnerable.

Complications

Possible complications following childhood pneumonia include:
■ Empyema – occurs when pus collects between the lung and the chest wall; if this is extensive it must be drained to allow the lung to recover
■ Lung abscess – often occurs after severe bacterial pneumonia.

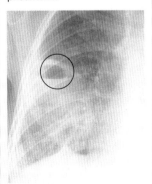

An abscess (circled) has developed in the middle lobe of this patient's right lung. This may need surgical drainage.

Pertussis

Pertussis, commonly known as whooping cough, is a serious
respiratory infection which mainly affects children.
Effective prevention can be achieved by vaccination of infants.

Whooping cough is caused by a bacterium called *Bordetella pertussis,* which attaches itself to the ciliated cells of the respiratory tract. The condition is highly infectious and is transmitted by air-borne droplets during coughing.

The actual damage is the result of toxins produced by *Bordetella pertussis* which do not actually invade the body beyond the respiratory mucosa (lining cells).

MULTIPLYING BACTERIA

During an infection, there is severe congestion and swelling of the mucosal lining of the respiratory tract, which worsens as the bacteria multiply. There is a tremendously high production of mucus which can cause blockage of the air passages and collapse of areas of the lung. In addition, secondary infection with o ther organisms that cause pneumonia can develop.

EPIDEMICS

Whooping cough occurs worldwide, and although it affects some children all the time, epidemics of the infection can occur. The incubation period from infection to symptoms is about seven days. Within communities, whooping cough is highly infectious to susceptible individuals.

Following World War II, there has been a marked decline in the incidence of infection in the Western world. This was initially due to socio-economic changes and later due to mass vaccination.

This section of the lining of the trachea shows bacteria (green) lodged between cilia. These bacteria cause a loss of cilia that normally protect the respiratory tract from particles.

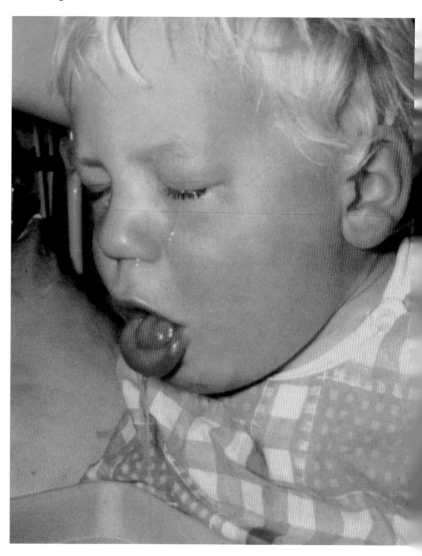

Whooping cough, which mainly affects children, carries a high rate of serious complications in small babies. The spasms of cough are often worse at night and may culminate in vomiting.

Symptoms and signs

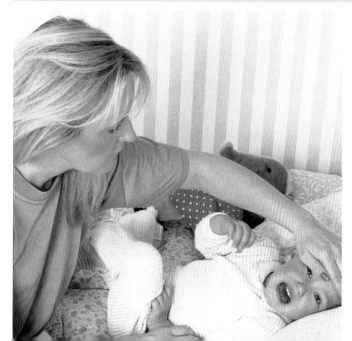

There are three phases in the progress of pertussis:
■ Catarrhal stage – this lasts for about a week and consists of a mild fever, blocked nose and sneezing. During this phase, the clinical features are the same as for any common cold
■ Paroxysmal stage – this lasts for two to four weeks and consists of bouts of coughing which may continue for 20–30 seconds. The child is unable to pause for breath during the coughing fit, and at the end there is a pronounced indrawing

Infants infected by the pertussis bacterium exhibit the typical clinical features of a common cold in the first stage. These include a mild fever.

of breath which is the 'whoop'. It is this sound that gives the disease its name
■ Convalescent stage – this may last many weeks during which the cough slowly improves. Because of the very prolonged cough, the Chinese call this infection 'the cough of a hundred days'.

Very young babies are typically the most severely affected and make up the bulk of paediatric pertussis admissions to hospital. In babies, the features may not be classic. The whoop is often not present and apnoea (temporary stopping of breathing) and choking spells are more typical. Infants frequently require help with feeding via a tube.

Possible complications

There is a high incidence of serious complications, particularly in small babies.

■ Pneumonia – this is the most common complication. It may be due to the *Bordetella pertussis* bacteria or may be a secondary infection from another organism

■ Brain damage – this is a major long-term concern due to a combination of raised intracranial pressure and lack of oxygen during bouts of coughing. This may manifest itself as seizures or inflammation of the brain – encephalitis. Long-term effects include paralysis, sensorineural deficits in vision or hearing and general learning difficulties

■ Conjunctival haemorrhage – the raised thoracic pressure during coughing can cause small blood vessels to rupture

■ Nosebleeds – the increased thoracic pressure can also lead to the bursting of tiny blood vessels in the nose

■ Lung damage – prolonged pneumonia as a result of pertussis infection may cause bronchiectasis (abnormal widening of the airways).

Nosebleeds can occur in children with pertussis owing to raised pressure causing blood vessels in the nose to rupture.

Making a diagnosis

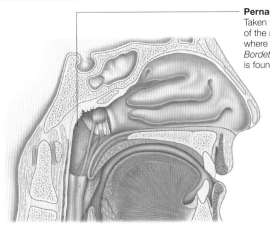

Pernasal swab
Taken from the back of the nasal cavity where the organism, *Bordetella pertussis,* is found

Characteristically the blood count demonstrates a very high number of lymphocytes, but this can apply to any infection and is not specific to pertussis. Definitive diagnosis can only be made by culturing the organism from the nasopharynx.

DETECTING BACTERIA
The difficulty with organism isolation is that it is most easily detected during the early phase

To diagnose pertussis a pernasal swab is taken through the nose. A special growth medium is needed to culture the bacterium.

of the illness (catarrhal stage) when clinical suspicion of pertussis is not very high. By the time there is a strong suspicion, the chances of a positive culture have diminished to less than 50 per cent.

Furthermore, samples must be taken from the nasopharynx rather than the nose, and must be transported rapidly to the laboratory before the organism dies. Detection of the DNA sequences of pertussis in secretions is more sensitive than looking for viable organisms; this may become the standard means of diagnosis in the future.

Treating pertussis

The clinical course of pertussis infection cannot be altered by antibiotics, since it is the toxins and not the bacteria that cause the damage. However, a course of erythromycin decreases the period of infectivity to others. Close contacts of confirmed cases, especially infants, may benefit from preventive use of erythromycin.

SUPPORTIVE MEASURES
General supportive measures are employed, such as attention to feeding. Breathing should be closely monitored to detect the problems of apnoea and oxygen desaturation (reduced levels of oxygen in the blood). Full respiratory isolation is necessary in cases of hospitalized children. If a secondary infecting agent is suspected, appropriate antibiotic cover is started.

An eight-week-old baby receives her first triple vaccination. The name of the vaccination is due to the fact that it protects against three diseases: diphtheria, pertussis and tetanus.

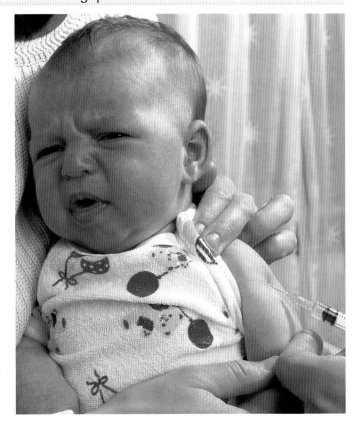

Immunization

Pertussis is largely preventable by active immunization of infants. In the UK, as in most countries, pertussis is included in the triple vaccine of DPT (diphtheria, pertussis and tetanus), of which three doses are given. The pertussis component has been implicated in some minor and more serious adverse vaccine reactions.

There is a risk of minor fever and erythema at the site of injection, and more seriously a rare risk of severe neurological reaction with subsequent brain damage.

In the 1970s there was considerable public concern about the risks involved, and vaccination rates plummeted. Parallel to this, rates of disease rose with a corresponding increase in the number of children with complications from pertussis.

A major inquiry in the UK calculated the risk of severe reaction as one per 300,000 vaccinations.

Tuberculosis in children

Tuberculosis is a disease found worldwide. Children usually catch it from infected adults and if adequate treatment is not given in time, tuberculous disease may occur, causing complications or death.

Tuberculosis, which is caused by infection with *Mycobacterium tuberculosis* bacteria, is the most common infectious cause of death throughout the world. It can affect both children and adults and occurs more frequently among populations living in crowded, substandard dwellings. The increasing prevalence of HIV infection has also led to the re-emergence of tuberculosis in many countries.

After exposure to *Mycobacterium tuberculosis* a patient may develop tuberculous infection or tuberculous disease, depending upon the balance

Testing for tuberculosis infection is done by injecting the skin with protein extract from the bacteria. This test can diagnose infection when no symptoms are evident.

between the ability of the organism to cause disease and the host's immune response.

TUBERCULOUS INFECTION
Tuberculous infection refers to a state in which the bacteria are established in the body, but there are no symptoms, and the patient will have a normal chest X-ray and negative bacteriological studies. In such cases, infection is diagnosed by carrying out a tuberculin test (Mantoux test).

The tuberculin test is carried out by the injection of a purified protein derivative of the bacterium into the skin of the forearm. Reactions occur two to three days later. A patch of redness and swelling greater than 10 mm in diameter is interpreted as a positive reaction.

TUBERCULOUS DISEASE
Tuberculous infection in children is often diagnosed when testing the contacts of a patient with tuberculosis. This is usually an adult with re-activation of a previous lung infection. Such people have tuberculous disease – an ongoing disease process involving the lungs or other organs of the body and causing symptoms.

Approximately 10 per cent of patients with tuberculous infection go on to develop the disease; however, all untreated infected individuals are at risk of this complication unless treated.

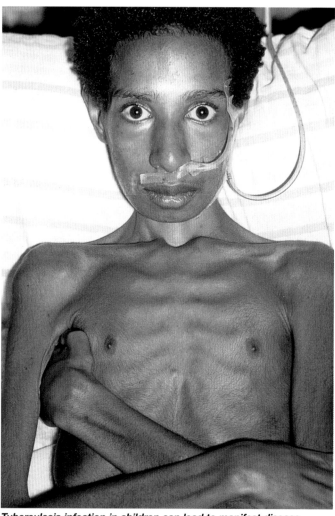

Tuberculosis infection in children can lead to manifest disease. The infection may then affect other organs of the body resulting in serious illness or even death.

Primary tuberculous infection

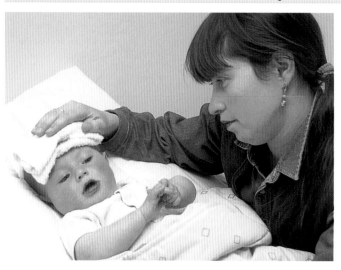

Primary tuberculosis follows infection of a non-immune child. *Mycobacterium tuberculosis* is spread by exhaled droplets, and primary infection may occur in the lungs, skin or intestines.

SYMPTOMS OF INFECTION
Once inside the body, the bacteria multiply slowly and the body reacts by forming granulation (inflammatory) tissue around them. The primary

Non-specific symptoms, such as coughing or wheezing, may occur as the bacteria multiply in the respiratory tract. Serious symptoms are uncommon with primary infection.

infection of the lungs is usually asymptomatic, although non-specific symptoms such as cough, wheeze, abdominal pain, diarrhoea, anorexia, weight loss and fever can occur.

In most cases the primary lesion within the lung undergoes caseation (breakdown), fibrosis and calcification. Similar changes may occur in the regional lymph nodes, with complete resolution. Sometimes persistent calcification can be seen on chest X-rays.

Primary infection of the tonsils and intestines may occur after drinking unpasteurized milk infected with *Mycobacterium bovis* or atypical mycobacteria.

Secondary complications

Most children do not suffer complications; however, there are a number of ways in which the primary infection can progress to cause severe tuberculous disease. There may be secretion of pus into the lining of the lungs (pleural effusions) – this is thought to be the result of hypersensitivity to the tuberculoid organism.

Malnourished children are at increased risk of progression of the primary focus of infection with dissemination to other lung areas. Enlargement of lymph nodes can cause bronchial obstruction leading to bronchiectasis, lung collapse or emphysema, depending on the extent of airway obstruction.

SPREAD OF INFECTION
Spread of the tuberculoid bacilli via the bloodstream can be a devastating complication and usually occurs in the first six months of infection. Infants are at particular risk. Widespread dissemination results in diffuse mottling throughout the lungs (miliary TB) and can also result in tuberculous meningitis. Other organs can be affected including bone, gut and the kidneys.

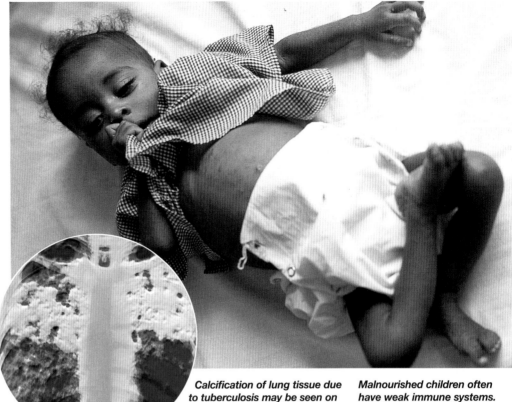

Calcification of lung tissue due to tuberculosis may be seen on X-ray as mottled patches in the lungs. These diffuse patches are found in miliary tuberculosis.

Malnourished children often have weak immune systems. They are therefore more at risk of the initial infection spreading to other parts of the lung.

Identifying bacteria

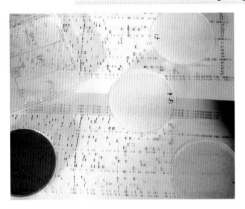

Special acid-fast stains are characteristically taken up by tuberculoid bacilli. Positive cultures are critically important to confirm the diagnosis of tuberculous disease. Gastric lavage (stomach washout) is sometimes an effective means of obtaining organisms for culture.

Bronchial secretions may be collected in order to culture the bacteria. This ensures that the organism is susceptible to specific antibiotic therapies.

Treating tuberculosis

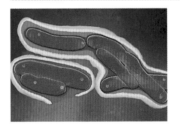

Mycobacterium tuberculosis (red rods seen in cross-section) can be treated using multiple antibiotics. Treatment is continued for up to nine months.

The most commonly used antibiotics for treating tuberculosis are Isoniazid, rifampicin and ethambutol. Multiple drug combinations are used for six to nine months to eradicate infection.

Children with positive Mantoux tuberculin skin tests and no signs of disease (tuberculous infection) are also treated with isoniazid for six to nine months to prevent the occurrence of complications at a later stage.

Preventing tuberculosis

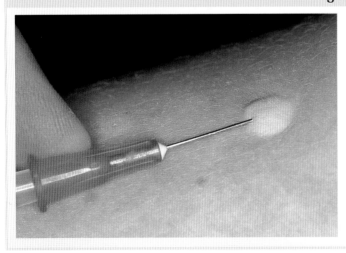

The BCG tuberculosis vaccine is injected superficially into the skin. The vaccination prevents secondary complications due to tuberculosis infection.

BCG vaccination is available to prevent tuberculosis in communities in areas where there is a high endemic rate of tuberculosis and for other individuals who are at risk. The bacillus of Calmette and Guérin (BCG) is an attenuated (reduced virulence) strain of *Mycobacterium bovis*. The vaccination does not prevent primary infection, but does prevent secondary complications from occurring. The BCG vaccination is thought to be up to 80 per cent effective.

Further considerations
Tuberculosis remains an important diagnosis to consider throughout the world. Its manifestations are such that the diagnosis should be considered as a cause for a wide variety of symptoms. Effective public health vaccination programmes and increased awareness of the condition by healthcare professionals will be important in the future eradication of this infective disease.

Inheriting cystic fibrosis

In the Caucasian population, 1 person in 25 is a carrier of the cystic fibrosis gene. However, as the gene is recessive, both parents must pass on the CF gene in order for their child to be affected.

In the Caucasian population, about one person in 25 carries a mutant CF gene. These individuals are called heterozygotes; they have no clinical symptoms and are not at any risk of developing cystic fibrosis.

In a population in which one in 25 people is a carrier, chance alone means that for one couple in 400, both partners will be carriers. Each carrier has a 50 per cent chance of passing a mutant gene to each of the children they have together.

When two partners are both carriers, each of their children has a recognized pattern of risk of inheriting the defective gene as follows:
■ Risk of being affected by CF

due to presence of two mutant genes: one in four
■ Risk of being a carrier from inheriting one mutant gene and one normal gene: one in two
■ Chance of being unaffected by mutant CF gene by inheriting two normal genes: one in four.

Children who inherit two mutant genes are called homozygotes, and those who inherit one mutant gene are called heterozygotes, or carriers. Carriers are at risk of having affected children if their future partners are also carriers. Individuals who do not carry a mutant gene are not at risk of having affected children. Each pregnancy for carrier couples has the same one in four risk of resulting in an affected child.

◀ *Atomic force microscope imaging is a method for visualizing human chromosomes. This can help the clinician diagnose a number of chromosome disorders.*

▶ *In this pedigree, each parent carries one copy of the mutant CF gene. The statistical chance of their offspring inheriting two copies of the gene is one in four. The risk is unaffected by the sex of the children.*

Inheritance pattern of recessive genes

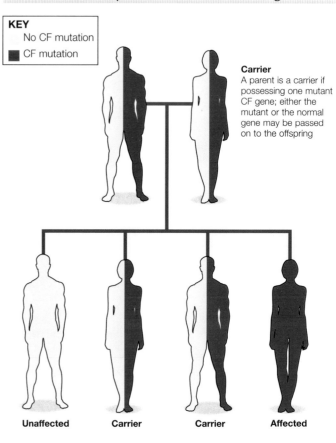

KEY
☐ No CF mutation
■ CF mutation

Carrier
A parent is a carrier if possessing one mutant CF gene; either the mutant or the normal gene may be passed on to the offspring

Unaffected   Carrier   Carrier   Affected

Incidence

Cystic fibrosis is one of the most common recessively inherited genetic diseases found in Caucasians and, on average, there is one affected child born in every 400 Caucasian births.

Not all ethnic groups have such a high incidence of the disease; for example, in the Hispanic population the incidence is one in 9,500 births and in native Africans and Asians it is estimated at fewer than one in 50,000 births.

Most ethnic groups which have been studied have a lower incidence than that of Caucasians, but with mixed cultural populations the local incidence can be difficult to predict.

About 25 per cent of northern Europeans are carriers of a mutant CF gene and thus

Couples at risk of having a child affected by cystic fibrosis can receive genetic counselling.

approximately one in every 4,000 children (including non-Caucasian children) born in the UK is affected by the disorder.

Diagnosing CF

The severity of the disease can range from mild to severe and although most patients are diagnosed by the age of one, patients with milder forms of the disease may not be diagnosed until middle age, or coincidentally when investigation of infertility problems is undertaken.

The increased amount of salt on the surface of the skin can be used as a diagnostic indicator of cystic fibrosis. The modern 'sweat test' is a more

sophisticated version of that used formerly when a midwife would lick the forehead of a newborn baby to taste if there were abnormally high levels of salt in the sweat. It was then known that high salt levels predicted pulmonary (lung) failure or cystic fibrosis.

Cystic fibrosis gene therapy research: protein electrophoresis gel showing the production of a human protein from a recombinant virus.

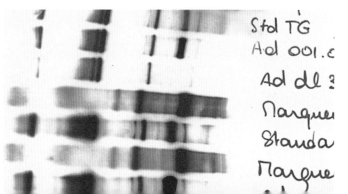

Testing and genetic counselling

Genetic testing is available to determine whether a person carries a CF gene, and counselling is useful to help couples make informed reproductive choices. Advances in technology may also lead to gene therapies in the future that can cure the disease.

Testing for the presence of mutations in the CF gene is available for confirmation of a diagnosis of cystic fibrosis and for those at risk of having an affected child. Such testing can be organized by a referring clinician such as a clinical geneticist, paediatrician or GP.

IDENTIFYING MUTATIONS

The mutations present in an affected individual can be identified and this information then used to offer testing to other family members to identify their carrier status. Testing is also available for individuals with a family history of the disease and for their partners.

Testing can be helpful with regard to informed reproductive decision-making. Individuals at risk of having an affected child should be referred to a genetics clinic, where counselling services are available. A clinical geneticist

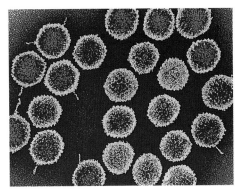

Genetically engineered adenoviruses are used in gene therapy for cystic fibrosis. Some of their own DNA is replaced with the human CFTR gene, and the patient is then infected.

can provide accurate information which will provide individuals with the opportunity to make decisions about their reproductive choices within a private and supportive environment.

FUTURE GENE THERAPY

Clinical treatments for cystic fibrosis have developed over the last three decades, and this has greatly increased the life expectancy of affected individuals. A major hope for future clinical management is in the development of gene therapy.

Gene therapy involves the transfer of a normal copy of the CF gene into cells of an affected individual. Since pulmonary problems are the greatest cause of early death in patients, the target for transfer of the normal gene is the epithelial cells of the lungs. The difficulty lies in how to get the normal copy of the gene into the cells and how to ensure it stays there. Many different methods are being tried

A researcher isolates an artificially produced human CFTR protein during research into gene therapy. The machine is operating in a temperature-controlled room.

with the purpose of ensuring that a normal CF gene is incorporated into sufficient numbers of cells to produce levels of CFTR protein that will support normal lung function.

Early experiments have shown that the gene can be successfully transferred into cells but the protein is only produced for periods of up to a few weeks.

Advantages of being a carrier of CF

The carrier rate of the mutation in cystic fibrosis is one of the highest known for a lethal disorder, which indicates that in quite recent times (in human evolutionary terms) there might have been a survival advantage for those individuals who carry the gene.

An explanation may be the response of carriers to intestinal bacterial infection. In normal individuals, bacterial infections of the intestines usually result in severe diarrhoea, which can be lethal to the individual.

However, some carriers of the mutant CF gene are resistant to such severe secretory diarrhoea due to the defective CFTR protein being unable to produce high levels of salt and fluid secretion. Carriers may therefore have a

resistance to other potentially life-threatening disorders, such as cholera and typhoid fever.

This resistance to infections could be the selective survival advantage which has resulted in such a high carrier rate in present populations. Why the mutations, all of which arise by chance, should have shown such strong selection in the Caucasian population and not in many other populations is not understood and there may in fact be other explanations for the high carrier frequency.

This light micrograph shows a section of the ileum (small intestine) affected by cystic fibrosis. Mucus obstructs the intestinal glands as well as the pancreas and bronchi.

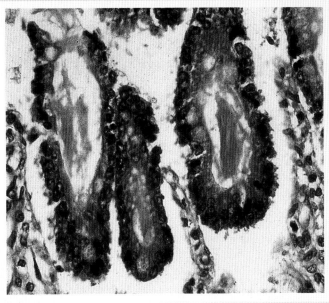

Managing cystic fibrosis

About 1 in 2,500 children suffers from cystic fibrosis (CF), an inherited genetic disorder affecting the chest. Prenatal diagnosis can identify the disorder, although, at present, treatment can only limit its effects.

Cystic fibrosis (CF) is a genetic disorder affecting the exocrine glands (those secreting mucus, tears and sweat), and results from the abnormality of just one gene. This faulty gene is recessive, meaning carriers are healthy and do not have any signs of the illness.

The genetic abnormality is carried by 1 in 25 of the UK population, but an individual will only develop CF if both parents carry the abnormal gene.

PROTEIN MALFUNCTION

This gene contains information for the production of a protein called the cystic fibrosis transmembrane regulator (CFTR). This protein is important in determining the movement of salt and water across cell layers, and abnormal versions of CFTR protein causes the production of salty sweat and a thickening of mucus. This leads to a clogging of the bronchi, intestinal glands and pancreas.

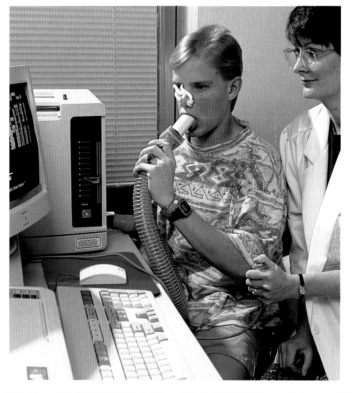

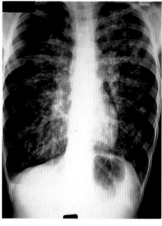

Chest X-rays of cystic fibrosis sufferers reveal areas clogged with mucus. As a result, crackles and wheezes are heard when the lungs are listened to with a stethoscope.

The lung function of a cystic fibrosis sufferer is assessed using a spirometer. This device measures lung capacity and expiratory flow rates.

Diagnosing cystic fibrosis

■ Measuring the increased saltiness of sweat in CF sufferers is one of the standard tests for verifying the diagnosis. Sweating is induced artificially by a method called pilocarpine iontophoresis, in which a weak electric current is used to help the penetration of the drug pilocarpine through the skin. The sweat is then collected on filter paper, and the concentrations of sodium and chloride ions are measured. At least 98 per cent

of patients who are homozygous for cystic fibrosis mutations (that is, they carry two copies of genes for cystic fibrosis) will have increased sweat saltiness.

■ Parents of affected children can be offered prenatal diagnostic testing in any subsequent pregnancies; this will determine whether or not the fetus will be affected in the same way.

■ Screening in the newborn period to detect the majority of affected children before the onset of symptoms is now feasible. A small spot of blood is obtained by pricking the heel, and blood tests are performed. This test is not yet widely available in the UK.

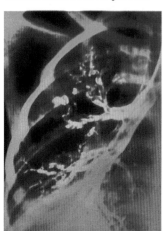

The bronchi of the lungs, seen in this X-ray of a CF sufferer, are filled with mucus (green). This is a result of chronic bacterial infection of the lungs.

Typical presentation of cystic fibrosis

■ Chronic, recurrent or severe wet cough
■ Failure to thrive in infancy
■ Intestinal obstruction in the newborn period (meconium ileus)
■ Frequent, loose, bulky and offensive stools

■ Rectal prolapse
■ Nasal polyps
■ Male infertility
■ Salty taste, apparent on kissing
■ Sibling/s with cystic fibrosis.

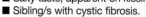

The 'wet cough' of a CF sufferer is caused by mucus filling the bronchi, the air passages branching from the windpipe into the lungs. The excess mucus can be seen on this CT scan: the lung tissue is shown in blue, and the red flecks are mucus-filled bronchi.

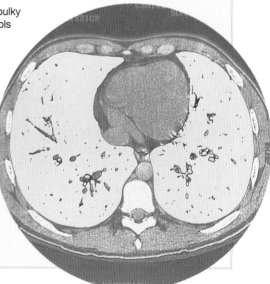

Living with CF

Early screening and diagnosis of CF may not improve long-term survival, but therapy can be started sooner, improving the lives of sufferers.

Once a diagnosis has been made, the family is invariably referred to the nearest CF specialist. Gradually, the patient and their family are taught the aspects of treatment that increase the chances of survival.

Up to 85 per cent of CF sufferers have malabsorption. Concentrated digestive enzymes accumulate inside the pancreas, leading to tissue destruction and organ failure. Fat absorption is particularly affected, and large greasy stools, which are difficult to flush away, are a typical feature. Fat-soluble vitamins (A, D, E and K) are not absorbed normally, and deficiencies occur.

These problems are countered by giving pancreatic enzymes orally prior to all meals, plus regular vitamin supplements. Modern enzyme supplements are packaged in enteric-coated microspheres – drugs that become activated in the appropriate part of the small intestine.

DIETARY CONSIDERATIONS

Dietary recommendations for cystic fibrosis patients appear to contradict current guidelines about healthy eating. Because CF patients have problems absorbing fat, lose increased amounts of salt in sweat and require an increased amount of calories to fight infection, they are encouraged to eat a high fat, energy dense diet with a generous salt intake.

CF patients with malabsorption must take pancreatic enzyme capsules before all meals. This maximizes the absorption of food.

Respiratory effects of cystic fibrosis

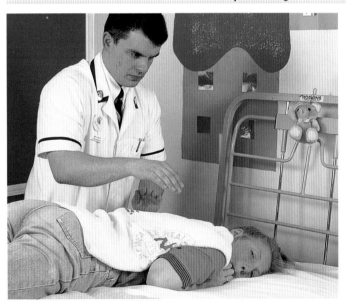

Respiratory complications have the most serious impact on long-term outcome, although the onset and progression of lung damage varies considerably between patients. Left untreated, recurrent infection with a variety of specific bacteria leads to irreversible lung damage called bronchiectasis. The airways become dilated, and the abnormal accumulation of secretions leads to a chronic cough and the production of large amounts of purulent (pus-containing) sputum.

Characteristically, there is a change in the fingertips, called

Percussion therapy involves clapping the chest with a cupped hand. This mobilizes secretions, which can then be coughed up.

clubbing, which parallels the progression of the lung damage. Curvature of the nail and soft-tissue swelling of the distal phalanges (fingertips) is typical.

One of the keys to preventing lung damage is physiotherapy, and all patients require treatment at least once daily. Postural drainage and percussion therapy (clapping the chest and back) encourage coughing and aid the clearance of secretions.

Older children are taught controlled breathing, thoracic expansion exercises and forced expiratory techniques. Patients are eventually able to treat themselves using a therapy known as the 'active cycle of breathing'. Physical exercise is also important, and patients are encouraged to participate in sporting activities.

COMPLICATIONS

As a result of improving long-term survival, late complications of CF have emerged as important problems. After the age of 10, endocrine insufficiency occurs, and diabetes mellitus becomes increasingly common.

Liver problems are also relatively common among older patients, although only a few develop severe complications that require liver transplantation. Bile-salt replacement is now commonly prescribed, and this may have an impact on the progression of liver damage.

Treating CF-related respiratory complaints

Frequent follow-up of CF patients is essential for detecting and treating respiratory complaints:
■ While most respiratory infections are due to viruses, CF sufferers are highly susceptible to secondary bacterial infection. Initially, courses of antibiotics are given orally, but organisms that are more difficult to treat require intravenous treatment.
■ Many CF sufferers also have asthma-like problems, and benefit from using bronchodilators. Recently, a new nebulized

medication called rhDNase has been developed to help liquefy and loosen sputum.
■ The body's own immune response to lung infection is a contributor to bronchiectasis, and research is addressing the use of anti-inflammatory medication to limit the natural immune response.

Inhaled nebulized medication can help loosen mucus. In the future, major breakthroughs in gene therapy may prevent the respiratory complications of CF.

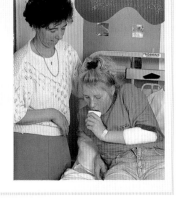

Viral encephalitis

Encephalitis is inflammation of the brain, and is often caused
by a virus. Affected children suffer increasing cerebral dysfunction,
shown by behavioural abnormalities, convulsions and coma.

Encephalitis is a serious neurological condition, which is generally caused by a virus that is toxic to brain tissue. It involves inflammation of the brain tissue itself, as opposed to inflammation of the meninges (the membranes that surround the brain), which occurs in meningitis. Sometimes, both the brain and the meninges become inflamed and this is known as meningoencephalitis.

CAUSES OF ENCEPHALITIS

The main viruses that cause encephalitis in the UK include:
■ Herpes simplex virus (types I and II) – the virus can be passed on to the baby by a mother during delivery (if she has genital herpes). Encephalitis can also be a complication of herpes simplex skin infection
■ Measles virus – about 1 in 5,000 children with measles develop encephalitis as a complication. The condition usually develops a few days after the rash becomes obvious
■ Mumps virus – this is a less common cause of encephalitis

■ Varicella virus (chickenpox) – this is usually a comparatively mild form of the illness
■ Influenza viruses.
  In the USA and Japan, the main causes of encephalitis are viral infections transmitted from animals to humans by ticks and mosquitoes. The rabies virus can also cause encephalitis.

Encephalitis involves inflammation and wasting of brain tissue. This can be identified through magnetic resonance imaging of the brain.

The herpes simplex virus (shown below) is a common cause of encephalitis in Europe. This form of the disease responds well to anti-viral therapy.

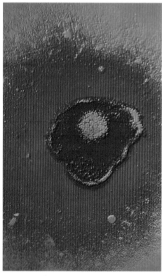

Recognizing the symptoms

The symptoms of viral encephalitis in a child vary greatly; they may be mild or severe and can either appear abruptly (with fits, for example), or develop as a gradual onset of abnormal drowsiness. The symptoms also depend on the cause. For example, if encephalitis is a complication of measles, the symptoms of measles will also be present.

Babies suffering from viral encephalitis may slowly develop a high fever and become drowsy and floppy, or experience the sudden onset of convulsions.

INITIAL SYMPTOMS

When a child develops encephalitis, symptoms may develop slowly or frighteningly fast, and include:
■ High fever
■ Intense headache – if a child is too young to articulate their pain, there may be obvious signs of distress such as persistent crying
■ Irritability and mental confusion
■ Abnormal behaviour
■ Weakness in one or more parts of the body
■ Speech disturbances – such as slurring of words
■ Hearing loss
■ Decreased level of consciousness, ranging from unusual drowsiness to unconsciousness
■ Convulsions or seizures
■ Abnormal reflexes.

Reye's syndrome

This is a very rare condition that may occur following a viral infection. It has been associated with taking aspirin in children under twelve years of age.
  Reye's syndrome causes an encephalopathy (clinically similar to encephalitis although there is no actual inflammation of the brain cells) and liver failure. Symptoms initially include vomiting, drowsiness and convulsions. As the disease progresses the child may lose consciousness and fall into a coma.

If doctors suspect Reye's syndrome the child will undergo blood tests to assess liver function and a CT scan or MRI of the brain to look for oedema (swelling). A liver biopsy may also be taken. There is no actual treatment for the condition itself, but artificial ventilation may help to reduce pressure in the brain.

Reye's syndrome is a very rare, potentially fatal condition. It shares many of the symptoms of encephalitis and may confuse diagnosis.

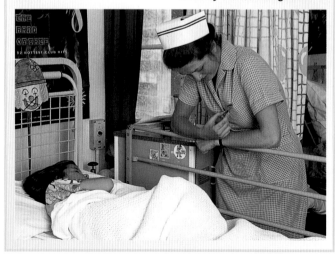

Confirming the diagnosis

Several diseases mimic the symptoms of encephalitis, preventing diagnosis on clinical examination alone. MR imaging and a lumbar puncture may be necessary.

If the doctor suspects that a child has viral encephalitis, prompt admission to hospital is usually arranged as the condition is serious and requires expert nursing and medical care.

The problem is that the symptoms could apply to a range of diseases that affect the brain, from infections to tumours, and investigations need to be carried out to exclude these other possibilities. After admission, doctors will carry out several tests both to confirm the diagnosis and to discover the cause of the inflammation.

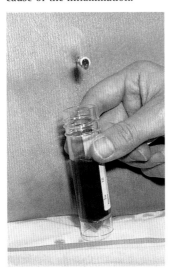

A lumbar puncture may be done to exclude bacterial meningitis. A hollow needle is used to obtain cerebrospinal fluid from around the spinal cord.

HOSPITAL TESTS

Initially doctors perform clinical examinations, such as testing reflex reactions, to assess the child's nervous system.

The child then undergoes a series of tests:

■ In most cases, a lumbar puncture is carried out. This can distinguish between a viral and bacterial infection, and will therefore exclude bacterial meningitis as the cause of the symptoms. A lumbar puncture involves taking a small sample of cerebrospinal fluid from around the spinal cord, under local anaesthetic. A narrow needle is inserted into the space between the vertebrae in the lower back and fluid is allowed to drip out. The sample is then examined for signs of inflammation or infection

■ Blood samples are taken to look for identifiable antibodies to particular viruses

■ An electroencephalogram (EEG) is performed – this shows the brain's activity as waves on a graph. In some types of encephalitis, particularly herpes

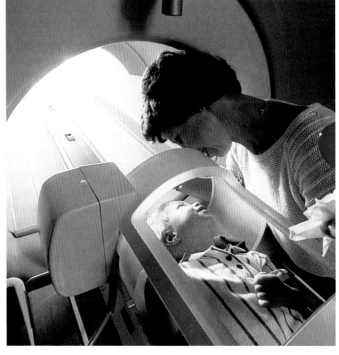

MR images provide the clearest pictures of the brain abnormalities associated with encephalitis. Rapid diagnosis of the disease is essential.

simplex encephalitis, the results show slow-wave abnormalities over one or other brain hemisphere

■ Scans of the brain are often carried out – both MRI (magnetic resonance imaging) and CT (computed tomography) scanning can reveal any swelling of the brain tissue or temporal lobe abnormalities, such as gross atrophy (wasting away) from loss of neural (nerve cell) tissue

■ Rarely, a brain biopsy may be performed – this enables laboratory technicians to check for the herpes simplex virus, which is one of the common causes of viral encephalitis. The virus can be cultured from the biopsy specimen.

Treating encephalitis

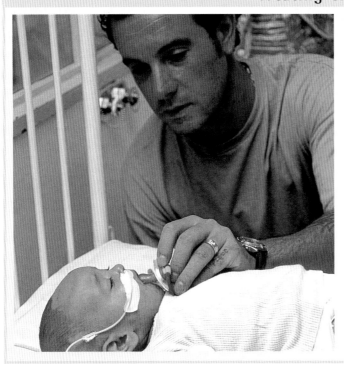

After a few days, children suffering from encephalitis may need to be fed through a nasogastric tube. Their condition requires constant monitoring.

Affected children are usually nursed in a specialist unit. The treatment has two aims:

■ Treating the specific cause of the inflammation

■ Treating the effects of the encephalitis.

Treating the cause

A rapid diagnosis is essential, as early treatment can make an enormous difference to the prognosis. Diagnosing infection with the herpes simplex virus is particularly important, as this is the most common form of viral encephalitis in the UK and the only one that responds to treatment with anti-viral therapy (intravenous injections of the anti-viral drug acyclovir).

Treating the effects

It is important to monitor a child's consciousness and, if he or she is drowsy or unresponsive, to make sure that the airway is kept clear. The following steps might be taken to ease symptoms:

■ Rehydrating the child with intravenous fluid therapy, which may also re-balance the body's chemical levels

■ If the illness persists for more than a few days, the child may be fed via a nasogastric tube

■ If there is increased pressure within the skull, artificial ventilation can reduce it.

Response to treatment may not be rapid, even in those cases where anti-viral therapy is appropriate. Some children recover fully but others may need physiotherapy or speech therapy for several months to fully regain motor skills. There may be permanent neurological damage in some children.

Epilepsy in childhood

Epilepsy is a recurrent condition affecting fewer than one per cent of children. In many cases, epilepsy resolves by adulthood, but it can also continue throughout life.

Epilepsy is characterized by recurrent, unprovoked seizures and is one of the most common brain disorders to affect children. The classification of the different types of epilepsy is complex, but there are a number of well-recognized epilepsy syndromes.

In many children the disorder follows a relatively benign course, with seizures ceasing in adult life. In others, seizures will continue to be a serious problem, despite medication. Some children with epilepsy that is difficult to control may require brain surgery.

SEIZURES

A seizure occurs when there is a sudden disturbance in the electrical activity of the brain. This can produce effects ranging from a convulsion with loss of consciousness and jerking of the limbs, to more subtle changes in behaviour and awareness, depending on which regions of the brain are involved.

There may be an obvious provoking factor such as fever, an acute head injury or drugs. Epilepsy is only diagnosed when

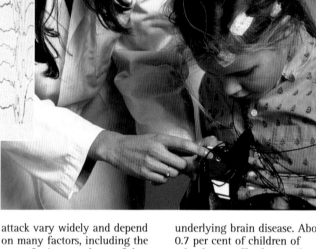

Electroencephalography (EEG) is frequently used to diagnose all types of epilepsy. The procedure involves attaching electrodes to the child's scalp.

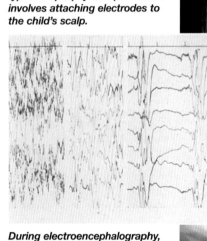

During electroencephalography, a visual display of the electrical activity in the brain is shown. This tracing shows epileptic spikes on the left side.

seizures recur spontaneously without any provocation.

RISK OF RECURRENCE

Estimates of the risk of further seizures after a first spontaneous attack vary widely and depend on many factors, including the type of seizure and age of the child. The recurrence risk is at least 33-50 per cent and higher if the seizure was a symptom of underlying brain disease. About 0.7 per cent of children of school age suffer from epilepsy, and about 60 per cent of adult epileptics will have suffered their first seizures in childhood.

Febrile convulsions

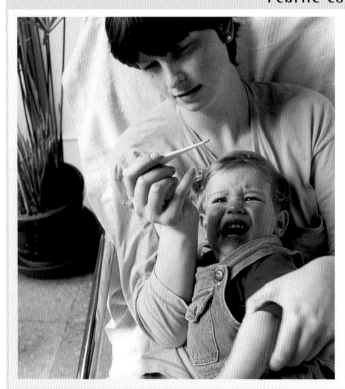

Febrile convulsions are defined as seizures that occur with a fever (excluding those caused by infections of the nervous system such as meningitis).

Strictly speaking, they are not classed as epilepsy, since there is a clear provoking factor. They are also characterized by the following:
■ They occur mainly from six months to five years of age
■ They affect up to four per cent of children within this age group
■ The risk is increased by 10–15 per cent when other family members have had convulsions
■ About 75 per cent of febrile seizures are simple, involving a generalized convulsion (tonic-clonic seizure) lasting no longer than around five minutes and with full recovery afterwards.

Very high fever can result in febrile convulsions in small children. Although frightening for parents, they rarely require treatment.

Complex seizures
These account for around 25 per cent of cases. They differ from simple convulsions in that:
■ They are prolonged (lasting 15-20 minutes or more) or recurrent
■ They involve focal features such as jerking of the limbs
■ They are followed by a neurological deficit, such as temporary paralysis.

Children with recurrent or prolonged febrile seizures may be treated in the acute stage with diazepam. These children have sometimes been given anti-epileptic medication on a regular basis, but there is no convincing evidence that this is very effective in preventing either further febrile convulsions or later epilepsy.

Epilepsy
The risk of a child with a history of simple convulsions going on to develop epilepsy is around ten per cent. This figure rises where seizures were complex and there is a family history.

Types of epilepsy

Several types of epilepsy are more prevalent in children than adults.
Some, like absence epilepsy, will often be outgrown by adolescence, while
others, such as temporal lobe epilepsy, represent a lifelong condition.

Absence seizures (often referred to as *petit mal*) involve a sudden interruption of awareness. During an attack, which typically lasts around 20 seconds, children stop whatever they are doing and stare blankly, often fluttering their eyelids, before returning just as suddenly to their tasks.

ABSENCE EPILEPSY
Typically, absence epilepsy:
■ Can cause many attacks a day
■ Can be brought on by hyperventilation
■ Shows a characteristic pattern in the electroencephalogram (EEG) brain wave tracing: a 3 Hz spike with wave activity
■ Accounts for around five per cent of all paediatric epilepsy

■ Is more common in boys than girls, with a peak age of onset at around six or seven years
■ Responds well to treatment with medication (most commonly sodium valproate)
■ Will stop in up to 75 per cent of children by adolescence
■ Will develop into tonic-clonic seizures (*grand mal*) in about 40 per cent of sufferers. The risk is increased in those with a family history of epilepsy or low IQ.

Juvenile absence epilepsy is a similar condition which starts at around 9-12 years. Although attacks are less frequent, they are more severe and the long-term outlook is not as good as for childhood absence epilepsy.

TEMPORAL LOBE EPILEPSY
This is a form of partial epilepsy, in which the electrical seizure activity begins in a localized area of the brain – in this case, the temporal lobe.

An attack commonly starts with an aura, involving odd tastes or smells, unpleasant sensations in the stomach and nausea. Typically progressing to a complex partial seizure, the child suffers a loss of awareness together with confusion and

Some forms of epilepsy respond well to medication. Drugs containing sodium valproate act to decrease brain activity and limit seizures.

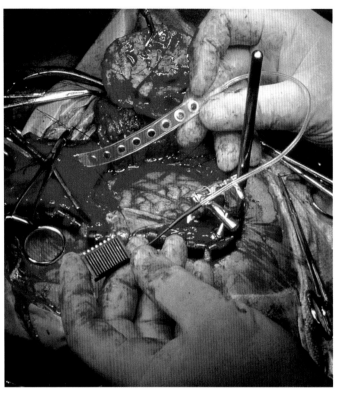

disturbed behaviour with automatisms, such as lip smacking or fumbling with clothing. Most complex partial seizures are over within three minutes or less, but may be followed by a further period of confusion before full recovery.

Children with partial epilepsy often show localized structural abnormalities in the brain.

Surgery may be used to treat children with severe epilepsy that has not responded to medication. The abnormal area of the brain is treated directly.

Where anti-epileptic drugs have proved ineffective, children occasionally undergo surgery to treat the abnormal area of the brain causing the seizures.

Photosensitivity

Reflex epilepsy is a type of epilepsy in which seizures are triggered by a particular kind of stimulation or activity. The most common form is photosensitive epilepsy.

Children with this condition are prone to attacks triggered by light flashing at certain rates. Strobe lights are a well recognized trigger, particularly where the flash rate is 12–20 per second.

The flicker from TV sets or computer games may also provoke attacks in photosensitive children. However, stimulation of this kind will only provoke

The flickering of light from a TV or computer screen can trigger epilepsy in children suffering from photosensitivity. It most commonly affects teenagers.

seizures in individuals who are already photosensitive and does not itself cause epilepsy.

Cause and prognosis
Photosensitivity is a genetically determined condition which affects about five per cent of all children with epilepsy.

More common in girls, the condition tends to develop between the age of six years and adolescence, with a peak around 12–16 years. Children often grow out of it as they develop into young adults and the response to medication (normally sodium valproate) is good.

Rarer forms of reflex epilepsy include those triggered by factors as wide ranging as eating, reading, doing mental arithmetic, or listening to music.

Hydrocephalus

Hydrocephalus is an abnormal increase in the amount of fluid in the ventricles of the brain. Symptoms are variable, and treatment is aimed at minimizing damage to the affected child's brain tissue.

Hydrocephalus is an uncommon condition, in which there is an abnormal increase in the volume of cerebrospinal fluid (CSF) within the ventricles (cavities) of the brain.

Hydrocephalus has three causes:
■ A blockage in the flow of CSF from the ventricles to the subarachnoid space (the space between two of the three membranes that surround and protect the brain)
■ Reduced reabsorption of CSF
■ Excess CSF production.

ASSOCIATED CONDITIONS
Blockage and reduced reabsorption of CSF may be associated with a number of conditions present at birth, most

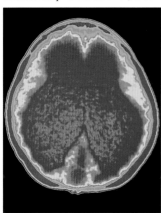

commonly spina bifida – an abnormality of the spinal cord. Congenital abnormalities of the brain itself, in particular a narrowing in the system around which the CSF circulates, may also result in hydrocephalus.

Alternatively, a blockage in the flow of CSF or reduced uptake may follow an intracranial haemorrhage (bleeding within the skull), an infection such as meningitis, in which the membranes covering the brain become infected and inflamed, or a brain tumour. Premature babies who have an intracranial haemorrhage are particularly at risk of developing this condition.

Excess production of CSF may occasionally occur in infancy as a result of a choroid plexus papilloma. This is a small tumour in the choroid plexus (a rich network of blood vessels) in the ventricles of the brain.

This CT scan shows a section through the brain of a child with hydrocephalus. The ventricles (red) are filled with an excessive amount of cerebrospinal fluid.

Hydrocephalus is an abnormal build-up of CSF in the cavities of the brain. This child, who has a shunt (drainage tube) in place, is undergoing physiotherapy.

The role of cerebrospinal fluid (CSF)

CSF is a clear, watery fluid that bathes and cushions the brain and spinal cord. It is continuously produced by the choroid plexus, a dense network of blood vessels within each of the ventricles.

The fluid circulates between the ventricles, the subarachnoid space between two of the three

membranes that surround the brain and spinal cord (the meninges), and the narrow canal in the centre of the spinal cord.

CSF is produced by the choroid plexus, a network of ventricular blood vessels. The function of CSF is to cushion the brain and spinal cord.

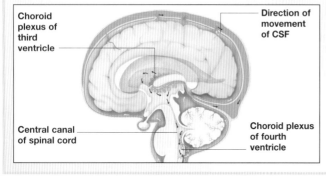

Choroid plexus of third ventricle

Direction of movement of CSF

Central canal of spinal cord

Choroid plexus of fourth ventricle

Neural tube defects and spina bifida

In early pregnancy, a fetal structure called the neural tube develops into the brain, spinal cord and meninges. If the tube does not close normally, a defect in the nervous system can result. The spinal cord is most often affected, causing the condition known as spina bifida. Spina bifida varies in severity between cases, but it is known to be associated with the development of hydrocephalus.

PREVENTION
It is now known that folic acid, taken around the time of conception and continued throughout early pregnancy, reduces the risk of spina bifida. Since folic acid supplementation was introduced, the incidence of the condition has declined by around 75 per cent.

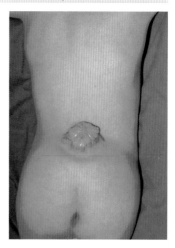

Hydrocephalus may be associated with spina bifida. Severe cases of spina bifida result in the exposure of part of the baby's spinal cord.

Signs and symptoms of hydrocephalus

The signs and symptoms are variable, their severity being largely determined by the age at which hydrocephalus begins and the speed at which the intracranial pressure rises.

ENLARGED SKULL
In infants, the bones of the skull have not yet fused and the skull can expand to accommodate the increasing amount of fluid. As a result, the head enlarges more rapidly than it should:
- The sutures, or joins between the skull bones, widen
- The fontanelles (the soft areas on an infant's head) become larger and may bulge due to the raised pressure
- The veins on the scalp may also become dilated (widened).

SYMPTOMS
In older children and adults, the skull cannot expand and the symptoms of raised intracranial pressure develop. These include:
- Headaches
- Nausea and vomiting
- Poor appetite.

Raised pressure can also affect infants if the expansion of the skull fails to keep pace with the increasing amount of fluid.

In addition, compression of specific areas of the brain may cause other symptoms:
- Unsteady walking
- Visual problems
- Hormonal disturbances, the most common manifestation of which is impaired growth.

SPEED OF ONSET
If the condition develops rapidly, headache and vomiting may soon be followed by drowsiness and, later, by coma. If hydrocephalus develops slowly, the symptoms tend to be subtle. Changes in an older child's behaviour and personality, and a gradual deterioration in schoolwork, may become evident.

Raised pressure in the skull eventually damages brain tissue, which may in turn result in disability.

One sign of hydrocephalus in children is an enlarged head. In most cases, however, the condition is treated before it reaches this stage.

Prenatal diagnosis

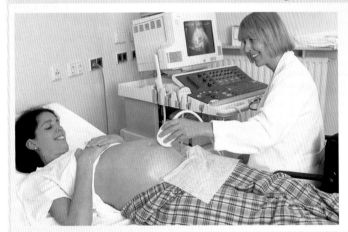

Hydrocephalus may be detected during pregnancy on a routine ultrasound scan.

Ultrasound and other scanning techniques, such as CT or MR imaging, may be performed on babies or children to confirm the diagnosis of hydrocephalus, look for an underlying cause and determine what treatment is required.

Hydrocephalus is sometimes noted during routine antenatal ultrasound scanning. The diagnosis is then confirmed with CT scanning or MRI.

Treating hydrocephalus

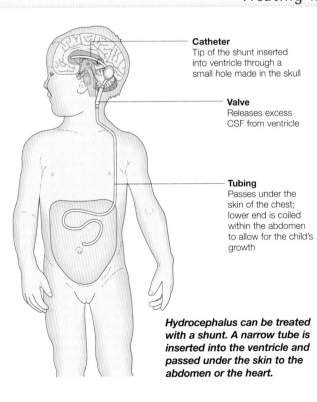

Catheter
Tip of the shunt inserted into ventricle through a small hole made in the skull

Valve
Releases excess CSF from ventricle

Tubing
Passes under the skin of the chest; lower end is coiled within the abdomen to allow for the child's growth

Hydrocephalus can be treated with a shunt. A narrow tube is inserted into the ventricle and passed under the skin to the abdomen or the heart.

The priority in treatment is to reduce the pressure in the ventricles, with the aim of minimizing damage to the surrounding brain tissue. Any underlying cause, such as a brain tumour, will be addressed.

In some cases, the obstruction to the flow or uptake of CSF is a temporary problem and the only treatment required may be drugs that slow the production of CSF.

INSERTING A SHUNT
Many children, however, require the insertion of a shunt – a narrow, flexible tube that diverts CSF from the ventricles to another part of the body, where it can be absorbed.

The tube is inserted into one of the ventricles through a small hole made in the skull and then directed under the skin to the abdominal cavity or, less commonly, the heart. Excess tubing can be coiled within the abdomen to allow for a child's growth.

Shunts may have two possible complications: blockages and infection. Parents need to be alerted to the signs of these and are advised to seek immediate medical help if they are apparent. Symptoms vary according to age, but include:
- Headache
- Lethargy
- Reduced appetite
- Changes in behaviour.

PROGNOSIS
The prognosis is very variable and depends on many factors, including the age of onset of the condition, the underlying cause and how soon the condition is effectively treated.

Children with hydrocephalus are at increased risk of developmental problems and learning disabilities. In some cases, however, if a shunt can be placed early enough, damage to the brain tissue may be averted and the child may develop normally.

211

Meningitis

Symptoms

Meningitis – inflammation of the meninges, membranes in the skull and spine – is often a childhood disease. There are two forms: viral and the more serious bacterial. The clearest sign of the illness is the appearance of bruise-like rashes, caused by bleeding from the small blood vessels (capillaries) in the skin.

The meningitis rash may appear suddenly and spread rapidly to cover the limbs and whole body. In extreme cases, the child may collapse within hours of this rash appearing, so treatment should be rapid.

The fontanelle (the soft spot on top of a baby's head) may be bulging and firm to the touch.

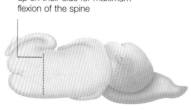

The appearance of blotchy rashes (known as petechiae) is the most ominous sign of meningitis. These rashes do not pale when pressure is applied, so test for this by pressing on the rash with a tumbler.

■ A baby that is irritable, vomiting repeatedly and has a high-pitched cry should be seen by a GP or A&E department without delay.

■ Older children will show sensitivity to light (photophobia) by closing or covering the eyes.

■ Headache will be present, as will vomiting and an inability to bend the head forward or, when sitting, to place the lips on the knees. This is due to back and neck stiffness.

Diagnosis

A lumbar puncture is performed to confirm the diagnosis of meningitis. In this procedure, a needle is inserted in the back into the spinal canal, and cerebro-spinal fluid (CSF) is extracted. This fluid, which surrounds the spine and brain and contains the meningitis bacteria or viruses, is then sent for detailed examination.

If the fluid is cloudy to the naked eye, it suggests infection due to meningitis. Microscopic examination, however, will reveal the number and type of cells present, and the type of 'bug' causing the infection. The organisms that cause meningitis are either bacterial or viral, and identification of these determines the correct therapy. Antibiotics, for instance, are only used for bacterial meningitis.

The most dangerous type of infection is from meningococcus bacteria, which enter the bloodstream and cause severe septicaemia (blood poisoning). Other bacteria that commonly cause meningitis are *Haemophilus influenzae* type B (Hib) and *Streptococcus pneumoniae.*

In a lumbar puncture, spinal fluid (CSF) is taken from the spinal canal, using a puncture needle with an added tap. Cloudy cerebro-spinal fluid suggests the presence of meningitis, and this may be confirmed after microscopic examination.

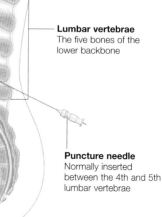

Lumbar vertebrae
The five bones of the lower backbone

Iliac crests
A line between the hip bones that delineates the level of the puncture. The patient lies curled up on their side for maximum flexion of the spine

Puncture needle
Normally inserted between the 4th and 5th lumbar vertebrae

Prognosis

The course of the infection depends on the organism responsible. Viral meningitis is usually self-limiting. In cases due to bacteria, early diagnosis and treatment are the keys to survival. Late diagnosis may lead to complications and death. Prognoses include:

■ Paralysis of cranial nerves, leading to squints, deafness and limb paralysis

■ Unconsciousness due to fluid build-up in the brain

■ Mental and behavioural problems; finally death

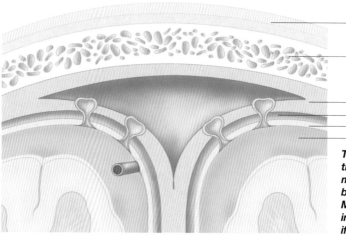

Scalp

Skull

MENINGES
Dura mater
Arachnoid
Pia mater

Brain

This skull cross-section shows the meninges, the three membranes that surround the brain and the spinal cord. Meningitis causes an inflammation of the layers, which, if not treated in time, can kill.

Causes

The bacterium that causes meningitis enters the bloodstream via the nose and throat, causing blood poisoning (septicaemia), which in turn infects the meninges.

The principle types of bacteria that cause meningitis are:
- Meningococcus
- Pneumococcus
- Haemophilus influenzae
- Streptococcus
- Staphylococcus

Sometimes other causes may be involved:
- In tiny babies, meningitis can be caused by *E. coli*, the source of infection being the umbilicus.

- Viral and fungal infections can be other causes of meningitis.

NOTIFIABLE
Because it is such a serious illness, meningitis is 'notifiable'. This means that any case must be immediately reported to the relevant Health Authority.

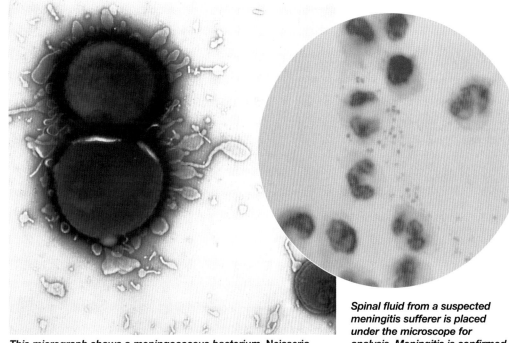

This micrograph shows a meningococcus bacterium, Neisseria meningitidis. It is one of the micro-organisms that causes meningitis. The bacterial infection spreads rapidly and results in meningococcal septicaemia, characterized by a haemorrhagic rash (one caused by blood loss) that spreads over the body.

Spinal fluid from a suspected meningitis sufferer is placed under the microscope for analysis. Meningitis is confirmed by the presence of bacteria (small dark-red spots) on the white blood cells that appear here as large red patches.

Incidence

Two-thirds of all meningitis cases occur in children under 15 years of age. Of these, 80 per cent occur before the age of five. Neonates (babies up to three months) and children between six and nine months are most at risk. In the neonatal period, infection is primarily due to the *E. coli* organism that lives in the gut and arises from umbilical infection.

- Most cases of bacterial meningitis begin as septicaemia; the germ enters the bloodstream from the nose.

- Ear infections may be responsible for introducing meningitis.

- In rare cases, meningitis will result from infection from a compound (open) fracture of the skull.

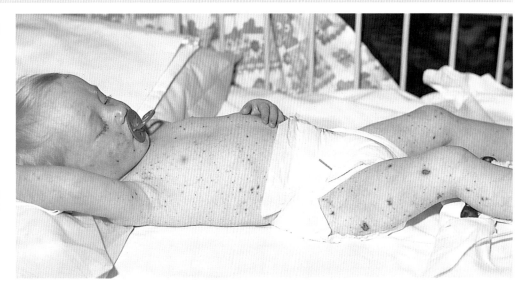

Meningococcal meningitis is characterized by the rapid spread of bruise-like haemorrhagic rashes over the patient's body. If the sufferer goes undiagnosed or untreated, the meningitis can prove fatal to a young child.

Treatment

If bacterial meningitis or septicaemia is suspected, penicillin (benzylpenicillin, or Crystapen) should be given as soon as possible, preferably by injection into muscle tissue. A single injection may be life-saving: fatality rates range from 7 to 20 per cent, depending on the type of infection.

Once the analysis has established the type of organism causing the meningitis, the appropriate antibiotic may then be prescribed. Treatment usually lasts for at least 10–14 days.

Viral meningitis will usually only require treatment with rest and painkillers; antibiotics are not effective against viruses.

Prevention

Hib vaccine now protects against *Haemophilus* meningitis and is routinely given at two, three and four months. Meningitis is infectious, so suspected cases should be isolated immediately. Local outbreaks can occur, so anyone in contact with sufferers should be immunized.

Causes of meningitis

Meningitis means inflammation of the meninges – the membranes that cover and line the brain. This occurs when microbes gain access to the subarachnoid space beneath the outermost pair of these membranes and multiply.

MENINGITIS IN CHILDREN

The bacteria responsible for meningitis in children after the first few months of life are among the common colonists of the nose and throat in healthy individuals. Three species are responsible for the great majority of cases:

Neisseria meningitidis, also known as meningococcus, is currently the main cause of meningitis in the UK, as well as causing the even more serious life-threatening infection, meningococcal septicaemia. Group B and group C strains are responsible for nearly all of the infections.

Streptococcus pneumoniae (the pneumococcus) is currently the next commonest in the UK. *Haemophilus influenzae* type b, otherwise known as Hib, used to be a common cause of meningitis in the UK. However, since 1992 all infants have been offered the very effective Hib vaccine, which has led to an enormous reduction in the number of cases.

MENINGITIS IN NEONATES

Around the time of birth, neonates (babies up to six weeks old) may be exposed to bacteria that colonize the maternal gastrointestinal and genital tracts, and some of these may cause meningitis. These include:
■ Enteric Gram-negative bacteria, particularly *Escherichia coli;* type K1 strains are

The bacterium species **Streptococcus pneumoniae** *(the pneumococcus) is a common cause of meningitis in the UK.*

particularly associated with invasive infection
■ Group B streptococcus
■ *Listeria monocytogenes* (a cause of bacterial food poisoning and septicaemia).

VIRAL MENINGITIS

Viral meningitis is generally a less serious condition than bacterial meningitis. However, as well as causing inflammation of the meninges, viruses can infect the brain itself, leading to encephalitis (inflammation of the brain), with fever, confusion and signs of brain dysfunction. Typically, viruses cause a mixed infection – meningoencephalitis – with

features of both meningitis and encephalitis.

Viruses that cause these conditions include:
■ Mumps virus. Mumps meningoencephalitis used to be very common, but wide use of mumps vaccine has greatly reduced its incidence.
■ Enteroviruses, among the common viruses causing diarrhoea and sore throats, can cause meningitis.

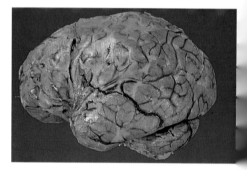

In paediatric intensive care, a nurse attends a young child who is suffering from a severe case of meningitis.

This brain was removed after a fatal case of pneumococcal meningitis. The meninges are thickened and the brain is covered with pus.

Signs and symptoms of meningitis

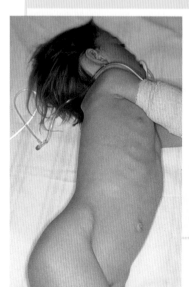

Spasm of the neck muscles causes the head to arch back, as seen in this severe case of meningitis.

General signs and symptoms of infection are seen from an early stage. At the beginning, the symptoms are similar to those of flu. These may include:
■ Fever
■ Nausea, and sometimes vomiting
■ Aches and pains
■ Shivering, and cold, pale or blotchy skin
■ In a baby, no interest in feeding.

Specific signs and symptoms of meningitis soon appear, relating to the fact that the meninges are inflamed. These include:
■ Very severe headache
■ Neck stiffness, arising from spasm of neck muscles as a result of irritation of nerves passing through the inflamed meninges
■ Severe discomfort from light (photophobia)

Other signs and symptoms, caused by a swelling of the brain as a result of inflammation, appear as the infection progresses:

■ Irritability, or, in a baby, moaning or high-pitched crying
■ Drowsiness or confusion
■ In a baby, floppiness or unusual stiffness
■ In a baby, bulging of the anterior fontanelle (soft spot between the skull bones) on the top of the head
■ Convulsions, as a result of pressure on vital centres of the brain, or as the consequence of disturbance of brain metabolism from the infection.
Unless urgent steps are taken to reduce the inflammation, the infection may prove fatal.

Transmission of the meningitis infection

Bacteria that may cause meningitis beyond the neonatal period are generally spread from one person to the next in droplets of secretions from the respiratory tract. This may be as a result of coughing and sneezing, or bacteria being passed through physical contact.

Acts such as kissing on the mouth or sharing a glass are also possible means for transmission. It is important to understand that transmission, or the resulting colonization, is extremely unlikely to lead to meningitis in an individual case.

Up to 40 per cent of older teenagers and young adults may be colonized with the meningococcus, but at present in the UK less than 4 people per 100,000 per year develop meningococcal disease.

As with many other communicable infections, the bacteria that cause meningitis can be transferred by a sneeze.

Protecting against meningitis

The bacteria that cause meningitis are common colonists of the nose and throat at all ages, and generally do no harm at these sites. Indeed, their presence may be useful in stimulating the immune system to generate subsequent protection. However, for reasons not yet understood, the bacteria occasionally invade the bloodstream and if they are not eliminated from the circulation, they may spread to the meninges and cause meningitis.

The chief protection against this lies in the immune system, and, in particular, the presence

Breast milk contains antibodies that can protect a child against meningitis. This is important in the early stages of life as a baby has an immature immune system.

of specific antibodies that bind bacteria and assist in their removal. Antibodies may be present as a result of prior exposure to the microbes, or through vaccination.

NATURAL ANTIBODIES

Another source of protection, for newborn infants, is passive acquisition of antibodies from the mother's blood, delivered through the placenta before birth. Babies are also protected by antibodies in their mother's milk. Antibodies that babies acquire via the placenta can last in the circulation for about the first three or four months of life at concentrations sufficient to protect against infection. After this period there are insufficient antibodies to clear bacteria adequately, and infants become susceptible to invasive infection. Thereafter, young children remain at risk of bacterial meningitis until they have acquired natural immunity through exposure to colonizing bacteria, or have received protection – where available – through vaccination.

Natural immunity will develop with age, but the process may take many years. For example, before Hib vaccine was available, nearly all children nevertheless acquired natural immunity to Hib infection by the age of five years, but until that age, and particularly in younger children, many were susceptible. The vaccine has reduced the period of susceptibility to close to zero, as the course of vaccination should be completed by four months of age. Other bacteria that cause meningitis, such as meningococcus, also generate natural immunity, but this may not develop until adult life, and many individuals remain susceptible throughout their life.

Antibiotic treatment for bacterial meningitis

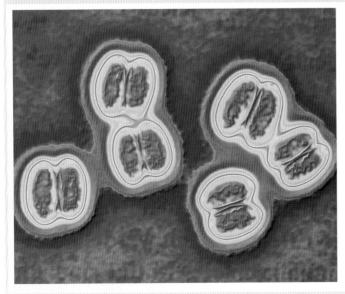

Bactericidal antibiotics must be administered without delay in cases of meningitis to minimize the risk of brain damage. As time is of the essence, treatment has to be started before the specific bacterial cause is identified. Therefore, broad spectrum antibiotics are used to ensure that all possibilities are covered.

A common choice to treat children beyond the neonatal period is a cephalosporin, such as ceftriaxone or cefotaxime.

Meningococci commonly colonize the nose and throat, but, rarely, they invade the blood-stream to cause septicaemia and meningitis. Urgent antibiotic treatment is then needed to reduce the risk of brain damage.

These are potent antibiotics that penetrate the meninges to kill bacteria in the cerebrospinal fluid. They are active against virtually all strains of the bacteria that commonly cause meningitis in this age group. Because very occasionally strains of pneumococcus may be resistant to these cephalosporins, an additional antibiotic such as vancomycin may be used in the initial stage of treatment.

In neonatal meningitis, it is necessary to prescribe a combination of antibiotics to cover the range of bacteria that may be responsible for the infection. Cefotaxime and ampicillin, or gentamicin and ampicillin, are widely used.

Meningococcal septicaemia

This condition is a serious complication of meningococcal infection that can quickly develop into life-threatening illness. Recognizing the characteristic rash can be life-saving.

As well as meningitis, meningococcus causes another life-threatening condition, known as meningococcal septicaemia. In meningococcal septicaemia, the bacteria circulating in the bloodstream cause a massive inflammatory response that leads to widespread damage to capillaries – capillary leak – in the skin and internal organs.

Leakage of blood and plasma out of the circulation into the tissues causes circulatory collapse, which can lead rapidly to multiple organ failure. Children who have contracted meningococcal septicaemia may progress from being well to fighting for their lives in a matter of hours, and may quickly need the full range of modern intensive-care services in order to survive.

MORTALITY RATE

While meningococcal meningitis has a mortality of around three per cent in the UK, septicaemia is much more dangerous, and 10–30 per cent of patients die. The outcome in meningococcal septicaemia depends critically on how quickly the seriousness of the condition is recognized, and how fast intensive-care measures to support the circulation and failing organs are instituted.

Signs and symptoms of meningococcal septicaemia

As meningococcal septicaemia may lead to brain inflammation and swelling as a result of capillary leak, many of the signs and symptoms of bacterial meningitis may also be seen in a case of septicaemia. However, as important exceptions, there is often no neck stiffness or photophobia. The lack of these signs should not be taken as reassurance that a sick child does not have meningococcal infection.

The appearance of red or purple spots or bruises on the skin can be a specific sign of meningococcal septicaemia. Caused by bleeding from capillaries into the skin, this can provide an early clue that a child has meningococcal septicaemia,

The characteristic rash of meningococcal septicaemia can be seen on this patient's arm. Recognizing such a rash can be life-saving.

and its recognition can be life-saving. The appearance is of a non-blanching red rash – sometimes hard to spot, but sometimes very obvious with bruises or whole areas of bleeding into the skin.

Red or purple spots and bruises on the skin are important signs that suggest meningococcal septicaemia. They are caused by blood leaking into the skin from broken capillaries.

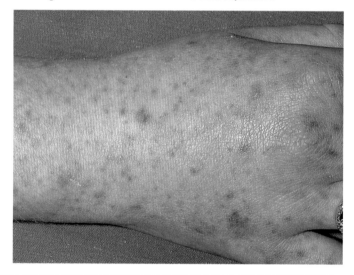

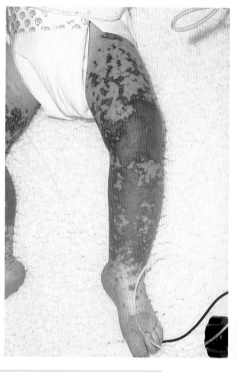

Glass test

The glass or tumbler test can be done simply at home to evaluate a rash. The side of a glass should be pressed over the area where spots have appeared, and the spot looked at through the glass. Under pressure, the skin will blanch and the common spots of many rashes – such as heat rash, or spots caused by viral infections – will blanch too and so disappear, returning when the glass is removed. If, however, a spot is caused by blood leaking into the skin, pressing a glass over it will make no difference.

The skin around the spot will become pale, but the spot will remain and perhaps become more obvious. In this is the case, the diagnosis could be meningococcal septicaemia. This is an emergency, and there should be no delay in getting medical help.

Placing a glass over a suspicious spot can help diagnose meningococcal septicaemia. A doctor should be contacted urgently if the spot does not blanch when pressed.

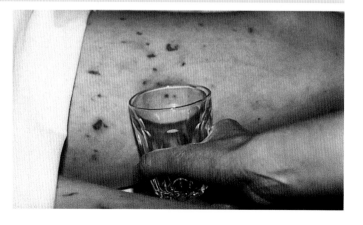

Managing meningococcal infection in the community

In England and Wales, guidelines on action to be taken in the event of an outbreak have been produced for Consultants in Communicable Disease Control (CCDCs) by the Public Health Laboratory Service Meningococcal Infections Working Group, and the Public Health Medicine Environmental Group. CCDCs take the lead in instituting public health measures.

Whenever a single case occurs, the aim is to reduce the risk of linked cases. There is good evidence that people who live in the same household are at higher risk of developing the disease than others in the community, through a combination of increased rate of exposure and perhaps (in families) genetic susceptibility.

Meningococcal disease occurs in a seasonal pattern, with most cases occurring in the winter. The period of increased risk is highest in the first week after a case, and thereafter quickly falls.

ANTIBIOTIC PROPHYLAXIS

The CCDC will arrange for oral antibiotics to be prescribed for these contacts as prophylactic treatment – that is, to eliminate carriage of meningococci and so prevent further cases from occurring. In the case of vaccine-preventable cases, vaccination is also offered.

There is no good evidence that more distant contacts of a single case are at increased risk as a result of their acquaintance with a sufferer. Antibiotics in these circumstances may do more harm than good, by eradicating protective strains that might otherwise generate valuable immunity, or by causing dangerous side effects. Much

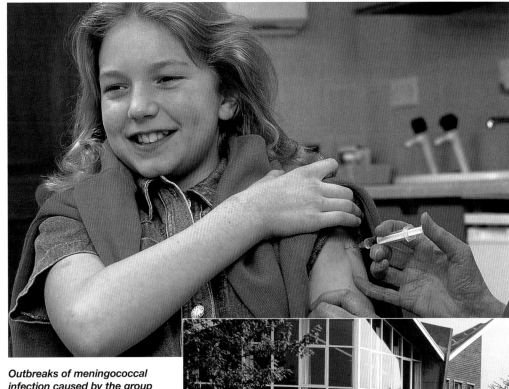

Outbreaks of meningococcal infection caused by the group C strain may be controlled by vaccination. For those caused by the group B strain, there is currently no vaccine available.

more important in these circumstances is that adequate information is given out; to be sure that friends and others in the community are aware of the signs and symptoms of infection; and of when and how to get medical help if they are concerned about the possibility of another case.

If more than one case of meningococcal disease occurs in a community in a period of four weeks, and there is evidence that the cases are linked by the strain being identical, this defines an outbreak. The CCDC will then

take urgent steps to establish a social network in which the virulent bacteria may be circulating, in order to identify a group to whom antibiotics and, where appropriate, vaccine should be prescribed.

Outbreaks of meningococcal infection, causing meningitis and septicaemia, occasionally occur in schools. This reflects increased transmission among individuals who spend a great deal of time together.

Aftereffects of meningitis and meningococcal septicaemia

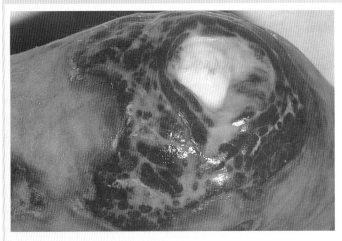

Although 90 per cent of patients who have bacterial meningitis recover completely, residual damage cannot be avoided in a small proportion. The consequence of infection in cerebrospinal fluid may be to cause a blockage of its circulation, leading to hydrocephalus (water on the brain). This may require neurosurgery to divert the fluid back into the blood circulation.

Meningococcal septicaemia can lead to major damage to skin and underlying soft tissue, requiring extensive plastic surgery.

The effect of inflammation of the brain during meningitis may cause persistent problems. The commonest of these is deafness, but blindness, epilepsy and physical or intellectual handicap may also occur. The circulatory collapse that is caused by the capillary leak in meningococcal septicaemia can lead to widespread and substantial tissue damage. Skin damage may be severe, requiring plastic surgery after the acute episode is over. More seriously, vascular damage can lead to muscle necrosis (death) and gangrene, leading to the loss of fingers, toes or even limbs.

Poliomyelitis

Poliomyelitis (polio) is a viral disease that is usually mild, but it can cause paralysis. Although rare in developed countries, it is still a major health problem among children in the developing world.

Poliomyelitis, commonly known as polio, is an important disease of childhood. Although it usually causes an insignificant illness it can, rarely, cause meningitis or even paralysis.

ROUTE OF INFECTION

Polio is spread by the faecal-oral route: in other words the virus is excreted in the faeces of infected people. Uninfected people contract the disease by ingesting contaminated food or water. Illness develops three to five days after exposure to the virus.

After infection with polio, the child may go on to develop:
- Inapparent infection
- Minor illness
- Aseptic meningitis
- Paralytic polio.

Polio is a major cause of disability in children in developing countries. Polio vaccination programmes are essential in eradicating the disease.

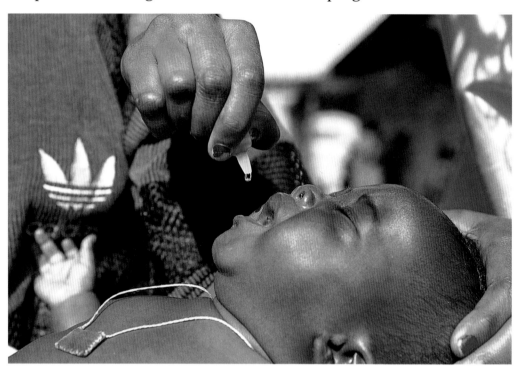

Types of polio

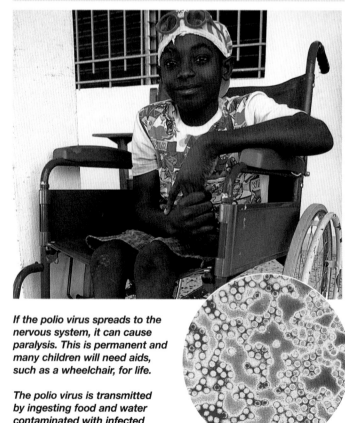

If the polio virus spreads to the nervous system, it can cause paralysis. This is permanent and many children will need aids, such as a wheelchair, for life.

The polio virus is transmitted by ingesting food and water contaminated with infected faeces. In most people the virus causes no symptoms.

■ Inapparent infection
In 90–95 per cent of cases, children infected with the polio virus have no evidence of infection and do not feel or look unwell. The infection is only confirmed through blood analysis.

■ Minor illness
Around five per cent of infected children show symptoms only of a minor viral illness. This form of polio is known as 'abortive polio'. These children have symptoms of a mild, non-specific illness with a slightly raised temperature. They may have a sore throat, be off their food and feel run down. However, such symptoms are so common that doctors rarely test for polio in such cases.

■ Non-paralytic polio
Children with this form of polio are moderately unwell with an aseptic meningitis (this is the name given to types of meningitis caused by viruses rather than bacteria).

Children with aseptic meningitis have a fever, with headache and vomiting. They usually develop aching muscles

and eventually complain of a stiff neck and sore back. Virtually all affected children make a full recovery.

■ Paralytic polio
This is the most severe form of polio. Affected children initially appear to have a marked form of aseptic meningitis. They have intense muscle pain, and look quite unwell with restlessness, agitation and a flushed appearance. They then go on to develop paralysis, which may begin suddenly or gradually over a three- to five-day period.

The paralysis typically affects one side of the body only, and paralysis of the legs is more common than the arms.

In severe cases, however, patients may develop paralysis of both legs and both arms. Some patients with paralytic polio may also develop temporary paralysis of the bladder or bowel.

The most life-threatening aspect of paralytic polio is weakness or paralysis of the muscles involved with breathing. If these are paralysed, the child cannot breathe efficiently and may die of asphyxia.

Treating and preventing polio

Polio only causes symptoms in more severe forms of the illness. A mildly ill child can be treated at home, but if the virus causes meningitis or paralysis the child will need hospitalization. Vaccination schemes have eradicated polio in many countries.

The diagnosis of polio will be made rarely, if at all, in children with no apparent evidence of infection or in those who have symptoms suggestive of a mild, non-specific viral illness.

DIAGNOSING POLIO

Diagnosis can be confirmed by culture of the cerebrospinal fluid (CSF). Virus growth in these cultures would allow the diagnosis of polio to be confirmed about one week after sampling. Analysis of two blood samples, taken after a 10-day interval, may reveal antibodies to polio; this confirms the diagnosis.

TREATMENT

As with most viral illnesses, there is no specific treatment available for polio. In mild disease, children are managed at home and are advised to take paracetamol for pain and fever.

Some children with aseptic meningitis (and all with paralytic polio) should be hospitalized. Those with paralytic polio should have their breathing assessed regularly to determine whether artificial ventilation is needed. If children have paralysis of the bladder they may need to be catheterized. This usually resolves after a few days.

Children affected by paralytic polio require physiotherapy. This mother is learning techniques which she can use on her daughter at home.

Paralytic polio causes paralysis of the muscles of the affected limb. Legs are most commonly affected, but the arms may also be paralysed.

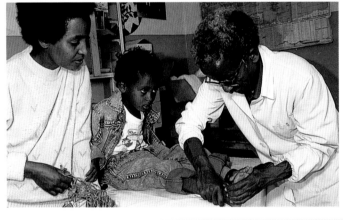

Immunization against polio

Polio vaccination was started in the late 1950s and this has led to the virtual elimination of polio in developed countries. In developing countries, however, polio is still a significant problem.

Oral polio vaccine has the advantage of conferring immunity to others as the inactivated virus is passed out in the child's faeces.

There are two types of vaccine:
■ Oral polio vaccine
■ Inactivated polio vaccine, administered by injection.

ORAL POLIO VACCINE

Oral polio vaccine (OPV) is a vaccine containing live but attenuated (reduced virulence) polio viruses. It is simple to administer, with drops of the vaccine being placed in the mouth. One major benefit with OPV is that it can allow indirect immunization of contacts of the

child receiving the vaccine. This is because the vaccine passes through the gut and is excreted in the faeces. It can, therefore, be passed on by contamination to those who are not vaccinated, reducing the spread of disease.

INACTIVATED VACCINE

Inactivated polio vaccine costs more to produce than OPV and needs to be injected. Unlike OPV it will not give immunity to any non-vaccinated contacts via the contamination route.

Giving the vaccine

In the United Kingdom vaccination programme, oral polio vaccine is used. The vaccine is administered from the age of two months. Three doses are given, with four weeks between each dose along with the diphtheria, pertussis and tetanus (DPT) vaccination. Booster doses are given at primary school entry and prior to leaving school.

Eradicating polio

World-wide polio eradication by the year 2000 was the aim of the World Health Organization in 1988. Although there was a 90 per cent reduction in cases between 1988 and 1996, complete eradication this year seems very unlikely.

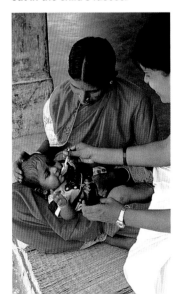

Incidence of polio worldwide

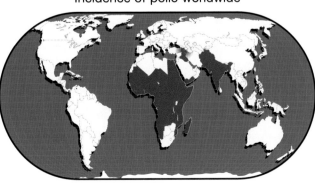

Polio was once a widespread disease of childhood. Since the immunization campaign started in the 1950s, it is now found only in the areas of the world shaded on this map.

219

Reye's syndrome

Reye's syndrome is a rare condition that may be
triggered by a viral infection. Treatment should be started as soon as
possible to reduce the risk of brain damage occurring.

Reye's syndrome is a rare disorder, characterized by damage to the brain and the liver. Almost exclusively a childhood disease, Reye's syndrome is a serious condition, requiring urgent treatment to avoid the risk of complications.

COMPLICATIONS
The condition may be fatal, usually due to swelling of the brain tissue. In addition to the brain swelling, Reye's syndrome is associated with the build-up of fat in the liver. As a result, the function of the liver is impaired.

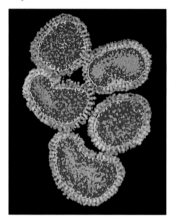

CAUSES
Reye's syndrome develops a few days after the onset of, or recovery from, a viral illness. A variety of viral illnesses may precede the syndrome, including chickenpox and influenza.

The cause is unknown, but there is thought to be an association with taking aspirin. Since 1986, therefore, it has been recommended that aspirin should not be given to children under 12 years. Paracetamol can be used as an alternative treatment.

DECLINE
The disorder was only recognized about 30 years ago. Over the last 15 years, there has been a dramatic decline in the number of cases diagnosed in the UK and the USA.

Reye's syndrome may follow a viral infection such as chickenpox. The condition can cause swelling of the brain and requires urgent treatment.

The influenza virus is shown here under the microscope. Rarely, a child with flu may go on to develop Reye's syndrome, but the connection is unclear.

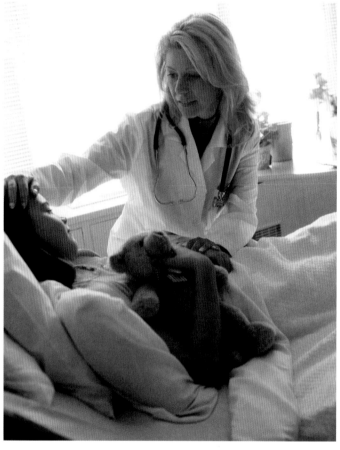

Pattern of symptoms

Reye's syndrome mainly affects children aged between six months and 15 years. However, small babies and young adults are occasionally affected. Boys and girls are affected equally.

RAPID DEVELOPMENT
The symptoms develop rapidly, in some cases over a few hours. Any of the following may occur:
■ Nausea and vomiting – the first symptom is usually profuse vomiting, followed or accompanied by lethargy
■ Disturbed consciousness – a characteristic feature; over a period of up to 24 hours an affected child may become disorientated and agitated
■ Visual hallucinations
■ Convulsions (fits) – these

occur in about 30 per cent of affected children
■ Low blood sugar levels – particularly in children under the age of two years
■ Breathing difficulties
■ Jaundice – the yellowing of the skin associated with impaired liver function.

Without treatment, drowsiness is likely to follow, leading to loss of consciousness.

VARIABLE PATTERN
The pattern of the syndrome is different in infants, in whom vomiting is a less common feature. In affected infants, the first symptoms tend to be breathing problems and convulsions. A history of a viral illness before the onset of symptoms is less common.

The rate at which the symptoms progress varies greatly in all those affected. The condition may stabilize at any stage.

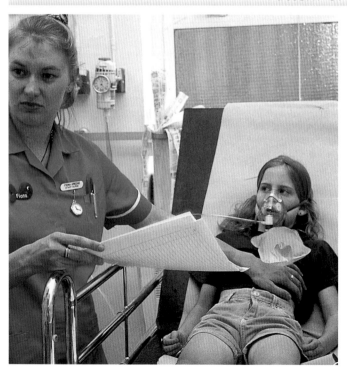

The onset of symptoms of Reye's syndrome is often rapid. A child may develop breathing problems and require oxygen or assisted ventilation.

Treating and diagnosing Reye's syndrome

Early diagnosis is essential to ensure the best treatment for Reye's syndrome. The outcome varies from child to child, but it largely depends on how quickly the symptoms develop and how soon medical attention is sought.

The outcome of Reye's syndrome depends on how early the condition is diagnosed and how effectively the swelling of the brain can be treated. Some children make a full recovery. For others, impairment of brain function persists, sometimes resulting in learning problems or movement difficulties.

For a number of children the condition is fatal; death occurs in up to 40 per cent of cases. The condition is more likely to be fatal if symptoms develop quickly and progress to coma.

MAKING THE DIAGNOSIS

Reye's syndrome is a medical emergency; the earlier the diagnosis can be made and treatment initiated, the better the prognosis. There are no specific tests for the condition. A careful examination will be carried out,

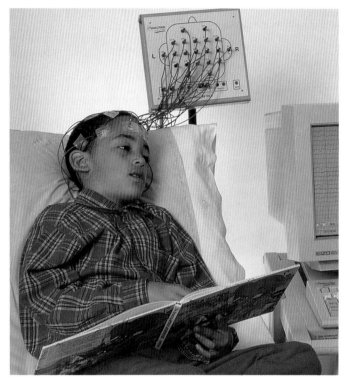

If a child has Reye's syndrome, an EEG may be carried out. This records electrical activity in the brain, which is shown as brain wave patterns on a monitor.

followed by tests to exclude other possible causes of the symptoms and to confirm the diagnosis. The examination may reveal signs of raised pressure in the skull caused by the brain swelling; the liver may be of normal size or enlarged.

Samples of blood may be taken and tested to check the levels of particular liver enzymes which, if raised, indicate impairment of liver function.

TESTING BRAIN AND LIVER FUNCTION

An EEG (electroencephalogram) may be performed to assess the electrical activity in the brain and look for signs of impairment of brain function.

The brain may be further examined by CT (computed tomography) scanning or MRI (magnetic resonance imaging). CT involves X-rays being passed through the body at different angles. The information is then processed by a computer to form cross-sectional pictures of the part of the body to be examined, in this case the brain.

MRI also produces detailed images of the body, but instead of

Liver cells (shown here) are examined to confirm a diagnosis of Reye's syndrome. The microscopic appearance may reveal damage.

using X-rays, the body is surrounded by a large magnet and is then exposed to short bursts of harmless radiowaves that cause hydrogen ions in the body to emit radio signals. Different types of tissue contain different amounts of hydrogen ions and produce strong or weak radio signals. These signals are analysed by the computer and formulated into images.

Finally, a liver biopsy may be

performed to confirm diagnosis. A sample of liver tissue is removed by a hollow needle passed through the skin and between the right lower ribs. Additional tests may be required to rule out other conditions.

Intensive care treatment

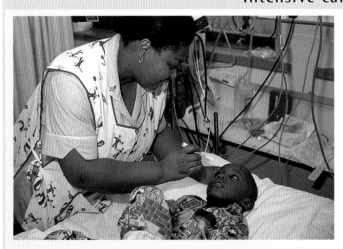

Children with Reye's syndrome are admitted to a paediatric intensive care unit. There they will be monitored closely and given medication.

Children with Reye's syndrome require admission to an intensive care unit, where they can be given constant specialist care.

Lowering pressure

There is no specific cure for Reye's syndrome, the treatment being particularly aimed at lowering the raised pressure within the skull, so reducing the risk of irreversible damage to the

brain. This usually involves treatment with intravenous drugs.

If breathing is affected, support with a mechanical ventilator may be necessary until the condition improves. Intravenous medication may also be required to control convulsions and this treatment may be continued in oral form for at least another six months. Throughout the illness, careful monitoring will be required.

Long-term follow-up will also be necessary, to monitor the child's progress and to assess the need for any continued support, such as physiotherapy and special help with education.

Spina bifida

Spina bifida is a failure of the bones of the vertebral column to develop normally and enclose the spinal cord. There are two degrees of spina bifida: occulta, the mild form; and aperta, the severe form.

Spina bifida is a congenital disorder in which there is incomplete closure of the spinal column at one or more levels. In the mildest form, the abnormality is only detectable radiographically (on X-ray). In the most severe form, the baby is born with abnormal nerve tissue visible on the surface of the back with varying degrees of lower limb paralysis and interference with bowel and bladder control.

Traditionally, spina bifida is divided into the mild form, called occulta, and the severe form, called aperta.

Spina bifida is a congenital defect where the spinal cord fails to develop properly. In severe cases, such as with this child, nerve tissue is visible.

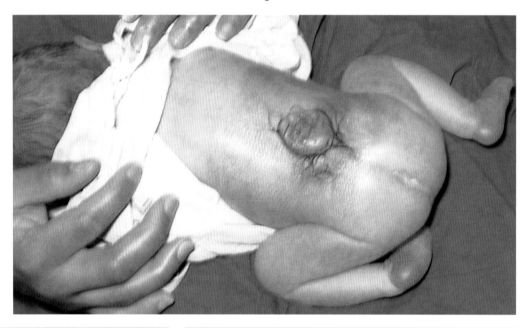

Advances in treatment

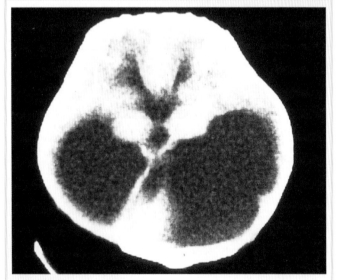

Treatment of spina bifida has advanced in the past two decades since the advent of improved methods of imaging the brain and spinal cord. In the 1970s, CT scanning revolutionized the ability to visualize physical abnormalities within the skull.

Over the past 10 years, magnetic resonance (MR) imaging has also evolved to reveal the subtle features of the anatomy of the brain and the spinal cord. Surgical techniques have also improved due to

This CT scan of the head shows a child suffering from hydrocephalus. Fluid collects in the ventricles of the brain (black), causing the skull to become distorted.

advances in pre-operative imaging and the introduction of the operating microscope, which have led to safer surgical procedures. More precise instruments and bipolar diathermy forceps (forceps with tips that cauterize tissue) have also changed surgical practice.

Types of spina bifida

SPINA BIFIDA OCCULTA

In spina bifida occulta, a split in the vertebral column (spinal column) may be seen on X-ray without any other evidence of neurological abnormalities.

A skin or subcutaneous (under the skin) abnormality may occur in conjunction with a bony defect of the vertebral column. The presence of these external signs may be a clue to underlying involvement of the spinal cord. The baby is usually, but not always, born without damage to the spinal cord; however, defects may develop at any age, although most often before four years of age.

SPINA BIFIDA APERTA

In babies with spina bifida aperta (also known as meningomyelocele), not only is there a defect in the vertebral column but normal spinal tissue is visible on the surface of the back. This form of spina bifida is usually associated with mild to severe neurological deficiencies, and is frequently associated with hydrocephalus ('water on the brain').

Antenatal care includes ultrasound scanning. Fetuses with spinal defects such as spina bifida may be detected on these routine ultrasound scans.

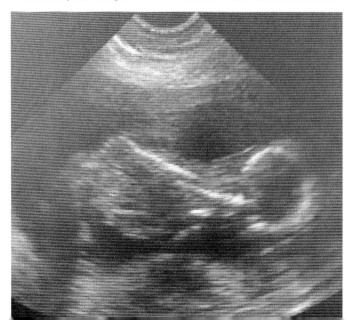

Spina bifida occulta

Spina bifida occulta is the mild form of the disorder where the physical defect is not normally visible. However, certain clinical signs, such as a patch of hair on the back, may suggest a deformity below the skin. Treatment is by surgical correction of the disorder.

Signs and symptoms

In spina bifida occulta, the pathology that involves the spinal cord is not visible on external examination. The clinical abnormality that is visible involves the skin and tissue under the skin.

SIGNS OF SPINA BIFIDA

The skin may be raised by an underlying lump which extends from the skin down through the bony defect and attaches to the spinal cord. This is where the spinal cord becomes fixed (tethered). The cord is therefore not free to move up and down during bending, and injury to the spinal cord results. The skin overlying the lump almost always contains soft, pinkish tissue. In the absence of a swelling, there may be a hairy patch or a dimple.

These abnormalities are warning signs of an underlying tethered spinal cord; however, there is one exception. If the dimple is very low and overlies the tip of the coccyx (the lower-most part of the vertebral column), the cord is not tethered.

The clinical picture in tethered cord syndrome is muscle weakness and wasting of the lower limbs, bowel and bladder incontinence, pain, loss of sensation of the lower limbs and deformity of the feet. Frequently, these symptoms are not present at birth but develop in the first few years. Symptoms may only develop in adulthood. Except in very young children, X-rays will show bony abnormalities and defects of the vertebral column.

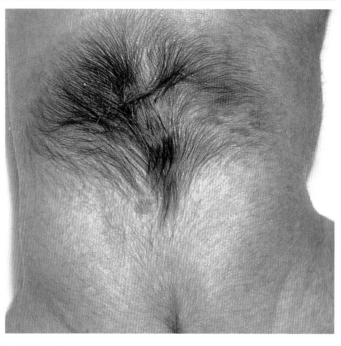

A hairy patch on the back is highly suggestive of the underlying disorder spina bifida occulta. Other signs may not develop for months or years.

Treatment

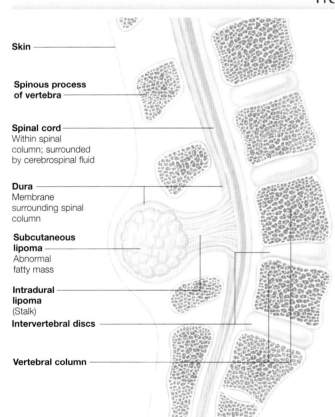

Skin

Spinous process of vertebra

Spinal cord
Within spinal column; surrounded by cerebrospinal fluid

Dura
Membrane surrounding spinal column

Subcutaneous lipoma
Abnormal fatty mass

Intradural lipoma
(Stalk)

Intervertebral discs

Vertebral column

The spinal cord is tethered to the abnormal mass of tissue under the skin. The cord is therefore unable to move with the spine, resulting in injury.

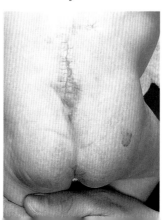

A recent post-operative scar is evident on this infant's lower back. It is a priority that the operation does not cause any further complications.

The goal of treatment of spina bifida occulta is to prevent neurological deficiencies and is therefore prophylactic (preventative). Once damage has developed, the chances of reversing the problem are very small unless surgery is undertaken as soon as possible after the onset of symptoms.

MR or CT scans are used to guide the surgical approach. The goal of surgery is to untether the lower end of the spinal cord in order to eliminate the chances of future injury and to correct the cosmetic abnormality. A consideration of surgery is that the procedure must not create new, or aggravate existing, neurological abnormalities.

CORRECTIVE SURGERY

In corrective surgery, an incision is made, and the underlying abnormal fatty mass

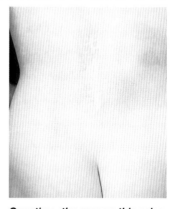

Over time, the scar on this spina bifida patient's back has faded. The cosmetic appearance of the final scar is a consideration during surgery.

(subcutaneous lipoma) is cut away from the normal tissue. The stalk beneath is identified and followed down to the dura – the membrane covering the spinal cord. The entire lipoma (subcutaneous and intradural) is then dissected free from the cord so that it can be removed. The cord is now untethered, enabling it to move freely with the movement of the spine.

The goal of surgical treatment of spina bifida occulta is to prevent new deficiencies with minimal complications.

Autism

Autism is a behavioural syndrome caused by an abnormality in developmental processes early in life. It is not a common condition, occurring in just 3–4 children in every 10,000.

The onset of autism is within the first 30 months of life, although abnormalities are generally apparent from birth. Autism is observable in very young children but it may not be diagnosed until age four or five. Autism is a serious condition, although there is a variation in the severity of the symptoms.

All children with autism will show the following difficulties to varying degrees:
- Language
- Getting on with others
- Behaviour patterns.

COMMUNICATION

In all children with autism there is a delay in the acquisition of language, and language difficulties manifest themselves early in life. Fifty per cent of autistic children never develop useful expressive language.

An autistic baby is unlikely to make attempts to communicate, such as through babbling. Some speech may develop but it is likely to be preservative – the child will go off on rambled tangents – or it might be echolalic, repeating what another person says without understanding the meaning.

Due to language difficulties, autistic children may come across as rude and insensitive. They are likely to confuse personal pronouns, for example talking about the self in the third person, and may have problems with taking turns in conversation. Finally, children with autism will have difficulties in terms of their play, which lacks creativity and imagination.

Autistic children tend to play alone and have a limited range of interests. They may find it difficult to interact with others.

Many children with autism will display repetitive or obsessive behaviours. Much of their behaviour is routine-led.

Social development and behaviour patterns

Autistic children have significant problems in terms of getting on with others. For example:
- They are averse to affection, particularly of a physical kind
- They will not naturally show an understanding of how another person feels or thinks
- Even if hurt, they tend not to seek comfort
- They will avoid looking another person in the eye.

As a result of these difficulties, autistic children will not show any interest in having relationships with others and will be very solitary.

BEHAVIOUR PATTERNS

Autistic children tend to organize themselves and the world around them very tightly and will become extremely distressed if their

One of the features of autism is an avoidance of eye contact. This can make communicating with an autistic child difficult.

routine is broken. This is because they are unable to extract meaning from their experiences and therefore fail to anticipate what will happen next; routines are therefore a means of avoiding surprises which might be distressing to them.

Autistic children may also have a restricted range of interests and often have attachments to unusual objects rather than people or other living things. Autistic children tend to play in repetitive ways, and their play will lack a story. They may have repetitive mannerisms, such as twirling around or circling their hands.

ABNORMAL RESPONSES

As well as these features, some children also have unusual responses to smells, sights and sounds. Some individuals might not respond to pain or might gain pleasure from inflicting pain on themselves.

Managing autism

Autism is a life-long condition, and once it is diagnosed the child
will need to be educated in a suitable setting with the help of a multidisciplinary team.
Behavioural therapy may be needed to manage difficult or obsessive behaviours.

Autism is three to four times more common in boys than in girls. The sex difference is most marked in those individuals who have a higher IQ; in children with a low IQ the numbers of boys and girls are more equal.

Fifty per cent of the autistic population have an IQ in the moderate to profoundly learning disabled range. Only 10-20 per cent have an IQ in the normal range. Autism is not linked to socio-economic status.

SPECIAL ABILITY

Overall, autism is much more common in children who have learning disabilities. However, in a minority of autistic individuals there may be areas of special ability, such as an exceptional rote memory.

Autism is also linked with seizures, which are present in 10-30 per cent of individuals.

Autistic children are socially withdrawn and have difficulties with language. They often have learning disabilities as well.

Coping with autism

Once the diagnosis of autism is made, it is essential that professionals are involved in helping families to understand and cope better with the autistic family member.

It is essential that children with autism are educated in a setting which is right for them. This is often at a special school with a structured curriculum and an emphasis on promoting language and communication skills.

THERAPY APPROACHES

Behavioural interventions are often used to help promote adaptive behaviours and to reduce behaviour which might get in the way of the child's learning, such as self-injurious or obsessional behaviour.

Medication is used in some instances, but only to a limited degree: fenfluramine is used to control repetitive mannerisms; haloperidol or pimozide are used for excitability.

A technique known as the Higashi approach, also called daily life therapy, uses movement, music and art to enable children with autism to learn through imitation in a structured environment.

Speech and language therapy play an important role in treatment. For individuals who do not use speech, communication can be taught using other strategies, and the co-operative aspects of communication might thus be facilitated.

Many children with autism have other learning difficulties associated with a low IQ which may complicate their schooling.

The Higashi approach to teaching children with autism uses music and art in its teaching practices.

Causes of autism

Owing to the fact that autism is heavily associated with learning difficulties and epilepsy, it is thought that the cause is biological.

However, at present no-one has been able to pinpoint for certain what has gone wrong in the brains of children with autism. It is suggested that it might be to do with higher levels of blood and platelet-bound serotonin, but the mechanisms are yet to be fully understood.

Although in any one case it may be difficult to ascertain a cause, there is evidence to suggest that autism is linked with a number of perinatal injuries, congenital rubella, phenylketonuria and infantile spasms.

'Theory of mind'

At the level of thinking, it is believed that autistic individuals have difficulties in terms of what has been called 'theory of mind'. What this means is that these individuals are unable to anticipate or think about what another person is thinking or feeling.

Attention deficit hyperactivity disorder

Children with attention deficit hyperactivity disorder (ADHD) have a limited attention span, which makes it difficult for them to complete tasks. They are also distractable, impulsive and overactive.

Attention deficit hyperactivity disorder (ADHD) refers to a pattern of difficulties with some aspects of thinking – including paying attention, concentration and organization – and behavioural difficulties, such as being overactive and impulsive.

These behaviours are all very common among normal children, and therefore the diagnosis of ADHD is only given when the difficulties are so severe that they have disrupted the child's life in more than one area, such as recreational activity, school work, getting on with his or her peers and with life at home.

DIAGNOSIS

ADHD is usually identified in early childhood and is generally diagnosed by a mental health professional such as a psychiatrist, although paediatricians, particularly those working in the community, may also diagnose the condition.

More boys are diagnosed with ADHD than girls, although the reasons for this are not clear. It has also been suggested that ADHD is more common in socially deprived areas.

About 33 per cent of children who are diagnosed with ADHD have reading problems. They are also likely to have difficulties in mixing with other children, often because they are aggressive.

PREVALENCE

It is difficult to say exactly how common ADHD actually is. This is because over time people are becoming more aware of it, and therefore the condition is now being recognized more readily. Estimates of the prevalence of ADHD among children range from about 0.5 to 1.5 per cent.

Children with ADHD may have difficulty carrying out everyday tasks such as washing, despite being intellectually and physically capable of doing so.

ADHD is only diagnosed when a child demonstrates severe difficulty in thinking or behaviour. This may affect peer relationships and school work.

What causes ADHD?

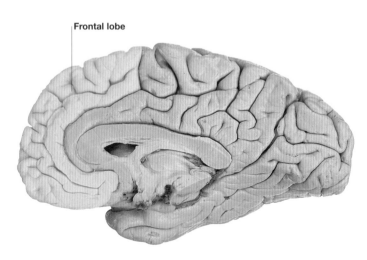

Frontal lobe

One theory for ADHD suggests that it may arise as a result of very subtle damage to the frontal lobes of the brain.

There is much debate as to what causes ADHD, though it is almost certain that it results from a combination of both environmental and genetic factors. However, any parent will recognize that some children are more difficult to parent than others. Children who have a diagnosis of ADHD are generally described as being difficult to soothe as babies.

ADHD may arise from a number of complications during the antenatal and post-natal periods. As a result, children with a diagnosis of ADHD have difficulties in regulating and organizing their behaviour. These are high-level skills which are controlled by the frontal areas of the brain, and it is thought that in ADHD these areas are not working properly. However, any damage is believed to be so subtle that it is unlikely to be picked up on brain scans.

It is likely that the development of these high-level skills is also influenced by factors in the child's environment. A child's ability to learn is influenced by stresses in the home, such as those caused by illnesses and the wider circumstances in which the child lives.

Treating ADHD

ADHD is commonly treated with medication to improve the child's attention span and alertness. Children with ADHD may also be taught techniques which enable them to change their behaviour and to identify and avoid problematic situations.

The most common form of treatment for a child with a diagnosis of ADHD is drug therapy. The medication that is most commonly used is methylphenidate (Ritalin). Less commonly used are dextroamphetamine (Dexedrine) or Pemoline (Volital). These drugs work by stimulating the parts of the brain which regulate arousal and alertness.

Ritalin may be used as part of a treatment programme for ADHD. It is only used under strict supervision, and is not suitable for children under six.

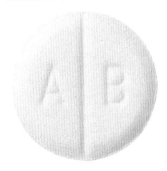

The drug selected is usually taken in several doses throughout the day. It starts working about 30–60 minutes after being taken and lasts for about three to five hours. The effects of the medication wear off very quickly.

SUCCESS RATE
Estimates suggest that medication works to some extent in about 90 per cent of cases of ADHD. Children undergoing such drug therapy often report that it gives them more 'thinking time'. As a result, they find that they are more likely to be able to work at school and to think before acting. In the long term, however, it is difficult to know how helpful medication is in terms of social and academic adjustment.

Children with ADHD may act aggressively in certain situations. Medication can help an affected child modify its unacceptable behaviour.

Other treatment approaches

It is known that children with a diagnosis of ADHD have difficulties getting on with other children of their age and with family members. It is generally helpful, therefore, to use other forms of intervention alongside medication.

There are a number of approaches which are beginning to emerge. These approaches include techniques that mental health professionals may use with children themselves, parent training techniques and techniques to be employed by educators.

CHANGING BEHAVIOUR
A 'cognitive behavioural' approach to modifying a child's behaviour is employed by the child psychologist. The idea is that the therapist helps the child to identify situations where a certain behaviour, such as aggression, is unhelpful for the child. These techniques would generally be used with older children.

With pre-school children, the therapist aims to help the parents. The techniques employed usually take the form of some sort of parent training. In particular, parents are helped to focus on and reward the child's positive behaviour rather than reprimanding negative behaviours, which tends to reinforce them, exacerbating the problem. This is also the approach favoured in the classroom.

LONG-TERM OUTLOOK
The symptoms that are part of ADHD are more common in all pre-school children and decrease over the course of development. However, the symptom patterns consistent with the diagnosis of ADHD tend to persist into

One approach to managing ADHD is to help the child work out what triggers problem behaviour. This may motivate the child to change its conduct.

Parents will be encouraged to focus on their child's positive behaviour and to offer rewards when it acts appropriately.

adolescence and beyond.

A child is more likely to continue to have difficulties into adulthood if it also has verbal deficits combined with learning and behavioural problems and poor family management practices. Children who have problems with aggression are the most likely to do poorly, both academically and socially.

Cerebral palsy

Cerebral palsy is a disorder of movement and posture associated with damage to the brain. It is not a progressive condition, although symptoms become more pronounced as children develop.

Cerebral palsy is a general term used to describe the symptoms that arise from a malformation or injury to the part of the brain concerned with body movement and posture.

The damage may develop during pregnancy, soon after birth or in early childhood. Some forms of cerebral palsy are apparent shortly after a child is born; others may not be noted until the child begins to walk.

SYMPTOMS AND SIGNS

The condition is not uncommon, and occurs in varying degrees of severity in around 1 in every 500 live births.

The symptoms vary, but general signs may include:
■ Abnormal muscle tone and posture in infancy
■ Delay in achieving developmental milestones, such as walking and speaking
■ Hearing loss
■ Lack of co-ordination
■ Abnormal gait
■ Feeding difficulties, such as difficulty swallowing.

Although children with cerebral palsy may have severely impaired movement, many lead fulfilling lives. Intellectual ability is not always affected.

What causes cerebral palsy?

Cerebral palsy is usually detected in the first few months of life. Babies with the condition are often 'floppy' because of reduced muscle tone.

Around 80 per cent of babies with cerebral palsy sustain damage to the developing brain during the first three months of pregnancy.

INFECTION

Cerebral palsy can develop from damage caused by an infection that passes from the mother to the unborn child. The most common of these infections, and the most well known, is rubella (German measles). For pregnant mothers, rubella is often mild, and can even go undiagnosed. For the developing fetus, however, the infection can be devastating as the virus interferes with the development of vital organs, particularly the nervous system and brain.

CHILDBIRTH

It is thought that only about 1 in 10 children with cerebral palsy develop brain damage during a difficult labour or delivery. In these babies, cerebral palsy is caused by birth trauma or oxygen starvation.

CHILDHOOD

During early childhood, cerebral palsy can occur as a result of meningitis, a serious infection of the protective membranes that surround the brain, or a head injury caused by trauma or, rarely, non-accidental injury.

Other causes include low blood sugar (hypoglycaemia), and high levels of bilirubin, a metabolic by-product of haemoglobin, which is normally found in the blood in small amounts.

Types of cerebral palsy

There are several types of cerebral palsy, which are characterized by varying abnormal limb function. Although many affected children have normal intellectual ability, some forms of the disorder cause varying degrees of mental impairment.

Cerebral palsy affects children in many different ways, so symptoms and signs vary immensely between individuals. It is, however, possible to describe three main types of cerebral palsy:
■ Spastic cerebral palsy – accounts for about 70 per cent of cases
■ Ataxic cerebral palsy – about 1 in 10 affected children have this form
■ Athetoid or dyskinetic cerebral palsy – affects 10 per cent of children with cerebral palsy.

Some children with cerebral palsy have difficulty with movement. Using a wheelchair helps them remain mobile and maintain their independence.

SPASTIC CEREBRAL PALSY

Babies born with spastic cerebral palsy may have hypotonia (reduced muscle tone) and appear floppy. Eventually, the limb muscles stiffen and often contract, rendering movement difficult. The main muscles affected are those that bend the joints, with the result that limbs are unable to straighten.

There are three sub-types of spastic cerebral palsy:

■ Hemiparesis – only one side of the body is affected, usually the arm more than the leg or vice versa. Delivery is usually uncomplicated and babies often appear unaffected at birth. However, from about four months onwards, parents may notice that one arm is held in an unusual position. The affected hand is held in a fist-like position and the arm is bent at the elbow and rotated abnormally. An affected child may use one hand much more than the other.

■ Diplegia – in children with diplegia, all four limbs are affected but the legs more so than the arms. These children may be unable to walk, or walk with difficulty using walking aids. Although at first glance they may appear to have normal arm movements, on closer examination hand function is limited.

■ Quadriparesis – about one child in 10 with spastic cerebral palsy has quadriparesis. It is usually diagnosed after a complicated birth and the child is likely to have suffered from birth trauma or birth asphyxia.

Affected babies have an unusual facial appearance, poor head control and reduced muscle tone. All four limbs are in

Regular exercise is vital to avoid stiff limb muscles becoming contracted further. Exercise can take many forms and is usually tailored to the individual.

spasm, with the arms abnormally bent and the hands held in a fist-like position. The legs are crossed due to spasm of the adductor muscles.

Rare forms of cerebral palsy

Often, people with cerebral palsy remain active and healthy. The provision of suitable care enables people to become more independent.

There are two other rare forms of cerebral palsy; these are known as ataxic cerebral palsy and athetoid or dyskinetic cerebral palsy. Each of these accounts for about 10 per cent of all cases of cerebral palsy.

ATAXIC HYPOTONIC

Children with this rare type of cerebral palsy at first have hypotonia and later ataxia, a general unsteadiness when walking or standing. This is due to a structural abnormality in a part of the brain called the cerebellum, which controls posture and balance.

ATHETOID/DYSKINETIC

This is a mild manifestation of cerebral palsy that is due to a structural problem affecting a part of the midbrain known as the basal ganglia. In health, the basal ganglia play a vital part in controlling body movement.

Children with this type of cerebral palsy have fluctuating muscle tone and experience involuntary body movements such as facial grimacing, jerking or uncontrolled, slow writhing movements. These movements increase with stress and decrease or disappear during sleep.

In addition, speech may be slurred due to poor tongue control and there are often hearing difficulties. There is no intellectual impairment and usually children are able to lead otherwise normal lives.

Difficulties associated with cerebral palsy

In addition to disorders of posture and movement, children with cerebral palsy often have learning difficulties. Although many benefit from mainstream schooling, special schools are available.

Many children with severe cerebral palsy have normal to above-average intelligence. However, learning difficulties are present in about 60 per cent of affected children.

LEARNING DIFFICULTIES
In particular, children with quadriparetic cerebral palsy often have moderate to severe learning difficulty. This reflects the degree of damage to an individual's brain.

In early childhood, the extent of individual learning difficulties may not be immediately apparent. It is only when a child begins to talk that significant delays in development of speech or communication become obvious to parents and medical professionals.

OTHER PROBLEMS
There are several other disorders that are associated with cerebral palsy, including:
- Constipation
- Epilepsy – found in 40 per cent of cases
- Squints, visual impairment and hearing loss – these are all common, each occurring in about 20 per cent of cases
- Problems with language development and speech – again the degree of impairment of these skills varies with the degree of overall disability
- Behavioural disorders – these are common. This is not surprising since children with cerebral palsy are likely to suffer from frustration and, possibly, depression, because of their day-to-day difficulties.

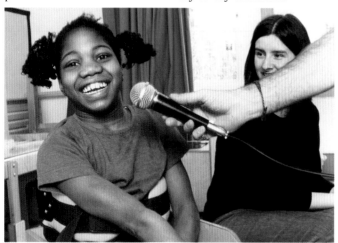

Many children with cerebral palsy have difficulties with language and speech. Music therapy can help to inspire confidence and improve communication skills.

Children with cerebral palsy often have learning difficulties. Education and play therapy are therefore a vital part of care for an affected child.

Education and intelligence

Education is a very important part of overall care for children with cerebral palsy. Some affected children are educated in a mainstream school and integrate well with other students.

SPECIAL SCHOOLING
Those children with cerebral palsy who have more severe learning difficulties and physical disability usually need special schooling in order to maximize their educational potential.

In these schools, affected children are cared for by a multidisciplinary team consisting of teachers, physiotherapists, educational psychologists and occupational therapists.

Using individualized teaching programmes, each child is encouraged to reach his or her maximum potential.

Children with severe learning difficulties may need teaching on a one-to-one basis. However, many children with cerebral palsy are able to integrate into mainstream education.

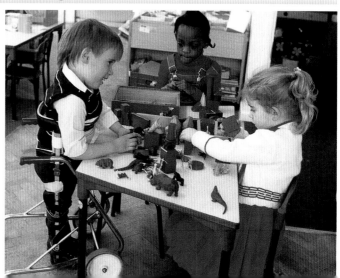

Caring for children with cerebral palsy

Although cerebral palsy cannot be cured, drug therapy, surgery or physiotherapy
help to alleviate symptoms. The child's physical and psychological needs are assessed
by a team of medical experts, who provide support for patients and their carers.

Cerebral palsy is diagnosed on the basis of a child's symptoms – often a failure to develop normally and reach milestones. In general , the earlier cerebral palsy is diagnosed, the better the outcome of treatment.

As there is no cure for cerebral palsy, this treatment revolves around keeping a child's muscles supple and helping him or her reach maximum potential, both physically and psychologically.

MEDICAL SUPPORT

A wide range of input and support is usually available from a multidisciplinary team including paediatricians, GPs, nurses, psychologists, social workers, physiotherapists, speech therapists and occupational therapists.

To some extent, the amount of help needed depends upon the degree of disability, the social circumstances, and how the children themselves and the carers are able to cope.

Each child is assessed and individual capabilities and difficulties are taken into account. Care is then planned according to each individual's needs.

DRUG THERAPY

Drug treatment can be of help in some cases. Anti-epileptic drug therapy may be needed, for example to control fits associated with epilepsy.

Muscle relaxants can also be of help in reducing muscle spasm. Diazepam and baclofen are commonly used muscle relaxants.

SURGERY

Surgery can sometimes be used to deal with muscular contractures. These are permanently contracted stiff muscles, which develop after prolonged periods of paralysis or significant muscular weakness. These contractures can make walking a very difficult task; surgical correction of contractures may therefore help to improve walking.

Despite restricted movement, many children are able to lead an active life. Therapists and parents will work together to encourage regular exercise.

The earlier treatment starts in childhood, the more successful the outcome is likely to be. Younger children with cerebral palsy are encouraged to learn through play.

The role of physiotherapy

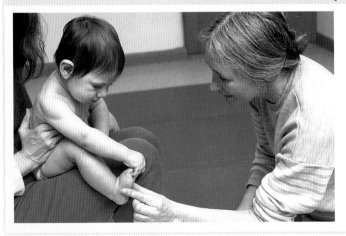

Physiotherapy plays an important role in managing cerebral palsy. It aims to improve muscle tone and teach correct movements.

Physiotherapy for cerebral palsy is vital in preventing severe joint deformities and contractures. There are three main techniques used by physiotherapists:
■ Bobath technique – inhibits the existing 'inborn' reflexes and increased muscle tone and teaches correct patterns of movement. The baby is placed in particular positions and specific exercises are used
■ Proprioceptive technique – through guiding certain activities with a child, the physiotherapist inhibits spasticity in some muscle groups and enables contraction of others. The proprioceptive senses, stretch, pressure, touch, and visual and auditory stimulation are used
■ Peto technique – a single movement is broken down into its smallest components. These individual components are practised over and over again, and then combined to produce the single action.

Down's syndrome

Down's syndrome is the most frequent genetic abnormality and the commonest genetic cause of mental retardation. One in 700 babies has the condition, which can have serious health implications.

Down's syndrome (named after J. L. H. Down, a 19th-century British physician) was initially called mongolism because of the similar facial appearance – a broad face and slanted eyelids – to certain Asian people.

The genetic basis of the Down's phenotype (the observable characteristics determined by the genes) was not discovered until 1959, when researchers linked the syndrome to the presence of an additional chromosome 21, giving the syndrome its alternative name of trisomy 21.

The normal chromosome complement is 46 – 2 sex chromosomes and 22 pairs of non-sex chromosomes (autosomes). A person with Down's syndrome has 47 chromosomes in all – 2 sex chromosomes, 21 pairs of non-sex autosomes and three copies of chromosome 21.

IMPLICATIONS

Approximately 75 per cent of Down's syndrome fetuses are aborted spontaneously or are stillborn. Of those that survive birth, many die in the first year because of heart defects. Other than the characteristic mental retardation, people with Down's syndrome have increased susceptibility to infections. This is due to immune system problems, although medical advances have improved life expectancy to over 30 years; 25 per cent of affected people live to the age of 50.

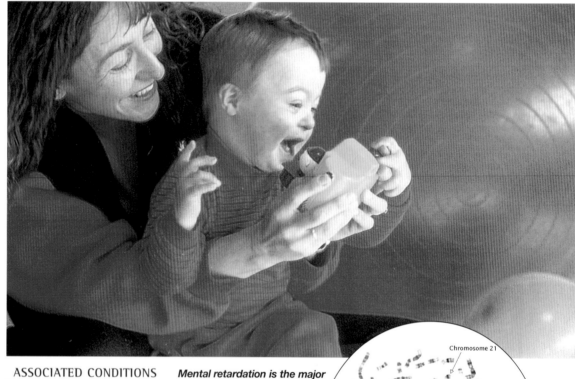

ASSOCIATED CONDITIONS

Leukaemia is more common in children with Down's syndrome than in the general population. In addition, a particular type of disorder – transient abnormal myelopoiesis – is seen in some young babies. This transient leukaemia usually resolves within weeks with little or no treatment, and does not recur in most cases. Heart defects affect about 40 per cent of children with Down's syndrome.

Mental retardation is the major feature associated with Down's syndrome, but the degree of this is extremely variable. However, children with the condition can be very cheerful, affectionate and lively.

Three copies (instead of two) of chromosome 21 are evident in this cell from an amniocentesis sample. Down's syndrome results from this genetic abnormality.

Chromosome 21

Chromosome 21

Chromosome 21

Trisomy 21

Clinical features of Down's syndrome

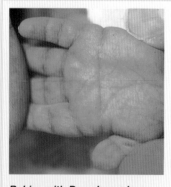

Babies with Down's syndrome may have hands that are broad and short-fingered, with a single crease across the palm.

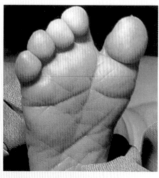

There is often a large gap between the big toe and the second toe. This is sometimes known as the 'sandal gap'.

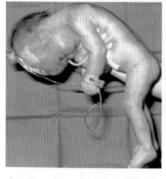

Another sign of the condition in newborns is hypotonia, a lack of muscle tone. This is also known as 'floppy baby'.

The clinical features of Down's syndrome vary from slight abnormalities to severe medical problems. These include a large, protruding tongue, a gap between the big and second toe, neonatal hypotonia, heart defects and malformations of the gastro-intestinal tract, kidneys and thyroid gland.

Males with the syndrome often have underdeveloped genitalia and are usually sterile; females may have irregular periods and ovarian problems. Most Down's syndrome children have moderate to severe mental handicap, with an average IQ of 69 (95–120 is the norm).

Genetic causes

Down's syndrome is caused by an extra (third) copy of chromosome 21. The extra copy can only be acquired at certain points in the cycle of cell division.

The failure of chromosomes to separate properly during meiotic cell division is termed meiotic non-disjunction. This can occur during the formation of germ cells (the precursors for sperm and ova) in either parent, and can lead to an unequal number of chromosomes in the daughter cells.

A small fraction (one per cent) of Down's syndrome cases are due to non-disjunction of mitotic (non-sex) cells, which results in a mosaic karyotype.

This means that while some cells have a normal set of 46 chromosomes, a proportion of cells have 47 chromosomes. The phenotype is variable, depending on the proportion of normal cells and the tissues affected.

TRANSLOCATION
Four per cent of Down's syndrome cases are due to unbalanced rearrangements of chromosome 21, where genetic material is exchanged between chromosomes. These are known

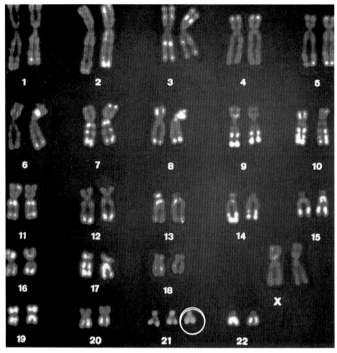

This karyotype (diagram of a chromosome set) shows the extra copy of chromosome 21 found in Down's syndrome. This abnormality can be detected by prenatal diagnosis.

as Robertsonian, or reciprocal, translocations. The 14;21 Robertsonian translocation is the most common rearrangement.

MATERNAL AGE
A woman's risk of having a child with Down's syndrome increases with her age. This is thought to be because a woman

is born with all her eggs in place in the ovaries. As the woman ages, the eggs are likely to accumulate more errors, such as non-disjunction. The risk is negligible until a woman reaches her late 30s, when there is a much greater chance of having a baby with Down's syndrome.

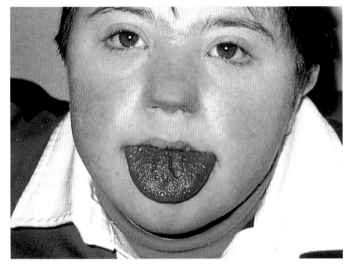

As a result of the genetic causes of Down's syndrome, children often have heart disorders. This child's tongue is cyanosed (blue) due to a lack of blood oxygen.

Screening and prenatal diagnosis

Amniocentesis is the ultimate diagnostic test for Down's syndrome. It is usually performed in the second trimester of pregnancy.

Women who have a high risk of having a Down's syndrome pregnancy are offered prenatal diagnosis.

ASSESSING RISK
The levels of certain chemicals in a woman's blood, combined with her age, are used to calculate a risk figure. This detects 65 per cent of Down's pregnancies.

An anomaly ultrasound scan at 13–26 weeks identifies many Down's syndrome pregnancies; however, only 50 per cent are detected this way. Another method involves an ultrasound scan in the first three months of pregnancy to measure the thickness of an area at the back of the baby's neck – the nuchal translucency. From this measurement a risk figure is given.

This ultrasound scan shows the face of a fetus with Down's syndrome in profile. The face is seen looking up with the typical short nose visible (circled).

PRENATAL DIAGNOSIS
The most frequently used test is amniocentesis. This involves taking a sample of the amniotic fluid that surrounds a fetus, in order to examine chromosomes of fetal cells shed into it and identify any abnormalities.

Women who have had a previous child affected by Down's syndrome due to non-disjunction have a risk of one per cent of having another affected child, and so they are offered prenatal diagnosis in any future pregnancies.

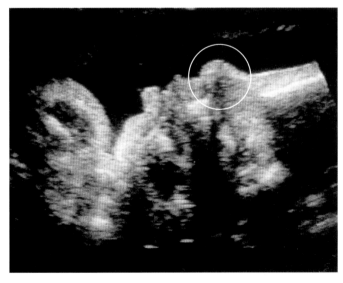

233

Accidental poisoning

Most cases of accidental poisoning occur in children under five years of age. Medicines, household chemicals, alcohol and poisonous plants can all cause serious illness and, occasionally, fatalities.

Accident and Emergency departments in the UK deal with more than 10,000 cases of accidental poisoning each year, and around 80 per cent of these involve children under five years of age. Fortunately, the vast majority of cases in this young age group are not fatal, although some children may be very seriously ill for a while.

PRE-SCHOOL CHILDREN
Children, especially those between the ages of two and four, are very curious and will put all kinds of objects into their mouths without being able to understand the risks involved. This inquisitiveness leads them to swallow medicines, household chemicals and even poisonous plants, especially if they mistake them for something interesting to eat or drink.

Medicines, usually those of an adult family member, account for over half of the cases of poisoning in young children. The increased use of childproof containers for medicines and household chemicals has done much to reduce the number of cases, however.

OLDER CHILDREN
As children become older, they are less likely to suffer accidental poisoning, with a steady decline being seen in the accident rate as children approach 10 years of age. However, between the ages of 10 and 14, there is an increase in the rates of poisoning due to alcohol ingestion. Many of these cases are serious.

Medicines are a common cause of accidental poisoning. Young children are naturally curious, and any pills lying around risk being played with or eaten.

Types of accidental poisoning

A range of substances can cause accidental poisoning in children. These include:
■ Medicines – including aspirin, paracetamol, antidepressants, drugs for heart disease (such as digoxin), tranquillizers, iron and antihistamines
■ Caustic liquids such as drain cleaners, bleach and dishwasher detergents
■ Petroleum distillates (petrol, paraffin), insecticides and weedkillers
■ Lead – usually ingested in small amounts over a long period (for example, from lead-containing paint)
■ Plants – common poisonous garden plants include laburnum, deadly nightshade and holly berries.

First aid

If poisoning is suspected, medical advice should always be sought. If the child is unwell, he or she should be taken to hospital immediately.

In many cases of suspected poisoning, the child will be found to have ingested a relatively harmless substance, or may not have actually swallowed any at all, having disliked the taste.

GUIDELINES
As there may be serious consequences from ingestion of some substances, however, medical advice should always be sought. Points to remember are:
■ If a child is unwell, he or she should be taken to hospital, or an ambulance called
■ If a child seems well, a doctor or the local Accident and Emergency department should be contacted for advice. Medical staff can contact a 24-hour poison information unit, which

Once at hospital, the child will be carefully examined. Medical staff themselves can contact a 24-hour poison information unit for specific advice on toxins.

will be able to tell them whether the substance could be harmful
■ To aid identification of the poison, a sample of the substance, medicine or plant should be given to the doctor.

This is important as treatment varies according to the poison
■ Vomiting should not be induced in children as it may be dangerous, especially if a caustic substance has been swallowed.

234

Caustic substances

Caustic liquids, such as drain cleaners, bleach and disinfectants, can be very
toxic if swallowed as they burn body tissues. Affected children should be admitted to
hospital, where they will be treated with antibiotics and steroids.

Caustic substances burn tissue with which they come into contact, and can cause a great deal of damage if they are swallowed. Young children are most likely to come across common household caustics, the most toxic of which are drain cleaners, which are the liquid form of sodium or potassium hydroxide.

Other caustic agents that might be swallowed include bleach (sodium hypochlorite), dishwasher detergents and disinfectants. These substances tend to be kept in the kitchen,

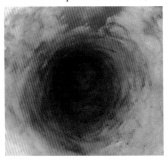

Caustic solutions can damage to the mucous membranes of the digestive tract. Oesophagitis (inflammation of the oesophagus) is shown here.

If swallowed, caustic liquids can be extremely toxic. If poisoning with caustics is suspected, early medical attention is vital.

which must be considered a danger area for young children.

SYMPTOMS
The symptoms of ingestion of caustic substances vary according to how strong the substance is, and how much has been swallowed. Burns around the mouth will alert the parents and doctor to the fact that a substance has possibly been ingested, but cannot reveal the extent of the damage.

The mouth and oesophagus, or gullet, are most likely to be damaged if a child swallows a caustic substance, but the affected area can stretch further down the gastrointestinal tract if large amounts are ingested.

If strongly caustic, the substance can perforate the wall of the oesophagus and reach the surrounding tissues.

HOSPITAL ADMISSION
When a child has ingested a caustic substance, hospital

admission is usually necessary. It is vital that no attempts are made to induce vomiting in the affected child as this would result in further exposure to the regurgitated caustic. Milk and water will dilute the agent.

TREATMENT
Depending on the severity of the damage, antibiotics and corticosteroid drugs may be prescribed. An endoscopy may be performed to assess the extent of the damage.

Prevention

The most effective way to prevent accidental poisoning in children is to keep potential poisons out of their reach, and preferably where they cannot be seen.

Household chemicals should never be left unattended when in use as children can harm themselves very quickly.

All medicines should be kept inside a locked cabinet, and children should never be allowed to play with empty medicine containers. Medicines are often kept in handbags, especially those belonging to older people who may have a number of prescription medicines.

Children should be warned of the dangers of harmful plants. They should be told never to eat berries or plants without first checking with an adult.

Restricted pack sizes
In the UK, the Medicine Control Agency leads the way in trying to prevent accidental poisoning with over-the-counter and prescription medicines. Legislation has been introduced to restrict the pack sizes of paracetamol and aspirin so that these drugs will not accumulate in large quantities in the home.

In addition, all pharmacists supply medicines in childproof containers unless specifically asked not to. All medical labelling in the UK is required to include the warning statement, 'Keep out of the reach of children'.

Harmful plants
Keeping children safe from poisonous plants can be more difficult. Gardens and play areas should ideally be cleared of

harmful plants. Older children can be taught which plants are harmful and advised not to eat any leaves or berries they find without first asking an adult. Some garden centres label plants with a specific warning if they are potentially toxic.

Precautions should be taken to ensure that harmful substances are kept out of the reach of children. All medicines should be locked away.

Alcohol and drug poisoning

Children, both young and old, can be poisoned by alcohol,
but most make a full recovery. A dose of a drug, however, can have
serious consequences, especially if taken in large amounts.

Acute alcohol poisoning occurs mainly in two groups of children: the under-fives who accidentally come across alcohol in the home, and the 10–14 year olds who drink to excess, usually outside the home.

Drinking alcohol holds hazards for both groups; young children because of their small, immature bodies and older children because of potential accidents while drunk. Older children are less likely than young ones to poison themselves accidentally, but they usually do not realize that alcohol is extremely toxic if taken in excess.

SIGNS
The common signs of alcohol poisoning are nausea, vomiting and ataxia (clumsiness and

Children are susceptible to poisoning from alcohol. They should therefore be warned of the dangers of drinking alcohol in excess.

difficulty in walking). There may also be progressive loss of consciousness. Aspiration pneumonia (infection caused by inhalation of vomit into the lungs) is one of the more serious consequences, along with brain damage.

The diagnosis of alcohol poisoning is usually fairly easy to make from the history, and can be confirmed by a blood test for alcohol levels.

If there has been no vomiting, the child may be given a gastric lavage. The blood sugar may be low, which may require treatment with dextrose (a type of sugar). With supportive treatment, the child usually recovers although, sadly, some cases are fatal. Older children should be educated about the risks they are taking, but some may need further help if it is a habit which they cannot stop.

Gastric lavage

Gastric lavage is a method of emptying the stomach contents if accidental poisoning is suspected.

The procedure should be carried out within two to four hours of the ingestion of toxic substances, but should still be considered if a longer time period has elapsed.

Performing gastric lavage
The child is placed on a bed, the foot of which is raised. A lubricated tube is passed into the stomach via the mouth. Tepid water is then poured down the tube so that it gently washes out the stomach, and the water and tablets are then allowed to flow back down the tube. This is repeated until no tablets are visible in the siphoned fluid. Activated charcoal is then introduced into the stomach; this acts as an adsorbent and as a decontaminant for most toxic substances.

Solvent abuse

Solvent abuse, or 'glue sniffing', is most common among children aged 12 to 16, although younger children may experiment as well. Most children who abuse solvents do so in small groups, with only a few continuing the habit alone.

SOLVENTS
Products which can be 'sniffed' include butane gas lighter refills, text correction fluids, glues, dry cleaning fluids and aerosol sprays. The substance is either put into a plastic bag or onto a sleeve to be sniffed, or sprayed directly into the face.

The effects which are being sought include feelings of drunkenness and light-headedness. Children may feel 'dreamy' or have hallucinations. Afterwards, they may feel as though they have a hangover. Solvent abuse carries hazards

that are potentially life-threatening. Under the influence of the solvent, children may become unconscious and choke on their own vomit and if plastic bags are placed over the head,

they can cause suffocation. As solvent abuse usually takes place outdoors, children are at risk from traffic accidents while they are disorientated, or they may fall from a height, or into water.

Solvent abuse is a very risky activity. Solvents may be 'sniffed' to induce feelings of euphoria, but unconsciousness and disorientation may ensue.

BEHAVIOUR
Often, it is not easy for parents to tell if their children are abusing solvents. Signs of solvent abuse include:
■ Sudden changes of mood
■ Unusual irritability or aggression
■ Loss of appetite
■ Loss of interest in hobbies or friends
■ Unusual drowsiness
■ Furtive or dishonest behaviour, including stealing from home.

Many of the above signs, however, may just indicate normal teenage behaviour, so parents should not rush to make assumptions.

Ingestion of medicines

If accidentally swallowed, painkillers, vitamins and prescription drugs can all be harmful to children. Treatment usually comprises gastric lavage or, if time permits, an antidote may be given.

Over half of the cases of accidental poisoning in children are due to medicines that belong to the adults who are caring for them. Young children cannot understand that the brightly coloured 'sweets' they find will do them harm, and may continue to swallow them even if they taste peculiar.

The types of medicines that are most likely to be swallowed accidentally by children include painkillers such as paracetamol and aspirin, vitamins such as iron, and prescription drugs such as antidepressants, antihistamines, tranquillizers and drugs for heart conditions.

EFFECTS
Some of these medicines cause severe consequences in the children who take them. For instance, paracetamol may cause liver failure, antidepressants can cause serious heart arrhythmias and iron may cause severe bleeding. These and many other drugs can be fatal if taken in sufficient amounts, or if treatment is delayed.

TREATMENT
In most cases of accidental swallowing of medicines, the initial treatment will involve the child being given a gastric lavage, or stomach washout, to remove any residual drug which has not yet been absorbed.

In some cases of poisoning, there is a specific antidote which can be administered, although there is often a time limit within which treatment must be started.

Medicines may be swallowed by children who mistake pills for a type of sweet. Painkillers are some of the most likely drugs to be taken by children.

Common sources of poisoning (medicines)

Drug	Type	Symptoms	Antidote
Paracetamol	Painkiller	Nausea, vomiting, abdominal pain	N-acetylcysteine
Aspirin	Painkiller, anti-clotting medicine	Vomiting, tinnitus, overbreathing, fever	No specific antidote
Imipramine, amitriptyline	Antidepressants	Drowsiness, clumsiness, agitation	No specific antidote
Iron tablets, such as ferrous sulphate	Vitamins	Severe vomiting, diarrhoea, vomiting or passing blood, pale skin, serious bleeding	Desferrioxamine

Toxic plants

Although there are relatively few types of very poisonous plants in the UK, there are many which can cause a young child to feel unwell if eaten. Plants, flowers and berries are some of the commonest sources of accidental poisoning in young children.

Accidental poisoning occurs when young children are attracted to brightly coloured berries, leaves or flowers, and try to eat them. Children old enough to play 'make believe' may use plants and berries they find in the garden as part of their games. Fortunately, these plants usually have a very bitter taste and most young children do not eat enough of the plant to make themselves seriously ill.

Poison information centre
If a child is believed to have ingested a potentially harmful plant, it is very important for the parent or carer to bring a sample of that plant to the hospital with the child. With a sample of the plant directly available to them, the hospital staff will be able to contact the local poison information centre, who should be able to identify it and advise on its possible harmful effects, perhaps suggesting treatments.

UK plants which are poisonous when swallowed include: laburnum (flower), deadly nightshade (root and berries), iris (root and flower), lupin (seed and flower), holly (berries), mistletoe (berries) and yew (berries).

Mushrooms
In addition to these, there are many kinds of poisonous mushrooms such as 'spotted fly agaric' and 'death cap', although all mushrooms should be considered hazardous until proven otherwise.

Mistletoe (Viscum album) berries are poisonous if eaten. Appearing from September to January, the berries have a translucent white appearance.

The effects of the fly agaric mushroom are unpredictable. The fungus is strongly hallucinogenic and affects the central nervous system.

Both the flowers and seeds of the lupin plant are toxic. The plant is a member of the pea family and has tall, colourful spikes of flowers.

Holly berries can cause severe poisoning. Holly poses a danger both outside and inside the home, sprays being used to decorate interiors at Christmas.

Head injuries

Head injuries are the most common form of injury in infants and children.
The flexible nature of the child's skull normally protects the brain from
permanent damage, but in a few cases, the consequences can be more serious.

Each year, around one in 200 children will stay the night in hospital with a head injury. The actual number of head injuries each year, however, is probably greater than this because not all injuries are reported to a hospital. Such injuries are the commonest cause of acquired disability in children, affecting approximately 3,000 children aged between 1 and 15 years each year in the UK.

CAUSES OF HEAD INJURY
The cause in each case is often related to the child's age and sex. Head injuries in infants under the age of one occur mainly as a result of non-accidental injury, in other words, child abuse.

In children between one and five years old, domestic accidents, such as falling down flights of stairs or out of windows, are a common cause of head injury. Over the age of five, however, most head injuries result from pedestrian road-traffic accidents (RTAs).

Overall, boys suffer head injuries more frequently than girls by a ratio of about 2:1 throughout childhood (up to the age of 15). The largest group to suffer is boys in their teenage years – again, because of RTAs.

Other, less common, circumstances in which children suffer head injuries include car crashes involving the child as a passenger, riding accidents – falling off a bicycle or a horse – or, occasionally, sporting accidents, particuarly in contact sports.

INITIAL ASSESSMENT
Most children with head injuries are taken to their local A&E department, where they will be assessed and stabilized. If necessary, they will be referred to the neurosciences department for further care and assessment, but this depends on the severity of the injury. Doctors in A&E will consult with the relevant doctors in the neurosciences department as to whether the child should be transferred for specialist treatment.

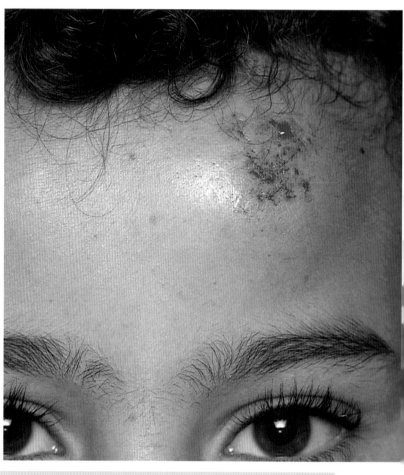

In the majority of head injuries – such as this bruising and swelling as a result of a playground fall – there are no long-term effects. However, if the child is knocked unconscious, they may be hospitalized for at least 24 hours.

Emergency transfer after serious injury

A child who has suffered a serious accident, for example after a road traffic accident, would be brought in by ambulance or, in extreme cases, helicopter air-ambulance to the nearest suitable hospital.

The immediate priority for the paramedic staff at the scene is to achieve a good airway, because hypoxia (deficiency of oxygen in the tissues) may result in serious brain damage. The child will be ventilated manually or intubated (have a tube inserted into their throat if normal breathing is difficult) by the paramedics.

During the journey to hospital, the main aim is to keep the child stable before further treatment.

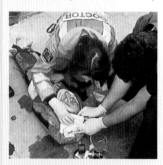

1. When a five-year-old boy falls from a window, it's obvious that urgent medical attention is required. The paramedic team is accompanied by a doctor, seen here assessing the boy's injuries and stemming initial blood loss.

2. The emergency is serious enough to warrant an air-ambulance. Once the boy is strapped on to the stretcher, with his neck supported and a 'back-board' in place to stabilize his spine, he is transferred to the waiting helicopter.

3. To maintain respiration in his critical state, the boy is 'bagged' with a hand-held respirator that administers air directly through a face-mask. Blood is being given intravenously to replace that which he lost from the injuries to his head.

4. The hospital has been given advance warning of the incoming case, so the 'crash' team is ready as the paramedics arrive at the intensive therapy unit. Specialists in neurosciences and paediatric trauma will also be present.

Assessment and treatment

The extent of a child's head injury must be established quickly – especially if the patient is unconscious. In order to do this, doctors use a three-part scoring system.

If the child is unconscious, the head will have been injured significantly. If the child is conscious, the doctor will check over the scalp for bruising and swelling. In either case, the level of consciousness will be tested to assess what further action is required.

GLASGOW COMA SCALE
The child's level of consciousness following a head injury can be assessed using the Glasgow Coma Scale, a standardized scoring system that is modified

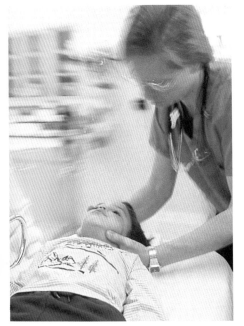

for use with children.

The scale looks at the overall level of responsiveness to stimuli by the eyes, limbs (motor response) and by speech (verbal response). The scores are added to make an aggregate that gives an idea of the child's condition.

From a potential maximum of 15, a score of 13 or over indicates that the child has not suffered a significant head injury. However, the score is often good to begin with and then deteriorates because of internal bleeding.

SERIOUS CASES
A score of less than eight means that mechanical ventilation will be required if this has not already been administered during the transfer to hospital. These are very serious cases; the child is extremely ill and may not survive. Many such cases will not make it to the hospital alive, and others will die in the Intensive Care Unit. Those who do survive with such a low score on the scale are not likely to do well in the long-term.

Children with head injuries must be assessed rapidly. Initially, A&E doctors look for alertness and responsiveness to voice and pain. Thereafter, a full Glasgow Coma Score should be obtained, determining the course of action.

Paediatric Glasgow coma score

4–15 YEARS		0–4 YEARS	
Response	**Score**	**Response**	**Score**
Eyes		**Eyes**	
Open spontaneously	4	Open spontaneously	4
Open to verbal command	3	React to speech	3
Open in response to pain	2	React to pain	2
No response	1	No response	1
Motor response		**Motor response**	
Obeys verbal command	6	Spontaneous or obeys verbal command	6
Response to painful stimulus		*Response to painful stimulus*	
Localizes pain	5	Localizes pain	5
Flexes limb with pain	4	Withdraws in response	4
Flexes abnormally	3	Flexes abnormally	3
Extension	2	Extension	2
No response	1	No response	1
Verbal response		**Verbal response**	
Orientated, converses, interacts, appropriate words	5	Smiles, orientated to sounds, objects, interacts	5
Disorientated, converses	4	Cries, inappropriate words	4
Inappropriate words	3	Inappropriate crying	3
Incomprehensible sounds	2	Inconsolable crying, irritable	2
No response	1	No response	1

SPECIFIC INVESTIGATIONS
The early tests done in A&E look at general brain function. More detailed investigations will be undertaken in the neurosciences and intensive care units. These tests include measuring the intracranial pressure (ICP) – the pressure inside the brain – using a probe inserted through the skull. By subtracting the ICP reading from the mean (average) arterial blood pressure, the resulting figure is the 'mean cerebral perfusion pressure', the pressure at which oxygen is being supplied to the brain.

Doctors also look at the pattern of the brainwave using an electroencephalograph (EEG). Even when the child is unconscious, signals are still sent between the retina and the brain, via the 'visual pathway'. The activity of the pathway is detected by EEG, which therefore provides a good warning sign if the brain has been badly injured.

X-ray and CT scans

After the severity of a child's head injury has been established clinically, the patient may be further examined if the signs warrant it. Once the child is stable, they will undergo X-ray examination and a CT (computerized tomography) scan. An X-ray of the neck is usually taken with the first skull X-rays to confirm or discount cervical spine damage. If there is any doubt about the neck it is kept in a collar, because the chance of fracture and dislocation is high.

Scanning takes from 30 to 60 minutes to complete and cannot

In computerized axial tomography (CT or CAT scan), the X-ray emitter and detector rotate around the patient. Unlike normal X-rays, this technique can produce 3-D images.

If the coma score is less than eight, a CT scan will usually be taken as soon as possible. This will highlight brain tissue damage or blood clots.

therefore be carried out on a patient who is still in need of resuscitation.

As well as the damage to the head, chest injuries must be assessed as the resulting hypoxia (low blood oxygen) will exacerbate any brain injury.

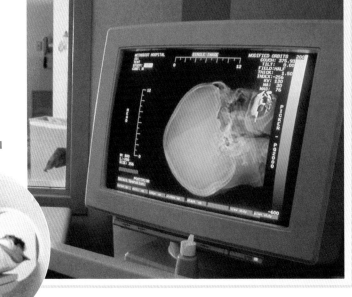

Types of head injury

About 1 in 800 children with head injuries develop serious problems that can lead to death. An understanding of the three main types of head injury is therefore vital, as seemingly simple injuries can often hide internal complications.

Localized skull fracture

One of the most common types of head injury is a direct, localized blow to the head. This may cause a fracture of the skull and haemorrhage (bleeding) beneath – indicative of a bruise on the brain.

Children with such injuries usually wake up quite quickly, but often have a neurological deficit depending on which side of the head they are hit. This will usually be a weakness or loss of speech, which improves as the bruise recovers. For these children, the outlook is good because the rest of the brain is usually undisturbed.

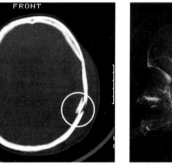

This CT scan shows a fracture (circled) in the right parietal bone of the skull.

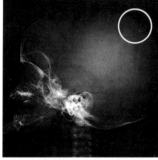

A simple, linear fracture in the skull such as this would probably not have affected the brain.

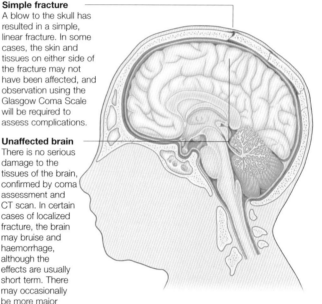

Simple fracture
A blow to the skull has resulted in a simple, linear fracture. In some cases, the skin and tissues on either side of the fracture may not have been affected, and observation using the Glasgow Coma Scale will be required to assess complications.

Unaffected brain
There is no serious damage to the tissues of the brain, confirmed by coma assessment and CT scan. In certain cases of localized fracture, the brain may bruise and haemorrhage, although the effects are usually short term. There may occasionally be more major bleeding around the brain.

Larger impact injury

Major trauma to skull
Multiple fractures and possible penetration by foreign objects. Skull is significantly deformed.

Haemorrhaging
Intracranial (within the skull) bleeding from the meninges (membranes surrounding the brain), and the brain. As the brain is compressed, extradural haematoma (blood clotting within the outer membrane) may occur.

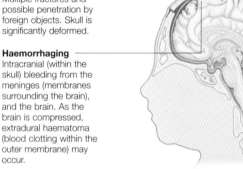

If the blow to the head is more forceful or over a larger area, multiple fractures of the skull and penetration by the object are possible. Common causes of such potentially devastating injury include falling and hitting the head on concrete, or receiving a blow to the head. Such injuries cause distortion of the brain, micro-tears of the tissue and sometimes massive bleeding can result. Immediate surgery may be needed to rectify the damage when bleeding has stopped, and more long-term neurological problems are to be expected.

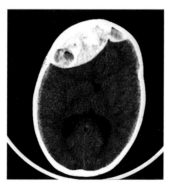

This scan of a large fracture shows an extradural haematoma (white) – an accumulation of blood from the membranes of the brain.

Diffuse axonal injury

The diffuse axonal injury is the typical injury suffered when a child is flung through the air at high velocity in a road traffic accident. It may produce no visible bleeding in the brain but it causes very severe swelling and long-term damage. The priority in this case is to reduce the pressure inside the head, such as by giving diuretic drugs.

These injuries are a matter for concern, because in diffuse injury, all parts of the brain are affected, and may also be accompanied by brainstem damage due to angulation and whipping of the head relative to the neck.

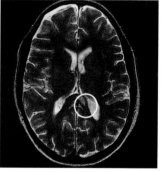

MR scans are needed to see the subtle lesions of diffuse axonal injury. This injury causes swellings in the brain (circled) and may result in long-term disability.

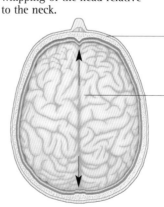

Skull
With diffuse axonal injury, the skull – and sometimes the brain – may show no visible signs of damage.

Brain movement
A rapid change in direction, such as when a child is hit by a car or falls out of a window, causes the brain to smash against the inside of the skull and rebound.

Widespread damage can result from microscopic shearing of delicate nerve tissue.

Long-term management

After initial assessment and treatment, the procedure involves waiting for the child to regain complete consciousness and managing the waking-up process.

When the child comes round after the injury, which may be a few minutes or several days later, further neurological examination (include additional scanning) may give an indication of any permanent damage.

The child will go through an initial state of confusion as they wake up, but many make quite a rapid recovery. However, the learning difficulties can take several months to assess fully; it is not until about six months after the accident that problems likely to persist in the long-term can be fully identified.

RECOVERY MANAGEMENT

During these crucial months, many different approaches will be needed for the patient's recovery. These include physiotherapy, occupational therapy, speech therapy and neuropsychology. Patients with severe injuries can also be very irritable and difficult to manage.

The age of the child can affect the severity of the possible resulting brain damage, being worse in younger children. Furthermore, the younger the child, the more likely they are to die from a severe head injury.

AFTEREFFECTS

With any head injury, there are many possible sequelae (medical disorders resulting from the injury). A child with a minor

Post-traumatic stress is common after a head injury, so the careful management of the child is required to help them overcome the resulting phobias and insecurities.

head injury can have short-term problems – typically classified as post-traumatic stress disorder. These may be manifested as behavioural difficulties, nightmares, phobias, and disturbances of their learning due to loss of concentration. However, this is not evidence of brain injury, but rather a response to a life-threatening occurence.

In more severe cases, brain damage may result in physical disabilities. A child who has a physical disability is also likely to have some learning difficulties. Many patients will have no physical disability, but still have problems with memory, concentration, behaviour and the ability to learn at speed. They may find it difficult to keep up with the rest of the class once they are back at school, so counselling may be offered.

FRONTAL LOBE TRAUMA

Frontal lobe injuries are very serious and can be devastating because they affect not only behaviour but also personality. Frontal lobe damage also affects the brain's 'executive function'. This is the ability to assimilate

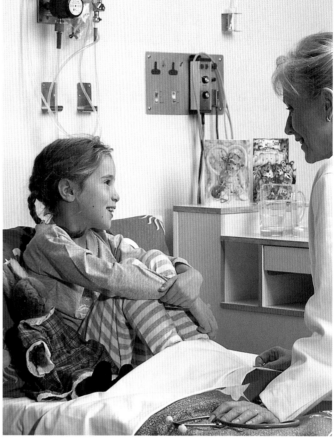

individual components of information into a whole and is the key to our understanding of and interaction with the world. Affected children therefore have difficulty planning, organizing and co-ordinating thoughts. The production of speech may also be difficult, and the child may have social disinhibition.

Fortunately, because most paedatric head injuries are not severe, the majority of affected children will make a complete recovery. Despite the relatively common occurrence of such injuries, long-term neurological effects such as epilepsy and cranial nerve damage following head trauma are very rare.

Shaken baby syndrome

The majority of head injuries in children under a year old result from abuse. A cause of bleeding around the brain and diffuse axonal injury in infants is so-called 'shaken baby syndrome', in which frustrated parents or child-minders shake a crying baby in order to silence it.

An infant's head control is not as effective as an adult's because of their undeveloped neck muscles. As a result, rapid back and forth motion during shaking causes the brain tissue to suffer rapid acceleration and deceleration stresses combined with rotational movement and whiplash. This trauma affects the entire brain, and the resulting disability is severe. In most cases, there will be no external evidence of injury.

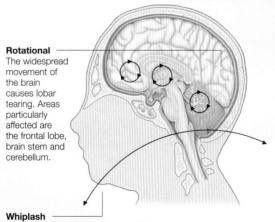

Rotational
The widespread movement of the brain causes lobar tearing. Areas particularly affected are the frontal lobe, brain stem and cerebellum.

Whiplash
Rapid movements of the head relative to the neck. Causes acceleration and deceleration injuries.

DAMAGING MOVEMENT:
Shaking causes two main types of damaging movement: rotational and whiplash.

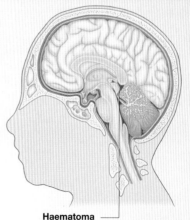

Haematoma
Small tears in brain tissue result in intracranial bleeding. Immediate effects range from confusion to coma or death.

AXONAL DAMAGE:
Potentially fatal results are diffuse axonal injury and haematoma (bleeding and clotting).

Sudden infant death syndrome

Sudden infant death syndrome (SIDS) accounts for the deaths of seven babies each week in the UK. While certain risk factors have been identified, the actual causes remain unknown.

Sudden infant death syndrome (SIDS) is the term used to describe the sudden and unexpected death of a baby for no obvious reason. The post-mortem examination may later yield an explanation in some cases, but those that remain unexplained are registered as SIDS or cot death.

The term 'cot death' can be misleading as death can occur anywhere. Some SIDS babies die in their parents' arms or in a pram, but usually they are found to have died in their cots.

INCIDENCE AND RISK FACTORS

The causes of SIDS are unknown, but researchers believe that a number of different factors are involved, rather than a single over-riding cause. Several factors acting together at a vulnerable stage of development may, in some cases, overwhelm a baby's ability to cope.

Research has shown that certain babies, such as boys, twins and premature and low-weight babies, are more at risk.

Although cot death can

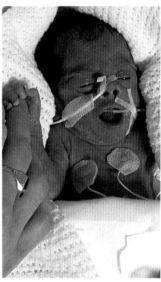

The causes of SIDS remain unknown, despite extensive research. Certain babies, such as twins, are thought to be at greater risk.

happen within any family, it is more likely to occur in families living in disadvantaged circumstances. In the UK one baby dies every day from SIDS, representing an incidence of 0.57 per 1,000 live births.SIDS is the leading cause of death of

babies over one month old, with a higher death rate than meningitis, road traffic accidents or leukaemia. Over 80 per cent of SIDS babies are under six months old, with a peak at 2–3 months. The risk reduces as babies get older.

Pre-term babies have an increased risk of sudden infant death. This may be due to problems within their immature respiratory systems.

Sleeping position

In most countries the traditional sleeping position for babies is on the back (supine), as was the case in the UK until the 1970s.

However, around this time it was reported that babies in special care baby units in the UK were placed on their fronts (prone), as this had been shown to improve breathing in pre-term babies with respiratory distress and reduce vomiting in babies

with gastro-oesophageal reflux.

CHANGING PRACTICE

As a result, in subsequent years this practice was extended to healthy full-term babies. Several studies since then, however, have shown that lying sleeping babies on their back significantly reduces the risk of SIDS, and the death rate from this has fallen considerably since 1991, when

supine sleeping was recommended and put into general practice. It has been suggested that putting healthy babies to sleep on their backs will put them at greater risk of death through choking. However, there is no evidence to support this.

Side sleeping is also not recommended as babies are more likely to roll onto their fronts. Babies should sleep on a firm, well fitting, waterproof mattress and should never be left sleeping with a pillow or on a bean-bag or cushion.

Since 1991, the UK government health department has advised that babies sleep on their backs. The baby's feet should also touch the foot of the cot.

Reducing the risk

Parents can take steps to reduce the risk of SIDS by:
- Placing their baby on its back to sleep
- Not smoking during pregnancy
- Not allowing anyone to smoke in the same room as the baby
- Making sure the baby does not become too hot
- Keeping the baby's head uncovered and placing the baby with its feet touching the foot of the cot, to prevent wriggling

down under the covers
- Seeking medical advice promptly if the baby is unwell
- Not falling asleep together with the baby on the sofa
- Keeping the baby's cot in their bedroom for the first six months
- Not sharing a bed with the baby if either parent has been smoking, drinking or taking medication or drugs that cause drowsiness, or if either is extremely tired.

SIDS and smoking

Since the success of the 1991 campaign to reduce SIDS by placing sleeping babies
on their backs, smoking has become one of the major contributory factors in cot death.
Smoking both during pregnancy and after birth significantly increases the risk.

Smoking in pregnancy is one of the risk factors linked to SIDS, with the risk increasing as the number of cigarettes smoked per day rises. It is thought that this may be due to the effect of smoking on either the baby's

control of breathing or lung growth at a critical stage of development.

PASSIVE SMOKING
Passive smoking after birth is also linked with SIDS, and there is an increased risk of SIDS if either parent smokes in the home or if the baby is taken into a cigarette smoke-filled environment.

The risk of SIDS is especially increased where the baby sleeps in the same bed as parents who smoke, even if they do not smoke in bed; the reason for this is unclear.

People who smoke around babies are putting them at increased risk. Passive smoking is thought to be a major contributory factor to SIDS.

Smoking during pregnancy increases the risk of SIDS in direct relation to the number of cigarettes smoked. At 20+, the risk increases by eight times.

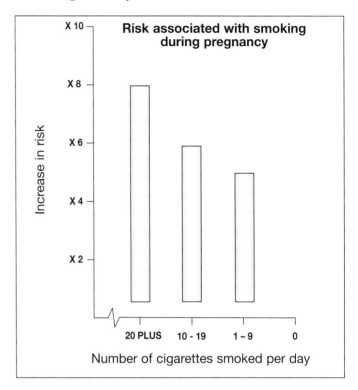

Risk associated with smoking during pregnancy

Increase in risk (Y-axis: X 2, X 4, X 6, X 8, X 10)

Number of cigarettes smoked per day (X-axis: 20 PLUS, 10 - 19, 1 – 9, 0)

Temperature

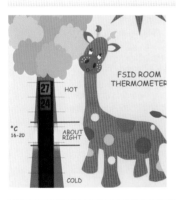

FSID ROOM THERMOMETER

°C 16-20 — HOT 27 24 — ABOUT RIGHT — COLD

Placing a thermometer in the baby's bedroom will help to ensure the correct temperature. These are accurate and easily available.

Overheating is thought to increase the risk of cot death. Babies can overheat either because the room temperature is too high, or because they have been wrapped in excessive bedding or clothing. The ideal room temperature for a baby is

around 18°C (65°F). The easiest way to check whether a baby is too warm is to feel his or her abdomen, as hands and feet may be cool even when body temperature is high.

Babies under one year should:
■ Never sleep with a hot water bottle or electric blanket; next to a radiator, heater or fire; or in direct sunshine
■ Not be overwrapped when unwell or feverish, even in winter
■ Not be put to bed with a

duvet or quilt which could accidentally cover the head. Placing the baby with its feet touching the foot of the cot helps prevent it from wriggling under any blankets
■ Be placed in a cot or pram with covers tucked in so that they cannot slip over the head
■ Not wear a hat while asleep indoors and they should have any extra clothing removed when moving from outside to inside.

Apnoea and respiration monitors

Apnoea is a temporary cessation of breathing. Irregular breathing and short apnoeic pauses are normal in young babies and have no adverse effect. In relation to SIDS, it is not known whether a baby dies because breathing has stopped, or whether breathing has ceased because the baby has died.

Home respiration or apnoea monitors can be used to detect any cessation of breathing over

a set time (usually 20 seconds), triggering an alarm. There is no evidence that they reduce SIDS, but they may offer reassurance to parents who have previously suffered a cot death.

Respiration monitors can serve to reassure parents who have already lost a baby. The monitor alarms if it detects an extended period of apnoea.

Prompt medical advice

Most SIDS babies are apparently healthy prior to death. While most parents and doctors know when a baby is unwell, in a proportion of babies the severity of a baby's illness may not be fully recognized.

Non-specific signs such as unusual drowsiness or floppiness, altered character of cry or breathing, or excessive sweating may indicate a serious illness.

Similarly, a baby who takes

less than a third of its usual fluids, passes much less urine than usual, vomits green fluid or passes blood in their stools should also be medically examined.

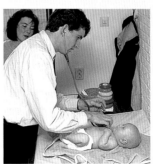

In a small number of SIDS deaths, a pre-existing condition was not diagnosed. Babies should be examined by a doctor at any sign of illness.

Childhood cancers

Cancers in children are rare and little is known of their causes.
Treatments, such as chemotherapy or surgery, and their success rates
depend on the type of malignancy and how far it has spread.

Childhood cancers affect about 1–2 children per thousand of the population, and they are an important cause of illness and mortality. Despite major advances in treatment over the last two decades, malignancies are the third most common cause of childhood deaths after accidents and congenital abnormalities.

CARE ISSUES

Quality of life for the patient has become an increasingly important issue among the rising number of long-term cancer survivors. A careful balance between treatment to eradicate

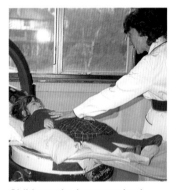

Children who have received transplanted organs will be closely monitored. The drugs used to stop rejection are associated with tumours.

tumours and the side effects of this treatment is essential to optimizing the overall results of therapy.

Centralizing care in specialist centres and the inclusion of all cases in carefully conducted controlled trials to assess the benefits of new therapeutic methods has been essential in achieving consistently improved survival rates.

There are a number of complications that can arise from either the treatment of cancer, or the cancer itself. These include:

■ Modern immunosuppressive intensive therapy, used to treat tumours or to suppress the rejection of a transplanted organ, is in itself associated with an increased risk of secondary tumours occurring

■ HIV infection, which profoundly depresses the number of T-cell lymphocyte cells in the immune system, is also associated with an increased incidence of lymphoma

■ Kaposi's sarcoma is a slow-growing tumour of the blood vessels in the skin. It is generally associated with patients infected with HIV.

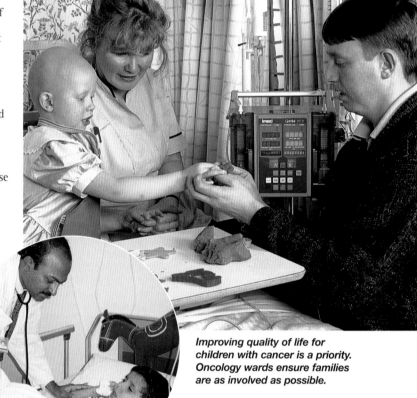

Improving quality of life for children with cancer is a priority. Oncology wards ensure families are as involved as possible.

Chemotherapy may be administered by an intravenous drip. The therapy has many side effects, particularly nausea and loss of appetite.

Predisposing factors

Relative incidence of the most common childhood malignancies

- Leukaemia 48 per cent
- Others 16 per cent
- Nephroblastomas 5 per cent
- Neuroblastomas 7 per cent
- Lymphomas 8 per cent
- Central nervous system 16 per cent

Relatively little is known about the cause of the majority of childhood tumours, but some rare genetic disorders have increased incidences of cancers. For example, acute leukaemia is 15 times more common in children with Down's syndrome compared with normal children. Other causes of cancer in children include:

■ The Epstein–Barr virus (a common cause of glandular fever) is associated with B-cell lymphomas in malarial areas of Africa

■ Some immunodeficiency disorders also have an increased

This pie chart shows a breakdown of the incidence of common cancers that affect children. Leukaemia is the most prevalent childhood cancer.

risk of tumour. Pre-natal exposure to radiation during the first trimester might also increase the risk of subsequent childhood cancer. For this reason, radiology departments take appropriate precautions to avoid exposure of pregnant women to X-rays

■ Reports of increased childhood malignancy among children in close proximity to nuclear-waste processing plants have been difficult to explain, with no obvious route of exposure to chemicals or nuclear materials

■ Studies investigating the relation between childhood cancers and high-voltage electric cables have been inconclusive

■ Ultraviolet radiation from sunlight is the most common known cause of cancer in adults, but skin tumours in childhood are very rare.

Treating children with cancer

Treating children with cancer is a balance between destroying the malignant cells and avoiding the severe side effects of the treatment. The treatment plan can run for several years, and the patients need regular check-ups for relapse for the rest of their life.

Leukaemia

Approximately half of all malignancies in childhood are associated with leukaemia. In 80 per cent of these cases, the tumour type is acute lymphoblastic leukaemia.

The majority of children present after a period of several weeks. Symptoms include:
■ Increasing malaise and pallor
■ Recurrent fever and infection
■ Bone pain
■ Abnormal bruising.
Examination may reveal enlarged lymph nodes, enlargement of the liver and spleen and bony tenderness. Diagnosis is confirmed by examination of blood and a bone marrow sample.

CANCER TREATMENT
Treatment consists of a combination of chemotherapy and radiotherapy. The scheme of management is to induce remission, followed by blocks of further intensive therapy to decrease the chances of relapse. This is followed by treatment aimed at eradicating cells from the central nervous system, and finally by continuation of therapy for a further two years.

SIDE EFFECTS
The treatment invariably suppresses red cells, white cells and platelets, and patients frequently require blood transfusions and specific anti-microbial agents. Bone marrow transplantation, providing a source of healthy cells to repopulate bone marrow, is an option for those who relapse after treatment.

Leukaemia causes an uncontrolled proliferation of white blood cells (stained purple in this microscope image). These cancerous cells have an altered DNA structure.

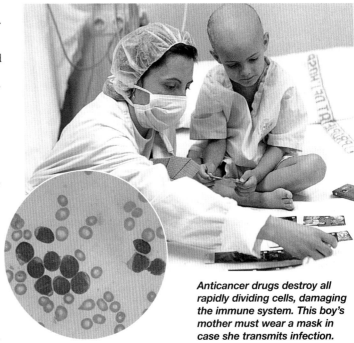

Anticancer drugs destroy all rapidly dividing cells, damaging the immune system. This boy's mother must wear a mask in case she transmits infection.

Neuroblastoma

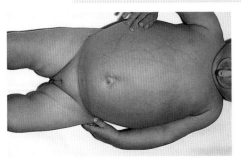

This child is suffering from an abdominal neuroblastoma (malignant tumour). A mass in the abdomen is a common sign.

Neuroblastoma tumours arise from neural cells, most commonly from the adrenal glands. They are highly malignant tumours that usually produce an abdominal mass which typically contains speckles of calcification on X-ray.

Most patients have an excess of catecholamine hormones and elevated levels of the products of their metabolism, which can be detected in urine. Surgery aims to excise tumours whenever possible, but the prognosis for advanced disease is poor.

Wilms' tumour

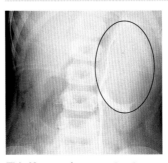

This X-ray, using a contrast medium, shows an enlarged kidney (circled) due to Wilms' tumour (nephroblastoma).

Wilms' tumour occurs as a result of abnormal proliferation of embryonal kidney cells. Most tumours occur in pre-school children and come to attention as an asymptomatic abdominal mass. Occasionally, patients have abdominal pain and blood in their urine.

Treatment involves surgically excising the tumour. Subsequent treatment, using chemotherapy and radiotherapy, is determined by the extent of tumour spread, and the long-term prognosis is good.

Long-term complications

While more aggressive therapy has resulted in improved survival rates for many childhood cancers, this has to be balanced against the occurrence of long-term problems related to treatment:
■ Cranial irradiation has been associated with subtle learning difficulties and can also impair growth hormone production, affecting final adult height

All patients require life-long follow-up to assess the long-term outcomes from current treatments.

■ Acute cardiac effects can occur after using anthracycline drugs, and many tumour survivors have reduced lung function. Drugs and irradiation might also affect gonadal function. The occurrence of long-term psychological problems is remarkably low, and time missed from school has the potential to affect long-term achievement.

Children with cancer have long periods of time away from school. Parents may choose to educate their child in the ward.

Paediatric intensive care

Paediatric intensive care is specifically for the treatment of critically ill children. The doctors and nurses involved have expert training to deal with the children's needs, and those of their parents.

A paediatric intensive care unit (PICU) is a special ward which undertakes the care of critically ill children who have failure of one or more of the vital body systems. Mortality rates of these patients have decreased as services have developed.

Until recently, particularly in the UK, much of the intensive care of children was provided by general hospitals with no specific PICU. Increasing recognition that children are not just 'scaled down adults' has led to expansion of dedicated children's units in major centres.

These units provide a 'flying squad' who travel from major treatment centres to smaller hospitals and stabilize the patient before undertaking transfer to the PICU in a mobile intensive care ambulance.

In a PICU, specialized equipment – such as ventilators – provides support for critically ill children. Heart rate and breathing are monitored at all times.

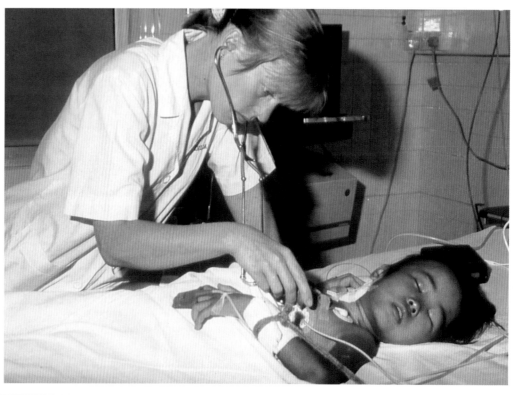

What care is provided in a PICU?

In a PICU there are many different forms of treatment provided for ill children:

■ **Ventilation**
Ventilation is the most common reason for intensive care and is due to actual or potential respiratory failure. This may be because of a respiratory infection such as bronchiolitis, which occurs particularly in small babies and those born prematurely. Respiratory compromise may also be part of multi-organ failure.

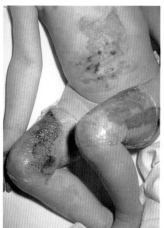

Children with serious burns will be treated in a PICU. This child has suffered burns to the abdomen and upper legs.

■ **Drugs to support the heart and blood pressure**
Low blood pressure is a common problem in critically ill children. This may be due to the action of toxins on the heart, so reducing its ability to pump blood, or to substances in the blood causing the blood vessels to relax. Certain drugs increase blood pressure, heart rate and the heart's force of contraction.

■ **Nutrition**
This is vital for a child with a serious illness as the demand for energy is very great and the patient cannot eat normally. Nutrition is provided intravenously or via a tube into the stomach (gastrotomy).

■ **Kidney therapy**
The kidneys fail due to poor blood circulation. Fortunately

they are able to recover after a temporary shutdown. The action of kidneys as filters of toxins can be substituted by filtration or dialysis. The child's blood is withdrawn via a large cannula and passes through a machine that removes excess fluid and toxins.

■ **Antibiotics**
In all patients with sepsis (bacterial infection) as the primary diagnosis, antibiotic cover is needed to combat likely organisms. In most patients in intensive care, infection is likely to become an important consideration.

■ **Care of the skin**
Patients with burns offer a huge challenge to intensive care specialists as they have lost the protection from loss of fluid and infection that the skin normally provides. In all PICUs care must be taken to prevent damage to the patient's skin from pressure or other trauma.

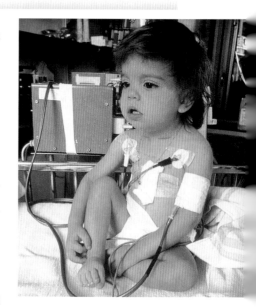

Children with kidney failure should have their circulation and fluid balance monitored. Dialysis treatment is used to replace the functions of the kidneys.

Critical conditions

Children who require paediatric intensive care treatment will have a variety
of critical conditions. Special medical skills and equipment are needed
to diagnose and care for these critically ill children.

There are numerous reasons why children need intensive care:

■ **Severe systemic infections**
Certain organisms have the capacity to produce systemic collapse and multi-organ failure. The meningococcus (*Neisseria meningitidis*) is the most notorious.

■ **Respiratory failure with need for ventilation**
Respiratory failure may occur as a single problem, such as in bronchiolitis, or it may be a feature of a multi-organ problem, for example after severe trauma or burns.

■ **Trauma**
Road traffic accidents (RTAs) involving children as pedestrians, cyclists or car passengers are the commonest cause of trauma, but other causes, such as falls or non-accidental injury, may be involved.

■ **Burns**
Burns from house fires are associated with smoke inhalation which is usually the primary threat to life. Specialist plastic surgery/PICU facilities are required for affected children.

■ **Following major surgery**
Cardiac, neurological and other

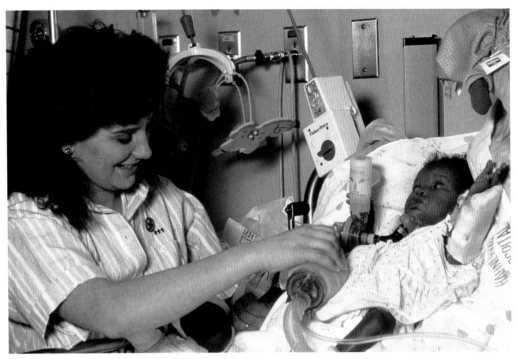

major surgical procedures require a period of stabilization post-operatively in a PICU. Special skills are required over and above normal intensive care practice.

■ **Severe fits or coma**
Fits or coma may occur for a large number of reasons. Poisoning, metabolic disturbance – such as hypoglycaemia (low blood sugar) – and unrecognized trauma must be considered by the medical staff in the differential diagnosis.

Children with bacterial meningitis suffer from fever, sore throat, headaches, neck stiffness and vomiting. This infection is treated in a PICU with large doses of intravenous antibiotic drugs.

Looking after the family

The admission of a child to a PICU can be a shock to parents, especially if the admission involves the transfer of the child to a unit far from home. Every effort must be made to explain the situation to the parents and give them the opportunity to ask questions.

Facilities are provided for families to spend time with the

child; they may need to stay overnight or longer.

WHEN A CHILD DIES
Sometimes the outcome of an admission to a PICU may be the death of the child. In such cases the family should be allowed as much time as possible to spend with their child. A child may be diagnosed brain dead, raising

the possibility of donation of organs. This sensitive issue must be handled very carefully but families may find it helpful in the future for something positive to have come from their loss.

In a PICU the death of a child is a possibility. Counselling is always available to help families cope with their loss.

Transport teams

Transport teams provide expert assistance at the hospital where the child was originally admitted and aim to provide intensive care on the move before arrival at the PICU. A doctor and nurse or larger team require specific training in transport as well as PICU skills.

Transport teams are vital for transferring children to PICUs as quickly as possible. If necessary, urgent treatment can be administered on the way.

Index

A

abdominal bloating 154
abdominal examination
   at birth 12-13
   at six weeks 21
abdominal pain
   from appendicitis 151
   intussusception 152
'abortive polio' 218
absence epilepsy 209
academic excellence 77
Accident and Emergency
   234, 238-9
accidental poisoning 234-5
   first aid 234
   medicines 237
   plants 237
   prevention 235
   types of 234
accidents
   head injuries from 238
   to toddlers 64-5
'accommodation' 104
acetabulum 158, 159
acetylcholine 115
acid-fast stains 201
action pathway 78-9
activated charcoal 236
activating hormones 63
'active cycle of breathing' 205
activity levels 82
acute lymphoid leukaemia
   182, 184-5
acute myeloid leukaemia
   182, 183
acute rheumatism
   see rheumatic fever
acute viral bronchiolitis
   see bronchiolitis
acyclovir 207
adaptability 83
'adaptive' reflexes 26
adenoids, enlarged 107, 193
adenosine 191
adenovirus 106, 110, 194, 203
ADHD see attention deficit
   hyperactivity disorder (ADHD)
adolescents
   alcohol abuse 236
   end of language learning 69
   growth rates in 96-7
   immunization 32
   solvent abuse 236
adrenal glands 245
aerosol sprays 236
Afro-Caribbean babies,
   umbilical hernia 47
aggression 227
Agpar score 12
AIDS see HIV
air-ambulance 238
airways
   obstruction of 112, 115
   upper airways problems
      103, 106-7, 110
alcohol
   consumption in pregnancy
      63, 188
   poisoning 236
alertness 52
alkaline phosphatase 165
alkylating agents 184

alleles 99
allergic conjunctivitis 102
allergies
   cows milk 38, 172
   gluten 36, 39, 41
   from weaning too early 36
   see also asthma; eczema
allergy testing 113
alopecia 185
alpha globin 175, 177
alpha thalassaemia 174, 177
aluminium thermal blanket 49
alveoli, inflammation of 196
Alzheimer's disease,
   reflexes and 27
ambulance 238
aminophylline 114
amitriptyline 237
ammonia dermatitis 42-4
amniocentesis 232-3
amniotic fluid, in the lungs
   18-19
amoxicillin 109
ampicillin 215
amplification 179
anaemia 172-3
   causes 172
   from late weaning 39
   in premature babies 51
   tests for 163, 174-5
   from thalassaemia 174-7
   treatment 173
anaesthetic gels 55
anal canal 122
ankylosing spondylitis 162
anterior uveitis 162
anthracyclines 245
antibiotics
   for eye problems 102-3
   and gastroenteritis 149
   in intensive care 246
   for meningitis 215
   prophylaxis 217
   for rheumatic fever 171
   for tonsillitis 109
   tuberculosis 201
   for urinary infections 125
   see also penicillin
antibodies
   absence of 28-9
   acquisition of 215
   anti-nuclear 163
   from breast milk 22-3
   HIV-specific 179
   maternal 28
   from vaccination 32
anticancer drugs 245
anti-D injection 15
antidotes 237
anti-emetics 185
antifungal creams 44
antihistamines 102, 126, 135
anti-inflammatories 126, 191
anti-nuclear antibodies 163
antiretrovirals 179-81
antivirals 206-7
aortic arch 188
aortic stenosis 190
apnoea 50-1, 107, 109, 194-5
apnoea monitors 243
appearance, and good teeth
   95
appendicectomy 151

appendicitis 150-1
   symptoms 151
appendicular artery 150
appendix 150
approach response 82
arithmetic 71
arthritis
   juvenile idiopathic 162-3
   rheumatoid 172
   from rubella 132
arthrogryposis 160
artificial ventilation
   195, 207, 246-7
Asian children, and rickets 165
aspiration
   bone marrow 173, 182-3
   meconium 19
   pneumonia 236
   suprapubic 125
aspirin 206, 220
   pack sizes 235
   poisoning from 237
assessment
   at eight months 35, 52-3
   newborns 12-13
   at six weeks 20-1
associative play 80
asteatotic eczema 127
asthma 112-15, 192
   clinical symptoms 112
   incidence of 112
   investigating 113
   life-threatening 114
   monitoring 113
   prevention 115
   from respiratory tract infections
      106
   treatment 114-15
'asymmetric tonic neck reflex'
   27
ataxic cerebral palsy 229
athetoid cerebral palsy 229
atomic force microscope imaging
   202
atopic eczema 126
atria 188
atrial septal defect 187-8
atrioventricular septal defect 188
attachment 77
attention deficit hyperactivity
   disorder (ADHD) 9, 226-7
   causes 226
   treatment 227
attention span 83
audiology assessment 57
aura 209
auscultation 189, 196
autism 9, 33-4, 224-5
   behaviour patterns 224
   causes 225
   coping with 225
   management 225
automatisms 209
autosomal recessive disorder 169
AZT 180-1

B

babbling 66, 68
babies
   developmental delay 34-5
   eight month check 52-3
   eye problems 102-5

failure to thrive 40-1
feeding and weaning 38-9
healthy 8
hearing problems 56-7
immunization 32-3
intussuseption 152-3
learning to eat 36-7
learning to walk 58-9
nappy rash 44-5
non-accidental injuries
   238, 241
SIDS 20, 42, 242-3
skin problems 42-3
teething 54-5
see also newborn;
   premature babies
baby clinics 16, 62
baby rice 36-7, 39
bacille Calmette-Guérin (BCG)
   32, 180, 201
baclofen 231
bacterial infections
   conjunctivitis 102
   cystic fibrosis 202-5
   gastroenteritis 148-9
   meningococcal 212-17, 247
   mycobacterial 29, 180, 200-1
   and nappy rash 45
   pneumococcal 176
   resistance to 203
   and rheumatic fever 170-1
   tonsillitis 106-9
   urinary tract 124
   whooping cough 198-9
balance, sense of 89
balanced diet 86-7, 95
   for healthy bones 164-5
barium enema 153, 155
Barlow's test 158
barrier creams 43-5
basal ganglia 229
B-cells 29
BCG (bacille Calmette-Guérin)
   32, 180, 201
Becker muscular dystrophy
   168
bedtime
   difficulties 25
   routines 85
bed-wetting 73-5
   causes of 74
   and drinking 75
   primary enuresis 74
   secondary enuresis 74
   treatment 75
behavioural problems
   in ADHD 226-7
   in cerebral palsy 230
   from dyslexia 143
   from dyspraxia 140-1
   and head injuries 241
   obsessional 224-5
benzylpenicillin 213
beta globin 175
beta thalassaemia 174-7
   intermedia 177
   minor 175
beta thalassaemia major 175
   diagnosis 177
   treatment 176
bile salt replacement 205
biliary atresia 15
bilirubin 13-15

biological washing powders 42, 45
biopsy
  bone marrow 182
  bowel 155
  brain 207
  liver 221
  muscle 169
bipedal gait 58
bipolar diathermy forceps 222
birth
  asphyxia 56
  breech presentation 158
birth canal 181, 197
bisphosphonates 167
bladder emptying 72-3
blast cells 182
bleach 235
blindness 162
  see also eye problems
blockage
  of the airways 112, 115
  digestive tract 13, 152
  tear ducts 103
blood, contaminated 178
blood count depression 185
blood flow
  abnormal 186-7
  newborns 13
blood groups
  inheritance of 99
  and jaundice 15
blood loss 172
blood oxygen saturation levels 194
blood tests
  for alcohol levels 236
  for anaemia 163, 172, 174-5
  for leukaemia 183
blood transfusions 176
blood-brain barrier 182
bloodshot eyes 46
Bobath technique 231
body proportions, changing 97
bone marrow aspiration 173, 182-3
bone marrow transplantation 184
bone remodelling 31
bone structure 164, 166
books see picture books
Bordetella pertussis 198
bottle-feeding
  and HIV prevention 181
  problems 38, 41, 120
bowel 122
  biopsy 155
  blockage 13
  disorders 148
  emptying 72-3
  intussusception 152-3
  muscles of the 154
  perforation 51
boys
  muscular dystrophy 168-9
  see also gender differences
bradycardias 51
brain
  biopsy 207
  development 30-1
  dysfunctions 142
  frontal lobes 226
  and need for sleep 24-5
  primitive responses 26
  role in eyesight 78-9
  role in walking 58-9
brain disorders
  cerebral palsy 228
  encephalitis 206-7
  epilepsy 208-9, 225
  from head injuries 239-41

hydrocephalus 21, 51, 210-11, 217, 222
  Reye's syndrome 220-1
  tests for 13
  tumour 211
  and whooping cough 199
  see also cerebral palsy; meningitis
brain tissue, inflammation 206
brainstem damage 240
breast enlargement 46
breast milk, constituents of 22, 149
breast pump 23
breast-feeding 22-3
  advantages of 22, 28
  and anaemia 173
  establishment of 13
  and HIV prevention 181
  and jaundice 15
  and meningitis 215
  problems 23, 38, 40, 120
  and rickets 164-5
  social issues 23
breathing
  at birth 12, 18
  rapid 18-19
breech presentation at birth 158
brittle bone disease
  see osteogenesis imperfecta
Broca's area 142
bronchi 112
bronchial obstruction 201
bronchiectasis 193, 199, 201, 205
bronchiolitis
  complications 195
  drug therapy 194
  nursing care 194
  recent advances 195
bronchitis 171
bronchodilators 112-15, 194, 205
bronchopneumonia 196
bronchoscopy 107
burns 246-7
butane gas lighter refills 236
buzzer treatment for bed-wetting 75

C
C reactive protein 163
caecum 150, 152
Caesarean section
  and HIV prevention 181
  lung complications after 19, 50
  prevention of virus transmission 103
calamine lotion 135, 137
calcium 164-6
calorie requirements 87
cancer 244-5
  long-term complications 244
  pre-disposing factors 244
  treatment 245
  see also leukaemia; lymphoma
candidiasis 29, 42, 44
capillary leak 216, 217
carbaryl 139
carbohydrates 86-97
cardiac catheterization 189-90
cardiac cycle 186-7
cardiac examination
  newborns 12-13
  at six weeks 21
cardiac surgery 190
cardiomyopathy 191
cardiopulmonary bypass 190
cardiorespiratory system
  fetal 51
  see also heart; lung

cardioversion 191
carriers, cystic fibrosis gene 202-3
CAT scan 239
cataracts 133
catecholamines 245
  released during labour 19
catheter
  cardiac 189-90
  intravenous 184
caustic substances 235
CCDCs (Consultants in Communicable Disease Control) 217
CD4 protein 179
cefotaxime 215
ceftriaxone 215
cell culture 183
centile charts 40, 96
central nervous system disorders
  and HIV 180
  and leukaemia 182
  see also brain
cephalosporins 215
cerebellum 58-9, 229
cerebral palsy 9, 26, 228-31
  caring for children with 231
  causes of 228
  difficulties with 230-1
  education and intelligence 230
  rare forms of 229
  and squint 79
  types of 229
cerebrospinal fluid 182, 207
  cloudy 212
  diagnosing polio 219
  role of 210
CFTR protein 203, 204
CHD see congenital dislocation of the hip
check-ups see assessment
chemical pneumonitis 19
chemotherapy 244, 245
  for leukaemia 182, 184-5
  side effects 185
Chernobyl 184
chest problems see respiratory diseases
chewing 55
chickenpox 134-5
  complications of 135
  and encephalitis 206
  and Reye's syndrome 220
  symptoms 134
  treatment 135
Child Health Promotion programme 20
child record book 34, 40, 53
childhood
  entering 76-7
  good eating habits 86-7
  growth rates in 96-7
  inherited characteristics 98-9
  play in 80-1
  starting school 92-3
  stimulation in 80-1
  teeth 94-5
  temperament and personality 82-3
  see also pre-school children; toddlers
childproof containers 235
chipmunk face 175
chlamydia 46, 103
chloramphenicol 102
cholera, resistance to 203
chorea 171
chorionic villus sampling 177
choroid plexus papilloma 210
chromosome 21 232-3

chromosomes
  abnormal 183, 188, 202
  sex chromosome 169
ciliary dyskinesia 192-3
cleft palate 13, 106
climbing stairs 70
closed reduction 159
clotrimazole 44
club-foot see talipes
clumsiness 140
cochlea 56-7
cochlear implants 57
coeliac disease 36, 39, 41
cognitive behavioural approach 227
cognitive skills, toddlers 70
colchicine 183
colds 106
  in children 29
  in infants 17
colic 9, 17
colitis 172
collagen deficiency 166, 167
colon 122, 143, 152
colonoscopy 155
colostomy 155
colour, at birth 12
colustrum 23
coma 239, 247
communication
  and autism 224
  competence of 69, 71
  maxims of 69
  in toddlers 65-7
complement deficiency 29
complex seizures 208
computed tomography (CT) scan 207, 210, 221-2, 239-40
computerized axial tomography (CAT) scan 239
concentration, developing 81
concomitant squint 104
conditioning, and toilet training 72-3
condoms 181
conductive deafness 56-7
congenital abnormalities
  of the brain 210
  health screening for 13, 158
  hearing loss 56
  heart disease 41
  Hirschprung's disease 154
  myotonic dystrophy 168
  from rubella 133
  spina bifida 222-3
  upper airway problems 106
  vertical talus 160
congenital dislocation of the hip (CHD) 158-9, 161
  clinical tests for 158
  treatment 159
congenital heart disease
  causes of 188
  diagnosis 189
  identifying 188
  treatment 190-1
  see also heart disease
conjunctival haemorrhage 199
conjunctivitis 102
  newborn 46
connective tissue problems 162, 170
consciousness
  disturbed 220
  lack of 239, 247
  regaining 241
consolidation chemotherapy 185
constipation 39, 122-3
  acute 123
  chronic 123

from Hirschsprung's disease 154
treatment 123
construction toys 80-1
Consultants in Communicable Disease Control (CCDCs) 217
contact dermatitis 45, 126
contact lenses 79
contractures 163, 169
contrast X-ray 155
convergent squint 104-5
conversation see speech
convulsions 208, 214
Coombs' test 15
co-operation
  learning of 71, 76-7
  in play 80, 91
  pre-school children 89
co-ordination
  difficulties with 140-1
  learning 80-1
  of motor skills 71
  pre-school children 89
  see also hand-eye co-ordination
copying see mimicry
corticosteroids 50, 115, 163, 171
cot death see sudden infant death syndrome
coughing 198
  'wet cough' 204
counselling 247
'cover test' 105
cows' milk allergy 38, 172
Coxsackie virus 136-7
cradle cap 43, 45
cranial irradiation 245
cranial ultrasound scanning 51
cranial vault 30-1
craniotabes 164
cranium see skull
'crash' team 238
crawling 52, 59
creatine phosphokinase 169
creative play 81
croup 110-11
  causes 110
  complications of 111
  start of 110
  treatment 111
'crowded card' 78
'cruising' 59
crying, in newborns 9, 17, 25, 152
CT scan
  see computed tomography scan
culture, and breast-feeding 23
curiosity in toddlers 64-5, 70, 80
cyanosis 18, 21, 41, 188-9, 233
'cyclicity' 93
cystic fibrosis 15, 41, 152
  and chest problems 192-3
  diagnosis 202, 204
  incidence 202
  inheritance 202-3
  living with 205
  management of 204-5
  and pneumonia 197
  respiratory effects 205
  testing and counselling 203
cytogenetics 183
cytokines 115
cytomegalovirus 15, 56
cytotoxic drugs 184
  side effects 185
cytotoxic T-cells 179

D

dactylitis 162
deadly nightshade 237
deafness
  conductive 56-7

linguistic isolation 69
sensorineural 56
see also glue ear; hearing
death 247
defecation 122-3
dehydration 75
  from gastroenteritis 148-9
  management 149
  types of 149
dental check-ups 55, 118
dental problems 118-19
  and diet 119
  tooth decay 119
dermatitis
  ammonia 42-4
  contact 45, 126
  seborrhoeic 43, 45
desferrioxamine 176
'detection ritual' 138-9
developing world
  polio 218-19
  and rheumatic fever 170
developmental delay 52
  babies 34-5
  causes of 34
  specialist referral 35
developmental dysplasia of the hip 53, 158, 161
developmental progress 52
  from 18 to 36 months 70-1
  to eighteen months 64-5
  language skills 65-9
  up to five years 90-1
  see also social interaction
Dexedrine 227
diabetes, from cystic fibrosis 205
diabetic mothers
  and jaundice 14
  and respiratory distress 50
dialysis 246
diarrhoea
  in babies 41
  from gastroenteritis 148-9
  resistance to 203
diathermy scissors 121
diazepam 208, 231
diet
  and anaemia 172
  healthy 86-7, 95, 164-5
  and tooth decay 119
  see also eating
'difficult' children 82
diffuse axonal injury 240-1
digestive problems
  babies 13, 39
  see also constipation; croup; diarrhoea
dilated cardiomyopathy 191
diphtheria vaccine 32, 109
diplegia 229
discharge examination 13
discoid eczema 127
disinfectants 235
distractability 83
distraction hearing test 53, 57
diuretics 240
divergent squint 104
DMSA scanning 125
DNA
  analysis 169
  damage to 183-4
dolls 81
dominant gene 98, 166
donation of organs 247
Doppler ultrasound 187
dorsal pathway 78
double-vision 105
Down's syndrome 9, 232-3
  clinical features 232
  feet 232
  genetic causes 233
  hands 21, 232

hypotonia 34
  and leukaemia 184, 244
  screening 233
  and squint 79
DPT vaccine 199, 219
drain cleaners 235
dreaming, in babies 25
dribbling 54-5
drinking, and bed-wetting 75
drugs
  see medicines; types of drug
dry cleaning fluids 236
dry skin 42
DTP-Hib vaccine 32-3
Duchenne muscular dystrophy 168
ductus arteriosus 51, 188
dura 223
dyskinetic cerebral palsy 229
dyslexia 78, 142-5
  diagnosis 144
  effects of 143
  misconceptions 143
  prognosis for 145
  treatment for 145
dysplasia of the hip 53
dyspraxia 140-1
  assessment and diagnosis 141
  identifying children with 140
  treatment 141
dystrophin 169

E

ear damage 53, 56
ear infections 213
earache 130
eardrum 107, 116-17
'easy' children 82
eating
  good habits 86-7
  learning to 36-7
  problems 87
  see also diet; feeding
EBV (Epstein-Barr virus) 107, 244
echocardiogram 169, 186-7, 189-91
echocardiography 171
eczema 126-7
  endogenous 126
  exogenous 126
  in infants 43
  and nappy rash 45
  treatment 126-7
education
  and autism 225
  and cerebral palsy 230
  and dyslexia 143-5
  and dyspraxia 140-1
  on HIV 181
  influences on 92-3
  pre-school 71
  see also learning; school
EEG see electroencephalogram
eight-month check 35, 52-3
elderly, reflexes in 27
electrocardiography 171
electroencephalogram (EEG) 207-9, 221, 239
electromyography 169
electrophoresis 202
elimination diets 43
ELISA 148
emergencies, from head injuries 238
emollient creams 42-3, 45, 126-7
emotional factors
  bed-wetting 74
  dyslexia 142-3
  and toddler development 77

emotions
  expressing 84-5
  revealing 66
empathy 88
emphysema 201
empyema 197
encephalitis 206-7
  confirming diagnosis 207
  from measles 129
  from mumps 131
  from rubella 132
  symptoms 206
  treatment 207
encephalopathy 206
endocarditis 171, 189, 191
endochondral ossification 31
endocrine disorders 97, 205
endotracheal tube 18-19, 197
enemas 123, 153, 155
energy requirements, newborns 37
enlarged skull 211
enterocolitis 154
enteroviruses 214
enthesitis 162
enuresis see bed-wetting
environment
  and genes 98-9
  and personality 82-3
enzyme deficiency, and rickets 165
enzyme-linked immunosorbent assay 148
epididymis 157
epididymitis 157
epiglottis 29, 106-7, 110
epilepsy 208-9
  and autism 225
  and cerebral palsy 230
  types of 209
Epstein-Barr virus (EBV) 107, 244
eruption 54-5
  permanent teeth 94-5, 118
erysipelas 170
erythema 171, 199
erythrocytes see red blood cells
erythromycin 199
  for tonsillitis 109
Escherichia coli 124, 197, 213-14
etanercept 163
ethambutol 201
ethnicity
  and cystic fibrosis 202
  and rickets 165
  and umbilical hernia 47
Europe, and HIV/AIDS 178
Eustacian tube 107, 116
evening primrose oil 126
exceptional children 77
exchange transfusion 15
exocrine glands 204
experimental play 80-1
exploration in toddlers 70
expressed milk 23
expressing ideas 67
'extensor thrust, placing and walking reflex' 27
external auditory canal 116
eye checks 78-9
eye contact 224
eye problems
  in children 102-5
  newborns 46
  physical 79
eyeballs 30-1
eyes
  focus 104
  whites of 166, 167
eyesight
  and cerebral palsy 230

development 20-1, 35
development in toddlers 78-9
at eight months 52
and learning to read 78
object and action pathways 78-9
and recognition 64

F

fabric conditioners 42, 45
faeces 122-3, 148, 152
infected 218
failure to thrive 38, 40-1
breast-feeding problems 40
medical problems 41
and rickets 164
false-colour X-ray 164
family
and autism 225
and chronic disease 163
HIV in the 178
and intensive care 247
living with cystic fibrosis 205
and serious conditions 9
see also parents
family clinics 180
fantasy 90-1
fathers see parents
fats 86-7, 165
malabsorption 205
febrile convulsions 208
feeding
at eight months 53
learning to 36-7
problems 38-9, 120
problems in infants 17
at six weeks 20
see also diet; eating
feet
Down's syndrome 232
hand, foot and mouth disease 136-7
six week assessment 21
see also talipes
femur 158-9, 164
fenfluramine 225
fetus
abnormalities 132-3, 135, 228
breathing 18
circulation 51
development of skull 30
Downs's syndrome 232-3
heart defects 188-9
HIV transmission 178-81
immune system 28
lung problems 19
thalassaemia trait 177
fever
and constipation 123
and convulsions 208
from hand, foot and mouth disease 136-7
and measles 128-9
in rheumatic fever 170-1
typhoid 203
from urinary infections 125
fibre 86-7, 123
fibula 164
fine motor skills 34-5, 37, 52
five year olds 90
toddlers 70
finger clubbing 192, 193, 205
finger feeding 36, 37, 39
first aid, for accidental poisoning 234
first teeth see milk teeth
first-born children 91
five year olds 90-1
growth 91
key features 91

personality and social awareness 91
reality and fantasy 90
'floppy' babies 34, 228-9, 232
fluid intake see water
fluoride toothpaste 119
fly agaric mushroom 237
focus, eyes 104
folic acid 210
fontanelles 31
food fads 41, 53, 87
food groups 87
foreign bodies, inhaled 107, 193
foreign languages, learning 69
'foremilk' 22
formula milk 22-3
strength 38
and vitamin D 164-5
fovea 104
fractures 166, 167
freckles 98
frenulum 47, 120-1
friends, playing with 81, 88
frontal bone 30-1
frontal lobe trauma 241
fungal infections 179
fusidic acid 102

G

gait
control of 58-9
development of 70
galactosaemia 15
galactose 149
gangrene 217
gastric lavage 201, 236-7
gastro-colic reflex 72
gastroenteritis 148-9
and breast-feeding 22
causes of 148
symptoms 148
treatment 149
gastrointestinal system
see bowel; colon; oesophagus
gastrotomy 246
G-CSF (granulocyte colony stimulating factor) 185
gender awareness, in toddlers 71
gender differences
autism 225
dyslexia 143
head injuries 238
height 97
hip dislocation 158
Hirschsprung's disease 154
size 62-3
in treatment 83
general practitioners
and child immunity 29
infant care 16
six-eight week check 20-1, 35
genes
abnormality 169, 175, 177
CF gene 203
dominant 98, 166
and environment 98-9
recessive 98, 202, 204
therapies 202-3
genetic counselling 166, 169, 175
cystic fibrosis 202-3
genetic factors
in anaemias 172-3
asthma 112
baby size 62
beta thalassaemia 175
cystic fibrosis 202-3
Down's syndrome 233
dyslexia 142
and eczema 126
hip dislocation 158

Hirschsprung's disease 154
inherited 98-9
and muscular dystrophy 169
osteogenesis 166
and squint 79
in temperament and personality 82-3
genital checks
in newborns 13
at six weeks 21
genital herpes 206
genital tract infections 103
genotype 99
German measles see rubella
gestational age, and survival 48
giant-cell pneumonia 129
Giardia 148
girls
growth chart 62
see also gender differences
'glabellar tap' reflex 27
glandular fever 108
Glasgow coma scale 239
glass test 216
globin 174
glucose 149
glue ear 53, 56, 106-7, 129
surgery 116-17
gluten 36-7
allergy to 41
intolerance 39
gluten-free cereals 36
gonorrhoea 103
good eating habits 86-7
Gower's sign 168
G6PD 172
graft-versus-host disease 184
graft-versus-leukaemia effect 184
grammar, learning of 68
grand mal 209
granulation tissue 200
granulocyte colony stimulating factor (G-CSF) 185
grasp reflex 26-7, 52
Griffiths Mental Development Scales 35
grommets 116-17
tools for insertion 117
gross motor skills 34
toddlers 70
Group B beta-haemolytic streptococcus pneumonia 197
growth
abnormalities 97
assessment 96
changing proportions 63
common patterns of 63
first eighteen months 62-3
five year old 91
measurement 62
and multiple births 53
pre-school children 89
problems 63
growth charts 53, 96
for girls 62
growth hormone 63, 97
growth rates, in childhood 96-7
growth spurts 62
gum disorders 55
Guthrie card test 13, 178

H

haem 174
haematernesis 23
haemoglobin 172-3
abnormal production 174-5
haemolysis 172
haemophilia 172, 178
Haemophilus 102, 107

Haemophilus influenzae type B (Hib) 20, 32, 107, 110, 212-14
haemorrhage
conjunctival 199
intracranial 51, 210
intraventricular 240
haemorrhagic disease 46
haemotomas 172, 240, 241
'hair-on-end' skull 175
haloperidol 225
hand, foot and mouth disease 136-7
signs and symptoms 136
treatment 137
hand-eye co-ordination 35-7, 80
in toddlers 70
hard palate 106
HbA2 175
HbH 177
head see skull
head circumference 96-7
babies 62
at birth 12, 30
monitoring 40
at six weeks 21
head injuries 238-41
assessment and treatment 239
and cerebral palsy 228
diffuse axonal injury 240-1
emergency transfer after 238
larger impact injury 240
localized skull fracture 240
long-term management 241
head lice
detection 138
life cycle 138
preventing spread of 139
treatment 139
health record book 34, 40, 53
health screening
for Down's syndrome 233
eight-month check 52-3
lung problems 18
newborns 8, 12-13, 34, 158, 186
six-eight weeks 8, 16-17
see also developmental progress
health visitors
eight-month check 52-3
infant care 16-17
healthy diet see balanced diet
hearing
in babies 66
defective 53, 56-7
development 20, 35
impairments 57, 239
see also deafness
hearing aids 56-7
hearing test, at eight months 52-3, 56-7
heart
fetal 51
neonatal 51
heart disease
and Down's syndrome 232-3
newborn 190-1
in the newborn 188-9
from rheumatic fever 171
from rubella 133
heart failure 189, 191, 193
heart murmurs 21, 172, 186-7, 189, 191
abnormalities producing 187
diagnosing and assessing 187
heart transplant surgery 190
heart valves, defective 186, 188
heel prick test 13, 15
height
during childhood 96-7
determination 63
helper T-cells 179
hemiparesis 229

hepatosplenomegaly 176
'herd' immunity 33
hernia 39
  inguinal 47, 156
  umbilical 47
hernia sac 156
herniotomy 156
herpangina 137
herpes simplex virus 103, 206-7
heterozygotes 202
heterozygous genotype 99
Hib vaccination 29, 32, 213, 215
Hickman line 184
Higashi approach 225
'hindmilk' 22
hip, bone marrow aspiration
  182-3
hip dislocation 13, 21, 53
  congenital 158-9, 161
Hirschprung's disease 123, 154-5
  diagnosis 155
  symptoms 154
  treatment 155
histamine 115
HIV 178-81
  and cancer 244
  caring for children with 180-1
  contracting 178
  diagnosis 179
  and eczema 127
  education 181
  immune deficiency 29
  infections with 180
  and pneumonia 197
  prevention 181
  and tuberculosis 200
hole in the heart 190
holly 237
homozygotes 202
homozygous genotype 99
house dust mite 113, 115, 126
household chemicals 235
HTLV-1 virus 184
human immunodeficiency virus
  see HIV
humidifier 111
hydrocele 47, 157
hydrocephalus
  21, 51, 210-11, 217, 222
  signs and symptoms 211
  treatment 211
hydrocortisone 43, 45
hygiene
  bacterial conjunctivitis 102
  bottle feeds 41
hypermobility 166
hyperpyrexia 171
hypersensitivity of the airways
  112
hypertrophic cardiomyopathy
  191
hypodermic syringes 178
hypothyroidism 97
hypotonia 34, 229, 232

I

identity 76
IgA 28
IgM 28
ileum 152
iliac crests 212
imaginative play 81
imipramine 237
immune deficiency syndromes
  29
  and chest problems 192
immune system
  babies 28-9
  before birth 28
  failure in HIV 179, 180
  infections and defences 28-9

and juvenile arthritis 162
and meningitis 215
patterns of infection 29
strengthening of 9
immunity
  from breast milk 22
  see also infections
immunization
  for bronchiolitis 195
  complications with 180
  against diphtheria 109
  infants 29, 32-3
  against measles 129
  against meningitis 213, 215
  meningococcal septicaemia 217
  against mumps 131
  polio 219
  against rubella 133
  schedule 32
  throughout childhood 9
  against tuberculosis
    32, 180, 201
  against whooping cough
    32-3, 199
  see also MMR vaccine
immunocompromised patients
  and chicken pox 134-5
  and measles 129
  and pneumonia 179, 197
immunofluorescence 194
immunoglobulins 28-9, 195
  injection 135
immunosuppresants 163, 244
impedance audiometer 57
impetigo neonatorum 42
inactivated vaccine 219
inborn character traits 82
incomcomitant squint 104-5
incubators 28, 48-9, 51, 190
independence
  bid for 76
  at eighteen months 65
  in feeding 36-7
  increase of 9
  pre-school 71, 89
  striving for 84
  from walking 59
independent will 65
indirect inguinal hernia 156
indomethacin 51
induction chemotherapy 185
infants see babies; pre-school
  children; toddlers
infections
  and defences 28-9
  and eczema 126
  nappy rash 44-5
  neonatal 19, 28
  opportunistic 179, 180
  patterns of 29
  sexually transmitted 181
  skin problems 42
  see also bacterial infections;
    immunity; viral infections
infective endocarditis 191
inferior vena cava 188
infertility 185
inflammation
  of the airways 112, 115
  alveoli 196
  in the brain 206-7, 216-17
  of the heart 171
  in infants 43
  of the meninges 212-15
  from mumps 131
inflammatory markers 163
influenza
  and encephalitis 206
  and Reye's syndrome 220
  virus 106, 194
  see also Haemophilus
    influenzae type B (Hib)

influenza vaccine 180
inguinal hernia 47, 156
inguinalscrotal disorders 156
inhalers 112-14, 205
inheritance see genetic factors
injuries 162
  see also accidents; head
    injuries; non-accidental injuries
'inspiratory stridor' 110
intensity of reaction 83
intensive care treatment
  221, 239
  see also paediatric intensive
    care unit
interaction
  mother and baby 20, 49
  parents and baby 58
  parents and toddler 76-7
  in play 80-1
  social 68-9, 71
  between toddlers 76-7, 88-9
intercostal muscles 112
intracranial haemorrhage 51, 210
intracranial pressure 211, 239
intramembranous ossification 31
intravenous catheter 184
intravenous chemotherapy 184-5
intravenous drip 149
intravenous drug users 181
  and HIV/AIDS 178
intraventricular haemorrhage 51
intussusception 152-3
  diagnosis and treatment 153
  recovery and outlook 153
  symptoms 152
involuntary reflexes 72
iron deficiency anaemia
  39, 51, 172-3
iron supplements 53, 173, 237
iron toxicity 176
isoniazid 201

J

jaundice 13, 56
  causes of 15
  physiological 14
jaws 30
jealousy 65
joint pain 170
junk food 87
juvenile idiopathic arthritis
  162-3
  caring for child 163
  classifying 162

K

'kangaroo care' 49
Kaposi's sarcoma 244
karyotype 183, 233
kernicterus 15
kidney disease 36
  causing rickets 165
  scarring 124-5
kidney failure 172-3, 246
Koplik spots 128
kwashiorkor 63

L

laburnum 237
lacrimal sac 103
lactase 149
lactose intolerance 38, 149
lactulose 123
language skills
  and autism 224-5
  and cerebral palsy 230
  communicative competence 69
  development 65-9
  and dyslexia 142

five year old 91
  foreign languages 69
  innate 68
  parental involvement 68
  pre-school children 89
  sign language 57, 69
laparoscopy 153
laparotomy 153
large intestine see bowel
laryngitis 129
larynx 107, 110
laser treatment 79
latent squint 105
latex agglutination 148
laughing 63, 65
laxatives 123
'lazy eye' 79, 105
lead poisoning 172
leadership skills 77
learning
  to eat 36-7
  and language 68-9
  motor skills 34-5
  non-curricular 93
  to read 78
  to talk 66-7
  thinking logically 88, 93
  through play 80
  and toilet training 73
  to walk 8
  see also education
learning disabilities
  in ADHD 226-7
  and autism 225
  with cerebral palsy 230
  and Down's syndrome 232
  see also dyslexia
length, babies 8, 12
lessons 92
leukaemia 162, 163
  bone marrow transplant 184
  causes of 184
  chemotherapy 185
  diagnostic tests 183
  and Down's syndrome 232
  incidence of 244
  treatment 184-5, 245
  types of 182
lice see head lice
light micrograph 203
limb-girdle muscular dystrophy
  168, 169
'linguistic isolates' 69
LIP 180
Listeria monocytogenes 214
liver
  biopsy 221
  enlarged 176
  enzymes 14
liver disease
  causing jaundice 15
  causing rickets 165
  in cystic fibrosis 205
  in Reye's syndrome 206, 220-1
lobar pneumonia 196
localized skull fracture 240
logical thinking 88, 93
long-sightedness 79, 105
low birth weight 62
low blood pressure 246
lumbar puncture 182, 207, 212
lung
  chronic infection 193
  tissue calcification 201
lung collapse 201
lung damage
  abscess 197
  and cystic fibrosis 205
  in newborn 18-19, 50-1
lung function 245
  monitoring of 113, 204
lupin 237

lymph glands
  enlargement 201
  neck 108
lymphocytes 179
  low count 185
  production 29
lymphocytic interstitial
  pneumonitis 197
lymphoma 109, 162, 163
  and HIV 244

M

macrophages 196
maculopapular rash 128
magnetic resonance imaging
  (MRI) 207, 221, 222, 240
maintenance chemotherapy 185
malabsorption 205
malaria, thalassaemia from
  175, 177
malathion 139
malnutrition 86
  and growth 63
  and tuberculosis 201
mandible 30-1
manifest squint 105
Mantoux test *see* tuberculin test
manual dexterity
  see fine motor skills
mastitis 38, 131
'mean cerebral perfusion
  pressure' 239
meanings of words 67
measles 128-9
  causing croup 110
  complications 129
  diagnosis 128
  and encephalitis 206
  mumps and rubella (MMR)
    vaccine 32-3, 129, 131, 133
  see also MMR vaccine
measurements
  after birth 12
  see also head circumference;
    height; weight
measuring mat 62
mechanical ventilation
  195, 207, 238-9
meconium 122, 154
  aspiration 19
medicines, accidental poisoning
  from 234-5, 237
Mediterranean, and thalassaemia
  175
medullary canal 183
meiotic non-disjunction 233
melaena 23
memory, evidence of 64
meninges 212, 240
meningitis
  9, 19, 28-9, 207, 210, 247
  after effects 217
  antibiotic treatment 215
  causes 213-15
  and cerebral palsy 228
  complications 56
  diagnosis 212
  incidence 213
  from mumps 131
  and polio 218
  prognosis 212
  protection against 215
  symptoms 212, 214
  treatment and prevention 213
  vaccines 32
  viral rashes 43
meningococcal septicaemia
  216-17
  after effects 217
  management in the community
    217

signs and symptoms 216
meningococcus bacteria
  212-17, 247
meningoencephalitis 206, 214
menstrual blood loss 172
mental handicap 232
messy play 81
metered dose inhaler 113-14
micturating cystourethrogram
  125
middle ear 116
Middle East, and thalassaemia
  175
midwives, handling newborns 17
milia 42
miliary tuberculosis 201
milk *see* breast milk; cows' milk
  allergy; formula milk
milk teeth 54-5
  caring for 55
  growth of 55
  importance of 55, 95
  losing 94-5
mimicry 66, 69
  in play 77
  and toilet training 72
minerals 86-7
mistletoe 237
'mixed dentition' 95
MMR vaccine
  32-3, 129, 131, 133
  adverse publicity 9
mobility
  difficulties with 228-9
  hypermobility 166
  independent 65
  toddlers 70-1
Mongolian blue spots 42
mongoloid face 175, 232
Moraxella catarrhalis 107
'Moro reflex' 27
mothers
  age in pregnancy 233
  antibodies 28
  and baby interaction 20, 49
  diabetic 14, 50
  HIV transmission 178-81
  rhesus-negative 15
  support from health visitors
    16, 53
  see also parents
motor skills 37
  coordination of 71
  development 76
  difficulty with 140-1
  at eight months 52
  five year olds 90
  learning 34-5
  toddlers 70-1
mouth ulcers 137
MRI *see* magnetic resonance
  imaging
mucositis 185
mucus 204, 205
multiple births
  early gestation 48
  and growth 53
multiple genes 98
mumps 130-1
  causing meningitis 214
  complications of 131
  and encephalitis 206
  symptoms of 130
  see also MMR vaccine
muscle biopsy 169
muscle tone
  at birth 12
  lack of 34
  at six weeks 21
muscular dystrophy 168-9
  caring for a child 169
  diagnosis 169

inheriting 169
  symptoms of 168
mushrooms 237
musical instruments
  70-1, 81, 230
mutations, in CF gene 203
mycobacteria infections
  29, 180, 200-1
Mycobacterium bovis 201
Mycobacterium tuberculosis (TB)
  29, 200-1
myelopoiesis, transient abnormal
  232
myocarditis 171
myotonic dystrophy 168

N

nappy, red staining in 46
nappy rash 42-5
  healing sore areas 44
  less common types 45
  prevention 44-5
  what to avoid 45
nasal cavity 106
navel 13, 17, 47
nebulizer 112, 113-14
neck
  stiffness 214
  swellings 108
necrotizing enterocolitis 51
Neisseria meningitidis *see*
  meningococcus bacteria
neonatal screening hearing test
  57
neonatologist 48
nephroblastomas 244
nerve palsy 182
nervous system *see* central
  nervous system disorders
neural tube defects 210
neuroblastomas 244-5
neurocranium 30
neurological development,
  from 18 to 36 months 70-1
neurological problems, and reflex
  testing 26-7
neuromuscular disease, and chest
  problems 192
neutrophils 196
newborn
  anaemia in 172
  breast milk and 22-3
  care of 16-17
  circulation in 188
  constipation in 122
  health screening
    12-13, 34, 158, 186
  health screening at six weeks
    20-1
  heart disease 188-9, 190-1
  immune systems 28-9
  jundice in 14-15
  learning to eat 36-7
  lung problems 18-19
  meningitis in 214-15
  minor abnormalities in 46-7
  pneumonia 197
  reflexes 26-7
  skull 30-1
  sleep patterns 24-5
  see also babies
night terrors 25
nipples, sore and cracked 38
nit comb 138
nits 138-9
noises *see* sounds; speech
non-accidental injuries
  166-7, 238, 241
non-paralytic polio 218
non-steroidal anti-inflammatory
  drugs (NSAIDs) 163

nosebleeds 199
notifiable diseases 213
NSAIDs (non-steroidal anti-
  inflammatory drugs) 163
nuchal translucency 233
nuclear waste 184, 244
numbers 71
nursery school 71, 77, 81
  benefits of 88, 92
  and toilet training 73
nutrition *see* diet; eating;
  malnutrition

O

obesity 87
  and growth problems 63
  reasons for 98-9
object pathway 78-9
obsessional behaviour 224-5
obstruction *see* blockage
occipital bone 30-1
occlusive bandaging 43
occupational therapy, for
  dyspraxia 141
oesophageal atresia 106
oesophageal reflux 39, 41
  and chest problems 192-3
oesophagitis 235
oesophagus 106
  blockage 13
oestrogen, reaction to 46
oligoarthritis 162
oncology wards 244
ondansetron 185
open platform 49
open reduction 159
ophthalmia neonatorum 103
ophthalmoscopy 50, 52
opportunistic infections 179, 180
oral rehydration 149
orchitis, from mumps 131
Ortolani's manoeuvre 158
ossicles of the middle ear 30
ossification 31
osteoclasts 94
osteogenesis imperfecta 166-7
  collagen deficiency 166
  common symptoms 166
  treatment and prognosis 167
osteomalacia 164
osteomyelitis 162
osteoporosis 166, 167
otitis media *see* glue ear
oto-acoustic emission hearing test
  53
otoscope 116
outgoing personality 83
outlet valve stenosis 187
overheating in babies 42
oximeter 194
oxygen desaturation 199

P

paediatric intensive care unit
  (PICU) 246-7
  critical conditions 247
pain
  abdominal 151, 152
  in joints 170
painting 81, 88-9
  for toddlers 64
palmar grip 52
palpation, fontanelles 31
pancreas, inflammation 131
pancreatic enzyme capsules 205
paracetamol 33, 109, 125, 220
  pack size 235
  poisoning from 237
para-influenza virus
  106-7, 110, 194

parallel play 71, 80
paralytic polio 180, 218-19
paramedics 238
paramyxovirus 130
parathyroid hormone 164
para-tonsillar abscess 107
parents
 and ADHD 227
 baby interaction 58
 and child behaviour 83
 coping with serious disease 9
 desires during pregnancy 8
 and dyspraxia 141
 eight-month check 52
 and inheritance 98-9
 involvement in language 68
 and learning 93
 premature babies 49
 role in play 80
 and SIDS 242-3
 sleep deprivation 24-5
 toddler interaction 76-7
 and toothbrushing 119
 see also family; mothers
parietal tuberosity 30
parotid glands 130
passive immunity 195
passive smoking 243
'patching' an eye 105
patent ductus arteriosus 51, 187
Pavlick harness 159, 161
peak flow meters 113
pedestrian road-traffic accidents
 238, 240, 247
pelvis 158, 182-3
penicillin 171, 176, 191
 for meningitis 213
 for tonsillitis 109
percussion therapy 205
perforated eardrum 56
pericarditis 171
periorbital cellulitis 29
peristalsis 154
peritonitis 150, 152-3
permanent teeth 94-5
 eruption 94-5, 118
 order of emergence 94
pernasal swab 199
persistence 83
personal health record book
 34, 40, 53
personality 82-3
 definition 74
 five year olds 91
 influences on 83
 types of 82
pertussis
 see whooping cough
petechiae 212
petit mal 209
Peto technique 231
pets 126
 and asthma 115
pharyngitis 106, 108
pharynx 106
phenotype 99
phenylalanine 13
phenylketonuria 13
phosphates in the body
 164-5, 166
photophobia 214
photosensitivity 209
phototherapy, and jaundice
 14-15
physical abuse
 see non-accidental injuries
physical development at school
 93
physical examination
 at eight months 53
 at six weeks 21
physical play 80

physiotherapy
 and cerebral palsy 231
 for cystic fibrosis 205
 and hydrocephalus 210
 for juvenile arthritis 163
 for muscular dystrophy 169
 for polio 219
 for talipes 161
picture books 64-5, 67, 69, 71
PICU (paediatric intensive care
 unit) 246-7
Pierre Robin sequence 106
pimozide 225
pincer grip 52
pituitary gland 63, 97
Pityrosporum ovale 127
plants, harmful 235, 237
plaque 55
plaster cast 159
 for talipes 161
plastic surgery 217
play
 and autism 224
 creative 81
 experimental 80-1
 five year olds 90-1
 with friends 81
 imaginative 81
 learning through 80
 messy 81
 pre-school children 88-9
 stages of 80
 in toddlers 70-1, 76-7
 vigorous physical 80
play school see nursery school
playgroup therapy 169
pleural effusions 201
Pneumococcus 176, 213
Pneumocystis carinii
 29, 179, 197
pneumonia 19, 28, 171
 aspiration 236
 causes 196
 factors predisposing to 197
 giant-cell 129
 and HIV 179-80
 in newborns 197
 types of 196
 and whooping cough 199
 see also Streptococcus
 pneumoniae
pneumonitis 19
pneumothorax 114
poison information unit
 234, 237
poisoning
 accidental 234-5, 237
 from alcohol 236
 solvent abuse 236
polio 218-19
 eradication of 9
 immunization 219
 treatment 219
 types of 218
polio vaccine 32-3, 180, 219
pollen 113, 126
polyarthritis 162, 163
polycythaemia 14
polygenic inheritance 98
pompholyx eczema 127
positional talipes 47
possessiveness 65, 85
posseting 17, 39
post-natal depression 53
post-traumatic stress 241
postural drainage 205
postural talipes 47, 160-1
potty training 72-4
poverty
 and rheumatic fever 170
 and tuberculosis 200
pre-eclampsia 48, 63

pregnancy
 desires of parents 8
 and rubella virus 132-3
 and varicella-zoster virus 135
 see also fetus; mothers
premature babies
 and anaemia 172
 and breast-feeding 23
 breathing 18
 and bronchiolitis 195
 caring for 48-9
 chances of survival 48-9
 danger of infection 28
 developmental delay 34
 and hydrocephalus 210
 jaundice in 14
 preparing for delivery 48
 problems with 50-1
 sudden infant death syndrome
 242
 vaccination 32
pre-school children 88-9
 accidental poisoning 234
 changing needs 88
 developmental progress 90-1
 growth and co-ordination 89
 head injuries 238
 immunization 32
 social development 89
 understanding in 89
 upper airway problems 106-7
pre-school education 71
 see also nursery school
primary enuresis 74
primary tuberculous infection
 200
primary vaccination programme
 32
primitive responses 26, 59
processus vaginalis 157
prodromal phase of infection
 128
projectile vomiting 39, 41
prolactin 23
proprioceptive technique 231
protease inhibitors 180
protein electrophoresis 202
proteins 86-7
psoriasis 162
psychologist, cognitive
 behavioural 227
psychomotor skills 77
puberty see adolescents
public health measures 217
pulse, checking 21
purpura 171
pyloric stenosis 39, 41
pyrethroids 139

Q

quadriparesis 229, 230
quality of life, for cancer patients
 244
quality of mood 83
quinsy 109

R

rabies 206
radiation
 and cancer 244
 and leukaemia 184
radiotherapy 245
 for leukaemia 182, 184-5
rapid breathing 18-19
rapid eye movement (REM) sleep
 25
rashes
 maculopapular 128
 from meningitis 212-13
 meningococcal septicaemia 216

nappy 42-5
 skin problems 17
 sweat 42
 transient 43
RDS (respiratory distress
 syndrome) 18-19, 29, 50
reading
 acquiring skills 68-9
 and ADHD 226
 and dyslexia 142-5
 learning to 78
reality and fantasy 90
reason, development of 88, 93
recessive gene 98
 inheritance of 202, 204
reciprocal translocations 233
recognition 64
rectum 122, 152, 154
red blood cells
 and anaemia 172-3
 and jaundice 14-15
 sedimentation rate 163
reflex epilepsy 209
reflexes
 at birth 12
 involuntary 72
 in the newborn 26-7
 primitive responses 26, 59
 testing for 27
 vital for survival 26
reflux, oesophageal
 39, 41, 192-2
refraction test 105
regularity 82
regurgitation see posseting
rehydration 149, 207
REM sleep 25
respiration monitors 243
respiratory diseases
 causes of 193
 chronic 192-3
 croup 110-11
 predisposing factors 192
 upper airway 106-7
 see also asthma; bronchiolitis;
 cystic fibrosis; pneumonia;
 whooping cough
respiratory distress syndrome
 (RDS) 18-19, 29, 50
respiratory failure 246-7
respiratory syncytial virus 51,
 106, 110, 194-5
retinopathy 50
Reye's syndrome 206, 220-1
 symptoms 220
 treatment and diagnosis 221
rhDNase 205
rhesus-negative mothers 15
rheumatic fever 170-1
 complications 171
 diagnosis and treatment 171
 and heart problems 191
 symptoms 170
rheumatoid arthritis 172
rhinitis 193
rhinovirus 106, 194
rhythmicity 82
ribavarin 129
ribavirin 195
rickets 164-5
 causes of 165
 clinical signs 164
 diagnosis and treatment 165
 ethnic considerations 165
 link with vitamin D 164
'rickety rosary' 164
rifampicin 201
ritalin 227
rituals 85
road-traffic accidents
 238, 240, 247
Robertsonian translocations 233

rodding 167
Romanian orphanages 178
'rooting reflex' 26
rotaviruses 148, 152
routines
 and autism 224
 importance of 85
rubella 28, 56, 132-3
 and cerebral palsy 228
 congenital 133
 diagnosis 132
 prevention of 133
 see also MMR vaccine

S

safety, and toddlers 65
salbutamol 114, 115, 194
salivary glands 130
salivation 54-5
Salmonella 148-9
satellite lesions 44
scabies 42
scanning
 CAT scan 239
 cranial ultrasound 51
 DMSA scan 125
 see also computed tomography
  (CT) scan; ultrasound scanning
school
 and common illnesses 9
 coping at 92
 and dyspraxia 141
 lunches 86
 non-curricular learning 93
 other influences 92-3
 pre-school education 71
 problems 74
 special schools 225, 230
 starting at 92-3
 see also nursery school
SCID (severe combined immune
 deficiency) 29
scoliosis, and chest problems
 192
scratch mittens 43
screening see health screening
scrotum 157
seborrhoeic dermatitis 43, 45
seborrhoeic eczema 127
secondary enuresis 74
secondary squint 105
seizures 208
 and autism 225
self-esteem 76
SEN (Special Educational Needs)
 code of practice 144
sensorineural deafness 56
sentences, forming 67
septic arthritis 162
septicaemia 19, 28, 212-13
 meningococcal 216-17
sequelae 241
severe combined immune
 deficiency (SCID) 29
sex chromosome 169
sexually transmitted infections
 181
shaken baby syndrome 241
Shigella 148
short-sightedness 79, 98, 105
shunt 210, 211
shyness 65, 83
siblings
 effect of 83
 impact of 91
 see also family; twins
sickle cell disease 172-3
sickle knife 117
SIDS see sudden infant death
 syndrome (SIDS)
sign language 57, 69

silver nitrate 47
sinusitis 193
sitting up 52, 59
situs inversus 193
six-eight weeks check 16-17, 35
skin colour 99
skin problems 217
 babies 42-3
 infections 42
 inflammatory 43
 rashes 17
skull
 craniotabes 164
 enlarged 211
 fontanelles 31
 growth of 63, 97
 newborn 30-1
 proportions 30
 see also head injuries
skull fracture, localized 240
sleep
 apnoea 107, 109
 definition 24
 deprivation 24-5
 early patterns 24-5
 at eight months 53
 necessity of 25
 newborn 20
 position in babies 242
 problems 17, 25
sleep and behaviour support
 groups 53
slit-lamp 105
'slow to warm up' children 82
small intestine see bowel
smallpox, eradication of 9
smiling 64
smoking
 and asthma 115
 maternal 63
 and SIDS 243
snacks 87
'snout reflex' 27
social interaction
 and ADHD 226
 and autism 224
 five year old 91, 93
 and language skills 68-9
 pre-school children 88-9, 89
 toddlers 71
sodium cromoglycate 102, 114
sodium valproate 209
solids
 problems with 120
 starting on 36-7
solvent abuse 236
sore throat 108
sounds
 from babies 34-5, 66
 at eight months 53
 exploring 65, 70-1
 recognizing 66
 response to 56
 transmission 56
soya-based milk 149
spastic cerebral palsy 229
special care unit 49
Special Educational Needs (SEN)
 code of practice 144
special needs 35
special schools 225, 230
specialist referral 9, 35
spectacles 79
speech
 and good teeth 95
 in toddlers 65, 69, 71
speech problems
 and hearing 56, 66
 and tongue-tie 47, 121
speech therapy 57, 225
spermatic vessels 156
spherocytosis 172

spina bifida 160-1, 210
 averta 222
 occulta 222-3
 signs and symptoms 223
 treatment 222-3
spinal canal 212
spinal cord 222-3
spirometry 113, 204
spleen 176
splenectomy 176
splint 159, 169
spoon feeding 36-7, 39
squint 52, 230
 cause of 105
 diagnosis 105
 risk factors for 79
 types of 104
standing 52, 59
Staphylococcus 102, 213
star chart, and bed-wetting 75
'startle reflex' 56, 66
stenosis
 aortic 190
 outlet valve 187
 pyloric 39, 41
sternum 182-3
steroids
 for eczema 126-7
 see also corticosteroids
stertor 106
stethoscope 186-7, 189-90
sticky eyes 46, 102-3
stimulation
 in a five year old 91
 in toddlers 77, 80-1
stoma 155
'stork patches' 42
strabismus 104
strapping, for talipes 161
strawberry naevi 42
Streptococcus 102
 during birth 19, 28-9
 causing rheumatic fever
  170-1, 191
 causing tonsillitis 106-7, 109
Streptococcus pneumoniae
 196, 212-14
stress
 and bed-wetting 74
 post-traumatic 241
stridor 106-7
structural talipes 47, 160, 161
subacute sclerosing
 panencephalitis 129
subarachnoid space 210
subcutaneous lipoma 223
suck and swallow reflex 26
sudden infant death syndrome
 (SIDS) 20, 242-3
 causes 42
sunlight and vitamin D 164-5
superior vena cava 188
supine sleeping 242
suppositories 123
suprapubic aspirate 125
supraventricular tachycardia 191
surfactant 50, 197
surgery
 after-care 247
 for appendicitis 150-1
 blocked tear ducts 103
 cardiac 190
 for congenital hip dislocation
  159
 for epilepsy 209
 glue ear 116-17
 Hirschsprung's disease 155
 inguinal hernia 156
 intra-operative procedures 151
 laparoscopy 153
 plastic 217
 post-operative procedures 151

pre-operative procedures 151
spina bifida 222-3
 for talipes 161
 for tongue-tie 121
 tonsillitis 109
 torsion of the testis 157
 upper airway problems 107
sutures 31
sweat rash 42
'sweat test' 202
systemic arthritis 162

T

tachycardia 191
tachypnoea 18-19
taking turns 77, 88
talipes 160-1
 calcaneovalgus 160
 calcaneovarus 160
 causes of 160
 diagnosis 161
 equinovalgus 160
 equinovarus 47, 160, 161
 postural 47, 160, 161
 treatment 161
 types of 160
tantrums 65, 84-5
 definition 84
T-cells 29, 115, 179
team sports 93
tear ducts, blockage 103
teenagers see adolescents
teeth 30
 decay 119
 dental problems 118-19
 development of 37, 54
 form, shape and number 118
 misalignment 95
 see also milk teeth
teething 54-5
 problems 55
teething ring 54
television, five year olds 92
temper tantrums 84-5
temperament 82-3
 characteristics 77
 definition 74
 variations 82-3
temperature, and SIDS 243
temporal lobe epilepsy 209
teniae coli 150
teratogenicity 185
terbutaline 194
'terrible twos' 84
testicles
 examination 53
 undescended 21, 156
testicular hydrocele 47
testis, torsion of the 157
tetanus vaccine 32
tethered cord syndrome 223
text correction fluids 236
thalassaemia 172-7
 treatment 176-7
 types of 174
theophylline 194
'theory of mind' 225
thinking
 and ADHD 226-7
 logical 88, 93
thoracolumbar scoliosis 192
threshold of responsiveness 83
throat infections 170-1
thrush 29, 42, 44
thumb-sucking 95
thyroid
 gland 63
 test in newborn 13, 15
thyroxin 63
tibia 164
time, learning about 93

titanium alloy rods 167
toddlers
  bed-wetting 74-5
  constipation in 122
  developmental progress
    64-5, 70-1
  entering childhood 76-7
  good eating habits 86-7
  growth 62-3
  language skills 68-9
  learning to talk 66-7
  potty training 72-3
  stimulation and play 80-1
  temper tantrums 84-5
  temperament and personality
    82-3
  vision problems 78-9
  see also babies;
    pre-school children
toilet timing 72
toilet training 72-4
tongue 232-3
  rolling 98-9
tongue-tie 47, 120-1
  feeding problems 120
  incidence 120
  speech problems 121
  surgery for 121
tonic-clonic seizures 209
tonsillectomy 109
tonsillitis 106-9, 137, 193
  causes 109
  diagnosis 108
  prognosis and prevention 109
  symptoms 108
  treatment 109
toothbrushing 55, 119
torsion of the testis 157
toxoplasmosis 15, 56
toys 80-1
trachea 106, 112
tracheo-oesophageal fistula 106
traction 159
transient abnormal myelopoiesis
  232
transillumination 157
transplantation 184, 190, 244
transport teams 247
trauma see head injuries
triamcinolone 163
tricycles 89
trisomy 21 232
tuberculin test 192, 200
tuberculosis 32, 200-1
  and pneumonia 197
  prevention 201
  primary infection 200

secondary complications 201
  treatment 201
  vaccination 32, 180, 201
tumbler test 43, 216
tunica vaginalis 157
Turner's syndrome 63
twins
  early gestation 48
  and growth 53
  postural talipes 160
  and secret language 69
  sudden infant death syndrome
    242
tympanic membrane 116-17
typhoid fever, resistance to 203

U

ultrasound scanning
  51, 125, 153
  for Down's syndrome 233
  heart defects 188-9
  hip dislocation 158
  hydrocephalus detection 211
  for osteogenesis 166
  spina bifida 222
umbilical
  cord 13-14, 17
  granuloma 47
  hernia 47
  problems 47
understanding
  pre-school children 89
  in toddlers 65-7, 71
underweight babies 40
undescended testicles 21
United Kingdom, and HIV/AIDS
  178
upper airways problems
  103, 106-7, 110
  see also respiratory diseases
ureters 124
urinary tract infections 124-5
  causes and symptoms 124
  treatment 125
urine 124-5
urticaria 42
uveitis 162

V

vaccination see immunization
vaccines 32
  risks of 33
  side effects 33
  see also individual vaccines
vaginal bleeding in newborns 46

vaginal discharge in newborns
  46
vancomycin 215
vaporizer 111
varicella-zoster virus 134-5
Vas deferens 156
vascular ring 106
'venous hum' 186
ventilation 195, 207, 246-7
ventilators 48-51
ventral pathway 78
ventricles 188
ventricular septal defect
  186-7, 188, 189
vertical talus 160
vesicoureteric reflux 124-5
vestigial structure 150
videorefractor 79
viral encephalitis see encephalitis
viral infections
  bronchiolitis 194-5
  causing croup 110
  chickenpox 134-5
  conjunctivitis 102
  ear damage 56
  hand, foot and mouth disease
    136-7
  from lung damage 51
  measles 128-9
  meningitis 212-13, 214
  mumps 130-1
  pneumonia 196-7
  rashes 43
  respiratory tract 106-7
  rubella 132-3
  see also HIV
viscerocranium 30
vision see eyesight
visuomotor tasks 79
visuospatial tasks 79
vitamin C 176
vitamin D 164-5
vitamin K 46
vitamins 86-7
  deficiencies 205
vocabulary, toddlers 64-5, 67, 69
vocal cords 110
Volital 227
voluntary bladder control 72-3
vomiting, excessive 39, 41, 152

W

walking
  difficulties 168
  learning to 8
  process of 58

refining basic skills 59
reflex 27
  toddlers 70
water
  benefits of 75
  high intake 123, 149
  intake 75
wax 56
weaning 36-7, 53
  problems 39
weight
  babies 8, 62-3
  at birth 12
  during childhood 96
  monitoring 38, 53, 149
  over first year 20
  problem in babies 40-1
Wernicke's area 142
'wet cough' 204
wheelchairs 167-8, 218, 229
whiplash 241
whooping cough 198-9
  complications 199
  diagnosis 199
  signs and symptoms 198
  treatment 199
whooping cough vaccine
  32-3, 199
Wilms' tumour 245
wisdom teeth 95
'witch's milk' 46
withdrawal 83
words
  association 69, 142, 145
  first 65, 67
writing
  beginnings of 71
  and dyslexia 142-4

X

X chromosome 169
X-ray examination 153, 239
  contrast 155
  hip dislocation 159
  osteogenesis 167
  for rickets 164

Y

yeast infection 44
  gastroenteritis 148

Z

zidovudine 180, 181

PICTURE CREDITS

Apart from those photographs listed below, all of the images contained in this book were originally sourced for the partwork *Inside the Human Body,* produced by Bright Star Publishing plc. For picture credit information please contact Amber Books Ltd.

Corbis: 15, 20, 23, 38, 73, 76, 80, 89, 113, 149, 153, 162, 220
Getty Images: 8, 9, 10, 60, 64, 86, 100, 109, 119, 146, 242
Photos.com: 95